CHILDHOOD LEUKEMIA

A Guide for Families, Friends & Caregivers

CHILDHOOD LEUKEMIA

A Guide for Families, Friends & Caregivers

Nancy Keene

O'REILLY™

Cambridge • Köln • Paris • Sebastopol • Tokyo

Childhood Leukemia: A Guide for Families, Friends & Caregivers
by Nancy Keene

Published by O'Reilly & Associates, Inc., 101 Morris Street, Sebastopol, CA 95472.

Editor: Linda Lamb

Printing History:

June 1997: First Edition

Many of the designations used by manufacturers and sellers to distinguish their products are claimed as trademarks. Where those designations appear in this book, and O'Reilly & Associates, Inc. was aware of a trademark claim, the designations have been printed in caps or initial caps.

This book is meant to educate and should not be used as an alternative for professional medical care. Research about childhood leukemia is ongoing and subject to interpretation. Although we have exerted every effort to ensure that the information presented is accurate at the time of publication, there is no guarantee that this information will remain current over time. Appropriate medical professionals should be consulted before adopting any procedures or treatments discussed in this book.

This book is printed on acid-free paper with 85% recycled content, 15% post-consumer waste. O'Reilly & Associates is committed to using paper with the highest recycled content available consistent with high quality.

ISBN: 1-56592-191-7

To my daughters
Katy and Alison

Contents

Foreword   xiii

Introduction   xvii

1. Diagnosis   1
    Signs and symptoms   1
    Where should your child receive treatment?   3
    Physical responses   4
    Emotional responses   5
    The immediate future   11
    Resources   13

2. What Is Leukemia?   20
    Leukemia is a disease of the blood   20
    Who gets leukemia?   22
    How is leukemia diagnosed?   23
    How is leukemia best treated?   24
    Types of leukemia   24
    Acute lymphoblastic leukemia (ALL)   25
    Acute myeloid leukemia (AML)   29
    Chronic myelogenous leukemia (CML)   32
    Telling your child   34
    Resources   40

3. Coping with Procedures   43
    Planning for procedures   43
    Pain management   46
    Procedures   51
    Resources   66

4. What Is a Clinical Trial?   72
    Why are children enrolled in clinical trials?   72
    What is standard treatment?   73
    What is randomization?   74
    Who designs clinical trials?   74
    Who supervises clinical trials?   75
    What questions should parents ask about clinical trials?   75

What is informed consent? 76
What is a protocol? 77
Should parents receive the entire trial document? 79
What happens if parents say no to a clinical trial? 80
Can parents remove their child from a clinical trial? 81
Pros and cons of clinical trials 81
Resources 83

5. *Family and Friends* 84
The extended family 84
Friends 90
Restructuring family life 100
Resources 105

6. *Forming a Partnership with the Medical Team* 108
The hospital 108
Finding an oncologist 111
Choosing a hospital 112
Types of relationships 112
Communication 114
Getting a second opinion 121
Conflict resolution 122
Changing doctors 125
Resources 126

7. *Surviving Your Child's Hospitalization* 129
The room 129
Food 131
Parking 131
The endless waiting 132
Befriending the staff 132
Being an advocate for your child 133
Where do the kids play? 134
Resources 135

8. *Choosing a Catheter* 137
External catheter 137
Subcutaneous port 142
Choosing not to use a catheter 146
The decision: Which catheter for your child? 147
Resources 148

9. *Sources of Support* 150
Hospital social workers 150
Support groups for parents 153
Support groups for children with cancer 156

Support groups for siblings 158
Parent-to-parent programs 159
Clergy 160
Individual and family counseling 161
Camps 166
Resources 169

10. *Chemotherapy* 173
How do chemotherapy drugs kill cancer cells? 173
How are chemotherapy drugs given? 174
Dosages 174
Chemotherapy drugs and their possible side effects 175
Antinausea drugs used during chemotherapy 194
Drugs used to relieve pain 196
Adjunctive treatments 197
Alternative treatments 198
Resources 200

11. *Common Side Effects of Chemotherapy* 204
Hair loss 204
Nausea and vomiting 207
Low blood counts 209
Diarrhea 216
Constipation 218
Fatigue, weakness, and loss of coordination 219
Bed wetting 221
Dental problems 223
Mouth and throat sores 224
Changes in taste and smell 225
Skin and nail problems 225
Learning disabilities 226
Eating problems 226
Resources 227

12. *Radiation* 229
What is radiation? 229
Possible short-term side effects 238
Possible long-term side effects 240
Resources 243

13. *Record Keeping and Finances* 245
Keeping medical records 245
Keeping financial records 249
Coping with insurance 254
Sources of financial assistance 257
Resources 259

14. *Nutrition*   262
    Treatment side effects and eating   262
    What is a balanced diet?   265
    Are vitamin supplements necessary?   267
    Making eating fun and nutritious   268
    What kids really eat   274
    Parent advice   276
    Commercial nutritional supplements   277
    Feeding by tube and IV   278
    Resources   280

15. *School*   282
    Keeping the school informed about treatment   283
    Keeping teacher and classmates involved   284
    Keeping up with schoolwork   284
    Siblings need help, too   285
    Returning to school   286
    Avoiding communicable diseases   289
    What about preschoolers?   290
    The terminally ill child and school   291
    Identifying cognitive late effects   293
    Your legal rights   295
    Record keeping   300
    On accepting disabilities   301
    Resources   303

16. *Siblings*   307
    Emotional responses of the siblings   307
    Sibling experiences   312
    Helping siblings cope   324
    Positive outcomes for the siblings   328
    Resources   329

17. *Feelings, Communication, and Behavior*   331
    Feelings   331
    Communication   332
    Common behavioral changes of children   334
    Common behavioral changes of parents   339
    Improving communication and discipline   345
    Resources   352

18. *End of Treatment and Beyond*   355
    Emotional issues   355
    Last day of treatment   357
    Catheter removal   358
    Ceremonies   359

What is normal? 362
One year after treatment 365
Possible long-term side effects 367
Follow-up care 372
Keeping the doctor informed 374
Employment 377
The military 379
Insurance 379
Resources 383

19. *Relapse* 389
Signs and symptoms 389
Emotional responses 392
Deciding on a treatment plan 393
Resources 397

20. *Bone Marrow Transplantation* 400
When are transplants necessary? 400
Types of transplants 401
Finding a donor 405
Choosing a transplant center 408
Paying for the transplant 410
Donating the marrow 411
The transplant 412
Emotional responses 414
Complications 416
Long-term side effects 420
Resources 423

21. *Death and Bereavement* 431
Making the decision to end treatment 431
Supportive care 435
Dying in the hospital 436
Dying at home 437
Siblings 439
The funeral 439
The role of family and friends 441
Sibling grief 449
Parental grief 451
Looking back after many years 457
Resources 461

A. *Photographs of Our Children* 471

B. *Blood Counts and What They Mean* 477

C. *Resource Organizations* 486

D. How to Get Information From Your Library or Computer   493

E. Wish Fulfillment Organizations   505

Glossary   511

Index   523

Foreword

EVERY YEAR IN THE UNITED STATES approximately 11,000 children and adolescents under the age of twenty years are diagnosed with cancer. Of these children approximately 2,500 will be afflicted with acute lymphoblastic leukemia and 500 with other types of childhood leukemia. Significant progress has been made in the treatment of childhood cancer over the past four decades, best illustrated by the dramatically improved cure rate for children diagnosed with acute lymphoblastic leukemia. A leading textbook on childhood cancer published in 1960[1] described leukemia in childhood as being "incurable." Today the cure rate for children diagnosed with acute lymphoblastic leukemia is 70 percent overall, and over 85 percent in certain groups of children with particular types of leukemia.

Not every child with acute lymphoblastic leukemia, however, is guaranteed cure, and progress in the treatment of other types of leukemia, such as the myeloid leukemias and other types of cancer, has been definite but slow. Long-term effects following childhood cancer and its treatment are now common as more children are cured of cancer. Thus the diagnosis of any form of cancer in a child remains devastating to a family suddenly thrust into a foreign and threatening world of new and frightening words, medical tests and treatments, uncertainty about the future and, perhaps worst of all for a parent, loss of control in guiding their child's life.

The best resource to help survive this new world is knowledge. Nancy Keene has taken her experience following the diagnosis of leukemia in her three-year-old daughter, Katy, melded this with the experiences of over thirty other families, and produced an invaluable source of knowledge for parents whose child has been diagnosed with cancer. Although the book focuses on leukemia, it contains information which will prove extremely helpful to parents and families coping with any type of childhood cancer.

---

[1] Ariel, I.M., and A.T. Pack, eds. *Cancer and Allied Diseases of Infancy and Childhood.* Boston: Little, Brown & Company, 1960.

She writes in her introduction that "I wanted to provide the insight and experiences of veteran parents who have all felt the hope, helplessness, anger, humor, longing, panic, ignorance, warmth, and anguish of their children's treatment for cancer. I wanted parents to know how other children react to treatment, what to expect, and provide tips to make it easier." She has clearly succeeded.

This most complete parent guide available covers not only detailed and precise medical information about leukemia and the various treatment options from chemotherapy to bone marrow transplantation, but also day-to-day practical advice including how to handle procedures, hospitalization, family and friends, school, social and financial issues, communication, feelings and, if therapy is not successful, the difficult issues of death and bereavement. The cumulative experiences of so many families who have faced the entire spectrum of what can happen in caring for a child with leukemia, and the comprehensive bibliographies at the end of every chapter, make this such an unique and helpful resource.

This book, however, is not only for parents. It will prove equally instructive for anyone, but particularly for all health care professionals involved in the treatment of children with cancer. The honest and candid opinions expressed by children being treated for cancer, their siblings and parents serve as a reminder of the continual need for the highest standards of competence and compassion in helping families manage the difficult, and sometimes overwhelming, physical, emotional, social, and financial burdens they face. *Forming a Partnership with the Medical Team* is an especially important chapter because it is this partnership and honest sharing of knowledge which returns as much control as possible to parents in making necessary decisions about the care of their child. Every child is different, as is every hospital, and not every physician or medical center will necessarily follow all of the guidelines described in the book. Treatments evolve and change. Nonetheless, the knowledge gained by reading this book will enable parents to ask the right questions and to become an integral part of the partnership in their child's treatment.

We still strive for the universally "truly cured child." As described by Dr. Jan van Eys, a pioneer in childhood cancer treatment: "Truly cured children are not just biologically cured, free of disease, but developmentally on a par

with their peers and at ease with their experience of having had cancer."[2]
Parents who read this book will have the opportunity to insure that, as
much as possible, they can give their child the very best opportunity to be
"truly cured."

F. Leonard Johnson, M.D.
The Robert C. Neerhout Professor of Pediatrics
Chief, Division of Pediatric Hematology/Oncology
Oregon Health Sciences University
Portland, Oregon

---

[2] Van Eys, J., ed. *The Truly Cured Child: The New Challenge in Pediatric Cancer
Care.* Baltimore: University Park Press, 1977.

Introduction

We are all in the same boat, in a stormy sea, and we owe each other a terrible loyalty.

—G. K. Chesterton

MY LIFE ABRUPTLY CHANGED on Valentine's Day, 1992, when my three-year-old daughter was diagnosed with acute lymphoblastic leukemia (high risk). At the time, I was the full-time mother of two small daughters, Katy, three years old, and Alison, eighteen months.

The phone call from my pediatrician informing me of Katy's probable diagnosis began my transformation into a "hospital mom." On the two hour trip to the nearest children's hospital, I naively thought that my background would equip me to deal with the difficulties ahead. I had a degree in biology, and had worked my way through the university in a series of hospital jobs. I had experience in the blood bank, the emergency room, the coronary care unit, and the IV (intravenous) team. After college, I was a paramedic with a busy rescue squad and for several years taught Emergency Medical Technician courses at the local community college. I understood the science and could speak the jargon; I thought I was prepared.

I was wrong. Nothing prepares a parent for the utter devastation of having a child diagnosed with cancer. My brain went on strike. I couldn't hear what was being said. I felt like I was trapped in a slow-motion horror movie.

I came home from Katy's first hospitalization with two shopping bags full of booklets, pamphlets, and single sheets containing information on a wide variety of topics. I didn't know how to prioritize what I needed to learn, so I started by researching everything that I could about leukemia. With the help of my wonderful family and hardworking friends, I began to rapidly fill several file cabinets with information on the medical aspects of the disease.

Emotionally, however, I felt lost. Since most of Katy's treatment was outpatient, I lived too far away to benefit from the hospital's support group, and I knew no local parents whose child had leukemia. I felt isolated. Then I discovered Candlelighters (see Chapter 1, *Diagnosis*). This marked a turning point in my ability to deal effectively with my daughter's disease. I began networking with other parents and made marvelous friends. I soon realized that we shared many of the same concerns and were dealing with similar problems. Advice from "veteran" parents became my lifeline.

Why I wrote this book

Experience is a jewel, and it had need to be so, for it is often purchased at an infinite rate.

—Shakespeare
The Merry Wives of Windsor

As I approached the end of Katy's treatment, I realized that I had amassed not only a library of medical information, but scores of first-person accounts of how individual parents coped. It saddened me to think that most parents of children with leukemia would, like me, have to expend precious time and energy to collect, assess, and prioritize information vital to their child's well-being. After all, parents are busy providing much of the treatment that their child receives. They make all appointments, prepare their child for procedures, buy and dispense most medicines, deal with all of the physical and emotional side effects, and make daily decisions on when the child needs medical attention. In a sense, this book grew out of my concern that other overwhelmed parents should not have to duplicate my efforts to gather and organize information.

What this book offers

Forewarned, forearmed; to be prepared is half the victory.

—Cervantes
Don Quixote

This book is not intended to be autobiographical. Instead, I wanted to blend basic technical information in easy-to-understand language with stories and advice from many parents and survivors. I wanted to provide the insight and experiences of veteran parents, who have all felt the hope, helplessness, anger, humor, longing, panic, ignorance, warmth, and anguish of their children's treatment for cancer. I wanted parents to know how other children react to treatment, what to expect, and provide tips to make the experience easier.

Obtaining a basic understanding of topics such as medical terminology, common side effects of chemotherapy, and how to interpret blood counts can only improve the quality of life for the whole family suffering along with their leukemic child. Learning how to develop a partnership with your child's physician can vastly increase your family's comfort and peace of mind. Hearing parents describe their own emotional ups and downs, how they coped, and how they molded their family life around hospitalizations is a tremendous comfort. Just knowing that there are other kids on chemotherapy who refuse to eat anything but tacos or who have frequent rages makes one feel less alone. My hope is that parents who read this book will encounter medical facts simply explained, will find advice that eases their daily life, and will feel empowered to be a strong advocate for their child.

The parent stories and suggestions in this book are absolutely true, although some names have been changed to protect children's privacy. Every word has been spoken by the parent of a child with cancer, a sibling of a child with cancer, or a childhood cancer survivor. There are no composites, no editorializing, and no rewrites—just the actual words of parents who wanted to share what they learned with others.

How this book is organized

I have organized the book sequentially in an attempt to parallel most families' journey through treatment. We all start with diagnosis, learn about leukemia, try to cope with procedures, adjust to medical personnel, and deal with family and friends. We all seek out various methods of support, and struggle with the strong feelings of our child with cancer and our other children. We try to work with our child's school to provide the richest and most appropriate education for our ill child. And, unfortunately, we must grieve, either for our child, or for the child of a close friend we have made in our new community of cancer.

Because it is tremendously hard to focus on learning new things when you are emotionally battered and extremely tired, I have tried to keep each chapter short. The "Resource" section at the end of each chapter deals only with the topic covered. I have not footnoted facts; the citations at the end of each chapter are the sources for information in that chapter.

The first time that I introduce a medical term, I define it in the text. If you do not read the book sequentially and encounter an undefined term, it will be explained in the glossary at the end of the book.

Since half of the children diagnosed with leukemia are boys, and half girls, I did not adopt the common convention of using only masculine personal pronouns. Because I do not like using he/she, I have alternated personal pronouns within chapters. This may seem awkward as you read, but it prevents half of the parents from feeling that the text does not apply to their child.

All of the medical information contained in this book is current for 1997. As treatment is constantly evolving and improving, there will inevitably be changes. However, most of the medicines now in use have been used for many years. Their use in combination and changes in dosages have accounted for the tremendous increase in treatment effectiveness in the last two decades. Scientists are currently studying some biological agents, however, that may dramatically improve treatment for leukemia. You will learn in this book how to discover the newest and most appropriate treatment for your child.

To meet some of the children you will read about in this book, and to give you more places to find help for your cancer journey, I have included five appendices for reference: a photo gallery of children during and after treatment, blood counts and what they mean, resource organizations, resources for additional information, and wish trip organizations.

How to use this book

While researching this book, I was repeatedly told by parents to "write the truth." Because the "truth" varies for each person, over forty parents, children with leukemia, and siblings share portions of their experiences. This book is full of such snapshots in time, some of which may be hard to read, especially by those families of children newly diagnosed. Here are my suggestions for a positive way to use the information contained in this book:

- Consider reading only sections that apply to the present or immediate future. Even if your child's prognosis indicates a high probability of cure, reading about relapse or death can be emotionally difficult.

- Realize that only a fraction of the problems that parents describe will affect your child. Every child is different; every child sails smoothly through some portions of treatment while encountering difficulties in others. The more you understand about the variability of cancer experiences, the better you will be able to cope with your own situation as well as be a good listener and helpful friend to other families you meet with differing diagnoses and circumstances.

- Take any concerns or questions that arise to your oncologist and/or pediatrician for answers (or more questions). The more you learn, the better you can advocate for your family and others.

- I have struggled to keep each chapter short and the technical information easy to read. If you want to delve into any topic in greater depth, the end-of-chapter resources are a good place to start. These sections contain a short list of pamphlets and books for parents as well as children of all ages. Reading tastes are a very individual matter, so if something suggested in the bibliography is not helpful or upsets you, put it down. You will probably find something else on the list that is more appropriate for you. Appendix D, *How to Get Information From Your Library or Computer,* explains how to locate any of the materials contained in the "Resources."

- Share the book with family and friends. Usually they desperately want to help and just don't know how. This book not only explains the disease and treatment but offers dozens of concrete suggestions for family and friends.

Best wishes for a smooth journey through treatment and a bright future for the entire family.

• • • • •

Katy finished her treatment in May 1994, rapidly regained her strength, and started kindergarten that fall. She is now a rosy-cheeked second grader, who enjoys bike riding and art. Each new school year, we watch her stride off with hope in our hearts and tears in our eyes.

Acknowledgments

THIS BOOK IS TRULY a collaborative effort for, without the help of many, it would simply not exist. My heartfelt gratitude to my brother, Bill Keene, whose subtle support included buying a computer, configuring it, then shipping it 3,000 miles with the suggestion that I begin to write, and who also spent countless hours researching, proofreading, and making valuable suggestions. Tim O'Reilly, old friend and now publisher, reminded me that this was a book for people who were in severe "information pain" and provided the infrastructure, personnel, and support to make it happen. Linda Lamb, editor and mentor, nurtured and shaped this project from its inception with unerring instincts, deep knowledge, and kind words. The entire staff at O'Reilly & Associates has been not only knowledgeable and efficient, but unbelievably kind to this fledgling author.

My deep appreciation also goes to my parents, Bill and Doris Keene, who provided proofreading, a printer, and a lifetime of love and encouragement.

Many well known and respected members of the pediatric oncology community, and professionals in related fields, graciously carved time out of busy schedules to make invaluable suggestions and to ensure that the material contained in this book is factually correct. Thank you: Wendy Hobbie R.N., M.S.N., P.N.T., Barbara Clark M.D., Lynne Conlon Ph.D., Debra Ethier R.T., Daniel Fiduccia B.A., JoAnne Holt M.A., Leonard Johnson M.D., Susan J. Leclair M.S., CLS (NCA), Grace Monaco J.D., Mary Riecke, pharmacist, Sheryl Lozowski Sullivan M.P.H., and Heidi Suni M.S.W.

The text of *Childhood Leukemia* was read by many people of disparate backgrounds, whose comments proved extremely helpful. Thank you, Belinda Buescher, Mary Ellen Keene, Patricia Keene, Cynthia Krumme, Christina O'Reilly, Hazel Reed, Donna Santora Vovcsko, and the many parents of children with cancer who graciously took time from their families to review and improve this book.

And finally, more than words can possibly express, my deepest gratitude to the parents, siblings, and children with leukemia, who generously opened their hearts and relived their pain while sharing their experiences with me. Raylene Walls, who introduced me to scores of parents and donated countless hours reviewing the manuscript, has been a beacon of hope and constant support to the rest of us in the decade since her son was diagnosed with leukemia. Mark Newman M.D, and Anne Newman R.N., combined medical knowledge with the emotions of parents of a child with leukemia, to continually review and improve this book. Wendy Corder Dowhower has been my friend and sounding board through it all. To all of the parents, children with cancer, and their siblings, whose words form the heart and soul of this book, thank you: Brenda Andrews, Robin B., Sue Brooks, Alicia Cauley, Naomi Chesler, Allison E. Ellis, Lisa N. Ellis, Dana Erickson, Mel Erickson, Alana Freedman, Jenny Gardner, Shirley Enebrad Geller, Kris H., Lisa Hall, Erin Hall, Kathryn G. Havemann, Douglas L. Herstrom, Connie Higbee-Jones, Chris Hurley, Fr. Joseph, Cynthia Krumme, Madeline LaBonte, Missy

Layfield, Wies & Julie Matejko, Caitlin McCarthy-King, Deirdre McCarthy-King, Sara McDonnall, Wendy Mitchell, Amanda Moodie, Jean Morris, Leslee Morris, Laura Myer, M. Clare Paris, Jeff Pasowicz, Donna Phelps, Mary Riecke, Jennifer M. Rohloff, Steve and Shirlene S., Carole Schuette, Susan Sennett, Lorrie Simonetti, Cathi Smith, Carl and Diane Snedeker, Anabel Stehli, Kim Stimson, Kathleen Tucker, Brigit Tuxen, Annie Walls, Jean Wilkerson, Ellen Zimmerman, and those who wish to remain anonymous.

Despite the inspiration and contributions of so many, any errors, omissions, misstatements, or flaws in the book are entirely my own.

Diagnosis

A journey of a thousand leagues begins with a single step.

—Lao-tzu

"WE HAVE THE RESULTS of the blood work back. I'm afraid it's bad news. Your child has leukemia." For every parent who has heard those words, it is a moment frozen in time. In one shattering instant, life forever changes. Many parents equate cancer with death and are staggered by the thought of losing their beloved child. Strong emotions will batter every member of the family. However, with time and the knowledge that most children survive childhood leukemia, hope will grow.

Signs and symptoms

Leukemia is cancer of the spongy blood-forming tissues that make up the bone marrow inside large bones. The diseased bone marrow floods the body with abnormal white cells. These cells do not perform the infection-fighting functions of healthy, mature white cells. Moreover, production of red cells, which carry oxygen, and platelets, which help prevent bleeding, is decreased. Chapter 2, *What Is Leukemia?*, provides an in-depth explanation of the various leukemias, their causes and treatments.

Diagnosis of leukemia is extremely difficult because many symptoms mimic those of normal childhood illnesses. The onset of the disease can be slow and insidious or very rapid. Initially, children begin to tire easily and rest often. Frequently, they have a fever which comes and goes. Interest in eating gradually diminishes, but only some children lose weight. Parents usually notice pale skin and occasional bruising. Some children develop back, leg, and joint pain which makes it difficult for them to walk. Often lymph nodes in the neck or groin become enlarged, and the upper abdomen protrudes due to enlargement of the spleen and liver. Children become cranky and irritable, and occasional nosebleeds develop.

Usually parents have an uneasy feeling that something is wrong but cannot pinpoint the cause for their concern:

> Preston (10 years old) had an incredible diagnosis. We were very lucky. We were at our beach cabin for Thanksgiving. Preston was tired and listless and had a low-grade fever (99-100) that had persisted for several days. We were bringing his younger sister into town to attend a birthday party, so we decided to bring Preston in to have him checked by the pediatrician on call. The doctor asked Preston what was wrong, and he said, "I don't know, I just feel awful." The doctor ordered blood work and a chest x-ray, and within thirty minutes I was told that he had a "blood cancer." I wanted to take Preston back to the cabin, but was told we needed to go immediately to the hospital, where Preston was admitted, and treatment began.

Most parents react to their concerns by taking their child to the doctor, as Preston's parents did. Usually, the doctor performs a physical exam and frequently orders a complete blood count (CBC). Sometimes the diagnosis is not so easy or fast as Preston's:

> I had been worried about Christine (three years old) for two weeks. She was pale and tired. She ate nothing but toast, and had developed bruises on her shins. At preschool, she was unusually irritable, and would utter a high-pitched scream whenever upset. She told me that she didn't want to go to preschool anymore, and when I asked why, she said, "It's just too much for me, Mommy."

> I took her to the doctor on an afternoon when he was very busy. He measured Christine's weight and height, pronounced them normal, and described her lack of appetite as "nothing to worry about." I told him that all she was doing was lying on the couch and asked why she would have bruises on her legs. He said bruises on shins always take a long time to heal. When I pointed out how pale she was, he stated that all children are pale in the winter.

> I grew more and more concerned and took her back the next week. The doctor discovered an ear infection and prescribed antibiotics. I asked why her eyelids were puffy and he thought it was from sinuses. When I told him of Christine's withdrawal from preschool, he suggested that I read a book entitled, "The Difficult Child."

Things continued to deteriorate, and I called three days later to say that she seemed to be sicker. Her prescription for antibiotics was changed without the doctor seeing her. I was starting to feel frantic, and went to talk to my neighbor who had recently retired after forty years of nursing. I told her I was afraid Christine had leukemia, and I cried. She said I should take her back to the doctor and insist on blood work. When I took her in that afternoon, her white count was over 200,000 (normal is 10,000, the rest were cancer cells) and her hematocrit (percentage of oxygen-carrying red cells) was 12, far lower than the normal 36.

Where should your child receive treatment?

After a tentative diagnosis of leukemia, most physicians refer the family for further tests and treatment to the closest major medical center with expertise in treating children. It is very important that the child with leukemia be treated at a facility that uses a team approach, including pediatric oncologists/hematologists, pediatric nurse practitioners, radiologists, rehabilitation specialists, education specialists, and social workers. State-of-the-art treatment is provided at these institutions, offering your child the best chance for remission and ultimately, cure.

For families that live long distances from the center, this referral can cause major disruptions. In these cases, one parent often remains behind to work, keep the household running, and make arrangements for the other children (if any).

When we were told that Katy had leukemia, for some reason I was worried that she would miss supper during the long road trip to Children's Hospital. Why I was worried about this when she wasn't eating anyway is a mystery. The doctor told us not to stop, just to go to a drive-through restaurant. I was so upset that I only packed Katy's clothes; my husband, baby and I had only the clothes on our backs for that first horrible week.

Usually the child is admitted through the emergency room or the oncology clinic, where a physical exam is performed. An intravenous line (IV) is started, more blood is drawn, and a chest x-ray is obtained. Early in your child's hospitalization, the oncologist will perform a spinal tap to determine if any leukemia cells are present in the cerebrospinal fluid and a bone marrow aspiration to identify the type of leukemia. Details of these procedures are described in Chapter 3, *Coping with Procedures*.

Physical responses

Many parents become physically ill in the weeks following diagnosis. This is not surprising, given that most parents stop eating or grab only fast food, normal sleep patterns are a thing of the past, and staying in the hospital exposes them to all sorts of illnesses. Every waking moment is filled with excruciating emotional stress, which makes the physical stress so much more potent.

> *I lost 35 pounds in the six weeks after my son was diagnosed. I had almost constant diarrhea and frequent vomiting.*

· · · · ·

> *My husband and I seemed to take turns getting sick. As soon as one of us got well, the other got sick.*

· · · · ·

> *The second week in the hospital I developed a ferocious sore throat, runny nose, and bad cough. Her counts were on the way down, and they ordered me out of the hospital until I was well. It was agony.*

· · · · ·

> *That first week, every time my son threw up, so did I. I also had almost uncontrollable diarrhea. Every new stressful event in the hospital just dissolved my gut; I could feel it happening. Thank God this faded away after a few weeks.*

Parental illness is a very common event. To attempt to prevent its occurrence, it is helpful to try to eat nutritious meals, get a break from your child's bedside to take a walk outdoors, and find time to sleep. Care needs to be taken not to overuse drugs or alcohol. Whereas physical illnesses usually end after a period of adjustment, emotional effects continue throughout treatment.

Emotional responses

The shock of diagnosis results in an overwhelming number of intense emotions. The length of time people experience each of these feelings greatly differs, depending on preexisting emotional issues and coping ability. These preexisting states vary from person to person, with some whose worlds are stable and good better able to move quickly through powerful emotions than those who are also dealing with other crises. Many of these emotions reappear at different times during the child's treatment. Some of the feelings that parents experience are described below.

Confusion and numbness

In their anguish, most parents cannot remember anything from the doctor's early explanations about their child's disease. This dreamlike state is an almost universal response to shock. The brain provides protective layers of numbness and confusion to prevent emotional overload. This allows parents to examine information in smaller, less threatening pieces. Oncologists understand this phenomenon and are usually quite willing to repeat information as often as necessary. It is sometimes helpful to write down instructions, record them on a small tape recorder, or ask a friend to help keep track of all the new and complex information.

> *The doctor ordered a CBC from the lab. All the while I'm still convinced his bleeding gums were caused by his six-year molars. The rest happened so fast it's hard to recount. We ended up at the hospital getting a bone marrow test. My husband and I tried to tell the doctor that we would go home and let Stephen rest and that when we came back in the morning they could do another CBC. We were positive that his cell counts would go up in the morning. He said that we didn't have until morning. He said Stephen was very, very sick. After the bone marrow test the doctor called us in a room and said that Stephen had leukemia. After that word I couldn't hear a thing. My ears were ringing, and my body was numb. There were tears in my eyes. It was actually a physical reaction. I asked him to stop explaining because I couldn't hear him. I asked for a book and went back to the hospital room to read and to cry.*

· · · · ·

For the longest time (in fact still, three years later) I can hear the doctor's voice on the phone telling me that Brent had leukemia. I remember every tiny detail of that whole day, until we got to the hospital, and then the days blur.

• • • • •

I felt like I was standing on a rug, which was suddenly yanked out from under me. I literally found myself sitting there on the floor, and I just didn't know how to get up.

Denial

In the first few days after diagnosis, many parents use denial to shield themselves from the terrifying situation. They simply cannot believe that their child has a life-threatening illness. In order to convince themselves that the diagnosis is not a mistake, some parents find comfort in seeking a second opinion (see Chapter 6, *Forming a Partnership with the Medical Team*). Denial may serve as a useful method to survive the first few days after diagnosis, but a gradual acceptance must occur so that the family can begin to make the necessary adjustments to cancer treatment. Life has dramatically changed. Once parents accept the doctor's encouraging statistics, push their fears into the background, and begin to believe that their child will survive, they will be better able to provide support for their child.

After our daughter's diagnosis, we had to drive two hours to the hospital. My husband and I talked about leukemia the entire trip, and, I felt, started to come to grips with the illness. However, after the IV, the x-rays, and the blood transfusions, he became extremely upset that they were going to admit her. He thought that we could just go home and it would be finished. I had to say, "This will be our life for years."

• • • • •

My husband and I sat and waited in silence until the doctor came back with the test results. The next thing I knew we were in his office with a primary nurse, a social worker, and a resident listening to the sickening news that our son had leukemia. I couldn't stop crying, and just wanted to grab my two-year-old son and run far, far away.

Guilt

Guilt is a common and normal reaction to childhood leukemia. Parents feel that they have failed to protect their child, and blame themselves. It is especially difficult because the cause of their child's cancer cannot be explained. There are questions: How could we have prevented this? What did we do wrong? How did we miss the signs? Why didn't we bring her to the doctor sooner? Why didn't we insist that the doctor do blood work? Did he inherit this from me? Why didn't we live in a safer place? Maybe I shouldn't have let him drink the well water. Was it because of the fumes from painting the house? Why? Why? Why? It may be difficult to accept, but parents need to remember that nothing they did caused their child's illness. One method to reduce the burden of guilt is to seek information about the causes of leukemia from medical staff and books.

Nancy Roach describes some of these feelings in her booklet *The Last Day of April*:

> Almost as soon as Erin's illness was diagnosed, our self-recrimination began. What had we done to cause this illness? Was I careful enough during pregnancy? We knew radiation was a possible contributor; where had we taken Erin that she might have been exposed? I wondered about the toxic glue used in my advertising work or the silk screen ink used in my artwork. Bob questioned the fumes from some wood preservatives used in a project. We analyzed everything—food, fumes, and TV. Fortunately, most of the guilt feelings were relieved by knowledge and by meeting other parents whose leukemic children had been exposed to an entirely different environment.

Some parents want to do everything possible to make sure that the child's environment does not pose additional risk. One mother explained how she checked on the possibility of electromagnetic fields in her home and yard:

> We have two transformers on our property. After Preston's diagnosis, I wanted to check for electromagnetic fields (EMF). I called our power company about the free service they offer to check EMF in the home and yard of customers. After my call, they came out promptly with testing equipment. Surprisingly, the highest readings that they found were from Preston's alarm clock next to his bed and some baseboard heaters with fans in our kitchen. These emitted far higher EMFs than the transformers did.

And another parent's thought:

> *A year before my daughter's diagnosis, we moved into a rural area and relied on water from a well. When we moved in, I had the water tested for all known contaminants. However, within a year, both of our dogs became ill, and my daughter was diagnosed with leukemia. I decided that for my peace of mind, we should buy water which had been extensively treated.*

Fear and helplessness

A diagnosis of leukemia strips parents of control over their child's daily life. Previously, parents established routines and rules which defined family life. Children woke up, washed and dressed, ate breakfast, perhaps attended day care or school, played with friends, and performed chores. Life was predictable. Suddenly, the family is thrust into a new world populated by an ever changing cast of characters (interns, residents, fellows, oncologists, IV teams, nurses, social workers) and containing a new language (medical terminology): a new world full of hospitals, procedures, and drugs.

Until adjustment begins, parents sometimes feel utterly helpless. Physicians whom they have never met are making life or death decisions for their child. Even if parents are comfortable in a hospital environment, feelings of helplessness may develop because there is simply not enough time in the day to care for a very sick child, deal with their own ever changing emotions, begin to educate themselves about the disease, notify friends and family, make job decisions, and restructure the family to deal with the crisis.

Parents also experience different levels of anxiety, including fear and panic. Many develop problems sleeping and feel overwhelmed by fears of what the future holds. Their world has turned inside out—they have gone from adults in control of their lives to helpless people who cannot protect their child.

Many parents state that helplessness begins to disappear when a sense of reality returns. They begin to make decisions, study their options, learn about the disease, and grow comfortable with the hospital and staff. However, feelings of fear, panic, and anxiety periodically erupt for many parents at varying times throughout their child's treatment.

> *A friend who had lost her husband to cancer called soon after my daughter's diagnosis with acute lymphoblastic leukemia (ALL). I told her that I felt helpless, confused, overwhelmed, and teary. I cried, "When will*

I be my usual competent self again?" She assured me that the beginning was the worst, but to expect to be on an emotional roller coaster for the entire two years of treatment. She was right.

Anger

Anger is a universal response to the diagnosis of cancer.

> *We were sent to the Emergency Room after my son's diagnosis with leukemia. After the inevitable delays, an IV was started and chest X-rays taken. I struggled to remain calm to help my son, but inside I was screaming NO NO NO. A resident patted me on the shoulder and said, "We'll check him out to make sure that everything is OK." I started to sob. She looked surprised and asked what was the matter. I said "He's not OK, and he won't be OK for a long time. He has cancer." I realized later that she was trying to comfort me, but I was very angry. Surprisingly, by the end of my son's hospitalization, we trusted and felt very close to that resident.*

It is nobody's fault that children are stricken with cancer. Since parents cannot direct their anger at the cancer, they target doctors, nurses, spouses, siblings, and sometimes even the ill child. Because anger directed at other people can be very destructive, it is necessary to devise ways to express the anger. Some suggestions from parents for managing anger follow.

Anger at doctors:

- Try to improve communication with doctors.
- Discuss feelings with one of the nurses.
- Discuss feelings with social workers.
- Talk with parents of other ill children.

Anger at family:

- Physical exercise.
- Do yoga or relaxation exercises.
- Keep a journal or tape-record feelings.
- Cry in shower or pound the walls.
- Listen to music.
- Read other people's stories about cancer.
- Talk with friends.

- Talk with parents of ill children.

- Join or start a support group.

- Improve communication within family.

- Try individual or family counseling.

- Live one day at a time.

Anger at God:

- Discuss feelings with clergyman or church members.

- Reexamine faith.

- Trust in God.

- Pray.

It is important to remember that angry feelings are normal and expected. Discovering healthy ways to vent anger is a vital tool for all parents.

Sadness and grief

Parents feel an acute sense of loss when their child is diagnosed with leukemia. They feel unprepared to cope with the possibility of death and fear that they may simply not be able to deal with the enormity of the problems facing the family. Parents describe feeling engulfed by sadness. Grieving for the child is common, even when the prognosis is good. Parents grieve the loss of normalcy, the realization that life will never be the same. They grieve the loss of their dreams and aspirations for their child. Shame and embarrassment are also felt by some parents. Cultural background, individual coping styles, basic temperament, and family dynamics all affect the type of emotions experienced.

Cynthia Krumme's book *Having Leukemia Isn't So Bad. Of Course It Wouldn't Be My First Choice* describes a message tacked on the Massachusetts General Clinic bulletin board:

> *How do I feel? Don't ask!...aside from nervousness, irritability, exhaustion, faintness, dizziness, tremors, cold sweats, depression, insomnia, muscle pains, mental confusion, internal trembling, numbness, indecisiveness, crying spells, unsocial, asocial, and anti-social behavior... I feel fine... Thank you.*

Parents travel a tumultuous emotional path where overwhelming emotions subside only to resurface later. All of these are normal, common responses to a catastrophic event. For the majority of parents, these strong emotions begin to fade as hope grows.

Hope

Daylight will peep through a very small hole

—Japanese proverb

After being buffeted by illness, anger, fear, sadness, grief, and guilt, most parents welcome the growth of hope. Hope is the belief in a better tomorrow. Hope sustains the will to live and gives the strength to endure each trial. The majority of children conquer childhood leukemia and live long and happy lives. There is reason for hope.

Think of what it was like for families twenty-five years ago—very few children were cured. Over the last two decades, due to research and participation in clinical trials (see Chapter 4, *What Is a Clinical Trial?*), we can now expect 70 percent of our children to be cured. In another twenty-five years, we can hope it will be 100 percent.

Many families discover a renewed sense of both the fragility and beauty of life after the diagnosis. Outpourings of love and support from family and friends provide comfort and sustenance. Many parents speak of a renewed appreciation for life and consider each day with their child as a precious gift.

The immediate future

The next several chapters will provide information to help you deal with immediate decisions that must be made in the first week of treatment: How to get the best doctors and treatment plan, what is leukemia, how (and when) to tell your child, what type of catheter to choose, whether your child be enrolled in a clinical study, and chemotherapy. Veteran parents will explain what choices they made, how they adjusted, learned, and became active participants in their children's treatment. Sharing experiences with parents and survivors of childhood leukemia may help your family to develop its own unique strategy for coping with the challenges ahead.

A Mother's View

Memory is a funny thing. I'd be hard pressed to remember what I had for dinner last night but like many people, the day of the Challenger explosion and, even further back, the day of John Kennedy's death, are etched in my mind to the smallest detail.

And like a smaller group of people, the day of my child's cancer diagnosis is a strong and vivid memory, even seven years later. Most of the time, I don't dwell on that series of images. It was, after all, a chapter in our lives, and one that is now blessedly behind us. But early each autumn, when I get a whiff of the crisp smell of leaves in the air, it brings back that dark day when our lives changed forever.

Many of the memories are painful and, like my daughter's scars, they fade a little more each year but will never completely disappear. While dealing with the medical and physical aspects of the disease, my husband and I also made many emotional discoveries. We sometimes encountered ignorance and narrow-mindedness, which made me more sad than angry. Mistakes were made, tempers were short, and family relations were strained. But we saw the other side, too. Somehow, our sense of humor held on throughout the ordeal, and when that kicked in, we had some of the best laughs of our lives. There was compassion and understanding when we needed it most. And people were there for us like never before.

I remember two young fathers on our street, torn by the news, who wanted to help but felt helpless. My husband came home from the hospital late one night to find that our lawn had been mowed and our leaves had been raked by them. They had found a way to make a small difference that day.

Another time, a neighbor came to our house bearing a bakery box full of pastries and the message that his family was praying for our daughter nightly around their supper table. The image of this man, his wife, and his eight children joining in prayer for us will never leave me.

A close friend entered the hospital during that first terrible week we were there to give birth to her son. I held her baby, she held me, and we laughed and cried together.

Sometimes, when I look back at that time, I feel as though everything that is wrong with the world and everything that is right is somehow distilled in one small child's battle to live. We learned so very much about people and about life.

Surely people who haven't experienced a crisis of this magnitude would believe that we would want to put that time behind us and forget as much of it as possible. But the fact is, we grew a little through our pain, like it or not. We see through new eyes. Not all of it is good or happy, but it is profound.

I treasure good friends like never before. I view life as much more fragile and precious than I used to. I think of myself as a tougher person than I was, but I cry more easily now. And sure, I still yell at my kids and eagerly await each September when they will be out of my hair for a few hours each day. But I hold them with more tenderness when they hop off the school bus into my arms. And I like to think that some of the people around us, who saw how suddenly and drastically a family's life can change, hold their children a little dearer as well.

Do I want to forget those terrible days and nights seven years ago? Not on your life. And I hope the smell of autumn leaves will still bring the memories back when I'm a grandmother, even if I can't remember what I had for dinner last night.

—Kathy Tucker
CURE Childhood Cancer Newsletter
Rochester, NY

Resources

Organizations

In the days after the diagnosis, most families need basic technical information and housing close to the hospital. The following are invaluable resources for assistance and information.

Ronald McDonald Houses

For families who have to travel long distances for treatment, a Ronald McDonald House can be a tremendous help. There are Ronald McDonald houses close to hospitals in many major cities. The rates are extremely low, and can be adjusted in cases of financial hardship. In addition to offering a place to stay in a very stressful time, Ronald McDonald Houses provide an emotional haven, a place where families facing similar situations can both give and receive support, advice, warmth, and understanding. Children and parents frequently start lifelong friendships at Ronald McDonald Houses. For information, ask at the medical center or contact:

Ronald McDonald House Coordinator
c/o Golin Communications Inc.
500 North Michigan Ave.
Chicago, IL 60614
(312) 836-7100

Candlelighters Childhood Cancer Foundation

The motto of Candlelighters is, "It is better to light one candle than to curse the darkness." This wonderful organization was founded in 1970, and has over 40,000 members worldwide. Their mission is "to educate, serve, and advocate for families of children with cancer, and the professionals who care for them."

Some of the free services provided by Candlelighters are:

- Library containing over 2,800 journal articles related to childhood cancer.

- Yearly bibliography and resource guide.

- Computerized searches for protocols and treatment options.

- Ability to match families with sources of help.

- Quarterly Newsletter full of articles and poetry by and for parents, children, and the professional community.

- Youth Newsletter by and for children with cancer, survivors, and siblings.

- Various handbooks on topics such as bone marrow transplant and educating the child with cancer.

- Toll Free Hotline 1-800-366-CCCF (in the U.S.).

When you subscribe to Candlelighters (no charge), they will send you a packet of information describing all of the services they provide. This organization has educated and comforted thousands of parents and professionals. A subscription to Candlelighters is a tremendously helpful thing for extended family, friends, or clergy to provide.

Candlelighters Childhood Cancer Foundation
7910 Woodmont Ave. Suite 460
Bethesda, MD 20814
1-800-366-CCCF
FAX: (301) 718-2686
World Wide Web: *http://www.candlelighters.org*
email: *info@candlelighters.org*

Candlelighters Childhood Cancer Foundation Canada
National Office
Suite 401, 55 Eglinton Avenue East
Toronto, ON Canada M4P 1G8
1-800-363-1062 (Canada only)
(416) 489-6440
FAX: (416) 489-9812
World Wide Web: *http://www.candlelighters.ca*
email: *staff@candlelighters.ca*

The Leukemia Society of America

This organization provides financial assistance to families, funds research, sponsors a national program in education for the public and the medical community, and publishes a large number of booklets on cancer-related topics. Outpatients are eligible for assistance of up to $750 per patient per year for costs not covered by other sources. The financial assistance program includes payments for:

- Drugs used in the care, treatment, and/or control of leukemia and allied diseases.

- Processing, typing, screening, and crossmatching of blood components for transfusion.

- Fees for transfusions of red cells, leukocytes, and platelets.

- Transportation to and from a doctor's office, hospital or treatment center.

- X-ray therapy up to $300 annually for cranial (not spinal) radiation for patients with acute leukemia.

To apply for financial aid, write or call:

Leukemia Society of America, Inc.
600 Third Avenue, 4th Floor
New York, NY 10016
(212) 573-8484 or 1-800-955-4LSA
FAX: (212) 856-9686
World Wide Web: *http://www.leukemia.org/*

The Leukemia Society will give the caller the address and phone number for the nearest local chapter. Application for financial aid is made to the local chapter. It is important to apply as soon as possible after diagnosis, because only bills incurred after application are eligible for reimbursement. For instance, if your child receives cranial radiation before you apply, you will not receive aid to cover that expense.

Because it is necessary to contact the national office, then the local chapter, then apply, then submit bills (you have up to a year to submit bills), it is quite helpful for a close friend or family member to make the initial calls and acquire the necessary forms to help an already overburdened family to obtain some financial assistance.

American Cancer Society and Canadian Cancer Society

The American Cancer Society and the Canadian Cancer Society have a national network of both employees and volunteers who implement count-less research, education, and patient service programs. Although programs differ according to state and province, some widely available programs are:

- Patient-to-patient visitation.

- Transportation—a network of volunteer drivers is available in many communities.

- Housing—some hotels and motels near major treatment centers offer rooms to those who must travel for treatment.

- Equipment and supplies—items not covered by insurance loaned for home use.

- Support groups—available for parents, siblings, and young cancer patients in some communities.

- Literature—booklets on a large variety of topics available free upon request.

- Summer camps for children with cancer—available in some communities.

- Research—public-donation funding of numerous researchers exploring the cause, prevention, and treatment of cancer.

- Educational programs—professionally taught programs on coping with various aspects of living with cancer are available in most communities.

- Core support grant for Candlelighters.

For information on the American Cancer Society programs in your community, write or call:

American Cancer Society
1599 Clifton Road NE
Atlanta, GA 30329-4251
1-800-ACS-2345
World Wide Web: *http://www.cancer.org/*

For information on the Canadian Cancer Society programs in your community, write or call:

Canadian Cancer Society
565 W 10th Ave.
Vancouver, BC Canada V5Z 4J4
(604) 872-4400
World Wide Web: *http://www.bc.cancer.ca/ccs/*

Reading for adults

Some of the books, booklets, and articles listed in this section of each chapter might also be appropriate for mature teen patients and siblings, depending on the level of their desire for information.

Adams, David, and Eleanor Deveau. *Coping With Childhood Cancer: Where Do We Go from Here?* rev.ed. Toronto: Kinbridge Publications, 1993. A guide for parents of children with cancer written by a pediatric social worker and nurse. Chapters 1 and 2 deal with the emotional and social impact of diagnosis, with a section on special problems for single parents.

Gravelle, Karen and Bertram A. John. *Teenagers Face to Face with Cancer.* New York: Julian Messner, 1986. Seventeen teenagers talk openly about their cancer, including diagnosis, dealing with doctors, chemotherapy, relationships with others, planning for the future, and relapse. A heartfelt, honest, yet comforting book.

Johnson, Joy, and S. M. Johnson. *Why Mine?: A Book for Parents Whose Child is Seriously Ill*. Omaha, NE: Centering Corporation, 1981. To order, call (402) 553-1200. Quotes from parents across the country make this a valuable book for families of seriously ill children. Addresses fears, feelings, marriages, siblings, and the ill child.

Krumme, Cynthia. *Having Leukemia Isn't So Bad. Of Course It Wouldn't Be My First Choice*. Winchester, MA: Sargasso Enterprises, 1993. To order, call (617) 729-9037; 14 Wildwood Street, Winchester, Ma. 01890. Personal story of Catherine Krumme, diagnosed with leukemia at age 4, relapsed at age 7, finished treatment at age 10. Catherine began college in 1994.

Kushner, Harold. *When Bad Things Happen to Good People*. Boston: G.K. Hall, 1982. A rabbi wrote this comforting book on how people of faith deal with catastrophic events.

Leukemia Society of America. *Emotional Aspects of Childhood Leukemia*. To obtain a free copy, call 1-800-955-4LSA. 34-page booklet describes the emotions of parents at diagnosis, changes in family life, dealing with hospitalizations, siblings, school, and bereavement.

National Institute of Health. *Young People With Cancer*. 67-page booklet. NIH Publication No. 89-2378. To obtain a free copy call 1-800-4-CANCER. This booklet describes leukemia, treatment for different types of childhood cancer, medical procedures, dealing with the diagnosis, family issues, and sources of information.

Rosenfeld, Isadore, M.D. *Second Opinion: Your Comprehensive Guide to Treatment Alternatives*. New York: Simon & Shuster, 1981. Chapters 1, 2, and 27 contain basic information from a physician on why second opinions are important and how to obtain one.

Roach, Nancy. *The Last Day of April*. Atlanta, GA: American Cancer Society, 1974. Out of print. To see if any copies are still available, call 1-800-ACS-2345. Booklet written by a mother of a child who dies from ALL; simply and movingly describes the emotions of the cancer experience.

Reading for children

Baker, Lynn, M.D. *You and Leukemia: A Day at a Time*. Philadelphia: W. B. Saunders Company, 1988. Very detailed but easy-to-read book for both children and parents. Written by a doctor, it describes the disease, procedures, and drugs.

Leukemia Society of America. *What It Is That I Have, Don't Want, Didn't Ask For, Can't Give Back, and How I Feel About It.* 1-800-955-4LSA. Booklet written by adolescents about their feelings about many different aspects of cancer treatment. In notebook form.

Monroe, Judy. *The Facts About Leukemia.* New York: Crestwood House, 1990. Describes leukemia in very clear, basic language appropriate for grade school children.

Rogers, Fred. *Going to the Hospital.* New York: G. P. Putnam's Sons, 1988. With pictures and words, TV's beloved Mr. Rogers helps to make preschoolers less fearful of hospitals.

Rogers, Fred. *Some Things Change and Some Things Stay the Same.* American Cancer Society. Order by calling 1-800-ACS-2345. Wonderful book for preschool age children with cancer and their siblings. Very comforting.

Video

Leukemia Society of America. *My Hug-A-Bear Friend.* To obtain free copy, call 1-800-955-4LSA. Sixteen-minute tape for young children, in which Hug-A-Bear (a comforting cartoon bear) explains how leukemia is diagnosed and treated.

CHAPTER 2

What Is Leukemia?

The world breaks everyone and afterward many are strong at the broken places.

—Ernest Hemingway
A Farewell to Arms

THE WORD LEUKEMIA literally means "white blood." Leukemia is the term used to describe a variety of cancers that begin in the blood-forming tissues of the bone marrow, the spongy material that fills the long bones in the body and produces blood cells. In leukemia, the bone marrow factory creates an overabundance of diseased white cells that cannot perform their normal function of fighting infection. As the bone marrow floods the bloodstream with diseased white cells, production of red cells (which prevent anemia) and platelets (which form clots to stop bleeding) slows and stops.

To better understand leukemia, it is necessary to become familiar with the function and composition of blood.

Leukemia is a disease of the blood

Blood is a vital liquid, which supplies oxygen, food, hormones, and other necessary chemicals to all of the body's cells. It removes toxins and other waste products from the cells. Blood helps the lymph system to fight infection and carries the cells necessary for repairing injuries.

Whole blood is made up of plasma, which is a clear fluid, and many other components, each with a specific task. The three main elements involved in leukemia are red blood cells, platelets, and white blood cells.

Red blood cells (erythrocytes or RBCs) contain hemoglobin, a protein which picks up oxygen in the lungs and transports it throughout the body. RBCs give blood its red color. When leukemia cells in the bone marrow slow down the production of red cells, the child develops anemia. Anemia can cause weakness, irritability, pale skin, and shortness of breath.

Platelets (thrombocytes) are tiny, disc-shaped cells which help form clots to stop bleeding. Leukemia can dramatically slow down the production of platelets, causing children to bleed excessively from cuts or in some cases from their nose or gums. Children with leukemia usually develop large bruises; sometimes small red dots (called petechiae) cover their skin.

White blood cells (leukocytes or WBCs) destroy foreign substances in the body such as viruses, bacteria, and fungi. They are produced and stored in the bone marrow and are released when needed by the body. If an infection is present, the body produces extra WBCs. There are three main types of leukocytes:

1. **Monocytes.** Theses cells contain enzymes that kill foreign bacteria.

2. **Lymphocytes.** There are two types that interact to prevent infection and provide immunity to disease:
   - T-cells attack infected cells, foreign tissue, and cancer cells.
   - B-cells produce antibodies which destroy foreign substances.

3. **Granulocytes.** There are three types that are the first defense against infection:
   - Neutrophils are the most numerous WBCs and are the first to respond to foreign bacteria.
   - Eosinophils respond to allergic reactions as well as foreign bacteria.
   - Basophils are the rarest of the white cells and play a special role in allergic reactions.

The different types of leukemia are cancers of a specific white blood cell type. For instance, acute lymphoblastic leukemia affects only lymphocytes. The specific types of leukemia are explained fully later in the chapter.

What is a blast?

"Blast" is a short name for an immature white blood cell such as lymphoblast, myeloblast, or monoblast. Normally, less than five percent of the cells contained in healthy bone marrow at any one time are blasts. Normal blasts develop into mature, functioning white blood cells, and are not usually found in the bloodstream. Leukemic blasts remain immature, multiply continuously, provide no defense against infection, and may be present in large numbers in the bloodstream.

How does leukemia begin?

When abnormal white blood cells appear in the bone marrow, they multiply rapidly and begin to crowd out the normal cells that develop there. After accumulating in the bone marrow, leukemic cells spill over into the blood and are carried to vital organs such as the lungs, liver, spleen, and kidneys. Leukemic cells may also cross the blood-brain barrier and invade the central nervous system (brain and spinal cord).

When the leukemic blasts begin to fill the marrow, production of healthy red cells, platelets, and white cells cannot be maintained. As the number of normal cells decreases, symptoms appear. Low red cell counts cause fatigue and pale skin. Low platelet counts may result in bruising and bleeding problems. If mature neutrophils and lymphoblasts are crowded out by the blasts, the child will have little or no defense against infections.

Who gets leukemia?

Acute leukemia is the most common childhood cancer. Although generally thought of as strictly a childhood disease, many more adults than children develop leukemia. Each year in the United States, approximately 25,000 adults and 2,500 children will be diagnosed with acute leukemia.

Childhood leukemia is most commonly diagnosed at ages two to seven, with the highest incidence at approximately four years of age. In the United States, leukemia is more common in whites than in blacks and boys have a slightly higher incidence than girls. Children with chromosomal abnormalities such as Down's syndrome, Bloom's syndrome, or Fanconi's anemia have a higher risk of developing leukemia than the general population. However, most children with these syndromes will not develop leukemia.

Although the exact cause of childhood leukemia is a mystery, certain factors are known to increase the risk of developing the disease.

Genetic factors

It is known that persons with extra chromosomes (genetic material contained in cells) or certain chromosomal abnormalities have a greater chance of developing leukemia. It is uncertain whether this is a cause or merely an association. In cases where one identical twin has leukemia, the other twin has a 25 percent chance of developing the disease within one year, but this risk decreases with an older age at diagnosis and with time. It is not known whether this is caused by an inherited trait or a simultaneous exposure to the same carcinogen. Leukemia is not contagious; it cannot be passed from one person to another.

Environmental factors

Exposure to ionizing radiation and certain toxic chemicals may predispose individuals to leukemia. Many Japanese who were exposed to fallout from the atomic bomb during World War II and some of the people living near the Chernobyl accident in the Ukraine have developed leukemia. Chronic exposure to benzene has been associated with leukemia in adults. However, most children are not exposed to large amounts of radiation or industrial chemicals. Risks to children from exposure to electromagnetic fields, herbicides, or pesticides are under investigation.

The National Institutes of Health maintain a free hot line to answer questions on health and the environment, at 1-800-643-4794. For questions about EMFs (electromagnetic fields), call the Environmental Protection Agency's EMF InfoLine at 1-800-363-2383. For information about the federal government's EMF research efforts, including public information materials developed by the EMF RAPID program, refer to the EMF RAPID home page on the World Wide Web: *http://www.niehs.nih.gov/emfrapid/home.htm*.

Viral factors

Viruses that cause leukemia in cows, cats, chickens, gibbons, and mice have been found. Recently, a T-cell virus has been identified which causes a rare type of leukemia-lymphoma in adults; however, no virus has been found which causes the types of leukemia commonly found in children.

Currently, it is thought that a complex interaction among genetic, environmental, immunologic, and possibly viral factors predispose individuals to leukemia. The most important point for parents to remember is that at present there is no way to predict or prevent leukemia.

How is leukemia diagnosed?

A tentative diagnosis is made after a physical examination of the child and microscopic analysis of a blood sample. Physical findings may include: pale skin, bruising or unusual bleeding, enlarged liver, spleen, or lymph nodes, ear or other infections (frequently resistant to treatment), weakness, and fever. Parents may describe irritability, night sweats, fatigue, bone pain, loss of appetite, and problems with balance. The blood test may show decreased red cells, decreased granulocytes, decreased platelets, and increased lymphocytes. There may be blast cells circulating in the blood.

To confirm a diagnosis of leukemia, bone marrow is sampled and tested (see Chapter 3, *Coping with Procedures*). The bone marrow is examined microscopically by a pathologist, a physician who specializes in body tissue analysis. If more than 25 percent blasts are discovered in the marrow, the pathologist will confirm the diagnosis of leukemia. A portion of the bone marrow is also sent to a specialized laboratory, which analyzes many other features of the leukemic cells to determine which type of leukemia is present and whether the child has a low, average, or high risk of relapse. Risk levels help the oncologist choose the appropriate treatment for each child.

How is leukemia best treated?

Over 70 percent of children with leukemia who receive optimal treatment are cured of the disease. At diagnosis, parents are confused about how to find the best doctors and treatment plan for their child. The best care available is obtained from institutions who are part of the Children's Cancer Group or the Pediatric Oncology Group (see Chapter 4, *What Is a Clinical Trial?*). These two study groups, composed of pediatric oncologists of every description, establish the standard of care for pediatric cancer patients, conduct new studies to discover better therapies or fine-tune the old ones, and now, with so many survivors, set the blueprint for follow-up. If the treatment center you are referred to is a member of one of these groups, you can rest assured that your child will have access to the best thinking on the treatment of pediatric cancers.

Types of leukemia

The two broad classifications of leukemia are acute (rapid progression) and chronic (slow progression). The acute leukemias are characterized by abnormal numbers of immature white cells (blasts). In chronic leukemia, mature white cells predominate. Chronic leukemia accounts for less than five percent of all childhood leukemia.

Acute leukemia is the most common type of cancer found in children. The two most common types of acute leukemia are acute lymphoblastic leukemia (ALL) and acute myeloid leukemia (AML). AML is also known as acute non-lymphoblastic leukemia (ANLL).

Acute lymphoblastic leukemia (ALL)

Seventy-five percent of all children with leukemia have ALL. It is caused by a rapid proliferation of immature lymphocytes, which would normally have developed into mature T-cells or B-cells. There are several subgroups of ALL based on whether the cancer cells developed from B-cells or T-cells, or display characteristics of both. The first sample of bone marrow taken from the child is analyzed to identify cellular characteristics to help plan the best therapy as well as predict response to treatment. Each different subgroup has a different response to treatment; some require less chemotherapy, while others require aggressive treatment to achieve a cure.

> I was walking around the hospital looking shellshocked the day after my daughter had been admitted to Children's Hospital with leukemia. One of the other mothers came up, introduced herself, and asked what we were in for. I told her leukemia. She told me that her son had just relapsed again from a brain tumor. She looked wistful and said how much she wished that her son had ALL. She said, "You might think that's strange, but I see those kids come, get better, and go home. We are still here."

Prognosis for the child with ALL

Treatment of childhood ALL is one of the major medical success stories of the last two decades. In the 1960s patients with ALL usually lived only for a few months, but by the early 1990s, 70 percent of children receiving optimal treatment were cured. The appropriate treatment for each child with ALL is determined by analysis of a multitude of clinical and biologic features. Most centers describe the child's chances of relapse as low, average, or high.

To determine the risk level, the following prognostic factors are considered: initial white blood count; age at diagnosis; sex; amount of chromosomal material; cell morphology (shape); immunologic type; presence or absence of tumor in chest; enlarged liver, spleen, and/or lymph nodes; presence or absence of chromosomal translocations; hemoglobin levels at diagnosis; race; platelet count at diagnosis; leukemia cells in the cerebrospinal fluid at diagnosis; and how quickly the child enters remission.

> High-risk ALL, in my daughter's clinical trial, was defined as a person between one and twenty years old with acute lymphoblastic leukemia or undifferentiated leukemia, who had either a white count greater than 50,000 or was older than ten years. They told me that she had a 65 percent chance of being cured. Once she finished treatment, that increased to an 85 percent chance of a cure. I asked what "cure" meant, and was told that if she made it five years from diagnosis without relapse, the leukemia was probably gone forever.

Treatment for ALL

ALL is now considered to be one of the most curable forms of childhood cancer. To receive the best available treatment, it is essential that the child with ALL receive treatment at a pediatric medical center from board-certified hematologists/oncologists with extensive experience treating acute leukemia. The intense treatment for ALL begins within days of diagnosis and requires aggressive supportive care. The goal of treatment is to achieve a complete remission by obliterating all cancer cells as quickly as possible. Complete remission occurs when all signs and symptoms of leukemia disappear and abnormal cells are no longer found in the blood, bone marrow, and cerebrospinal fluid.

The mainstay of treatment for ALL is chemotherapy—the use of various drugs to treat disease. In some cases radiation of the brain and spinal cord is also administered. Bone marrow transplantation is sometimes used in the treatment of ALL, but usually only after relapse. For the average-risk patient, treatment is typically divided into four phases: induction, central nervous system prophylaxis, consolidation, and maintenance.

Induction

Induction is the most intensive phase of treatment since its purpose is to kill as many abnormal white cells in the shortest amount of time possible. It usually lasts four weeks but can last up to twelve weeks, and for a portion of that time, children must remain hospitalized for monitoring and transfusions. For the remainder of the time, children are treated on an outpatient basis unless a complication arises. Children usually need to be readmitted on more than one occasion during induction due to fever and/or infection.

Chemotherapy is most effective if two, three, or four drugs are used simultaneously. In 1997, the majority of ALL induction programs include methotrexate, vincristine, prednisone, L-asparaginase, and sometimes daunomycin. Drugs are given intravenously (through a needle or tube in the vein), intramuscularly (injection in muscle), orally (by mouth), or intrathecally (injected into the cerebrospinal fluid). These drugs can cause numerous side effects. See Chapter 10, *Chemotherapy*, for an in-depth discussion of each drug and its side effects.

Ninety-five percent of children who receive three or more drugs during induction achieve a complete remission.

CNS prophylaxis

In most cases of childhood ALL, cancer cells are not found in the cerebrospinal fluid at diagnosis. However, prior to using drugs and/or radiation to the central nervous system (CNS), it was a frequent relapse site. Therefore, CNS prophylaxis (prevention) is an essential component of treatment for ALL. Because a blood-brain barrier exists which prevents chemotherapy drugs from crossing into the CNS to destroy leukemic cells, chemotherapy drugs are injected directly into the cerebrospinal fluid (called intrathecal medication) during spinal taps. Intrathecal medication is given during induction and periodically throughout treatment.

Low- and average-risk patients receive intrathecal methotrexate, or triple intrathecal therapy—methotrexate, hydrocortisone, and cytarabine—for CNS prophylaxis. Patients with a high risk of CNS relapse (e.g., high white cell count at diagnosis, T-cell ALL with a high white cell count, or those with mediastinal mass) require intrathecal therapy as well as cranial radiation.

CNS prophylaxis has been extraordinarily successful in preventing CNS relapse, and is partially responsible for the huge increase in cure rates. Unfortunately, the treatments can sometimes cause long-term disabilities such as decreased attention span, short-term memory problems, and lower ability in spatial and mathematical skills, particularly when radiation is used (see Chapter 15,). Current clinical trials are attempting to determine how much intrathecal medicine is necessary to prevent relapse while minimizing the chances for long-term side effects or whether high-dose intravenous methotrexate can replace radiation in some patients.

Consolidation

Even though the child is in remission, in children with intermediate or high risk ALL, a second series of drugs is necessary to prevent the reappearance of leukemia.

Consolidation therapy consists of new combinations of drugs to destroy any cancer cells that survived induction. In 1997, the most common drugs used in consolidation are: methotrexate, cyclophosphamide (cytoxan or endoxan), cytosine arabinoside (ARA-C), 6-mercaptopurine (6-MP), dexamethasone (decadron), L-asparaginase, adriamycin, and thioguanine. See Chapter 10, *Chemotherapy*, for detailed descriptions of these drugs.

More intensive regimens

Protocols for high risk ALL contain more drugs at higher doses. This treatment has increased toxicity but is more effective for the small percentage of children with high-risk features. In these high-risk protocols, a second induction (commonly called delayed intensification or reinduction) and a second consolidation are usually administered prior to maintenance. Cranial radiation, in addition to intrathecal chemotherapy, is currently the standard treatment to prevent CNS relapse for high-risk ALL.

The researchers studying childhood cancer are gaining understanding of what types and subtypes of particular cancers require more intensive therapy and for which ones therapy can be less aggressive. If you are at a center associated with the Children's Cancer Group or Pediatric Oncology Group, you can feel comfortable that your pediatric oncologist will not propose an aggressive treatment unless it is your child's best chance for a cure.

Maintenance

Maintenance therapy, the final phase of treatment for ALL, consists of daily low-dose chemotherapy for two to three years. Its purpose is to kill any remaining cancer cells. This portion of treatment is less toxic and easier to tolerate than induction and consolidation.

In most clinical trials, mercaptopurine (6-MP) administered daily and methotrexate given weekly are the standard drugs. In addition, other drugs such as vincristine, prednisone, or dexamethasone are given periodically. Many protocols also include intrathecal methotrexate during maintenance therapy. (See Chapter 10, *Chemotherapy*.)

At the end of maintenance, spinal tap and bone marrow samples are examined to ensure that the cerebrospinal fluid and bone marrow are free of leukemia. If no cancer is found, treatment ends.

Bone marrow transplantation (BMT)

Bone marrow transplants are not the treatment of choice for children newly diagnosed with ALL. However, for many children with ALL in second remission, bone marrow transplantation may be recommended (see Chapter 20, *Bone Marrow Transplantation*).

Newest treatment options

To learn of the newest treatments available, call 1-800-4-CANCER and ask for the PDQ (physicians data query) for ALL. These free statements explain the disease, state-of-the-art treatments, and ongoing clinical trials. There are two versions available: one for patients that uses simple language and contains no statistics and one for profesionals that is technical, thorough, and includes citations to the scientific literature.

Acute myeloid leukemia (AML)

AML is cancer of the granulocytes. Because treatment for AML and ALL are very different, it is crucial that sophisticated laboratory studies are performed on the bone marrow samples to determine whether the child has AML or ALL. Eight thousand cases of AML are diagnosed in the U.S. each year, most often in adults over forty. It is also seen in infants or older teens, but can also strike children at any age. AML accounts for approximately 15 percent of all cases of childhood leukemia. There are seven different classifications or types of AML (M1 to M7) based on the type of granulocyte involved.

> My six-year-old daughter had been getting bad headaches. The school would call me to pick her up, and she would throw up all the way home. She had an appointment with the optometrist who noticed an odd-looking vein in her eye and that she looked pale and had some bruising. He recommended taking her in for blood work. We did, and she was diagnosed with AML type M2.

Prognosis for the child with AML

Treatment for AML has dramatically improved in the last decade. Today, 75 to 85 percent of children who receive optimal treatment at a major pediatric medical center achieve a complete remission. Of the children who achieve remission, 40 to 50 percent remain in remission for five years, and are considered cured.

Treatment for AML

Treatment for AML is very intensive, lasts one to three years, and is potentially hazardous. It is vital that children with this disease are treated at a major pediatric hospital with expertise in treating acute leukemias. Chemotherapy is the primary treatment. Radiation of the brain and sometimes the spinal cord is also used in some protocols. Bone marrow transplantation (see Chapter 20) is used with increasing frequency to treat childhood AML in first or second remission.

As with ALL, chemotherapy drugs for AML are more successful if two, three, or four are used simultaneously. The most common drugs used to treat AML are: ARA-C (cytarabine), daunomycin (daunorubicin), etoposide, thioguanine, vincristine, and prednisone. Chemotherapy can be administered by mouth (orally), intravenously (through the IV), intramuscularly (injection in the muscle), or intrathecally (through a needle in the lower part of the back). See Chapter 10, *Chemotherapy*, for an in-depth discussion of each drug, possible side effects, and parent suggestions.

The two phases of treatment for AML are induction and post-remission therapy.

Induction

Induction is the most intense part of treatment; its purpose is to quickly kill as many cancer cells as possible. Several weeks of hospitalization are usually required, as the toxic chemotherapy drugs damage normal cells as well as leukemic cells, leaving the child susceptible to infections and excessive bleeding. Biologic response modifiers such as granulocyte-macrophage colony-stimulating factor or granulocyte colony-stimulating factor are used to shorten the duration of nutropenia (low white counts). Transfusions of blood and platelets are usually necessary, as is intravenous feeding (hyperalimentation).

If the disease has spread to the brain, the child is given intrathecal chemotherapy and sometimes radiation to destroy the cancer cells in the central nervous system. Even if leukemia cells have not been found in the brain, most protocols for childhood AML use some form of CNS treatment, usually intrathecal chemotherapy with or without cranial radiation.

During induction, the majority of patients go into remission, and then enter the second phase of treatment.

Post-remission therapy

Even though your child is in complete remission, residual cancer cells would multiply rapidly without additional treatment. Consequently, after a short period of recuperation from induction, children with AML receive either a bone marrow transplant or more chemotherapy called post-remission therapy.

Post-remission therapy consists of two parts: consolidation and intensification. Your child may receive one or both of these phases of treatment. The drugs used during post-remission therapy are high-dose cytarabine, etoposide, amsacrine, vincristine, azacitidine, cyclophosphamide, and methotrexate.

In the past, a third phase of treatment, called maintenance, has been used. This phase consists of low-dose chemotherapy given for a number of years. Currently no data conclusively shows that additional therapy after intensive induction and consolidation lengthens remission for children with childhood AML. In 1997, there are ongoing clinical trials using immunotherapy (interleukin-2) versus standard follow-up to see if this treatment extends length of remission.

Bone marrow transplantation (BMT)

BMT is being used increasingly to treat children with AML in first remission. High-dose chemotherapy, with or without total body radiation, is used to destroy the child's bone marrow and any remaining cancer cells. Healthy matched marrow is taken from another person, usually a family member, and is dripped into the patient's blood intravenously. The new marrow migrates to the bones and replaces the destroyed marrow. This is called an allogenic transplant. Nearly 60 percent of children with matched donors who undergo a BMT in first remission experience remissions in excess of three years without severe graft-versus-host disease.

Another method sometimes used for children without a matched, or closely matched, donor is called autologous BMT. In this type of transplant, marrow is removed from the child, may be treated chemically to remove all leukemia cells, and frozen. After the child's own diseased marrow has been destroyed, the frozen marrow is thawed and returned to the patient intravenously. Clinical trials have found autologous transplants to be no more effective than intensive chemotherapy in treating AML.

Chapter 20, *Bone Marrow Transplantation*, discusses in great detail the types of transplants, the procedures, side effects, and coping suggestions from parents and survivors.

Newest treatment options

To learn of the newest treatments available, call 1-800-4-CANCER and ask for the PDQ (physicians data query) for AML. These free statements explain the disease, state-of-the-art treatments, and ongoing clinical trials. There are two versions available: one for patients that uses simple language and contains no statistics and one for profesionals that is technical, thorough, and includes citations to the scientific literature.

Chronic myelogenous leukemia (CML)

CML is a rare type of leukemia, accounting for less than five percent of all childhood leukemias. This disease is characterized by increased production of granulocytes in the bone marrow, and progresses slowly. It is usually associated with a specific chromosomal abnormality. The two major forms are the juvenile form, which occurs mostly in infants, and the adult form, which occurs primarily in adults and adolescents.

Juvenile CML

Juvenile CML usually strikes children under five years of age. The symptoms are similar to that of the acute leukemias: pale skin, bruising, fatigue, headaches, sweating, and recurrent infection. Also usually present are a face rash, enlarged lymph nodes, enlarged spleen and liver, and low platelet count. Unlike the adult form of CML, the juvenile form does not have a chronic phase. Once diagnosed, progressive deterioration usually occurs.

Because chemotherapy has not proven to generally be a successful treatment for juvenile CML, bone marrow transplantation provides the only hope for cure. See Chapter 20, *Bone Marrow Transplantation*.

Adult CML

This disease is most common in adults, but occasionally is diagnosed in older boys and girls. It is characterized by a very large spleen and high white count of mostly neutrophils and other types of granulocytes. Other symptoms of CML are fatigue, weakness, headaches, irritability, fevers, night sweats, and weight loss. Some patients have no symptoms and are picked up on a routine blood test done for other reasons. There is no anemia or tendency to bleed. In over 90 percent of patients with CML, analysis of the cells of the bone marrow shows a genetic abnormality called the Philadelphia chromosome. This chromosome contains a "translocation" or swap of genetic material involving chromosomes 9 and 22, abbreviated as t(9;22).

Despite its name, adult CML can progress rapidly but it generally has:

- A chronic phase (less than 5 percent blasts in the peripheral blood or bone marrow), which can last several years.

- An accelerated phase (greater than 5 percent but less than 30 percent blasts in the peripheral blood or bone marrow).

- A blast crisis (greater than 30 percent blasts in the peripheral blood or bone marrow).

> Leah, eleven years old, enjoyed participating in basketball, soccer, and gymnastics. She developed severe hip joint pain, and we brought her back to the doctor three times in an unsuccessful attempt to find out what was wrong. The last time, my husband had to carry her in because she couldn't walk. They did blood work, and her white count was 176,000 and her platelets were one million. A bone marrow test confirmed that she had CML.

Treatment for children with adult CML

The goal of initial treatment is to lower the white count and reduce the size of the spleen. This is accomplished by taking oral medications, usually either hydroxyurea or busulphan (also called myleran). Two recent studies comparing the biologic agent interferon alfa with conventional chemotherapy (hydroxyurea or busulfan) showed that interferon resulted in more delay of disease progression and prolonged survival. The average length of the chronic phase of CML is three years, although some patients have remained in this phase for up to ten years.

The doctors did not know how long my daughter had had CML prior to diagnosis, so they estimated that she had three days to four years before the blast phase would begin. They told us that if the blast phase started, there was nothing they could do. She needed a bone marrow transplant as soon as possible.

If the spleen does not shrink after treatment with drugs, radiation or surgical removal may be required.

Although chemotherapy and interferon alpha slow the progress of CML, the only hope for cure is bone marrow transplantation. The highest cure rates occur when the patient is transplanted during the chronic phase with marrow from an identical twin, HLA-identical family member, or HLA-identical non-family donor. Refer to Chapter 20, *Bone Marrow Transplantation*, for detailed information.

The second stage or "accelerated phase" is usually brief. The number of both mature white blood cells and blast cells in the bloodstream increases. The number of red blood cells drops and platelets may increase or decrease. In 1997, treatment for this phase includes increased doses of hydroxyurea, 6-mercaptopurine (purinethol) or cytosine arabinoside (Cytosar-U or Ara-C). (See Chapter 10, *Chemotherapy*.)

The final phase is called "transformational phase" or "blast crisis." During this phase, white blood cells fail to mature and flood the bloodstream. This phase is usually resistant to chemotherapy, and children typically survive less than six months.

Once parents understand the basics about the type of leukemia their child has, it is time to begin to decide how and when to tell their child the news.

Telling your child

In the first harrowing days after a diagnosis of leukemia, parents must decide when and what to tell their children. Because parents are coping with a bewildering array of emotions themselves, sharing information and providing reassurance and hope may be difficult. In the past, shielding children from the painful reality was the norm. Most experts now agree that children feel less anxiety and cope with treatments better if they have a clear understanding of the disease. It is important to provide age-appropriate information soon after diagnosis and to create a supportive climate so that children feel comfortable asking questions of both parents and the medical team. Sharing strengthens the family, allowing all members to face the crisis together.

When should you tell your child?

As soon as possible. It is impossible to prevent a child from knowing that he is seriously ill. The child has been whisked to an unfamiliar hospital by frightened parents, endured painful tests, received drugs and transfusions. Cards and presents begin to arrive, and friends and siblings are absent or behave in a strange manner.

Delay in providing age-appropriate information escalates the child's fears. Well-meaning parents may cause great anguish by isolating their child in a conspiracy of silence. Parents may delude themselves into thinking that the diagnosis is a secret, but children are extraordinarily perceptive. They frequently keep their thoughts and feelings to themselves in order to protect their parents from more pain. In this case, not only must the child deal with having cancer, but he must do it on his own with no one to console him. Lacking accurate information, children can imagine scenarios far more frightening than the reality.

> We feel that you have to be very honest or the child will not be able to trust you. Meagan (5 years old) has always known that she has cancer and thinks of her treatments and medications as the warriors to help the good cells fight the bad cells.

Who should tell your child

This is purely a personal decision, influenced by ease of communication within the family, age and temperament of the child, religious beliefs, and sometimes physician recommendation. Small children (ages 1 to 3) primarily fear separation from parents. The presence of strangers in an already unfamiliar situation may cause additional fear. Many parents tell their small child in private, while others prefer to have family members, family physician, clergyman, or social worker present.

Older children (4 to 12) sometimes benefit from having the treatment team (oncologist, nurse, social worker or psychologist) present. This may create a feeling that all present will unite to help her get well. Staff members can answer the child's questions and provide comfort for the entire family. Children in this age group frequently feel guilty and responsible for their illness.

They may harbor fears that the cancer is a punishment for something that they did wrong. Social workers and nurses can help explore unspoken questions, provide reassurance, and identify the needs of parents, the sick child, and siblings.

> *My six-year-old son Brent was sitting next to me when the doctor called to tell me that he had leukemia. I whispered into the phone, "What should I tell him?" The doctor said to tell him that he had a disease in his blood and needed to go to a special children's hospital for help. As we were getting ready to go to the hospital, Brent asked if he had AIDS (it was right after Magic Johnson's announcement), if he was going to die, what were they going to do to him. We didn't know how to answer all the questions, but told him that we would find out at the hospital. My husband told him that he was a strong boy and we would all fight this thing together. I was at a loss for words.*

> *At the hospital, they were wonderful. What impressed me the most was that they always talked to Brent first, and answered all his questions before talking to us. When Zac (8-year-old brother) came to the hospital two days later, the doctors took him in the hall and talked to him for a long time, explaining and answering his questions.*

> *I was glad that we were all so honest, because Brent later confided to me that he thought he got leukemia because he hadn't been drinking enough milk.*

Adolescents' need for control and autonomy should be respected. Teenagers sometimes feel more comfortable discussing the diagnosis with their physician in private. At a time when teens' developmental tasks are to challenge authority figures and begin to become independent from their families, they are suddenly totally dependent on medical personnel to save their lives and parents to provide emotional support. In some families, a diagnosis of cancer can create an unwelcome dependence on parents and can add new stress to the already turbulent teen years. Other families report that leukemia helped to forge closer bonds between teenagers and their parents.

> *Preston was age ten to thirteen while on treatment, and we asked the doctor to never talk to us without Preston being invited to be present. Preston was included in most of our early conferences, but then he got bored and asked not to be included sometimes. I always told him when we were talking with the doctor, and he usually wanted to know what was discussed. I tried to have phone conversations (even the ones where I got*

*mad) within hearing distance of Preston so that he never felt that he
didn't know everything that was happening with his care. In some ways,
this was difficult because he rode the emotional ups and downs with his
dad and me, but I think it was better in the long run because there were
no secrets and he could ask us any questions.*

Children and teens react to the diagnosis of cancer with as wide a range of
emotions as their parents. They may lapse into denial, feel tremendous
anger or rage, or be extremely optimistic. Children, like their parents, will
experience a variety of emotions as treatment progresses.

What to tell your child

Children need to be told that they are seriously ill, that they will be spending some time in the hospital, that the treatment will last for a long time and
is sometimes painful, that the treatments are usually successful, and that the
doctors and nurses are experts and will provide the very best care available.
Depending on the child's age, this could vary from saying, "Part of your
blood is sick and we need to go to the hospital for medicine to make it
better" to reading many books together and answering hundreds of questions.

> *My daughter Kathleen Rae knew she had cancer when she was
> three. She knew that her motor oil wasn't running her engine right—but
> she called it cancer.*

Young children need to be reassured that they did nothing to cause the disease. It is important that they understand the disease is not contagious and
they cannot "give" it to their siblings or friends. They need to have procedures described realistically, so that they can trust their parents and medical
team.

> *My four-year-old daughter told me very sadly one day, "I wish that I
> hadn't fallen down and broken inside. That's how the leukemia started."
> We had explained many times that nothing she did, or we did, caused the
> leukemia, but she persisted in thinking that falling down did it. She also
> worried that if she went to her friend Krista's house to play that Krista
> would catch leukemia.*

Children should understand that it is expected they will have many questions throughout their treatment, and they should be assured they will be
answered honestly. Parents need to let their children know that being fright-

ened or upset is normal, indeed is felt by parents and children alike. Gentle and honest communication is essential for the child to feel loved, supported, and encouraged.

> When I told Christine (3 years old) that she had a disease in her blood, her first concern was that I might leave. Over the years, I have repeated many, many times that I would always be with her and that I would make sure that there were never any surprises (difficult sometimes in the hospital setting but it can be done). She is very artistic and wanted me to draw a picture of the cells that were a problem. We drew lots of pictures of white cells being carried off by chemo drugs to be "fixed." Although many of the other parents successfully used images of good cells killing off bad cells, I thought that would upset my extremely gentle daughter. So we imagined, drew pictures of, and talked about chemo turning problem cells into helpful cells.

Barbara Sourkes, Ph.D., explains the importance of first understanding the child's question prior to responding:

> Coping with the trauma of illness can be facilitated by a cognitive understanding of the disease and its treatment. For this reason, the presentation of accurate information in developmentally meaningful terms is crucial. A general guideline is to follow the child's lead: he or she questions facts or implications only when ready, and that readiness must be respected. It is the adult's responsibility to clarify the precise intent of any question and then to proceed with a step-by-step response, thereby granting the child options at each juncture. He or she may choose to continue listening, to ask for clarification, or to terminate the discussion. Offering less information with the explicit invitation to ask for more affords a safety gauge of control for the child. When these guidelines are not followed, serious miscommunications may ensue. For example, an adult who hears "What is going to happen to me?" and does not clarify the intent of the query may launch into a long statement of plans or elaborate reassurances. The child may respond with irritation "I only wanted to know what tests I am going to have tomorrow."

Telling siblings

A diagnosis of cancer is traumatic for siblings. Family life is disrupted, time with parents decreases, and a large amount of attention is paid to the ill child. Brothers and sisters need as much knowledge as their sick sibling.

Information provided should be age appropriate, and all questions should be answered honestly. Siblings can be extremely cooperative if they understand the changes that will occur in the family and their role in helping the family cope. However, parents may see behavior changes such as: jealousy, regression (bed wetting in potty-trained toddlers), guilt (thinking that they caused their sibling's illness), school problems, and symptoms of illness to gain attention. Sometimes these problems can be minimized by carving time out to devote to the healthy children. Maintaining open communication about feelings helps siblings continue to feel loved and secure. Chapter 16, *Siblings*, explores sibling issues in detail and contains many suggestions from both parents and siblings.

The following was written by Jenny Gardner and is reprinted from Candlelighters Youth Newsletter, Spring 1995, Vol. XVII No. 2. Jenny was diagnosed with ALL in 1984 and had five years of treatment. A resident of New Jersey, she is an accomplished horsewoman and also enjoys singing and acting.

> *When I was diagnosed with leukemia, I felt like I was trapped in a room with no windows or doors and the walls were closing in on me. I thought that I would never be able to smell my grandmother's hand cream, or feel the way my dad's face felt in the morning before he shaves or the way my mom's silk blouse feels when I hug her. I thought that I would never have the sensation of turning one year older again. I thought that I would never again be able to feel how I feel after it rains, when it smells so fresh and clean like the whole world just took a bath. I thought that I would never be able to taste my first glass of champagne on New Year's and feel all bubbly and warm like I was flying in a hot air balloon. And all of a sudden my dream popped, and I realized that this wasn't a dream, it was reality.*

> *Right now there are thousands of kids like me across the country who are feeling the same way I felt eight years ago, and I would just like to wish them good luck. Because it's a long, hard journey full of needles, blood tests, and chemotherapy, but when you finally get to the end, you feel like you've been freed after years and years of darkness, and I'll tell you one thing—that is the greatest feeling you could have!*

Resources

Reading for adults

Bearison, David J. *'They Never Want to Tell You': Children Talk About Cancer.* Cambridge, MA: Harvard University Press, 1991. Several children and teenagers living with cancer candidly discuss their feelings. Written by a developmental psychologist.

Bombeck, Erma. *I Want to Grow Hair, I Want to Grow Up, I Want to Go to Boise.* New York: Harper & Row Publishers, 1989. Funny, touching book about children surviving cancer.

Candlelighters Childhood Cancer Foundation. *Bibliography and Resource Guide.* 1993. 1-800-366-CCCF. Extensive listing of books and articles on childhood cancer, coping skills, death and bereavement, effects on family, long-term side effects, medical support, and terminal home care. Updated every year. Excellent resource.

Candlelighters Childhood Cancer Foundation Canada. *Resource Catalog.* 1996. 1-800-363-1062 (Canada only) or (416) 489-9812. Extensive listing of books, articles and videotapes on all aspects of childhood cancer. Excellent resource.

Gravelle, Karen, and Bertram A. John. *Teenagers Face to Face With Cancer.* New York: Julian Messner, 1986. Seventeen teenagers with cancer discuss their feelings and experiences.

Margolies, Cynthia P., and Kenneth B. McCreadie. *Understanding Leukemia.* New York: Charles Scribner and Sons, 1983. Extremely detailed text describes the biology of leukemia.

National Cancer Institute. *Talking with Your Child About Cancer.* NIH Publication No. 91-2761. 1-800-4-CANCER. Excellent 16-page booklet on talking with your child about diagnosis. Full of helpful hints on how to answer many commonly asked questions.

National Cancer Institute. *Young People With Cancer.* NIH Publication No. 92-2378. 1-800-4-CANCER. Very helpful 86-page book, covering a range of topics including types of cancer, treatment, common issues, coping with procedures, dealing with diagnosis, and support organizations.

National Institute of Environmental Health Sciences and U.S. Department Of Energy. *Questions and Answers About E.M.F. Electric and Magnetic Fields Associated with the Use of Electric Power.* To obtain a free copy, call 1-800-363-2383 and request publication number DOE/EE-0040. 66-page booklet clearly explains electric and magnetic fields, human health studies, biological studies, government actions, and environmental exposure.

Reading for children

Leukemia Society of America. *Learn About Leukemia*. To obtain free copy, call 1-800-955-4LSA. A coloring and activity book to help 3 to 6-year-old leukemia patients learn about leukemia and discuss their feelings.

Leukemia Society of America. *Someone Likes You Beary Much*. To obtain free copy, call 1-800-955-4LSA. An activity book for younger siblings of leukemia patients.

Leukemia Society of America. *What It Is That I Have, Don't Want, Didn't Ask For, Can't Give Back, and How I Feel About It:* 1-800-955-4LSA. Booklet about feelings of adolescents with cancer. In notebook form, this publication can be used as a diary by teens.

Nessim, Susan, and Barbara Wyman. *Draw Me a Picture*. A fun coloring book for children with cancer (ages 3 to 6). Marty Bunny talks about how it was when he was in the hospital for cancer and invites readers to draw about their experiences. To order, send $7.45 check to Cancervive, 6500 Wilshire Blvd., # 500, Los Angeles, CA. 90048.

Shultz, Charles. *Why Charlie Brown Why?* New York: Topper Books, 1990. Tender story of a classmate who develops leukemia. Available as a book or videotape. For video availability, call American Cancer Society 1-800-ACS-2345.

Technical reading

Cortes, J. E., M. Talpaz, et al. "Chronic Myelogenous Leukemia: A Review." *American Journal of Medicine* 100:5 (May 1996): 555-70. Discusses the various methods of treating CML, reviews existing studies, benefits and limitations of bone marrow transplantation, and newer forms of therapy.

Hess, J. C., and M. M. Zutter. "Juvenile Chronic Myelogenous Leukemia." *American Journal of Clinical Pathology* 105:2 (February 1996): 238-48. Discusses differential diagnoses of JCML with an emphasis on the pathologic findings and laboratory data necessary to confirm a diagnosis. Covers the current biology of JCML, and discusses some of the controversies regarding JCML.

National Institutes of Health. *Leukemia Research Report.* To obtain free copy, call 1-800-4-CANCER. NIH Publication Number 94-329. 63-page booklet describes function of blood cells, types of leukemia, survival rates, causes of leukemia, and treatment for each type of leukemia.

Ravindranath, Y., A. M. Yeager, et al. "Autologous Bone Marrow Transplantation Versus Intensive Consolidation Chemotherapy for Acute Myeloid Leukemia in Childhood." *New England Journal of Medicine* 334(22) (May 30, 1996): 1428-34. Compares autologous bone marrow transplantation with intensive consolidation chemotherapy for children with AML in first remission. The event free survival after three years was not significantly different between the two groups.

Pizzo, Philip, and David Poplack, eds. *Principles and Practice of Pediatric Oncology.* Philadelphia: Lippincott-Raven, 1996. Textbook used by many pediatric residents and fellows includes Chapter 17, "Acute Lymphoblastic Leukemia," Chapter 18, "Acute Nonlymphoblastic Leukemia," Chapter 19, "Chronic Leukemias of Childhood," and other extremely detailed chapters on all aspects of childhood malignancies.

Video

Leukemia Society of America. *Closing in on a Cure.* 1990. To obtain free copy, call 1-800-955-4LSA. Promotional tape from the Leukemia Society of America explaining the different types of leukemia, their treatments, and the various research efforts being made to increase cure rates.

Leukemia Society of America. *Acute Myelogenous Leukemia.* 1991. To obtain free copy, call the Leukemia Society of America's Communications Department at (513) 381-8088. An informative, 21-minute video which discusses AML, its diagnosis, treatment, and associated emotional issues. Discusses the recent advances in treatment (drugs, bone marrow transplants) that have greatly improved the chances of remission and cure. This video only interviews adult patients.

Shultz, Charles. *Why Charlie Brown Why?* See listing under "Reading for children."

Coping with Procedures

Mommy, I didn't cry but my eyes got bright.

—4-year-old with ALL

THE PURPOSE OF THIS chapter is to prepare both child and parent for several common procedures by providing detailed descriptions of each. Since almost all procedures are repeated frequently during the long treatment for childhood leukemia, it is important to establish a routine that is comfortable for your child. The procedure itself may hurt, but a well prepared, calm child fares far better than a frightened one.

Planning for procedures

As soon as possible after your child's diagnosis, find out if the hospital has a child life program. The purpose of these programs is to minimize psychological trauma, promote optimal development, and to maintain, as much as possible, normal living patterns during hospitalizations. Child life professionals provide play experiences that encourage expression of feelings and create a sense of mastery and understanding of procedures. They attempt to minimize the child's stress by giving the child developmentally appropriate explanations of the nature of, and reasons for procedures and hospital routines.

> Matthew was in sixth grade when he was diagnosed, and he was worried about the surgery for implanting the port. He didn't know what the scar would look like and he was concerned about AIDS, because it had been in the news a lot that year. The child life worker came in and really helped. She showed him what a port looked like, then they explored the pre-op area, the actual surgery room, and post-op. She showed him on a cloth doll exactly where the incision would be and how the scar would look. Then she introduced him to "Fred," the IV pump. She said that Fred would be going places with him, and that Fred would keep him from getting so many pokes. She told Matthew that he could bring some-

thing from home to hang on Fred. Of course, he brought in a really ugly stuffed animal. Throughout treatment, she really helped his fears and my feelings about losing control over my child's daily life.

Many child life specialists accompany children to and provide support during procedures. They establish relationships with children based on warmth, respect, empathy, and understanding of developmental stages. They also communicate with the other members of the health care team about the psychosocial needs of children and their families.

Discuss with the child life professional or social worker when and how to prepare your child for upcoming procedures. Usually, parents need to experiment with how much advance notice to give younger children about procedures. Some children do better with several days to prepare, while others worry themselves sick. Sometimes, needs change over the years of treatment, so good communication and flexibility are essential.

I started giving my four-year-old daughter two days notice before procedures. But she began to wake up every day worried that "something bad was going to happen soon." So we talked it over and decided to look at the calendar together every Sunday to review what would happen that week. She was a much happier child after that.

If possible, try to schedule procedures so that the same person does the same procedure each time. My daughter's oncologist always did her spinal taps and bone marrows, her nurse always accessed the Port-a-cath (catheter described in Chapter 8, *Choosing a Catheter*), and we went to the same technician for blood work. I called ahead to check for unexpected changes to prevent any surprises. Repetition can provide comfort and reassurance to children.

Giving children some control over what happens helps tremendously.

Katy and I wrote down her requests for each procedure that first week in the hospital. For example, during spinal taps she wanted me (not a nurse) to hold her in position, she wanted xylocaine to be given with a needle not the pneumatic gun, and she had a rigid sequence of songs that I sang. She felt in control.

One or both parents should try to be present, especially for small children, for all procedures. Parents set the tone. A calm parent and a well-prepared child give the best chance for a quick, peaceful procedure. If you find that you are unable to be of help to your child during procedures, ask the child life specialist or other member of the health care team to be present solely to comfort your child.

> *We decided from the very beginning that, even though it's no fun to have a bone marrow or a spinal, we were going to make something positive out of it. So we made it a party. We'd bring pizza, popcorn, or ice cream to the hospital. We helped Kristin think of the nurses as her friends. We'd celebrate after a procedure by going out to eat at one of the neat little restaurants near the hospital.*

Oncology clinics usually have a special box full of toys for children who have had a procedure. It sometimes helps for the child to have a treat to look forward to afterward. Some parents occasionally bring a special gift to sneak into the box for their child to find.

If given the chance, children have definite opinions about how they like things to go at the clinic. For instance, *Having Leukemia Isn't So Bad. Of Course It Wouldn't be My First Choice* describes a list of clinic rules written by then seven-year-old Catherine Krumme in the car on the way to the hospital:

1. Must have a good sense of humor.

2. Must always do a good LP (Lumbar Puncture) and Bone Marrow.

3. Must always remember the toy box.

4. Must tell the truth.

5. Must like people.

6. Must like junk food.

7. Must know a lot about chemotherapy.

8. Must not mind the sight of blood.

9. Must like bald heads.

10. Must never be grumpy.

Pain management

Before reviewing specific procedures, it may be helpful to discuss pain management. The goal of pediatric pain management should be to minimize suffering while performing a successful procedure. The two methods to achieve this goal are psychological (using the mind) and pharmacological (using drugs).

Psychological method

Preparation for every procedure is essential. There is no fear greater than fear of the unknown. Unexpected stress is more difficult for children to cope with than anticipated stress. If children understand what is going to happen, where it will happen, who will be there, and what it will feel like, they will be less anxious and better able to cope. Methods to prepare children are:

- Verbally explain each step in the procedure.

- If possible, meet the person who will perform the procedure.

- Tour the room where the procedure will take place.

- See the instruments that will be used.

- Small children can "play" the procedure on dolls.

- Older children can observe a "demonstration" on a doll.

- Adolescents may observe a videotape describing the procedure.

- Encourage discussion and answer all questions.

> For my child, playing about procedures helped release many feelings. Parents can buy medical kits at the store or simply stock their own from clinic castoffs and the pharmacy. We had IV bottles made from empty shampoo containers, complete with tubing and plastic needles. Several dolls had accessed ports, and many stuffed animals in our house fell apart after being speared by the pen during countless spinal taps. Katy's younger sister even ran around sometimes with her own pretend port taped onto her chest. Some suggestions for the child's medical kit are: gauze pads, tape, tubing, stethoscope, reflex hammer, pretend needles, syringes, medical chart, and toy box. Of course, lots of dolls or stuffed animal patients are required.

· · · · ·

My daughter (three years old) took an old stuffed animal to the
clinic with her. Having the nurse and doctor perform the procedure first
on "bear" helped her immensely.

Hypnosis is a well documented method for reducing discomfort during painful procedures. As it requires individualized treatment for each child, it would have to be an available option at your child's hospital.

Imagery, while similar to hypnosis, can be taught by parents. To be successful, the method must be practiced prior to the procedure. Have the child visually focus on one object in the room, hold the parent's hand, breathe deeply, and imagine a tranquil scene. Ask if the hospital has someone to teach your child this very effective technique.

When Kim was in the treatment room, I would look into her eyes
and tell her to take deep breaths and relax. It was similar to what you do
in natural childbirth classes. Her doctor said she was one of his best
patients.

Distraction can be used successfully with all age groups, but it should never be used as a substitute for preparation. Babies can be distracted by colorful, moving objects. Parents can help distract preschoolers by showing picture books or videos, telling stories, singing songs, or blowing bubbles. Many youngsters are comforted by hugging a favorite stuffed animal. School-age children can watch videos or TV, or listen to music. Several institutions use interactive videos to help distract older children or teens.

My daughter went through her therapy prior to the days when kids
were given any pain medications for procedures. She and I would make
up a schedule of songs for me to sing during the spinal tap or bone
marrow. I would stroke her skin and sing softly to her. She visibly
relaxed, and the staff found it soothing, as well. I'll never forget the time
that the oncologist, nurse, and I were all quietly singing "Somewhere
Over the Rainbow" during the spinal tap.

Other adjunctive therapies that are used successfully to help deal with medical treatments are relaxation, biofeedback, massage, and acupuncture. Ask the hospital's child life specialist, psychologist, or trained nurse to discuss and practice different methods of pain management with your child.

The following description of using imagery was written by Jennifer Rohloff, seventeen years old, and is reprinted from the *Free To Be Yourself* newsletter of Cancer Services of Allen County, Indiana.

My Special Place

Many people had a special place when they were young—a special place that they still remember. This place could be an area that has a special meaning for them, or a place where they used to go when they wanted to be alone. My special place location is over the rainbow.

I discovered this place when I was twelve years old, during a relaxation session. These sessions were designed to reduce pain and stress brought on by chemotherapy. This was a place that I could visualize in my mind so that I could go there anytime that I wanted to—not only for pain, but when I was happy, mad, or sad.

It is surrounded by sand and tall, fanning palm trees everywhere. The blue sky is always clear, and the bright sun shines every day. It is usually quiet because I am alone, but often I can hear the sounds of birds flying by.

Every time I come to this place I like to lie down in the sand. As I lie there, I can feel the gritty sand beneath me. Once in a while I get up and go looking for seashells. I usually find some different shapes and sizes. The ones I like the best are the ones that you can hear the sound of the ocean in. After a while I get up and start to walk around. As I walk, I can feel the breeze going right through me, and I can smell the salt water. It reminds me of being at a beach in Florida. Whenever I start to feel sad or alone or if I am in pain, I usually go jump in the water because it is a soothing place for me. I like to float around in the water because it gives me a refreshing feeling that nobody can hurt me here. I could stay in this place all day because I do not worry about anything while I am here.

To me this place is like a home away from home. It is like heaven because you can do anything you want to do here. Even though this place may seem imaginary or like a fantasy world to some people, it is not to me. I think it is real because it is a place where I can go and be myself.

Pharmacological method

Some pediatric oncology clinics offer sedation or anesthesia for painful procedures; others do not. Sometimes anesthesia is available only for infants or overwhelmingly anxious children. If you find that your child is distressed by painful procedures (bone marrow aspiration and spinal taps), it is reasonable to explore all available options for pain relief.

One father, a doctor just completing his anesthesia residency, explained:

> *That first bone marrow was horrible. To have my little three year old look up at me with tears in her eyes and ask "What else are you going to let them do to me, daddy?" was just too much. It was the worst day of my life.*

His wife, a nurse, said:

> *We really made waves by insisting that Meagan be sedated for her spinal taps and bone marrows. It was mostly a logistical problem, but we held firm, and now it has become much more routine for many other kids as well.*

The ideal pain relief drug for children should be easy to administer, predictable in effect, provide adequate pain relief, have a short duration, and have minimal side effects. There are two topical anesthetics in wide use for pediatric procedures. EMLA cream (see Chapter 10, *Chemotherapy*) is a cream put on the skin one to two hours prior to the painful procedure. Ethyl chloride spray is used immediately before the procedure to anesthetize the surface skin.

Other drugs for sedation and/or general anesthesia are given intravenously. Some facilities then take the child into the operating room (OR) for the procedure, while others use a preoperating area or clinic sedation room and allow the parent to be present the entire time.

Drugs used for pediatric anesthesia during procedures include:

- **Valium or versed plus morphine or fentanyl.** Valium and versed are sedatives which are used with pain relievers such as morphine or fentanyl. These drugs can be given in the clinic, but due to the possibility of slowed breathing, expert monitoring is required and emergency equipment should be present. The combination of a sedative and a pain reliever will result in your child's being awake but sedated. The child may move or cry, but will not remember the procedure. Often, EMLA (an anesthetic in a cream base; see Chapter 10, *Chemotherapy*) or lidocaine are also used to ensure that the procedure is pain free.

- **Propofol.** A milky liquid given by IV, propofol has rapid onset with a rapid recovery. Administration and monitoring by an anesthesiologist (doctor who specializes in giving anesthetics) are required. Propofol, a general anesthetic, will cause your child to lose consciousness. At low doses, propofol prevents memory of the procedure, but may not relieve all pain, so it is often used with EMLA or lidocaine.

- **Ketamine.** Ketamine needs expert monitoring. It has a much longer recovery time than the drugs listed above, and upon awakening, up to 30 percent of children may become confused and/or hallucinate. For these reasons, ketamine is no longer in wide use for pediatric sedation for procedures.

Be aware that there are many types of drugs and several methods used in administering them, from very temporary (ten minutes) mild sedation to full general anesthesia in the operating room. Discuss with your oncologist and anesthesiologist which method will work best for your child.

> Let's face it, kids don't care about blasts, lab work, or protocols, they just want to know if they are going to be hurt again. I think that one of our most important jobs is to advocate, strongly if necessary, for adequate pain control. If the dose doesn't work and the doctor just shrugs her shoulders, say you want a different dosage or drug used. If you encounter resistance, ask that an anesthesiologist be consulted. Remember that good pain control and/or amnesia will make a big difference in your child's state of mind during treatment.

Since children with leukemia are treated for years, many children build up a tolerance for sedatives and pain relievers. Often, over time, doses may need to be increased or drugs changed. If your child remembers the procedure, advocate for a change in drug and/or dosage. It is reasonable to request that an anesthesiologist be present to ensure adequate pain relief.

> My job as an oral surgery assistant required me to be very familiar with different types of sedation. From the first day of Stephan's diagnosis, I quietly insisted on Versed for bone marrows and spinal taps. We have been in treatment for two years, and they still fight me every time, saying that it's just not necessary. When I make the appointment I tell them we want Stephan sedated, and then I call and remind them so that all will go smoothly.

All sedation can result in complications, primarily to the airway. It is imperative that sedation occur under the care of trained, experienced personnel and that the child is monitored until fully recovered from the anesthesia.

Procedures

Understanding what will occur during a procedure and what other parents did to prepare their children will arm you with essential information. Knowing what to expect will lower your anxiety level and enable you to lay the foundation for years of tolerable tests.

Questions to ask before procedures

Parents need information prior to procedures in order to prepare themselves and their child. Some suggested questions to ask the physician are:

- Why is this procedure necessary and how will it affect my child's treatment?

- What information will it provide?

- Who will perform the procedure?

- Will it be an inpatient or outpatient procedure?

- Please explain the procedure in detail.

- Is there any literature available that describes it?

- Is there a child life specialist on staff who will help prepare my child for the procedure?

- If not, are there parents who can come talk to me about how to prepare my child?

- Is the procedure painful?

- What type of anesthetic or sedation is used?

- What are the risks, if any?

- What are the common and rare side effects?

- When will we get the results?

Bone marrow aspiration

Many current protocols require up to five bone marrow aspirations, a process by which bone marrow is sucked out with a needle, over the two- to three-year treatment for leukemia. Unless sedated, children and teens describe bone marrow aspirations as uncomfortable to unbearable.

The purpose of the first, or diagnostic, bone marrow is to see what percentage of the cells in the marrow are abnormal blasts. Then these cells are analyzed microscopically to determine which type of leukemia is present. The next bone marrow aspiration occurs on day 7 or 14 of treatment. At this time it is important to determine how many blasts are still present. This information helps the oncologists decide how intensive treatment should be. For instance, if the marrow shows less than 25 percent blasts, the child might continue on the intermediate risk protocol. But if the marrow is still crowded with blasts, the child might be described as a "slow responder," who would require a much more intensive course of treatment.

> Since the doctors knew that my daughter had leukemia from the blood work, they did her first bone marrow while she was under anesthesia to implant her Port-a-cath. This was a blessing as her marrow was packed tight with blasts.

Most centers require additional bone marrow aspirations at the end of each phase of treatment and at the end of maintenance (or post-remission treatment, if your child does not require the maintenance phase).

To obtain a sample of the bone marrow, doctors usually use the iliac crest of the hip (the top of the hip bone in back). This bone is right under the skin and contains a large amount of marrow.

The child is placed face down on a table, sometimes on a pillow to elevate the hip. The doctor will feel the site, then wipe it several times with an antiseptic to eliminate any germs. Sterile paper is placed around the site, and the doctor will wear sterile gloves. Then an anesthetic (usually xylocaine) is injected into the skin and a small area of bone. This causes a burning and stinging sensation that passes quickly. The physician usually rubs the area to allow the drug to fully anesthetize the area. The physician then pushes a hollow needle (with a plug inside) through the skin into the bone, withdraws the plug, and attaches a syringe. The liquid marrow is then aspirated (sucked out) through the syringe. Removing the marrow is very painful. Here are some descriptions from children who have experienced it:

> It was the worst thing of all. It felt really, really bad.
>
> — Elisabeth, 10 years old (treated from age 6 to 8)

• • • • •

It hurts a lot. It feels like they are pulling something out and then it aches. You know, it hurts so much that now they put the kids to sleep. Boy, am I glad about that.

—Brent, 10 years old (treated from age 6 to 9)

• • • • •

It feels like they are trying to suck thick Jell-O from inside the bone. Brief but incredible pain.

—Catherine, 22 (treated from age 3 to 6)

• • • • •

I would become very anxious when they were cleaning my skin and laying the towels down. Putting the needle in was a sharp, pressure kind of pain. Drawing the marrow feels tingly, like they hit a nerve. I always asked a nurse to hold my legs because I felt like my legs were going to jump up off the table.

—Laura, 30 (treated from age 8 to 17)

If all goes well, and a sample is obtained, the needle is removed and a bandage is put on. However, it may be necessary to do a bone biopsy if the marrow is too dense to be aspirated. This situation occurs most often when the marrow is packed full of cancer cells. If a sample cannot be obtained by aspiration, sometimes the same needle can be pushed further into the bone to obtain a sample. Occasionally, a small cutting instrument is needed to break off a chip of bone for analysis. The needle or instrument is then removed, and the site is bandaged.

Before any procedure in the hospital, Caitlin would politely inform the staff that she planned to scream loudly but she would not move. Once the procedure was over, Caitlin would say in the most sweet voice, "Thank you, thank you." As my heart broke, hearing those words, I wanted to scream, "Thank you for what, your pain?" But her eyes saw it all so differently. The people were only there to help her and become her friends.

Spinal tap (lumbar puncture or LP)

Due to the blood-brain barrier, systemic chemotherapy usually cannot destroy any blasts present in the central nervous system (brain and spinal cord). Chemotherapy drugs must be directly injected into the cerebrospinal fluid in order to kill any blasts present and prevent a possible central nervous system relapse. The drugs most commonly used intrathecally are methotrexate, ARA-C, and hydrocortisone. The number of spinal taps required varies depending on the child's risk level, the clinical study involved, and whether radiation is used.

Some hospitals routinely sedate children for spinal taps, and others do not. If the child is not sedated, EMLA cream is usually prescribed. EMLA is an anesthetic cream put on the spinal tap site two hours prior to the procedure. It anesthetizes deep into the tissue, preventing some or all of the pain associated with the procedure.

> *I would rather have several bone marrow aspirations than one spinal tap. Not only are spinal taps very painful, but they are slow. The area they use is a bundle of nerves. When the doctor puts the needle in there is sharp, intense pain. The only thing I can compare it to is try to imagine someone putting a sliver of wood under your fingernail very, very slowly, then pulling it back out after 15 minutes.*

To perform a spinal tap, the physician or nurse practitioner will ask the child to lie on her side with her head tucked close to the chest and knees drawn up. A nurse or parent usually helps hold the child in this position. The doctor will feel the designated spot in the lower back, and will swab it with antiseptic several times. The antiseptic feels very cold on the skin. A sterile sheet will drape the area, and the doctor will wear sterile gloves. One or two shots of an anesthetic (usually xylocaine) will be injected into the skin and deeper tissues. This causes a painful stinging or burning sensation that lasts about a minute. If EMLA was used, the doctor usually still injects anesthetic into the deep tissues. A few-minutes wait is necessary to ensure that the area is fully anesthetized.

> *My four-year-old daughter had finished 18 months of her treatment for ALL when EMLA was first prescribed. She had been terrified of going to the clinic. After using EMLA for her next LP, a dramatic change occurred. She was no longer frightened to go for treatment, and her behavior at home improved unbelievably. We use it for everything now: finger pokes, accessing port, bone marrows, even flu shots.*

It is essential that the child hold very still for the rest of the procedure. The doctor will push a hollow needle between two vertebrae into the space where cerebrospinal fluid (CSF) is found. The CSF will begin to drip out of the hollow needle into a container. After a small amount is collected, a syringe is attached to the needle in the back and the medicine is slowly injected, causing a sensation of coldness or pressure down the leg. The needle is then removed and the spot bandaged. The CSF is sent to the laboratory to see if any blasts are present and to measure glucose and protein. Occasionally, older children and teenagers get severe headaches from spinal taps. These can sometimes be prevented by lying still for up to an hour after the procedure.

> During spinals, Brent listens to rock and roll on his walkman, but he keeps the volume low enough so that he can still hear what is going on. He likes me to lift up the earpiece and tell him when each part of the procedure is finished and what's coming next.

Cynthia Krumme describes her daughter's technique in *Having Leukemia Isn't So Bad. Of Course It Wouldn't be My First Choice:*

> We faced the last two spinal taps the protocol demanded with renewed interest in helping Catherine refine her techniques of pain control and distress management. We showed her the Lamaze breathing techniques we had learned some years before. She learned to concentrate on breathing in a regular rhythm during procedures. She made up stories which she imagined she was in, and she concentrated on peaceful, restful, and enjoyable images. Catherine learned these techniques quickly and was able to reduce her own anxiety during treatment. She called these tricks, getting myself together.

After her relapse, Catherine refined her technique:

> Facing innumerable spinal taps, Catherine worked out her own position for the procedure, wherein she sat tailor fashion bent over a pillow which had the effect of rounding off her spine. The staff let her have her own way about this, and she seemed to handle the LPs better.

Starting an IV

Most children with leukemia have a permanent right atrial catheter implanted in their chest within a week after diagnosis (see Chapter 8, *Choosing a Catheter*) to avoid the pain of years of IV sticks. However, some hospitals still do not recommend catheters, and there are many medical reasons why surgery for a catheter may be postponed. We will, therefore, discuss methods for dealing with IVs, an alternative to using a permanent catheter.

Most pediatric hospitals have teams of technicians who specialize in starting IVs and drawing blood. They are usually extremely good at their job. The IV technician will generally use a vein in the lower arm or hand. First, a constricting band is put above the site to make the veins larger and easier to see and feel. The vein is felt by the technician, the area is cleaned, and the needle is inserted. Sometimes a needle is left in place and sometimes it is withdrawn leaving only a thin, plastic tube in the vein. The technician will make sure that the needle (or tube) is in the proper place, then cover the site with a clear dressing, and secure it with tape.

Some methods that help when having an IV started are:

- **Stay calm.** The body reacts to fear by constricting the blood vessels near the skin surface. The calmer the child is, the larger his veins will be. Small children are usually more calm with a parent present; teenagers may or may not desire privacy. Listening to music, visualizing a tranquil scene (mountains covered with snow, floating in a pool), or using the same technician each time can help.

- **Use EMLA cream**. EMLA—a cream anesthetic—is applied to the skin one hour prior to the procedure to prevent pain. In some cases, it can constrict the veins, so experiment to see if it works for your child.

- **Keep warm.** Cold temperatures also cause the surface blood vessels to constrict. Wrapping the child in a blanket and putting a hot water bottle on the arm can enlarge the veins.

- **Drink lots of fluids.** Dehydration decreases the fluid in the veins, so encourage lots of drinking.

- **Let gravity help.** If the child is lying in bed, have her hang her arm down over the side to increase the size of the vessels in the arm and hand.

- **Let the child be in control.** If the child has a preference, let him pick the arm to be stuck. If the child is a veteran of many IVs, let him point out the best vein. Good technicians know that patients are quite aware of their best bet for a good vein.

- **Stop if problems develop.** The art of treating children is lots of time on preparation and not much time on procedures. If a conflict arises between the child and technician, side with the child. It's far better to take a time-out and regroup, than to force the issue and lose the child's trust. Children can be remarkably cooperative if their needs are respected and they are given some control over the situation.

You'll think I'm crazy but I'll tell you this story anyway. After getting stuck constantly for a year, my daughter (5 years old) just lost it one day when she needed an IV. She started screaming and crying, just flew into a rage. I told the tech, "Let's just let her calm down. Why don't you stick me for a change?" She was a sport and started a line in my arm. I told my daughter that I had forgotten how much it hurt and I could understand why she was upset. I told her to let us know when she was ready. She just walked over and held out her arm.

Blood draws

Frequent blood samples are a part of life during leukemia treatment. A complete blood count (CBC) tells the physician how effective the drugs are and helps determine the child's susceptibility to infection. It is important to measure blood chemistries to make sure that the liver and kidneys are not being damaged by treatment. (For a list of normal blood counts, see Appendix B, *Blood Counts and What They Mean*.) During induction and consolidation, transfusions are necessary when the red cell count or platelet count gets too low.

Blood specimens are primarily used for three purposes: to obtain a CBC, evaluate blood chemistries, or culture the blood to check for infection. A CBC measures the types and numbers of cells in the blood. Blood chemistries measure substances contained in the blood plasma to determine if the liver and kidneys are functioning properly. Blood cultures help evaluate whether the child is developing a bacterial infection. If only a CBC is needed, a finger poke will provide enough blood. Blood chemistries or cultures require one or more vials of blood obtained from a vein in the arm or the right atrial catheter.

Blood is usually drawn from the large vein on the inside of the elbow using a procedure similar to starting an IV, except that the needle is removed rather than left in the arm. The advice for starting an IV also applies to drawing blood from the arm.

Catheters

Children with catheters have blood drawn from the catheter rather than the arm or finger. These procedures are described in Chapter 8, *Choosing a Catheter*.

Finger pokes

Finger pokes are different in several ways. First, EMLA can be used success-fully. Put a blob of EMLA on the tip of the middle finger. Cover the finger tip with Saran wrap, and tape it on the finger. Another method is to buy long, thin balloons with a diameter a bit wider than the child's finger. Cut off the open end, leaving only enough balloon to cover the finger up to the first knuckle. Fill the tip of the balloon with EMLA and slide it on the finger tip. EMLA needs to be applied an hour before a finger poke to be effective. At the laboratory, remove the saran wrap or balloon, wipe off the EMLA, and ask for a warm pack. Wrapping this heated pack around the finger for a few minutes opens the capillaries to allow the blood to flow out more readily. Now the child is ready for a pain-free finger poke.

The technician will hold the finger and quickly stick it with a small sharp instrument. Blood will be collected in narrow tubes or a small container. It is usually necessary for the technician to squeeze the finger tip to get enough blood. If EMLA is not used, the squeezing part is uncomfortable and the finger can ache for quite a while.

> Even though we use EMLA, Katy (five years old) still becomes angry when she has to have a finger poke. I asked her why it was upsetting if there was no pain, and she replied, "It doesn't hurt my body anymore, but it still hurts my feelings."

Blood transfusions

By the time a child is diagnosed with leukemia, she usually has a very low hematocrit (percentage of red blood cells in a sample of blood). A normal hematocrit for a girl is 35 to 46 percent, and for a boy is 38 to 50 percent. The normal life of a red cell is three to four months and, as old cells die, the diseased marrow cannot replace them. Most children require transfusions of red cells when first admitted, and periodically throughout treatment.

> Whenever my son needed a transfusion, I brought along bags of col-oring books, food, and toys. The number of VCR's at the clinic was lim-ited, so I tried to make arrangements for one ahead of time. When anemic (hematocrit below 20 percent), he didn't have much energy, but by the end of the transfusion, his cheeks were rosy and he had tremen-dous vitality. It was hard to keep him still. After one unit (bag) of red cells, his hematocrit usually jumped up to around 30.

Generally, doctors order a red cell transfusion when the hematocrit falls below 20 percent. One bag (called a "unit") of red cells takes approximately two to four hours to administer and is given through an IV or catheter.

Parents should check each sticker on the bag of red cells to ensure that it is the correct blood type, has been irradiated, and is cytomegalovirus (CMV) negative (only necessary if your child is CMV negative). Blood of the wrong type can cause a serious transfusion reaction as it will not be accepted by the child's immune system. If a child develops chills and/or fever during a transfusion, the nurse should be notified so that the transfusion can be stopped immediately.

There are some risks of infection from red cell transfusions. Since new tests have been devised to detect the AIDS virus, the risk of exposure is minuscule, less than 1 in 450,000. Although there are excellent tests for the various types of hepatitis, exposure to this disease is still possible (the risk is less than 1 in 4,000). The cytomegalovirus is also a concern. These risks are the reason transfusions are given only when absolutely necessary.

> *My daughter received several transfusions at the clinic in Children's Hospital with no problems. After we traveled back to our home, she needed her first transfusion at the local hospital. Our pediatrician said to expect to be in the hospital at least eight hours. I asked why it would take so long when it only took four hours at Children's. He said he had worked out a formula and determined that she needed two units of packed cells. I mentioned that she only was given one unit each time at Children's. He called the oncologist, who said it was better to give the smaller amount. We went to the hospital where a unit of red cells was given. Then, a nurse came in with another unit. I questioned why he was doing that and he said, "Doctor's orders." I asked him to verify that order, as we had already discussed it with the doctor. He went into another room to call the doctor, and came back and said the pediatrician thought she needed 30 cc more packed cells. I called Children's and they said she didn't need more, so I refused to let them administer any more blood. It just wasn't worth the risk of hepatitis to get 30 cc of blood. Even though I was pleasant, the nurses were angry at me for questioning the doctor. Luckily, I was never afraid to question a procedure or refuse treatment which was not in the best interest of my child.*

Platelet transfusions

A normal platelet count for a healthy child is 150,000/mm³ to 420,000/mm³. Chemotherapy will severely depress the platelet count for most children, and uncontrollable bleeding can result if there are too few platelets. Most centers require a transfusion when the child's platelet count goes below 10,000 to 20,000/mm³, and sometimes repeat transfusions are required every two or three days until the marrow recovers.

> *Brent (6 years old) had several platelet transfusions during induction and consolidation. He had no problems and his counts would immediately jump up to around 40,000/mm³.*

· · · · ·

> *After several relapses and many years of treatment Jesse developed platelet antibodies which was a frightening and serious complication. We found several matched donors who would come in to donate platelets whenever she needed them.*

· · · · ·

> *Justin had a platelet reaction which caused profuse sweating and difficulty breathing. They stopped the transfusion immediately, and he got over it.*

Infections transmitted by platelets are identical to those of other blood products: hepatitis, cytomegalovirus, and HIV (the virus that causes AIDS). The chance of contracting these infections, although small, is the reason that platelet transfusions are also given only when absolutely necessary.

Taking pills

In the 27 months of my daughter's treatment for high risk ALL, I gave her over 3,000 pills and 1,100 teaspoons of liquid medication. When giving oral medications, it is essential to get off to a good start and establish cooperation early. In the following suggestions from veteran parents, you may find one technique that works well for your child.

> *To teach Brent (6 years old) to swallow pills, when we were eating corn for dinner I encouraged him to swallow one kernel whole. Luckily, it went right down and he got over his fear of pills.*

· · · · ·

I wanted Katy (3 years old) to feel like we were a team right from the first night. So I made a big deal out of tasting each of her medications and pronouncing it good. Thank goodness I tasted the prednisone first. It was nauseating—bitter, metallic, with a lingering aftertaste. I asked the nurse for some small gel caps, and packed them with the pills which I had broken in half. I gave Katy her choice of drinks to take her pills with and taught her to swallow gel caps with a large sip of liquid.

Gel caps come in many sizes. Number 4's are small enough for a three or four year old to swallow, but big enough to hold half a 10 mg. prednisone tablet. Dexamethasone also tastes awful. Most of the others pills can be chewed or swallowed whole without taste problems. Just remember that children develop different taste preferences and aversions to medications, and gel caps are useful for any medication that bothers them.

After much trial and error with medications, Meagan's method became chewing up pills with chocolate chips. She's kept this up for the long haul.

· · · · ·

I always give choices such as, "Do you want the white pill or the six yellow pills first?" It gives them a little control in their chaotic world.

For younger children, many parents crush the pills in a small amount of pudding, applesauce, jam, frozen juice concentrate, or other favorite food.

Jeremy was four when he was diagnosed, and we used to crush up the pills and mix them with ice cream. This worked well for us.

· · · · ·

Carrie Beth was two when diagnosed. She hated the taste of the pills, so I would submerge them in teaspoonfuls of pure maple syrup. The next year when she just decided she didn't want to cooperate about taking pills, I'd say to her and her two older sisters, "Strawberry gum for everybody as soon as Carrie Beth finishes her pills." Then I would leave, and the older kids encouraged her to swallow the pills.

· · · · ·

We used the liquid form of prednisone for my son, mixed it with a chocolate drink, and followed this with M&M's. The chocolate seemed to mask the taste.

Most children on maintenance take SMZ-TMP (sulfamethoxazole and trime-thoprim) three times a week to prevent pneumonia. It comes in liquid or pill form, and is produced by several different manufacturers. Ask your pharmacist (you'll know her quite well after a few years) for a kid taste test. Letting your child choose a medicine that appeals to him encourages compliance.

> Whenever my son had to take a liquid medicine, such as antibiotics, he enjoyed taking it from a syringe. I would draw up the proper amount, then he would put it in his mouth and push the plunger.

Since children associate taking medicine with being sick, it is helpful to explain why they must continue taking pills for years after they feel well. Some parents use the Pac-man analogy, "The pills are needed to gobble up the last few bad cells." Others explain that the leukemia can return, so medicine is needed to prevent it from growing again. It is important that parents give children all the required medications; there are many studies showing low compliance results in lower survival rates.

Issues for teenagers about taking pills are completely different from those described for young children. The problems with teens revolve around autonomy, control, and feelings of invulnerability. It is impossible to force teenagers to take pills if they choose not to cooperate. If there is good communication within the family, discussing the reasons the pills are necessary is important. Many teenagers benefit by taking an active role in their own recovery and are responsible enough to take their medication. When this is not the case, the physician, nurse, or social worker may be able to reason a resistant teenager into compliance.

> I think the main problem with teens is making sure that they take the meds. Joel (15 years old) has been very responsible about taking his nightly pills. I've tried to make it easy for him by having an index card for the week and he marks off the med as he takes it. I also put the meds on a dry erase board on the frig as a reminder. As he takes the med, he erases it. That way it's easy for him (and me) to see at a glance if he's taken his stuff. The index card alone wasn't working because he couldn't find a pen, or forgot to mark it off.

> One of the biggest concerns with teens and maintenance is non-compliance. I think it's a delicate balancing act to allow the teen to be responsible for taking their own meds and yet have some supervision of the

process. Our meds are kept in a small plastic basket on the kitchen counter. All meds are taken there. I'd never want him to keep his meds in his room where I would have no idea if he had taken them or not.

On Friday nights when he is to take his weekly methotrexate—a 16 pill dose—I will count it out and put it in a medicine cup on the counter. I am not always an awake and alert person when he comes home at midnight on Friday night. When I get up Saturday morning, I know immediately if he's taken his meds.

If he had shown any resistance to taking the meds, or any sign of telling me that he had taken them when he had not, I'd be doing this differently. But he's aware of the importance of each dose and the importance of his participation in the team beating the leukemia.

My only other advice is to be sure and ask the doctors what to do about a missed dose for each med. In three plus years of treatment, you are going to have a missed dose and it helps to know how to handle it.

Taking a temperature

In the years a child is treated for childhood leukemia, fever becomes the enemy. Parents take hundreds of temperatures, often when their child is not feeling well. Temperatures can be taken under the tongue, under the arm, or in the ear using a special type of thermometer. Anal temperatures are not recommended due to the risk of tears and infection. Here are a few suggestions that might help.

- Digital thermometers can be purchased at any drug store. Some have an alarm that beeps when it is time to remove the thermometer.

  We bought a digital thermometer that we only use under his arm. It has worked well for us.

- Heat-sensitive paper strips are available at drug stores or pharmacies. They are inexpensive, and popular with some children.

  We used the paper strips with the dots that turned blue. She could choose whether to put it under her tongue or under her arm, and seemed to enjoy seeing the colors change.

- Tympanic thermometers measure infrared waves and are very easy to use. One manufacturer of the ear thermometer is Thermoscan. To locate the nearest dealer, call 1-800-EAR-TEMP.

When my in-laws asked at diagnosis if there was anything that we needed, I asked them to try to buy a tympanic (ear) thermometer. The device cost over a hundred dollars then, but it worked beautifully. It takes only one second to obtain a temperature. You can even use it when she is asleep without waking her. They are now sold at pharmacies and drug stores, and cost much less.

Before parents leave the hospital, they should know when to call the clinic because of fever. Usually, parents are told not to give any medication for fever and to call if the fever goes above 101° F. This allows the doctors to make a judgment on whether it is an infection that requires treatment, or just a minor fever that quickly disappears. It is especially important for parents of children with implanted catheters to know when to call the clinic, as an untreated infection may necessitate removal of the catheter. (See Chapter 8, *Choosing a Catheter.*)

Providing a urine specimen

If you have a teenage or younger boy who likes to "perform," you may have laughed when you read the title for this section. If, however, you are struggling with a just potty-trained girl who simply refuses to urinate into a cup, read on.

Chemotherapy requires frequent urine specimens. One way to help obtain a sample is to encourage lots of drinking the hour before or ask the nurse to increase the drip rate on the IV. Explain to the child why the test is necessary. Ask the nurse to show how the dip sticks work (they change color so they are quite popular with the preschoolers). Use a "hat" under the toilet seat. This is a shallow plastic bucket that fits under the seat and catches the urine.

Turn on the water while the child sits on the toilet. I don't know why it works, but it does.

As all parents learn, eating and elimination are areas that the child controls. If she just can't or won't urinate in the hat, go out, buy her the largest drink you can find, and wait.

Echocardiogram

Several drugs used to fight leukemia can damage the muscle of the heart, decreasing its ability to contract effectively. Many protocols require a baseline echocardiogram to measure the heart's ability to pump before any chemotherapy drugs are given. Echocardiograms are then given periodically during treatment and after treatment ends to see if any heart muscle damage has occurred.

An echocardiogram uses ultrasound waves to measure the amount of blood that leaves the heart each time it contracts. This percentage (blood ejected during a contraction compared to blood in the heart when it is relaxed) is called the ejection fraction.

The echocardiogram is performed by a technician, nurse, or doctor. The child or teen lies on a table and has conductive jelly applied to the chest. Then the technician puts a transducer (which emits the ultrasound waves) on the jelly and moves the device around on the chest to obtain different views of the heart. Pressure is applied on the transducer, and can sometimes cause discomfort. The test results are displayed on a videotape and photographed for later interpretation.

> Meagan used to watch a video during the echocardiogram. Sometimes she would eat a sucker or a popsicle. She found it to be boring, not painful.

Having Leukemia Isn't So Bad contains a different viewpoint:

> Catherine did not like participating in the echocardiogram...she said the pressure on her chest for the lengthy time it took to get a reading was too much. She complained more about this test than the spinals, even though it was a noninvasive test.

MUGA scan

MUGA stands for multiple-gated acquisition scan, which is another way to test cardiac function. Prior to having a MUGA scan, children are sometimes given a sedative to relax them and help them stay perfectly still for the 15 to 20 minute test. An injection of red cells or proteins tagged with a mildly radioactive substance (called technetium) is also given. The child lies on a table with a large movable camera above. This special camera records sequential images of the technetium as it moves through the heart. These pictures of the heart's function allow doctors to determine how efficiently the heart muscle is pumping and if any damage to the heart has occurred.

My three-year-old daughter had a MUGA scan before she received any chemotherapy. They gave her an injection, and she fell asleep. They laid her on her back on a big table and moved a huge contraption around her to take pictures of her heart beating. We watched on a screen, and they printed out a copy on paper for the doctors.

If either the echocardiogram or MUGA scan show heart damage, the oncologist may reduce the dosage or remove the drug causing the damage from the child's protocol.

Meagan is scheduled to go off therapy this May. She's doing well, and is very happy. A father at our support group was reminding a new set of parents to remember to view life from the child's perspective; he said that, especially with little ones, parents sometimes agonize more than the child. He said that at the end of the first year of treatment he and his wife were reflecting on how much misery their child had endured, and then she piped up and said, "This has been a great year for me!" Meagan is the same. When I have bad days and get preoccupied with the uncertain future, I see Meagan skipping along and saying as she frequently does, "I'm such a happy girl."

Resources

Organizations

The American Society of Clinical Hypnosis
2250 East Devon Avenue, Suite 336
Des Plaines, IL 60018
(708) 297-3317

A membership organization for doctors, Ph.D. psychologists, and dentists who use hypnosis in their practices. Provides a national referral service. For referral to a local member, send request with S.A.S.E. to above address.

The Academy for Guided Imagery
PO Box 2070
Mill Valley, CA 94942
1-800-726-2070

This organization can assist in locating a professional in your area to help your child learn visualization.

Starbright
1990 S. Bundy Drive, Suite 100
Los Angeles, CA 90025
(310) 477-9090
FAX : (310) 447-9090

There are many exciting intervention programs being developed to help children cope with the pain, stress, and anxiety caused by cancer treatments. One such intervention is the Starbright Pediatric Network. This group, led by Steven Spielberg, is comprised of pediatric health care professionals, experts in computer technology, and leaders in the field of entertainment. They have developed interactive, virtual-reality playgrounds where kids meet, talk, and play with other sick kids across the country. Starbright's mission is "to improve the quality of life of seriously ill children and their families by taking a leadership role in the development of entertainment-oriented therapeutic interventions integrating state-of-the-art pediatric and entertainment expertise." This new technology is being evaluated as a therapeutic tool to lessen fear, withdrawal, and pain of youngsters at six different pediatric hospitals across the U.S.

Reading for adults

Benson, Herbert. *The Relaxation Response*. New York: Avon Books, 1985. This is an excellent resource for the relaxation method of pain relief

Candlelighters Childhood Cancer Foundation. *Myths About Pain in Children*. To order, call 1-800-366-2223. Excellent. Debunks common myths about children's pain. Also uses case studies to discuss relaxation and self-hypnosis techniques that help children self-regulate pain.

Eland, Jo, R.N., Ph.D. "Current Problems and New Developments in Pediatric Pain Control." *Candlelighters Newsletter* Volume X No. 1 (1993). To order call 1-800-366-2223. Discusses methods to assess pediatric pain and describes several drugs currently used to alleviate pain.

Kellerman, Johnathan. *Helping the Fearful Child*. New York: W.W. Norton, 1981. Although this book was written as a guide for everyday and problem anxieties, it is full of excellent advice for parents of children undergoing traumatic procedures. Chapter 7, "Going to the Doctor," and Chapter 8, "Coping with Hospitalization," are full of real life examples and methods to help your child cope.

Krumme, Cynthia. *Having Leukemia Isn't So Bad. Of Course It Wouldn't be My First Choice*. Winchester, MA: Sargasso Enterprises, 1993. 14 Wildwood St., Winchester, MA 01890 (617-729-9037). Sprinkled throughout this book are the methods Catherine Krumme used to cope with painful procedures during her treatment for leukemia from ages 4 to 10.

LeShan, Lawrence. *How to Meditate*. Boston: Little Brown, 1974. For older children and teenagers, meditation is an excellent stress reducer. This book is a good guide for self-instruction.

Lewis, Sheldon, and Sheila Lewis. *Stress-Proofing Your Child: Mind- Body Exercises to Enhance Your Child's Health*. New York: Bantam Books, 1996. I highly recommend this book to all parents. It clearly explains easy ways to teach children techniques such as guided imagery, deep breathing, and meditation to decrease stress, increase a child's sense of control, and boost children's confidence. A wonderful, practical book.

McGrath, Patrick J., Allen G. Finley, and Catherine J. Turner. *Making Cancer Less Painful: A Handbook for Parents*. Produced by the Oncology Unit of the Izaak Walton Killam Children's Hospital, Halifax, Nova Scotia, 1992. If parents only read one book on children's pain control, this should be it. This 60-page booklet is an excellent, well-written guide for parents who wish to learn about methods to control their child's pain from disease, procedures, or treatment. Distributed in the U.S. through health care professionals only, ask your oncologist, pediatrician or social worker to order for you.

McKay, Judith, R.N., and Nancee Hirano, R.N., M.S.N. *The Chemotherapy Survival Guide*. Oakland, CA: New Harbinger Publications, 1993. Chapters 2, 3, 11 and 12 contain easy to understand descriptions of blood, blood tests, IV insertion, and methods for relaxation and stress reduction.

Roach, Nancy. *The Last Day of April*. American Cancer Society, 1974. Out of print. To see if any copies are available, call 1-800-ACS-2345. Forty-page booklet written by a mother about her daughter's struggle with ALL. Deals with issues such as adjusting to the diagnosis, coping with procedures, marital conflicts, getting along with medical staff, and grief after her child's death.

Spiegel, David, M.D. *Living Beyond Limits*. New York: Random House, 1993. This book was written by a Stanford psychiatrist active in the scientific exploration of the benefits of psychological support and pain control used in conjunction with appropriate medical care. Contains an excellent chapter on pain control that clearly describes imagery and hypnosis.

Wisconsin Cancer Pain Initiative. *Children's Cancer Pain Can be Relieved*. 1300 University Avenue, Room 4720, Madison, WI. 53706. (608) 262-0978. FAX: (608)265-4014. E-mail:wcpi@facstaff.wisc.edu. Twelve-page booklet helps parents determine if their child is in pain and provides methods to manage the pain. Single copy free. *Handbook of Cancer Pain Management*, 4th edition. $3.50 per copy. Single copy $4.

Reading for children

Baker, Lynn, M.D. *You and Leukemia: A Day at a Time*. Philadelphia: W.B. Saunders Company, 1988. Chapter 4 contains clear descriptions of procedures written for both children and adults.

Berglund, Rita. *An Alphabet About Kids with Cancer*. Children's Legacy, 1994. A book full of poems, stories, and photographs of children coping with cancer.

Krisher, Trudy. *Kathy's Hats: A Story of Hope*. Morton Grove, IL: Albert Whitman Co., 1992. 6340 Oakton St., Morton Grove, IL 60053 or 1-800-255-7675. $14.95. A charming book for ages 5 to 10 about a girl whose love of hats comes in handy when chemo makes her hair fall out.

Warmbier, J., and E. Vassy. *Hospital Days-Treatment Ways: Hematology/Oncology Coloring Book*. National Cancer Institute, 1981. To order call 1-800-4-CANCER. Designed to familiarize patients with hospital diagnostic and treatment procedures. Good way to spark discussion between parent and child.

Technical reading

Bearison, David, and Raymond Mulhern. *Pediatric Psychooncology: Psychological Perspectives on Children with Cancer*. New York: Oxford University Press, 1994. Excellent collection of technical articles on psychological aspects of pediatric oncology, with especially good sections on pain identification and management.

Greenbaum, Barbara, M.D., and Jay Herman, M.D. "Transfusion Therapy in Pediatric Oncology." *Pediatric Annals* 17:11 (November 1988). Detailed discussion of red blood cell transfusions, platelet transfusions, white cell transfusions, CMV, transfusion reactions, and irradiation of blood products.

Hockenberry, Marilyn, and Saba Bologna-Vaughan. "Preparation for Intrusive Procedures Using Noninvasive Techniques in Children with Cancer: State of the Art vs. New Trends." *Cancer Nursing* 8(2) (April 1985): 97-102. Pediatric Oncology Group study indicates that underutilized techniques such as distraction, imagery, relaxation, desensitization, and hypnosis are effective and low risk, and return control to the child.

McDowall, R. H., C. S. Scher, et al. "Total Intravenous Anesthesia for Children Undergoing Brief Diagnostic or Therapeutic Procedures." *Journal of Clinical Anesthesia* 7:4 (June 1995): 273-80. Study compared the quality of anesthesia with propofol, ketamine, or etomidate in 971 children undergoing brief diagnostic or therapeutic procedures. Found that ketamine was associated with vomiting (14.6%), agitation (15%), and rapid heart rate (19.5%); etomidate was associated with vomiting (9.9%) and agitation (1.2%). 15.7% of the patients receiving propofol required supplemental oxygen. The study concluded that anesthesia with the three anesthetics is safe and effective for children undergoing brief procedures. Propofol is associated with easily treated respiratory depression and has a decreased incidence of agitation and vomiting.

Schechter, N. L., S. J. Weisman, et al. "The Use of Oral Transmucosal Fentanyl Citrate for Painful Procedures in Children." *Pediatrics* 95:3 (March 1995): 335-9. A randomized, placebo-controlled clinical trial evaluated the efficacy and safety of oral fentanyl in providing analgesia and sedation for bone marrow aspiration and lumbar puncture. The children who received fentanyl reported significantly less pain than those in the placebo group, but those receiving fentanyl had highter rates of itching and vomiting.

Zappa, S. C., and S. B. Nabors. "Use of Ethyl Chloride Topical Anesthetic to Reduce Procedural Pain in Pediatric Oncology Patients." *Cancer Nursing* 15:2 (April 1992): 130-136. Studied the use of ethyl chloride spray prior to procedures such as port sticks, lumbar punctures, and bone marrow aspirations. Sixty-eight percent of parents reported that the patient had more of a sense of control and 78 percent of the patients reported less pain. Staff noted an increase in cooperation, less combativeness, and more compliance with treatment.

Zeltzer, Lonnie, M.D., Sysan Jay, Ph.D, and Dennis Fisher, M.D. "The Management of Pain Associated with Pediatric Procedures." *Pediatric Clinics of North America* Vol. 36, No. 4 (August 1989). In-depth review of psychological and pharmacological management strategies to help children cope with pediatric procedures.

Audio

The Stress Reduction Clinic of the University of Massachusetts Medical Center offers two audio tapes for $11 each, including shipping and handling. These tapes are appropriate for preteens or adolescents. For information, call (508) 856-2656, or write to:

Stress Reduction Tapes
P.O. Box 547
Lexington, MA 02173

CHAPTER 4

What Is a Clinical Trial?

The challenge in pediatric oncology remains clear: to strive for the cure and health of all children through the development of more effective yet less damaging treatment for our young patients.

—Daniel M. Green, M.D. and Giulio J. D'Angio, M.D.
Late Effects of Treatment for Childhood Cancer

WITHIN DAYS OF ARRIVING at a major pediatric medical center with a newly diagnosed leukemic child, parents may be asked to enroll their child in a clinical trial. A clinical trial is a research study that uses human volunteers to answer specific scientific questions. Pediatric clinical trials are all directed toward improving upon existing treatments. A trial can involve a totally new approach that is thought to be promising, fine-tune existing treatments, improve the results or reduce the toxicity of known treatments, or develop new ways to discern response to treatments. Seventy-five percent of children with cancer are enrolled in clinical trials throughout their experience with cancer.

Making an informed judgment on whether to participate is crucial, as it will determine what treatment your child will receive in the years to come. This chapter will explain the terms *clinical trial* and *protocol* and will give examples of how different parents made decisions on this important issue.

Why are children enrolled in clinical trials?

The enormous improvements in treating childhood leukemia have been the direct result of clinical trials. In order to accurately evaluate any new treatment, large numbers of patients are needed in each clinical trial.

Because clinical trials offer the most up-to-date treatment available, children who participate in a clinical trial may benefit from the newest research. Most parents derive comfort from knowing that the knowledge gained will make an important contribution to medical science, and may help other children with cancer.

What is standard treatment?

Standard treatment is the best treatment known for a specific type of cancer. For instance, in 1997, the standard treatment for intermediate-risk ALL is combination chemotherapy for two to three years. The standard treatment for high-risk ALL includes more drugs plus cranial radiation.

As results from ongoing and completed clinical trials are analyzed, more knowledge is accumulated, and standard treatments evolve. In the 1980s, most children with low- and intermediate-risk ALL received cranial radiation as standard care. Carefully controlled clinical trials compared three groups of children: those who received cranial radiation (the standard treatment), those who received high-dose IV methotrexate (an experimental treatment), and those who received only intrathecal methotrexate (an experimental treatment) to prevent central nervous system relapse. It was discovered that children with low- and intermediate-risk ALL did not require cranial radiation. The standard care was changed.

Most clinical trials divide patients into two or more groups (arms). One arm of the trial is the standard treatment, and the other arms are the experimental portions, which scientists hope will prove to be more effective or less toxic than the standard treatment. Each arm is based on preliminary, but not conclusive, information that it will be beneficial and is carefully reviewed by leaders in the field before implementation.

> My daughter's clinical trial for high-risk ALL had three arms. One arm was the standard treatment of four drug rotations of chemotherapy with a delayed intensification and consolidation, and 1,800 rads of cranial radiation. The second arm was identical except radiation was replaced with more frequent doses of intrathecal methotrexate. The third arm was for children who had CNS disease at diagnosis, or who were slow responders to initial therapy. They received a very aggressive chemotherapy regimen plus cranial radiation.
>
> The purpose of the study was to compare response to treatment, duration of disease control, and side effects. The investigators hoped to be able to eliminate radiation from the standard care for high-risk ALL.

What is randomization?

An unbiased scientific study requires a process called randomization. This means that after parents agree to enroll their child in a clinical trial, a computer will randomly assign the child to one arm of the study. If there are three arms, the parents will not know which of the three (one standard, two experimental) their child will receive until the computer assigns one. One group of patients (the control group) always receives the standard treatment to provide a basis for comparison to the experimental arms. Because neither the physician nor the parents choose the treatment option, a comparable mix of patients is assured.

> We decided not to participate in a study for several reasons. One arm would require extra spinal taps, and our son was just so little that we couldn't bear the thought of any more treatments than what was required in the standard arm. Another arm contained a second induction, and since we were on Medicaid, we just didn't feel it was right for the taxpayers to pay for anything extra. We felt we were only entitled to basic health care.

At the time the clinical trial is designed, there is no conclusive evidence to indicate which arm will prove to be superior. It is not possible to predict if the child will benefit from participating in the study.

> We had a hard time deciding whether to go with the standard treatment or to participate in the study. The "B" arm of the study seemed, on intuition, to be too harsh for her because she was so weak at the time. We finally did opt for the study, hoping we wouldn't be randomized to "B." We chose the study basically so that the computer could choose and we wouldn't ever have to think "we should have gone with the study." As it turned out, we were randomized to the standard arm, so we got what we wanted while still participating in the study.

Who designs clinical trials?

In the United States and Canada, there are two primary pediatric research groups: Children's Cancer Group (CCG) and the Pediatric Oncology Group (POG). Most large pediatric medical centers work in close cooperation with one of these groups, although there are some centers of excellence which design their own clinical trials. Experts from many institutions usually collaborate in the design of clinical trials.

Who supervises clinical trials?

The ethical and legal codes ruling medical practice also apply to clinical trials. In addition, most research is federally funded or regulated (all CCG and POG trials are), with rules to protect patients. The CCG and POG also have review boards which meet at prearranged dates for the duration of a clinical trial to ensure that the risks of all parts of the trial are acceptable relative to the benefits. If one arm of the trial is causing unexpected or unacceptable side effects, that portion will be terminated, and the children enrolled will be given the better treatment. If one of the arms appears to be less effective than the standard, it will be terminated and if one arm is better than the standard the trial will also be terminated. Whenever a treatment is proven to be superior, all children receive it.

All institutions that conduct clinical trials also have an Institutional Review Board (IRB), or an Ethics Committee which approves and reviews all research taking place there. These boards, whose purpose is to protect patients, are made up of scientists, doctors, sometimes clergy, and often citizens from the community.

What questions should parents ask about clinical trials?

To fully understand the clinical trial that has been proposed, here are some important questions to ask the oncologist:

- What is the purpose of the study?
- Who is sponsoring the study? Who reviews it? How often is it reviewed? Who monitors patient safety?
- What tests and treatments will be done during the study? How do these differ from standard treatment?
- Why is it thought that the treatment being studied is better than standard treatment?
- What are the possible benefits?
- What are all possible disadvantages?
- What are the possible side effects or risks of the study? What are the side effects of the study compared to those of standard treatment?
- How will the study affect my child's daily life?

- What are the possible long-term impacts of the study compared to the standard treatment?

- How long will the study last? Is this shorter or longer than standard treatment?

- Will the study require more hospitalization than standard treatment?

- Does the study include long-term follow-up care?

- What happens if my child is harmed as a result of the research?

- Compare the study to standard treatment in terms of possible outcomes, side effects, time involved, costs, and quality of life.

- Have insurers been reimbursing for care under this protocol?

When discussing the clinical trial with the oncologist, it is perfectly reasonable to ensure that the information will be available for later review. Many parents bring a tape recorder or a friend to take notes. Some parents write down all of the doctor's answers for later reference.

What is informed consent?

Informed consent requires that (1) all the treatments available to the child have been laid on the table and discussed—not just the treatment available at your hospital or through your doctor, but all the treatments that could be beneficial, wherever they are given; (2) the parents and, to the extent possible, the child, have discussed these options and decided that they want to consider one of them; (3) the option selected is thoroughly discussed, with all its benefits and risks clearly explained. A fully informed medical decision weighs the relative merits of a therapy after full disclosure of benefits, risks, and alternatives.

During the discussions between the doctor(s) and family, all questions should be answered in language that is clearly understood by the parents, and there should be no pressure to enroll the child in the study. The objective of the informed consent process is that the participants are comfortable that they have made a good choice, one they can comply with and stand behind.

> We had many discussions with the staff prior to signing the informed consent to participate in the clinical trial. We asked innumerable questions, all of which were answered in a frank and honest manner. We felt that participating gave our child the best chance for a cure, and we felt good about increasing the knowledge that would help other children later.

The form that parents sign will have language similar to the following: "The study described above has been explained to me, and I voluntarily agree to have my child participate in this study. I have had all of my questions answered, and understand that all future questions that I have about this research will be answered by the investigators listed above."

> *The study that our institution was participating in at the time of my daughter's diagnosis was attempting to lessen the treatment to reduce neurotoxicity yet still cure the disease. My family began a massive research effort on the issue, and we had several family friends who were physicians discuss the case with the heads of pediatric oncology at their institutions. The consensus was that since my daughter was at the high end of the high-risk description, it was advisable to choose the standard care which was more aggressive.*
>
> *Although we believe strongly in clinical trials, we decided to opt for the standard treatment because she had a poor prognosis, and we felt that she would need the cranial radiation, despite the possibility of late side effects.*

Parents are experts on their children, but no matter how much reading they do, they are not experts on cancer. By the time a study is published in the literature, doctors on the cutting edge of treatment are six months to two years into improving that treatment or learning of its shortcomings. For this reason, it is best to make decisions in partnership with knowledgeable medical caregivers, rather than in isolation.

No matter how comfortable you are with your child's treating oncologist, it is helpful to have another medical caregiver help sort out your options. Often, that person will be the family's pediatrician or family doctor. Second opinions can also be arranged through the Childhood Cancer Ombudsman Program, which uses volunteer specialists to provide free help to families considering the range of treatment options and informed consent process. To avail yourself of this service, call (703) 492-0045.

What is a protocol?

A protocol is a recipe for treating cancer. Just like a recipe for baking a cake, it has ingredients that have to go in at certain times and in certain ways in order for the recipe to be successful. The protocol document lists the drugs, dosages, and tests for each segment of treatment. For instance, the first page of the protocol for the child with intermediate-risk ALL might list the following for the induction period: two bone marrow aspirations, four doses of vincristine, nine doses of L-asparaginase, two intrathecal doses of methotrexate, and twenty-seven oral doses of prednisone. It will state the dates and dosages for each chemotherapy drug and procedure.

If your child is enrolled in a clinical trial, the protocol will outline the treatment for each arm.

> The clinical trial that my child was enrolled in had three arms—A, B, and C. He was in the A portion, so we only referred to the A section of the protocol, which clearly outlined each procedure and drug to be given for the duration of the trial. It also listed the follow-up care required by that particular clinical trial.

If the family chooses not to enroll in a clinical trial, they will be given a protocol for standard treatment.

The protocol may be five to twenty pages long, and the family may also be given an abbreviated version (one to two pages) to provide quick and easy reference on a daily basis. Parents and teenage patients should review these documents carefully with the oncologist so that all portions are understood. It will be the parent's responsibility to make the appropriate appointments and give the many pills at the correct times.

Many parents expressed anguish when discussing their child's protocol. Below is a sampling of their comments.

> I didn't know what a protocol was when Preston was diagnosed, and I understood from the doctors that this was the "exact" regime which must be followed to cure Preston. It frightened me whenever changes were made in the protocol. After several years, I came to view the protocol as merely a guideline which is individualized for each patient according to his tolerance and reaction to the drugs. We ended up deleting whole sections of Preston's protocol due to extreme side effects. He has been off therapy for five years now with no relapse.

> • • • • •

> It took me a long time to get over my hang-up that things needed to go exactly as per protocol. Any deviations on dose or days was a MAJOR STRESS for me. It took talking to many parents, as well as doctors and nurses, to realize and feel comfortable with the fact that no one ever goes along perfectly and that the protocol is meant as the broad guideline. There will always be times when your child will be off drugs or on half

dose because of illness or low counts or whatever. It took a long time to realize that this is not going to ruin the effectiveness, that the child gets what she can handle without causing undue harm.

· · · · ·

I sobbed every night for an entire week when Katy was first taken off chemo for low counts. I was convinced that the immunosuppression was due to a relapse. That was two years ago, and we have changed her dosages almost every two weeks due to erratic counts. I wish I had known how normal it is to go off protocol.

Should parents receive the entire trial document?

The clinical trial protocol described above is actually a very small portion of an extensive document describing all aspects of the clinical study. The entire document often exceeds 100 pages and covers the following topics: study hypothesis, experimental design, scientific background and rationale with relevant references from the scientific literature, patient eligibility and randomization, therapy for each arm of the study, required observations, pathology guidelines, radiation therapy guidelines (if applicable), supportive care guidelines, specific information about each drug, relapse therapy guidelines, statistical considerations, study committee, record keeping, reporting of adverse drug reactions, and consent form.

Parents are sometimes not aware that this lengthy document exists. Admittedly, for some parents the full protocol could be overwhelming or boring. There are many parents, however, who throw themselves into research to better understand their child's illness. These parents may benefit from having a copy of the study document for several reasons. First, it provides a description of all the clinical trials that preceded the present one and explains the reasons the investigators designed this particular study. Secondly, it provides detailed descriptions of drug reactions, which comforts many parents who worry that their child is the only one exhibiting extreme responses to some drugs. Thirdly, motivated parents who have only one protocol to keep track of occasionally prevent serious errors in treatment. Physicians treat scores of children on dozens of protocols and sometimes make mistakes. And finally, for parents who are adrift in the world of cancer treatment, it can return a bit of control over their child's life. It gives the parents a job to do: monitoring their child's treatment.

Since knowledge is comfort for me, I really wanted to have the entire clinical trial document, despite its technical language. Whereas the brief protocol that I had listed day, drug, dose, the expanded version listed the potential side effects for each drug, and what actions should be taken should any occur. I learned the parameters.

Parents have a right to review all literature and information related to their child's treatment. There are no moral, ethical, or legal restrictions that come into play. If you wish to read all of the details of the study, simply insist that a copy be provided to you.

The following are excerpts from a letter to a doctor sent by a mother who discovered the study document two years into her son's treatment:

Until just recently, I thought that high-dose methotrexate was being tested against intrathecal methotrexate to determine if it was more effective in preventing CNS relapse. I believed that high-dose methotrexate was the untested drug. I didn't realize that data was available from a prior protocol showing good results with high-dose methotrexate. It would have been reassuring to me to have known this information earlier in Preston's treatment...

As a parent, I worry more about things I don't know. I have found that the more information I have, the less I worry. Please consider giving parents more information in future protocols about chemotherapy side effects and about the evolution and intent of the protocol...

Thank you for listening to me and thank you for all your efforts which benefit the health of my child and so many others.

What happens if parents say no to a clinical trial?

Parents have the legal right to decide not to participate in a clinical trial. If the parent chooses not to participate, her decision will be respected. The child will still be treated at the pediatric medical center and given the standard treatment for his type of leukemia.

Our son's doctor gave us the paperwork on the clinical trial to read and told us that it was our decision and that he would not pressure us. We really decided not to join the study for financial reasons. My husband was a student and we had no health insurance. One of the parts of the study required more clinic visits, and we just couldn't afford it.

Can parents remove their child from a clinical trial?

Yes. If parents have questions or concerns about any aspect of the trial, they should talk it over with their doctor. If the problem is not resolved, parents have the legal right to remove their child at any time from a clinical trial. This decision should not be held against the parent, and the child should still receive the best available care for her type of cancer. On the consent form signed by the parent, there will be language similar to this: "You are free not to have your child participate in this research or to withdraw your child at any time without penalty or jeopardizing future care."

Jesse was enrolled in a clinical trial to assess long-term neuropsychological consequences of cranial radiation. The testing was free, and we were glad to participate. Unfortunately, the billing department of the hospital continually billed us in error. We tried to correct the problem, but it became such a hassle that we withdrew from the study.

Pros and cons of clinical trials

Pros of clinical trials are:

- Patients receive either state-of-the-art investigational therapy or the best standard therapy available.

- Clinical trials can provide an opportunity to benefit from a new therapy before it is generally available.

- Information gained from clinical trials will benefit children with leukemia in the future.

- Children enrolled in clinical trials may be monitored more frequently throughout treatment.

- Review boards of scientists oversee the operation of clinical trials.

- Participating in a clinical trial often makes parents feel that they did everything medically possible for their child, possibly lessening guilt if child relapses.

- Some clinical trials provide all treatment and follow-up care at no cost to the family.

Cons to consider are:

- The experimental arm may not provide treatment as effective as the standard, or it may generate unexpected side effects or risks.

- Not all patients in a study receive the new treatment.

- Some clinical trials require more hospitalizations, treatments, or clinic visits than the standard treatment.

- Some families feel additional stress over which arm is the best treatment for their individual child.

- Participation may generate parental guilt if the child has unacceptable toxicity from the more aggressive experimental arm.

- Insurance may not cover investigational studies. Parents need to carefully explore this issue prior to signing the consent form.

If you are having trouble deciding whether to join the study or not, ask your pediatrician, oncologist, fellows, and nurses what they would do if it was their child. Then ask them why they would make that decision. Parents can acquire many perspectives on the issue this way.

> When we were struggling with the decision of whether to join the study, I asked the oncologist how would we ever know if we made the right decision. He said something very wise. "You will never know and you should never second guess yourself, no matter how the study turns out. Statistics are about large groups of kids, not your child. Your child might relapse no matter which arm she is on and she might be cured on an arm where most of the other kids relapse. Statistics for you will be either one hundred percent or zero because your child will either live or die. I can't tell you which will be the better treatment, that is why we are conducting the study. But no matter what, we will be doing absolutely the best we can."

Resources

Reading for adults

Brown, Elizabeth F., M.D. "Clinical Trials: What They Are, How They Work." *Cancer News* 6 (Autumn 1986). Defines the different types of clinical trials, informed consent, and advantages of participating.

Katz, Jay, M.D. *The Silent World of Doctor and Patient.* New York: Free Press, 1984. Each chapter deals with a different facet of informed consent: historical, legal, professional, psychological, scientific. Develops a strong argument for genuine dialogue between doctor and patient.

McAllister, Robert M., M.D., and Sylvia Horowitz, Ph.D. *Cancer.* New York: Basic Books, 1993. This book is divided into three parts: description of cancer, the cancer patient, and the ten most common cancers. Includes an excellent and detailed chapter on all aspects of clinical trials and a good basic description of how cancer cells operate.

National Cancer Institute. *What Are Clinical Trials All About?* NIH Publication No. 92-2706. To obtain free copy, call 1-800-4-CANCER. Twenty-two page booklet covers basic information about clinical trials.

Technical reading

Leventhal, Brigid, and Michael Graham. "Clinical Trials in Pediatric Oncology." *Seminars in Oncology* 15,5 (October 1988): 482-7. Discusses the different types of clinical trials, the ethics of using children as research subjects, and the existence of cooperative group studies.

National Cancer Institute. *Physician Data Query (PDQ).* 1-800-4-CANCER. PDQ is a computer data base that can provide information sheets (in either medical or nonmedical terms) on each type of cancer. PDQ can also provide lists of all the current clinical trials in the U.S., Canada, and abroad.

Video

National Cancer Institute. *Patient to Patient: Cancer Clinical Trials and You.* To obtain free copy, call 1-800-4-CANCER. Very clear, 15-minute tape which explains clinical trials and presents the views of four adult patients who participated in one.

CHAPTER 5

Family and Friends

Shared joy is double joy, shared sorrow is half sorrow.

—Swedish proverb

THE INTERACTIONS BETWEEN the parents of a child with cancer and their extended family and friends are complex. Potential exists for loving support and generous help, as well as for bitter disappointment. The diagnosis of leukemia creates a ripple effect first touching the immediate family, then extended family, friends, coworkers, schoolmates, church members, and the entire community. Parents are usually surprised at the diversity of coping abilities exhibited by relatives and friends.

This chapter discusses some of the experiences the family might encounter, as well as scores of ideas for helpful things that family and friends can do. To prevent possible misunderstandings between family members and friends, veteran parents also share ideas on things that do not help.

The extended family

Extended family—aunts, uncles, cousins, grandparents—can cushion the shock of a leukemia diagnosis by loving words and actions. Extended family members sometimes drop their own lives to rush to the side of the child with leukemia, and often remain steadfast for the years of treatment. Regrettably, family members may not be helpful, either from ignorance of what is helpful or simply because they are overwhelmed by events in their own lives. The following sections explore how some families notified extended family members, kept the lines of communication open, and dealt with grandparents.

Notifying the family

Notifying relatives is one of the first painful jobs for the parent of a child newly diagnosed with cancer. In times of crisis, family is refuge, and the news is usually quickly shared. Here are some ways that parents have told their relatives:

> *I called my mom and told her to make all the phone calls to family and friends. I couldn't choke out the word leukemia yet. Then I called our pastor.*

· · · · ·

> *I called my sister and asked her to take care of telling everyone. She called my other sister, and together they told my frail mother.*

· · · · ·

> *I waited three days after the diagnosis to call anyone. The doctors had trouble determining whether it was ALL or AML, and I wanted to be able to give the prognosis on the first call. I called my mom and asked her to notify everyone else but to request that they not call me for a week. I felt too fragile, and didn't want to continually cry in front of my daughter.*

Paradoxically, the family members who potentially may provide the greatest support may also be sources of added stress. Some extended families and even entire communities rally around the stricken family, while support never materializes for others. Several factors affect the strength of support: well-established community ties, good communication within extended family, physical proximity to extended family, and clear exchange of information on needs of the affected family. If any of these elements are missing, support may evaporate.

> *We had just moved three thousand miles away from family and friends for my husband to accept a new job. We had no family, no friends. Each family member and some close friends used their vacation to fly out and take two-week shifts at our new house to help out. Thankfully, they got us through the first months, but the two stressful years of maintenance were lonely.*

Other well-established families have support throughout treatment:

> *Shortly after Jesse relapsed, I was praying with my bible study group. With four children aged one to nine, I just didn't know how we would manage with one parent 100 miles away at the hospital and one*

parent working. The group decided to collect enough money to allow my sister to quit her job and move in to take care of the other three children while I was at the hospital with Jesse. She stayed for eight months. It was such a wonderful thing. They didn't even ask us; they just said they would support her financially so that she could care for my children and keep the household running.

Staying in touch

The most important first step for families is to set up clear communication over what truly will help. Sometimes, the child is too sick or too fatigued for company, and this needs to be expressed. Establishing a telephone chain is a good way to keep family informed of the child's progress. One family member can be delegated as communicator, and this person will relay the information to another person who will then phone another. Some families leave updates on their telephone answering machines. When visits are welcome, make them brief and cheerful. Not only do long visits distress sick children, but they can also overtax a tired parent.

Helpful things for family to do

The following are parents' helpful hints for family:

- Be sensitive to the emotional state of both child and parent. Sometimes parents want to talk about the leukemia; sometimes they just need a hand to hold.

- Encourage all members of the family to keep in touch through visits, calls, mail, videotapes, audiotapes, or pictures.

     Our relatives who lived close to the hospital had teenagers. One was a candy striper at Children's on Saturdays. Judd's aunts, uncles, and cousins came to visit several times a week any time he was in the hospital during his three years of treatment. They were all very supportive, very positive, and fun to be around.

- Be understanding if the parents do not want phone calls in the hospital. Remember that the child can hear all phone conversations when parents talk on the phone in the room.

     The first three days in the hospital I spent much of my time crying on the phone when talking to friends and relatives. Then I realized how frightening this must be to my two-year-old. So I just took the phone off the hook and left it there. Now, each time Jennifer is hospitalized, I call one friend and have her spread the news, then I take the phone off the hook again and concentrate on my daughter.

- A cheerful hospital room really boosts a child's spirits. Encourage sending balloon bouquets, funny cards, posters, toys or humorous books. Be aware that some hospitals do not allow rubber balloons, only mylar. Flowers are also not allowed in children's rooms.

  We plastered the walls with pictures of family and friends and so many people sent balloons that the ceiling was covered. It was a lovely sight.

- Laughter helps heal the mind and body, so send funny videotapes or arrive with a good joke.

  My brother Bill and his wonderful girlfriend Cathy created an exciting "trip" for my four-year-old daughter. She was bald, big-bellied from prednisone, and her counts were too low to leave the house, but her interest in fashion was as sharp as ever. Bill and Cathy bought ten outfits, rigged up a dressing room, and with Cathy as saleswoman, turned Katy's bedroom into a fashion salon. She tried on outfits, discussed all of their merits and shortcomings, and had a fabulous time. It was a real high point for her.

- Puzzles, games, picture books, coloring books, age appropriate computer games, and crafts are welcome. Remember that attention spans are shortened by treatment, so keep it simple.

  A friend who was a nurse came to my son's room shortly before Christmas and brought an entire gingerbread house kit, including confectioner's sugar for the icing. We had a very good time putting it together.

- Offer to give the parent a break from the hospital room. A walk outside, shopping trip, haircut, or just a long shower can be very refreshing.

- Donate frequent flyer miles to distant family members who have the time but not the money to help.

  A close friend (who lived three thousand miles away) had just lost her job and wished she could be there for us. My parents gave her their frequent flyer miles. She flew in for three weeks during a hard part of treatment and helped enormously.

- If you don't hear from a family member, call. Often silence means that he doesn't know what to do or say. Cynthia Krumme writes in her book *Leukemia Isn't So Bad*:

> *An irony that we felt and others expressed was that the difficulty of living with cancer is sometimes compounded when much of the reassurance must come from the patient and the family toward the rest of the world.*

Grandparents

Grandparents grieve deeply when a grandchild is diagnosed with leukemia. They are concerned not only for their grandchild, but for their own child (the parent) as well. Cancer wreaks havoc with grandparents' expectations, reversing the natural order of life and death. Grandparents frequently say "Why not me? I'm the one who is old." Parents express anguish at having to tell the grandparents the grim news. Cancer in a grandchild is a major shock to bear.

Surprisingly, in one major study on childhood cancer, only 19 percent of parents reported that grandparents were truly helpful. The parents in the study rated close friends, nurses, physicians, and other parents of ill children as greater sources of support.

In researching this book, descriptions of grandparents' reactions tended to fall into two categories: pillars of strength or additional burdens.

Many parents reported that the grandparents responded to the crisis with tremendous emotional, physical, and financial support.

> *My mother was a rock. She lived far away, but she put her busy life on hold to come help. She took care of the baby and kept the household running through both induction and reinduction when I was living at the hospital with my very ill child. She was strong, and it gave me strength.*

Some grandparents cancel all other activities to totally devote themselves to the crisis. Geralyn Gaes describes her experience in *You Don't Have to Die: One Family's Guide to Surviving Childhood Cancer*:

> *From the day Jason was diagnosed, she and my father selflessly responded to our family's needs. First, they turned over their business to someone else, then later that year sold their home in Storm Lake, and*

moved into a townhouse just blocks away from our rented home on West Ninth Avenue. The two of them dropped everything to help run our household, cooking meals, washing clothes, and so on.

Some parents express tremendous gratitude for the role played by the grandparents in providing much needed stability to the family rocked by cancer. Caring for the siblings and running the household allow the parents to care for the sick child and return to work.

> Because Judd had no neutrophils at diagnosis, he was put in isolation at Children's for a month. I stayed with him full time, and my husband took a month off work to be there. Luckily, my mother had moved to our town just the year before and was able to immediately move to our house to take care of Erin, my ten-year-old daughter. Grandma was great because she cooked special meals for Erin and helped with cleaning and transportation.

Other families are not so fortunate. Many grandparents are too old, too ill, or simply unable to cope with a crisis of this magnitude. Some simply fall apart:

> My mother became hysterical when my daughter was diagnosed with leukemia. She called every day, sobbing. Luckily, she lived far away, and this minimized the disruption. We had to ask her not to come because we just couldn't handle the catastrophe at home and her neediness too. It hurt her feelings, but we just couldn't cope with it.

Other grandparents allow preexisting problems with their adult child to color their perceptions of what the family needs. Sometimes cancer allows grandparents to renew criticism of the way grandchildren are being raised:

> While we stayed at the hospital the grandparents moved into our house to care for our eight-year-old daughter. They decided that this was their chance to "whip her into shape, teach her some manners, and get her room cleaned up." Our daughter was in tears, and we ended up saying, "We appreciate your help but we will take over."

Sometimes grandparents try to blame the parents for the cancer or make other hurtful comments:

> The first day in the hospital my mother told me I had caused the leukemia by coloring my hair blond during the pregnancy. My mother-in-law wasn't helpful either. Throughout the ordeal of treatment, all she did was to tell us to "put it in God's hand."

Grave problems can also result when grandparents try to take charge. Criticizing parents' choice of doctors, hospitals, or treatment can be very disruptive and further stress the family's resources.

Some grandparents simply cannot cope and withdraw from the situation. One mother was eight months pregnant, and her parents were visiting when her two-year-old son was diagnosed:

> I called my parents from the hospital and told them the news. While my parents were concerned and helped out while they were there, they did not offer to extend their visit, nor did my mother offer to stay and help while my father returned to Florida to work. I just didn't get the support that I needed from them at a very difficult time. I was truly disappointed and hurt.

> • • • • •

> I will never, ever be able to forget how my mother let me and my son down. She never came to the hospital, saying, "He's too sick for company." I told her he would love to see her, that his little face just would light up when he had visitors. But she never came. She never offered to help at home when he was so ill. She just disappeared.

It is hard to predict how anyone will react to the diagnosis of childhood leukemia. Grandparents are no exception. Some respond with the wisdom gleaned from decades of living, others become needy, and some withdraw. It is natural in a time of grave crisis to look to your parents for support and help, but it is important to remember that grandparents' ability to respond also depends on events in their own lives. If problems develop, help can be obtained from hospital social workers or through individual counseling.

Friends

Like family, friends can cushion the shock of diagnosis and ease the difficulties of treatment with their words and actions.

Notifying friends

The easiest way to notify friends is to delegate one person to do the job. Calling one neighbor or close friend prevents numerous tearful conversations. Most parents are at their child's bedside and want to avoid more emotional upheaval, especially in front of their child. Parents need to recognize that friends' emotions will mirror their own: shock, fear, worry, helplessness. Since most friends want to help but don't know what to do or say, giving cues of what would be helpful are welcome.

> I called a close friend to ask if she could drive our second car the 100 miles to the hospital so that my husband could return in it to work. She came with her family to the Ronald McDonald House with two big bags containing the following: snack foods, a large box of stationery, envelopes, stamps, books to read, a book handmade by her three-year-old daughter containing dozens of cut-out pictures of children's clothing pasted on construction paper (which my daughter adored looking at) and a beautiful, new, handmade, lace-trimmed dress for my daughter. It was full length and baggy enough to cover all bandages and tubing. She wore it almost every day for a year. It was a wonderful thing for my friend to do.

Helpful things for friends to do

We can do no great things—only small things with great love.

—Mother Teresa

It is a given that the family of a newly diagnosed child is overwhelmed. The list of helpful things to do is endless, but here are some suggestions from veteran parents.

Household

• Provide meals.

> One of the nicest things that friends did was to bring us a huge picnic basket full of food to the hospital. We spread a blanket on the floor, Erica crawled out of bed, and the entire family sat down together and ate. Most people don't realize how expensive it is to have to eat every meal at the hospital cafeteria, so the picnic was not only fun, but helped us to save a few dollars.

• Take care of pets or livestock.

• Mow grass, shovel snow, rake leaves, weed gardens.

> We came home from the hospital one evening right before Christmas, and found a freshly cut, fragrant Christmas tree leaning next to our door. I'll never forget that kindness.

- Clean house.

  My husband's cousin sent her cleaning lady over to our house. It was so neat and such a luxury to come home to find the stove and windows sparkling clean.

- Grocery shop (especially when the family is due home from the hospital).

- Do laundry. Drop off and pick up dry cleaning.

- Provide a place to stay near the hospital.

  The mother-in-law of a coworker of my husband's lived near the Children's Hospital which was 120 miles away from our home. We had never met her, but she called up and offered us the use of her basement apartment. Her mother had recently moved to a nursing home, and she said she would welcome the company. She was absolutely wonderful to us. I often came home from the hospital with my very ill child to find a lovely dinner sitting on the table. She was a nurse and never intruded, but always provided a sympathetic ear. We are still friends, and I hope to be able to repay her kindness someday.

  • • • • •

  One of the ladies from the school where I worked came up to the ICU waiting room where we were sleeping and pressed her house key into my hand. She lived five minutes from the hospital. She said, "My basement is made up, there's a futon, there's a TV, you are coming and staying at my house." I hardly knew her, but we accepted. Every day when we came in from the hospital there was some cute little treat waiting for us like a bowl of cookies, or two packages of hot chocolate and a thermos of hot milk.

Siblings

- Baby-sit whenever parents go to clinic, emergency room, or for a prolonged hospital stay.

  The mother of a secretary from my office called me, introduced herself, and offered to care for my newborn daughter while I spent time at the hospital. I had never met this woman, but she turned out to be a real lifesaver and a jewel. She would come every day, bathe, dress, and feed my daughter, clean up the house, and stay from morning until evening. She did this for several months. I will never forget her for being so kind. I would not have been able to get through those first few difficult months without this type of support—and to find it in a complete stranger certainly renewed my faith in mankind!

- When parents are home with a sick child, take sibling(s) to the park, sports event, or a movie.

- Invite sibling(s) over for meals.

- If you bring a gift for the sick child, bring something for the sibling(s), too.

    Friends from home sent boxes of art supplies to us when the whole family spent those first ten weeks at a Ronald McDonald house far from our home. They sent scissors, paints, paper, colored pens. It was a great help for Carrie Beth and her two sisters. One friend even sent an Easter package with straw hats for each girl, and flowers, ribbons, and glue to decorate them with.

- Offer to help sibling(s) with homework.

- Drive sibling(s) to lessons, games, or school.

- Listen to how they are feeling and coping. Siblings' lives have been shattered, they have limited time with their parents, and they need support and care.

Psychological support

- Call frequently, and be open to listening if the parents want to talk about their feelings.

- Call to talk about non cancer-related topics.

- If one parent had to leave work to stay in the hospital with the sick child, coworkers can send messages by mail or tape.

    One very neat thing that was an emotional boost was that my friends and former coworkers from Kansas faxed us messages and pictures and things to Meagan while we were in the hospital. It was very nice to get such fresh messages—it really shortened the miles.

- If you think the family might be interested, call Candlelighters, the American Cancer Society, or the social worker at the local hospital to find out if there are support groups for parents and/or kids in your area.

- Offer to take the children to the support groups, or go with the parents. For most families, the parent support group becomes a second family with ties of shared experience as deep and strong as blood relations.

- Drive parent and child to clinic visits.

- Buy books (uplifting ones) for the family if they are readers.

- Send cards or letters.

  Word got around my parents' hometown, and I received cards from many high school acquaintances, who still cared enough to call or write and say we're praying for you, please let us know how things are going. It was so neat to get so many cards out of the blue that said, "I'm thinking about you."

- Baby-sit the sick child so that the parents can go out to eat, exercise, take a walk, or just get out of the hospital or house.

- Ask parents if you could enroll them in Candlelighters and other helpful organizations.

  After I called our pastor the day Stephan was diagnosed, he called the Leukemia Society. They sent us some much needed information.

- Donate blood. Your blood will not be used specifically for the ill child, but will replenish the general supply, which is depleted by children with cancer.

- If the child has a type of leukemia that may require a bone marrow transplant, organize a drive to have lots of people typed and entered into the marrow registry. Contact: National Marrow Donor Program. 3433 Broadway St. NE, Suite 400, Minneapolis, MN, 55413. 1-800-654-1247.

- Send the family a gift certificate for professional photographs.

  My daughter wanted her picture taken several months into treatment. She was bald, sick, and frightened of strangers. I called Donnette Studio, asked to speak to the photographer who was best with kids, and explained the situation. I told him that how the pictures looked didn't matter, I wanted it to be a fun experience. He scheduled one and one half hours for the appointment, and he played with her the majority of that time. They did puppets, chased each other around, and just had a ball. She had a glorious smile on her face for the pictures, and we go back every six months to see Donny.

- Give lots of hugs.

Grandpa Fred is a seventy-one-year-old retiree who has been visiting pediatric oncology patients at Children's for almost twelve years. He begins his day at 9:30 every morning on the teens ward, then he moves on to visit the younger patients, the playroom, and the clinic. Grandpa Fred always takes pictures of his young friends, very good ones, and has filled twenty-three photo albums with them. Fred has two prints made of each picture he takes and gives one to the families. He also helps Santa on Christmas and visits on Halloween. He has been the camp manager at Camp Good Times every summer for eight years. Fred feels that a hug is more important than anything he can say to someone. "Listening and giving a hug," he says, "That's the best I can do."

Financial support

Helping families avoid financial disaster can be the next greatest gift after the life of the child and the strength of the family. It is estimated that even fully insured families spend 25 percent or more of their income on copayments, travel, motels, meals, and other uncovered items. Uninsured or underinsured families may lose their savings, or even their house. Most families need financial help. Here are some suggestions.

- Start a support fund.

A friend of mine called and asked very tentatively if we would mind if she started a support fund. We felt awkward, but we needed help, so we said OK. She did everything herself, and the money she raised was very, very helpful. We did ask her to stop the fund when people started calling us to ask if they could use giving to the fund as an advertisement for their business.

- Share leave. The federal government and some companies have leave banks that permit persons who are ill or taking care of someone who is ill to use other coworkers' leave so they won't have their pay docked.

- Job share. Some families with two working parents work out job-share arrangements in which a coworker donates time to perform part of one job to enable one parent to spend time at the hospital. Job sharing allows the job to get done, keeps peace at the job site, and prevents financial losses for the family. Another possibility would be for one or more friends with similar skills (e.g., word processing, filing, sales, etc.) to rotate through the job on a volunteer basis to cover for the parent of the ill child.

- Collect money at church or work to give informally.

  The day my daughter was diagnosed, my husband's coworkers passed the hat and gave us over $250. I was embarrassed, but it paid for gas, meals, and the motel until there was an opening in the Ronald McDonald House.

  • • • • •

  Finances were a main concern for us because I wanted to cut back on work to be at home with Meagan. Sometimes my coworkers would pool money and present it with a card saying, "Here's a couple of days work that you won't have to worry about."

  • • • • •

  My husband's coworkers didn't collect money, they did something even more valuable. They donated sick leave hours, so that he was able to be at the hospital frequently during those first few months without losing a paycheck.

- Collect money by organizing a bake sale, dance, or raffle.

  Coworkers of my husband held a Halloween party and charged admission for us. We were very uncomfortable with the idea at first, but they were looking for an excuse to have a party, and it helped us out.

- Keeping track of medical bills is time-consuming, frustrating, and exhausting. If you are a close relative or friend, you could offer to review, organize, and file (or enter into a computer) the voluminous paperwork. Making the calls and writing the letters over contested claims or errors in billing are very helpful.

Help from schoolmates

- Encourage visits (if appropriate), cards, and phone calls from classmates.
- Ask the teacher to send the school newspaper and other news along with assignments.
- Classmates can sign a brightly colored banner to send to the hospital.

Brent's kindergarten class sent a packet containing a picture drawn for him by each child in the class. They also made him a book. Another time they sent him a letter written on huge poster board. He couldn't wait to get back to school.

Religious support

- If the family goes to church, contact the pastor or rabbi.

- Arrange for the pastor, rabbi, or church members to visit the hospital, if that is what the family wants.

- Arrange prayer services for the sick child.

- Have the child's Sunday school class (or whatever class is appropriate for the family's denomination) send pictures, posters, letters, balloons, or tapes to the sick child.

The day our son was diagnosed, we raced next door to ask our wonderful neighbors to take care of our dog. The news of his diagnosis quickly spread, and we found out later that five neighborhood families gathered that very night to pray for Brent.

Accepting help

One father's thoughts on accepting help:

An egotistical thing about fathers is that they have a deep-seated need to protect their family. Yet here I was with a child with leukemia, and there wasn't a single thing that I could do about it. The loss of control really bothered me. The very hardest thing that I had to learn was to let go enough to let people help us.

One mother's thoughts on accepting help:

The most important advice I received as the parent of a child newly diagnosed with cancer came from a hospital nurse whom I turned to when I was overwhelmed with all the advice being offered by family and friends. This wise nurse said, "Don't discount anything. You're going to need all the help you can get." I think it is very important for families to remain open and accept the help that is offered. It often comes when least expected and from unlikely sources. I was totally unprepared at diagnosis for how much help I would need, and I'm glad that I remained open to offers of kindness. This is not the time to show the world how strong you are.

What to say

The following are some suggestions on what to say and how to offer help. Of course, much depends on the type of relationship that already exists, but a specific offer can always be accepted or graciously declined.

- I am so sorry.

- I didn't call earlier because I didn't know what to say.

- Our family would like do your yardwork. It will make us feel as if we are helping in a small way.

- We want to clean your house for you once a week. What day would be convenient?

- Would it help if we took care of your dog (or cat, or bird)? We would love to do it.

- I walk my dog three times a day. May I walk yours, too?

- The church is setting up a system to deliver meals to your house. When is the best time to drop them off?

- I will take care of Jimmy whenever you need to take John to the hospital. Call us anytime, day or night, and we will come pick him up.

Things that do not help

Tread softly, because you tread on [their] dreams.

—W. B. Yeats

Out of ignorance, people sometimes say unbelievably hurtful things to parents of children with cancer. If you are a family member or friend of a parent in this situation, please do not say any of the following:

- "God only gives people what they can handle." (Some people cannot handle the stress of childhood leukemia.)

- "I know just how you feel." (Unless you have a child with cancer, you simply don't know.)

- "You are so brave," or "so strong," etc. (Parents are not heroes; they are normal people struggling with extraordinary stress.)

- "They are doing such wonderful things to save children with leukemia these days." (Yes, the prognosis is good, but what parents and children are going through is not wonderful.)

- "Well, we're all going to die one day." (True, but parents do not need to be reminded of this fact.)

- "It's God's will." (Just not a helpful thing to hear.)

- "At least you have other kids," or "Thank goodness you are still young enough to have other children." (A child cannot be replaced.)

> *A woman whom I worked with, but did not know well, came up to me one day and out of the blue said, "When Erica gets to heaven to be with Jesus, He will love her." All I could think to say was, "Well, I'm sorry, but Jesus can't have her right now."*

Parents also make the following suggestions of things to avoid doing:

- Do not say, "Let us know if there is anything we can do." It is far better to make a specific suggestion.

> *Many well-wishing friends always said, "Let me know what I can do." I wish they had just "done," instead of asking for direction. It took too much energy to decide, call them, make arrangements, etc. I wish someone would have said, "When is your clinic day? I'll bring dinner," or "I'll baby-sit Sunday afternoon so you two can go out to lunch."*

- Do not make personal comments in front of the child: when will his hair grow back in, he's lost so much weight, she's so pale, etc.

- Do not do things that require the parent to support you (for example, call up repeatedly crying).

- Do not talk continually about the cancer; some normal conversations are welcome.

- Do not ask "what if " questions: What if he can't go to school? What if your insurance won't cover it? What if she dies? The present is really all the parents can deal with.

- Stories of children you know who have survived leukemia and are doing fine are welcome. Stories of those who have died or who have long term side effects should not be shared.

Losing friends

It is an unfortunate reality that most parents of children with leukemia lose friends. For a variety of reasons, some friends just can't cope and either suddenly disappear or gradually fade away. Many times this can be prevented by calling them to keep them involved, but sometimes, they just can't handle the stress.

Except for one good friend, none of my friends called when I was home. It seemed that after the initial three-month crisis, they removed themselves from the situation, as often happens.

· · · · ·

I had a friend who really thought herself to be empathetic, except that she just couldn't "deal with" hospitals. She said that they made her uncomfortable, so she wouldn't visit. I also got tired of her talking about the silver lining of the dark cloud that has been hanging over my head. I have a really hard time dealing with that.

· · · · ·

Friends? What friends? They disappeared, family, too. No one knew what to say to us.

Evan Handler, who was diagnosed with leukemia as a young adult, wrote a powerful memoir called *Time on Fire* about his experience. In it he discussed what his parents did to keep their friends informed:

They began to distribute a newsletter describing my progress as well as the stresses they were under...I saw it as a brilliant device. The exhaustion that is unavoidable to the parents of a sick child, even an adult child, is enough to overwhelm the strongest individual. My parents were simply accepting the offers coming forth and sharing their burden in a fashion that didn't increase their already superhuman load. By revealing themselves in the newsletter, both the good news and the bad, they gave their friends the option of tuning in or out, without having to suffer the indignity of those who could not cope with what my parents coped with daily.

Restructuring family life

Childhood cancer does not only strike families of brave children and heroic parents. In the United States, the popular press has responded to people's terror of cancer by churning out story after story of people who faced the diagnosis with almost superhuman hope and strength. Families rally round, the community cheers, and human will triumphs over the evil of cancer. As we know, this simply is not always the case. Cancer strikes all types of families: single-parent families, those with two parents in the home, financially secure families, those with no insurance, families with strong community ties, those who have just moved to a new community, families of every size, type, and color. Most parents do find unexpected reserves of strength to deal with the crisis. They survive the years of stress and pain, emerging different and sometimes stronger. Still, expectations of heroism are not appropriate.

Keeping the household functioning

Every family of a child with leukemia needs massive assistance. It is important for families to recognize this early and learn not only to accept aid gracefully but also to ask for help when needed. As discussed earlier in the chapter, most family members, friends, neighbors, and church members want to help, but they need direction from the family on what is helpful but not intrusive.

In families where both parents are employed, decisions must be made about the jobs. It is better, if possible, to use all available sick leave and vacation days prior to deciding whether one parent needs to terminate employment. Parents need to be able to evaluate their financial situation and insurance availability. This requires time and clarity of thought, both in short supply in the weeks following diagnosis.

> *I was eight months pregnant when my two-year-old son was diagnosed. I went on maternity leave, but we needed to make arrangements quickly with my husband's employer to allow him time off to care for Carl in the hospital after I had the baby. Even worse, I knew that I would need to deliver by caesarian section. Carl's protocol required him to be in the hospital for one week then home for one week from September through January. My husband worked out a schedule where he worked seventy hours the week that Carl was home, then was off work the week Carl was hospitalized. He then only needed to use ten hours of leave, and was able to stay at the hospital with Carl.*

Family and Medical Leave Act

In August 1993, the Family and Medical Leave Act (FMLA) became federal law. FMLA protects job security of workers in large companies who must take a leave of absence to care for a seriously ill child, to take medical leave because the employee is unable to work because of his or her own medical condition, or for the birth or placement of a child for adoption or foster care. The Family and Medical Leave Act:

- Applies to employers with 50+ employees within a 75 mile radius.

- Provides 12 weeks of unpaid leave during any 12-month period to care for seriously ill self, spouse, child, or parent. In certain instances, the employee may take intermittent leave, such as reducing his or her normal work schedule's hours.

- Requires employer to continue to provide benefits, including health insurance, during the leave period.

- Requires employer to return employee to the same or equivalent position upon return from the leave. Some benefits, such as seniority, need not accrue during periods of unpaid FMLA leave.

- Requires employee to give 30-day notice of the need to take FMLA leave when the need is foreseeable.

- Is enforced by complaints to the Wage and Hour Division, U.S. Department of Labor, or by private lawsuit. The nearest office of the Wage and Hour Division may be located by looking in the U.S. Government pages of your telephone directory.

Marriage

Cancer treatment places enormous pressure on a marriage. Couples are separated for long periods of time, emotions are high, and coping styles and skills differ. Initially, family life is shattered. Couples must simply survive the first few overwhelming weeks, then work together to rearrange the pieces in a new pattern. Here are parents' suggestions and stories about how they managed:

- Share medical decisions.

My husband and I shared decision making by keeping a joint medical journal. The days that my husband stayed at the hospital, he would write down all medicines given, side effects, fever, vital signs, food consumed, sleep patterns, and any questions that needed to be asked at the next rounds. This way, I knew exactly what had been happening. Decisions were made as we traded shifts at our son's bedside.

• • • • •

I made most of the medical decisions. My husband did not know what a protocol was, nor did he ever learn the names of the medicines. He came with me to medical conferences, however, and his presence gave me strength.

• • • • •

Curt and I discuss every detail of the medical issues. It is so helpful to hash things over together to get a clearer idea of what our main concerns are.

- Take turns staying in the hospital with the ill child.

We took turns going in with our son for painful procedures. The doctors loved to see my husband come in because he's a friendly, easygoing person who never asked them any medical questions. We shared hospital duty, also. I would be there during any crisis because I was the person better able to be a strong advocate, but he went when our son was feeling better and needed entertaining company. It worked out well.

· · · · ·

My husband fell apart emotionally when our daughter was diagnosed, and he never really recovered. He stayed with her once in the hospital and cried almost the whole time. She never wanted him to go again, so I did all hospital duty.

· · · · ·

Whenever Brent was in the hospital, we both wanted to be there. We were able to be there most of the time because our children have a wonderful aunt and uncle who stayed with them when needed. During Brent's second extended stay in the hospital, we both let go a little, and we each took turns sleeping at the Ronald McDonald House. That way we each got a decent night's sleep (or some sleep) every other night.

· · · · ·

My wife took care of most of the medical information gathering because she had a scientific background. But my work schedule was more flexible, so I took my son for almost all of his treatments and hospitalizations. I cherish my memories of those long hours in the car and waiting room, because we were always so very close.

- Share responsibility for home care.

My husband worked long hours, and therefore I had to do almost all of the home care. It was very hard on me, especially in the beginning when she was so ill and needed so many medications. I felt like I was doing all the horrible things to her; I wish that he could have done some of it.

· · · · ·

We had a traditional relationship in which I took care of the kids and he worked. I didn't expect him to cook or clean when I was staying at the hospital, it was all he could do to ferry our daughter to her various activities and go to work.

· · · · ·

We both worked full time, so we staggered our shifts. He worked 7 to 3, I worked 3 to 11. He did every single dressing change for the Hickman catheter—584 changes, we counted them up. Wherever I left off during the day, he took over. He was great, and it really worked out well for us. We shared it all.

· · · · ·

My husband really didn't help at all. I couldn't even go out because he wouldn't give the pills. He kept saying that he was afraid that he would make a mistake.

- Accept differences in coping styles.

We both coped differently, but we learned to work around it. I didn't want to deal with "what if" questions, but he was a pessimist and constantly asked the fellow questions about things that might happen. I felt that it was a waste of energy to worry about things that might never happen. I didn't want to hear it and felt that it just added to my burden. It was all I could do to survive every day. We worked it out by going to conferences together, but I would ask my questions and then leave. He stayed behind to ask all of his questions.

· · · · ·

My husband didn't have the desire to read as much as I did. However, whenever I read something that I felt he should read, he always took the time to do so and then we discussed it.

- Seek counseling.

I went for counseling because I couldn't sleep. At night, I got stuck thinking the same things over and over and worrying. I ended up spending two years on antidepressants, which I think really saved my life. They helped me sleep and kept me on an even keel. I'm off them now, my son is off treatment, and everything is looking up.

· · · · ·

My husband and I went to counseling to try to work out a way to split up the child rearing and household duties because I was overwhelmed and resenting it. I guess it helped a little bit, but the best thing that came out of it was that I kept seeing the counselor by myself. My son wanted to go to the "feelings doctor," too. I received a lot of very helpful, practical advice on the many behavior problems my son developed. And my son had an objective, safe person to talk things over with.

Most marriages survive, but some don't. It is usually marriages with serious preexisting problems that are further strained by cancer treatment.

My husband had a lot of problems that really brought my daughter and I down. The cancer really opened my eyes to what was important in life. We stayed together through treatment, but we divorced after the bone marrow transplant. I just realized that life is too short to spend it in a bad relationship.

• • • • •

My husband went to work rather than go with us to Children's when our son was diagnosed. It went downhill from there. He started using drugs and mistreating us, so we divorced.

Siblings

It takes an entire chapter to deal with the complex feelings that siblings confront when their brother or sister has leukemia. Chapter 16, *Siblings*, provides an in-depth examination of the issues from the perspective of both siblings and parents.

Resources

Reading for adults

Adams, David, and Eleanor Deveau. *Coping with Childhood Cancer: Where Do We Go from Here?* rev.ed. Toronto: Kinbridge Publications, 1993. Written by a pediatric oncology social worker and a nurse, this book is highly recommended for dealing with emotional issues.

Chesler, Mark, Ph.D., and Oscar Barbarin. "Dilemmas of Providing Help in a Crisis: The Role of Friends with Parents of Children with Cancer." *Candlelighters Progress Reports* V(4) (1985): 9-11.

Chesler, Mark, Ph.D., and Oscar Barbarin. *Childhood Cancer and the Family: Meeting the Challenge of Stress and Support.* New York: Brunner/Mazel Publishers, 1987. Written by two sociologists, one the parent of a young person with cancer, it is filled with parent commentary and analysis of a large group of parents. Excellent resource.

Dorfman, Elena. *The C-Word: Teenagers and Their Families Living with Cancer.* Portland, OR: New Sage Press, 1994. A cancer survivor (treated from age 16 to 18) spent four years interviewing and photographing the daily lives of five teenagers with cancer and their families. This book portrays in words and powerful pictures some of the deepest emotions experienced by teens with cancer and those close to them. Four of the five teens featured have leukemia.

Gaes, Geralyn, Craig Gaes, and Philip Bashe. *You Don't Have to Die: One Family's Guide to Surviving Childhood Cancer.* New York: Villard Books, 1992. Very well-written, uplifting biography of a young boy with cancer, which contains good chapters on how one large extended family coped with the stresses of treatment.

Handler, Evan. *Time on Fire: My Comedy of Terrors.* Boston: Little, Brown, 1996. Powerful personal account of a young adult's struggle with leukemia, and cure from a bone marrow transplant. Very graphic descriptions of procedures and emotions.

Maxwell, Katie. *Bedside Manners: A Practical Guide to Visiting the Ill.* Grand Rapids, MI: Baker Book House, 1990. Publisher's address: P.O. Box 6287, Grand Rapids, MI 49516. (616) 676-9185. Practical advice for visiting the sick in the hospital or home. Religious perspective, includes suggested scriptures.

Peterson, Sheila. *A Special Way to Care.* 1988. Available from: Friends of Karen, Box 217, Croton Falls, N.Y. 10519. Free guide for those who wish to provide financial/emotional support for families of ill children. Discusses how to differentiate between interference and advocacy. Explains how to organize, manage, and perpetuate a support fund. Excellent resource.

Technical reading

Speechley, Kathy Nixon, and Samuel Noh. "Surviving Childhood Cancer, Social Support, and Parent's Psychological Adjustment." *Journal of Pediatric Psychology* 17(1) (1992): 15-31. Assessment of emotional strain and social support of families of children with cancer.

Video

Childhood Cancer: Today's Crisis, Tomorrow's Challenge. Videotape and program guide. Rent from: Children's Hospital Medical Center, Hematology-Oncology Division, Elland & Bethesda Ave., Cincinnati, OH 45229. (513) 559-4266. How one family coped with their son's diagnosis of leukemia.

Family Portrait: Coping with Childhood Cancer. Videotape. 25 mins. VHS. Purchase from: Films for the Humanities and Sciences, P.O. Box 253, Princeton, N.J. 08543. 1-800-257-5126. Videotape of five family portraits covering issues such as guilt, sibling rivalry, divorce, the adopted child, and involvement of other family members in the care of the child. Introduction and closing by Bob Keeshan (Captain Kangaroo).

Mr. Rogers Talks About Childhood Cancer. 1989. Videotapes (2), guidebook, storybook. 45 mins. VHS. Available from American Cancer Society. 1-800-ACS-2345. Mr. Rogers talks to children and uses characters from the land of make believe to stress the importance of talking about feelings.

Mr. Rogers Talks with Parents About Childhood Cancer. Videotapes (2) guidebook, pamphlet. 47 mins. VHS. Available from American Cancer Society. 1-800-ACS-2345. The first tape consists of interviews with parents which illustrate ways to deal with emotions during diagnosis and treatment. The second tape sensitively deals with bereavement.

Forming a Partnership with the Medical Team

It is our duty as physicians to estimate probabilities and to discipline expectations;
but leading away from probabilities there are paths of possibilities, toward
which it is our duty to hold aloft the light, and the name of that light is hope.

—Karl Menninger
The Vital Balance

IT IS VITALLY IMPORTANT that parents and the health care team establish and maintain a relationship based on excellent medical care, good communication, and caring. In this partnership, trust is paramount. Unlike many other diseases, children with leukemia spend years being treated primarily on an outpatient basis. Physicians rely on parents to make and keep appointments, give the proper medicines at the appropriate times, prepare the child for procedures, and be vigilant in noticing any illness or drug side effect. Parents rely on physicians for medical knowledge, expertise in performing procedures, good judgment, caring, and clear communication. It is a delicate dance, which spans years of trauma and emotional upheaval.

A climate of cooperation and respect between the health care team and parents allows children to thrive. This chapter will explore ways to create and maintain that environment.

The hospital

After diagnosis, a steady parade of anonymous faces enters the life of a child with leukemia. To understand who is responsible for the child's treatment, an explanation of hospital pecking order is necessary.

The doctors

A medical student is a college graduate who is attending medical school. Medical students wear white coats, but do not have M.D. after the name on their name tags.

An intern is a graduate of medical school who is in her first year of post-graduate training.

A resident is a graduate of medical school in his second or third year of postgraduate training. Most of the residents at pediatric hospitals will be pediatricians upon completion of their residencies.

After residency, if the pediatric resident wishes to further specialize in oncology (the study of tumors), he applies for a fellowship in pediatric oncology. Fellowships generally last two to four years. A fellow who treats children with cancer is a doctor who has completed four years of medical school, one year of internship, two years of residency in pediatrics, and is taking additional specialty training in pediatric oncology.

Above fellows in the hospital hierarchy are attending physicians (called simply "attendings"). These well-established doctors are hired by the medical center to provide and oversee medical care and to train interns, residents, and fellows. They are frequently also professors on the staff of the medical school.

> When my daughter was first admitted, each new group of doctors
> that came in added to my confusion. I finally asked them not to introduce
> themselves, but just tell me whether they were an intern, resident, fellow,
> or attending. I told them I needed to sort them out by groups first, then I
> would learn names.

When a child arrives at a teaching hospital, he will be assigned a fellow and/or an attending. These physicians will provide continuous care throughout treatment. The physician in charge of your child's care should be "board-certified" or have equivalent medical credentials. This means that she has taken rigorous written and oral tests by a board of examiners in her specialty, and meets a high standard of competence. You can call the American Board of Medical Specialties at 1-800-776-2378 to find out if your child's physician is board-certified.

While an inpatient, your child will see a large number of other doctors. Residents usually rotate to different floors every four weeks, so they are an ever-changing group. If questions arise about your child's treatment or illness, it is better to ask only the fellow or attending assigned to your child, as they will be more familiar with your child's situation.

If your family is insured by a health maintenance organization (HMO), you probably will be sent to the affiliated hospital which will have one or more pediatric oncologists on staff.

The nurses

An essential part of the hospital hierarchy is the nursing staff. The following explanations will help you understand which type of nurse is caring for your child.

An L.P.N. is a licensed practical nurse. To be licensed as such, a person must complete a vocational training program. L.P.N.s have a narrow scope of practice; for example, they usually do not start IVs or give IV medications.

An R.N. is a registered nurse who obtained an A.A. degree or a B.A. degree in nursing, and then passed a licensing examination. These medical professionals give medicines, take vital signs (heart rate, breathing rate, blood pressure), monitor IV machines, change bandages, and care for patients in hospitals, clinics, and doctors' offices.

> At our hospital, each of our nurses is different, but each is wonderful. They simply love the kids. They throw parties, set up dream trips, act as counselor, best friend, stern parent. They hug moms and dads. They cry. I have come to respect them so much because they have such a hard job to do, and they do it so well.

A nurse practitioner or clinical nurse specialist is a registered nurse who has completed an educational program that has taught her advanced skills. For example, in some hospitals and clinics, nurse practitioners perform procedures such as spinal taps.

The head or charge nurse is the supervisor of all the nurses on the floor for one shift. If you have any problems with a nurse, your first step in resolving them would be to talk to the charge nurse.

The clinical nurse manager is the administrator for an entire unit such as an oncology floor or oncology clinic. He is in charge of all of the nurses on the unit.

Finding an oncologist

Few things are more delicate or important in dealing
with serious illness than the psychological environment
in which the patient is treated.

—Norman Cousins
Head First

Parents do not have the luxury of time in choosing a pediatric oncologist. At diagnosis, the family is usually referred to the nearest pediatric center of excellence. The young patient may be assigned the fellow or attending who happens to be on call at the time of diagnosis. If the child is insured by an HMO, sometimes there are only one or two oncologists on staff.

During induction and consolidation, your child may see a myriad of doctors. A permanent assignment should be made for all outpatient treatment. Be sure that you are working with a board-certified pediatric oncologist or an oncologist with equivalent credentials who participates in association with the Children's Cancer Group (CCG) or the Pediatric Oncology Group (POG). Your child's chance for a cure depends on getting the most up-to-date treatments available.

Often the assignment of oncologist is a good match, and the family finds the doctor to be easy to communicate with, competent, and caring. If the medical facility allows you to choose your child's oncologist, here are several traits to look for:

• Board-certified in the field of pediatric oncology.

• Establishes good rapport with child.

• Communicates clearly and compassionately.

• Skillful in performing procedures.

• Answers all questions.

• Consults with other doctors on complex problems.

• Uses language that is easy to understand.

• Makes available the results of all tests.

• Is willing to let parents participate in the decision-making process.

• Respects parent's values.

• Able to deliver the truth with hope.

If you don't develop a good rapport with the physician assigned to you, at large teaching hospitals it is common practice to ask to be assigned to a different physician that you have met on rounds or during clinic visits. Most parents are accommodated, for hospitals realize the importance of good communication between family and physician.

Choosing a hospital

At diagnosis, if your family is not initially referred to a specific hospital, or if there are several excellent pediatric hospitals in the area to choose from, it may be necessary to choose where you would like your child to be treated. Parents can obtain a free referral to an accredited center from either the National Cancer Institute (1-800-4-CANCER) or the offices of the Children's Cancer Group and Pediatric Oncology Group:

Children's Cancer Group
P.O. Box 60012
Arcadia, CA 91066
(818) 447-0064

Pediatric Oncology Group
645 N. Michigan Ave. Suite 910
Chicago, IL 60611
(312) 482-9944

Types of relationships

There are primarily three types of relationships that develop between physicians and parents:

- **Paternal.** In a paternal relationship the parent is submissive, and the doctor assumes a fatherly role. The problem with this dynamic is that although medical personnel never intend harm, they are human and mistakes occur. If parents are not monitoring drugs and treatments, these mistakes may go unnoticed. In addition, parents are the experts in their own child and his reactions to drugs and treatments.

    After we left Children's and returned home for outpatient treatment, the local pediatrician's nurse called and said, "Doctor wanted me to tell you that the blood results were normal." I thought that unlikely since she was on high-dose chemotherapy, so I politely asked for the actual numbers for my records. She read them off and my daughter's ANC [absolute neutrophil count—see Appendix B, *Blood Counts and What They Mean] had dropped far below 500. I said, "Would you tell the doctor that her counts have dropped dramatically from last week?" She said in a frosty voice, "Doctor said they were fine." So I called Children's, and they told me to keep her at home, take her off all medications for a week, and then have her blood retested. I was glad that I paid attention to the counts.*

A surprising number of parents are intimidated by doctors and express the fear that if they question the doctors their child will suffer. This type of behavior robs the child of an adult advocate who speaks up when something seems wrong.

- **Adversarial.** Some parents adopt an "us against them" attitude that is counterproductive. They seem to feel that the disease and treatment are the fault of medical staff, and they blame staff for any setbacks that occur. This attitude undermines the child's confidence in his doctor, a crucial component for healing.

    I knew one family who just hated the Children's Hospital. They called it the "House of Horrors" or the "torture chamber" in front of their children. Small wonder that their children were terrified.

- **Collegial.** This is a true partnership in which parents and doctors are all on the same footing and they respect each other's domains and expertise. Here the doctor recognizes that the parents are the experts on their own child and are essential in ensuring that the protocol is followed. The parents respect the physician's expertise and feel comfortable discussing various treatment options or concerns that arise. Honest communication is necessary for this partnership to work, but the effort is well worth it. The child has confidence in his doctor, the parents have lessened their stress by creating a supportive relationship with the physician, and the physician feels comfortable that the family will comply with the treatment plan giving the child the best chance for a cure.

    We had a wonderful relationship with the oncologist assigned to us. He blended perfectly the science and the art of medicine. His manner with our daughter was warm, he was extremely well qualified professionally, and he was very easy to talk to. I could bring in articles to discuss with him, and he welcomed the discussion. Although he was busy, he never rushed us. I laughed when I saw that he had written in the chart, "Mother asks innumerable appropriate questions."

· · · · ·

Justin's oncologist had remarkable interpersonal skills. At our first meeting he said, "Justin has leukemia. There are two kinds of leukemia, and both of them are treatable." So right away he emphasized the positive. He then wrote on his notepad what all of Justin's blood counts were, he told us what normal counts were and explained clearly what we needed to do next. He told us that Justin needed a blood transfusion; he said that it was safe and he would allow his own daughter to have one. He was very reassuring. It has been years since that day, and he has always been very caring. He still frequently calls us on the phone.

Another mother relates a different experience:

We tried very hard to form a partnership with the medical team but failed. The staff seemed very guarded and distant, almost wary of a parent wanting to participate in the decisions made for the child. I learned to use the medical library and took research reports in to them to get some help for side effects and get some drug dosages reduced. Things improved, but I was never considered a partner in the health care team; I was viewed as a problem.

Communication

Clear and frequent communication is the lifeblood of a positive doctor/parent relationship. Doctors need to be able to explain clearly and listen well, and parents need to feel comfortable asking questions and expressing concerns before they grow into grievances. Nurses and doctors cannot read parents' minds, nor can a parent prepare her child for a procedure unless it has been explained well. The following are parent suggestions on how to establish and maintain good communication:

* Tell the staff how much you would like to know.

    I told them the first day to treat me like a medical student. I asked them to share all information, current studies, lab results, everything, with me. I told them, in advance, that I hoped they wouldn't be offended by lots of questions, because knowledge was comfort to me.

    Another view:

    If the doctors at Children's told me to do something, I didn't question it. I did it because I trust them.

* Inform staff of your child's temperament, likes, and dislikes.

Whenever my daughter was hospitalized, I made a point of kindly reminding doctors and nurses that she was extremely sensitive, and would benefit from quiet voices and soothing explanations of anything that was about to occur, such as taking temperatures, vital signs, or adjustments to her IV.

- Encourage a close relationship between doctor, nurse, and child. Insist that all medical personnel respect the young person's dignity. Do not let anyone talk in front of the child as if she is not there. If a problem persists, you have the right to ask the offending person to leave. Marina Rozen observes in *Advice to Doctors and Other Big People*:

    The best part about the doctor is when he gives me bubble gum. The worst part is when he's in the room with me and my mom and he only talks to my mom. I've told him I don't like that, but he doesn't listen.

- Most children's hospitals assign each patient a "primary" nurse who will oversee all care. Try to form a close relationship with your child's nurse. Nurses usually possess vast knowledge and experience about both medical and practical aspects of cancer treatment. Often, the nurse can rectify misunderstandings between doctor and parents.

    The nurses at Children's were splendid. They were gentle with both kids and parents. Once, when I asked to have Christine's spinal done by the fellow rather than the resident, the fellow said in a nasty voice, "Well, we'll see about that!" and he disappeared. He didn't come in for two hours; my child was crying, we missed an appointment with radiation, and everyone was upset. The nurse ran back and forth between the fellow and us trying to get it resolved. In the end—after the resident had done the spinal—she hugged me, and told me that she was going to talk with the fellow because his actions were unacceptable.

- Older children and teenagers should be included as part of the team. They should be consulted about treatments and procedures and be given age-appropriate choices.

- Cooperate. If your home town pediatrician will handle all of your child's outpatient treatment, find ways to facilitate communication between oncologist and pediatrician.

Before we left Children's, I called our pediatrician to ask what paper-work he had received and what he needed. He had received nothing, so he gave me a list of what he needed, which I was able to get from the primary nurse and carry home with me.

When maintenance started, I asked if there was anything that he thought might help keep his staff aware of the cycles of blood work and chemo orders. He asked me to write a letter at the beginning of every three-month cycle listing the day of the cycle, the date, and the treatment. They put this in the front of her chart, and it helped keep the orders and communication flowing smoothly.

- Go to all appointments with a written list of questions. This prevents the exhausted parent from forgetting something important and saves the staff from numerous follow-up phone calls.

- Ask for definitions of unfamiliar terms. Repeat back the information to ensure that it was understood correctly. Writing down answers or tape recording conferences are both common practices.

  We found that sitting down and talking things over with the nurses helped immensely. They were very familiar with each drug and its side effects. They told us many stories about children who had been through the same thing and were doing well years later. They always seemed to have time to give encouragement, a smile, or a hug.

- Some parents desire to read their child's medical chart to obtain more details on their child's condition and to help in formulating questions for the medical team. Often, the doctor or nurse will let the parents read it in the child's hospital room or in the waiting room at the clinic. Most states have laws that allow patient access to all records. You may have to write to the doctor asking to review the chart and pay any photocopy costs.

- To avoid confusion, it is usually better to ask questions only of the child's assigned fellow or attending physician. Most residents or fellows are not as familiar with the details of each child's condition.

- The medical team is comprised of many specialists: doctors, nurses, physical therapists, nutritionists, x-ray technicians, radiation therapists, and more. At training hospitals, many of these persons will be in the early stages of their training. If a procedure is not going well, the parent has the right to tell the person to stop, and to request a more skilled person to do the job.

At our hospital, family practice residents rotate through, and are often assigned to do the spinal taps. My son was on a high-dose methotrexate protocol, which required a rescue drug to be administered at a certain time. Once, the resident tried for an hour to do the tap, and just couldn't do it. My son was very late getting the rescue drug, and I was worried. Later, I requested a conference with the oncologist and asked him to perform the spinal taps in the future to prevent the residents from practicing on my child. He agreed, but I didn't intervene that first time and I felt very guilty.

• • • • •

While I truly supported the teaching hospital concept, it was difficult to deal with a first-year resident who couldn't do a spinal tap or insert an IV. We had a tendency to lose patience rather quickly when our child was screaming and the doctor was getting impatient. More than once we requested a replacement and had someone else do the test.

- Know your rights. Legally, your child cannot be treated without your permission. If a procedure is proposed that you do not feel comfortable with, keep asking questions until you feel fully informed. You have the legal right to refuse the procedure if you do not think that it is necessary.

  However, if the hospital feels that you are wrongfully withholding permission for treatment (i.e., you reject standard treatment in favor of an unproven remedy, or you are so concerned about side effects that you are endangering the child's chance for cure) they can take you to court. The child is the important person in this equation, and both the hospital and the parents have input once you step into the legal arena.

One day in the hospital a group of fellows came in and announced that they were going to do a lung biopsy on Jesse. I told them that I hadn't heard anything about it from her attending, and I just didn't think it was the right thing to do. They said, "We have to do it," and I repeated that I just didn't think it needed to be done until we talked to the attending. They seemed angry, but we stood our ground. When the attending came later, he said that they were not supposed to do a biopsy because the surgeon said it was too risky of an area in the lung to get to.

• • • • •

An end-of-treatment testicular biopsy (surgically removing a piece of tissue for microscopic examination) was part of my son's protocol. I could think of few things worse for a thirteen year old to undergo, so I went to the medical school library to research the subject. I discovered many studies that showed that manual exams were as effective as the biopsies. I requested a conference with the oncologist. I was told at the conference that the biopsies had been eliminated from the protocol at an earlier date, but our institution had not received notification. By questioning this procedure, my son was saved from unnecessary surgery.

• Don't let problems build up until there is a long laundry list of grievances.

We had a problem with the pediatrician's office not calling me with the results of her blood work in time for me to call the clinic. This would result in worry for me and a delay in changes of her chemo doses. I told the pediatrician's nurse that I knew how busy they were and I hated having to keep calling to get the results. I asked her if it was possible for them to give the lab authorization to call me with the results. They thought it was a great idea, and it worked for three years. The lab would fax the doctor the results, but call me. Then I would call the clinic and get the dose changes. The clinic would then fax that information to the pediatrician's office. It was a win/win situation: the doctor's office received no interruptions, they got copies of everything in writing, and I got quick responses from the clinic on how to adjust her meds to her wildly swinging blood counts.

• Use "I" statements. For example, "I feel upset when you won't answer my questions" rather than, "You never listen to me."

• Assume mistakes will happen and be vigilant to prevent them.

Few children were on the high-risk protocol at the time my daughter was being treated. The attendings always knew exactly what was supposed to be done, but the fellows made quite a few mistakes. I was embarrassed to correct them, but I just kept reminding myself that they had dozens of protocols to keep track of, and I had only one.

• Ask your child's doctor every day what drugs and procedures are scheduled for that day, and make the final checks on all drugs (check for the correct dosage and for your child's name on the syringe) and transfusions (check that it is the right blood type and that your child's name is on the bag).

Once I was given syringes containing ondansetron to give at home which were ten times the proper dose. I noticed the error, and it was corrected.

• • • • •

When Meagan was in the hospital during induction, the nurse came in with two syringes. I asked what they were, and she said immunizations. I said that it must be a mistake, and the nurse said that the orders were in the chart. So I checked Meagan's chart, and the orders were there, but they had another child's name on them.

- Be specific and not confrontational when describing problems. Allow room for the staff to save face. For example, "My daughter has to go to radiation after this spinal tap. I want it to go smoothly, so I would appreciate it if Dr. Smith, the attending, does the procedure instead of the intern," rather than, "I'm not going to let that intern near my daughter again." Another example is, "My son gets very nervous the longer we wait for our appointment. We have waited over two hours for our last two appointments. Could we call ahead next time to see if the doctor is on schedule?" rather than "Do you think your time is more valuable than mine?"

- If you have something to discuss with the doctor that will take some time, request a conference. These are routinely scheduled between parents and physicians, and should allow enough time for a thorough discussion. Grabbing a busy doctor in the hallway is not fair to her, and may not result in a satisfactory answer for you.

- Do not be afraid to make waves if you are right.

    After I caught another error, the director of our clinic patted me on the back and said, "If the doctors think that you are a pain in the neck, then you are doing a good job for your child."

- Show appreciation.

    I sent thank you notes to three residents after my daughter's first hospitalization. The notes were short but sweet. I wanted them to know how much we appreciated their many kindnesses.

• • • • •

I always try to thank the nurse or doctor when they apologize for being late and give the reason. I don't mind waiting if it is for a good cause, and I feel they show respect when they apologize.

. . . . .

Erica's doctor would sometimes call up just to say "How's my little chickadee?" He really cared. It touched me that he took the time to call, and I told him that I appreciated it.

. . . . .

Early in my daughter's treatment, we changed pediatricians. The first was aloof and patronizing, and the second was smart, warm, funny, and caring. He was a constant bright spot in our lives through some dark times. So every year during my daughter's treatment, she and her younger sister put on their Santa hats and brought homemade cookies to her pediatrician and nurse. This year was the first time she was able to walk in, and she looked them in the eye and sang, "We Wish You a Merry Christmas." Her nurse went in the back room and cried, and her doctor got misty-eyed. I'll always be thankful for their care.

Norman Cousins in his book *Head First: The Biology of Hope* shares portions of his commencement talks at the medical schools of UCLA, Harvard, George Washington University, and Baylor University:

There are qualities beyond pure medical competence that patients need and look for in doctors. They want reassurance. They want to be looked after and not just looked over. They want to be listened to. They want to feel that it makes a difference to the physician, a very big difference, whether they live or die. They want to feel that they are in the doctor's thoughts. The physician holds the lifeline. The physician's words and not just his prescriptions are attached to that lifeline.

This aspect of medicine has not changed in thousands of years. Not all the king's horses and all the king's men—not all the tomography and the thallium scanners and two-D electrocardiograms and medicinal mood modifiers—can preempt the physician's primary role as the keeper of the keys to the body's own healing system.

I pray that you will never allow your knowledge to get in the way of your relationship with your patients. I pray that all the technological marvels at your command will not prevent you from practicing medicine out of a little black bag. I pray that when you go into a patient's room you will recognize that the main distance is not from the door to the bed but from the patient's eyes to your own—and that the shortest distance between those two points is a horizontal straight line—the kind of straight line that works best when the physician bends low to the patient's loneliness and fear and pain and the overwhelming sense of mortality that comes flooding up out of the unknown, and when the physician's hand on the patient's shoulder or arm is a shelter against the darkness.

I pray that, even as you attach the highest value to your science, you will never forget that it works best when combined with your art, and, indeed, that your art is what is most enduring in your profession. For, ultimately, it is the physician's respect for the human soul that determines the worth of his science.

Getting a second opinion

Good doctors welcome consultations and encourage second opinions. Because there are many gray areas in medicine where judgment and experience are as important as knowledge, consultations are frequent. In fact, the American Medical Association (AMA) recommends that patients obtain a second medical opinion before consenting to any invasive medical treatment, including surgery; many insurance companies require it. If, after discussions with the doctor, you are still uneasy about any aspect of your child's medical care, you should not hesitate to seek another opinion.

There are two ways to get a second opinion: see another specialist or ask the child's physician to arrange a multidisciplinary second opinion. Many parents seek a second opinion at the time of diagnosis. Do not do this in secret. Explain to your child's oncologist that before proceeding you would like a second opinion, and ask for his recommendation. The Childhood Cancer Ombudsman Program (703-492-0045), with dozens of participating board-certified pediatric oncologists, will review your child's treatment plan and offer second opinions without charge. To allow for a thorough analysis, arrange to have copies of all records sent ahead to the physician(s) who will give the second opinion.

Multidisciplinary second opinions incorporate the views of several different specialists. Parents who would like their child's case to be reviewed can ask to have it discussed at a tumor board, which usually meets weekly at major medical centers. These boards are comprised of medical, surgical, and radiation oncologists, as well as fellows and residents. Your child's oncologist will present the facts of your child's case for discussion.

Good doctors informally seek second opinions all the time. Residents confer with their fellow for complicated situations; fellows might confer with the attending when unusual drug reactions or responses to treatment occur. Parents should feel free to ask their physician if he has conferred with other staff members to gain additional viewpoints.

> Brent developed a seizure disorder after a rare drug reaction, so he
> was on anticonvulsant as well as chemotherapy for two years. We
> worried about the interaction of all the drugs, as well as the advisability
> of his continuing on the more aggressive arm of the protocol. We asked
> the fellow to arrange a care conference, and she met with the clinic direc-
> tor as well as Brent's neurologist to discuss how best to manage his case.
> The fellow told us she strongly supports second opinions.

Parents often fear seeking a second opinion because they are afraid of offending the doctor or creating antagonism. Good doctors will not resent a parent seeking a second opinion. If she does resist, consider changing doctors. Cancer is life or death, and you won't have a second chance.

Two opinions that agree are all that parents should require before proceeding. Treatment for the leukemia should begin within days of diagnosis. Parents who drag their child from doctor to doctor are denying the gravity of the situation; they hope that someone will give them more favorable news. But, the longer they delay treatment, the worse the possible outcome.

Conflict resolution

Don't find fault; find a remedy.

—Henry Ford

Conflict is a part of life. In a situation where a child's life is threatened, such as childhood leukemia, the heightened emotions and constant involvement with the medical bureaucracy guarantee conflict. Because clashes are inevitable, resolving them is of paramount importance.

Here are some suggestions from parents on how to resolve problems:

* Treat the doctors with respect, and expect respect from them.

I always wanted to be treated as an intelligent adult, not someone of lesser status. So, I would ask each medical person what they wished to be called. We would either both go by first names, or both go by titles. I did not want to be called mom.

- Expect a reasonable amount of sensitivity from the staff.

Soon after my daughter began treatment, I was walking by the open door of the residents room which was directly across from the nurses station. Written in large letters on the blackboard were the words "Have a blast of a day!" with a picture of a smiling leukemia blast drawn below. I felt like I had been punched in the stomach. I was too upset to say anything, but I always regretted not complaining.

• • • • •

On my son's first night of chemotherapy, he had several frightening reactions including chills, vomiting, and a very high fever. I was scared to death and asked the resident if we shouldn't call the attending in since things were not going as expected. He put his arm around me and said, "I know that this is terrifying for you, but it is a routine night for us." He was very kind, I relaxed, and we all made it through the night.

- Treat the staff with sensitivity. Recognize that you are under enormous stress, and so are the doctors and nurses. Do not blame them for the disease or explode in anger. Be an advocate, not an adversary.
- If a problem develops, state the issue clearly, without accusations, and then suggest a solution.

I found out late in my daughter's treatment that short-acting, safe sedatives were being used for many children at the clinic to prevent pain and anxiety during treatments. Only parents who knew about it and requested it received this service. I felt that my daughter's life would have been incredibly improved if we had been able to remove the trauma of procedures. I was angry. But I also realized that although I thought that they were wrong not to offer the service, I was partially at fault for not expressing more clearly how much difficulty she had the week before and after a procedure. I called the director of the clinic and carefully explained that I thought that poor staff/parent communication was creating hardships for the children. I suggested that the entire staff meet with a panel of parents to try to improve communication and to educate the doctors on the impact of pain on the children's daily life. They were very supportive and scheduled the conference. This is a classic example of how something good can come out of a disagreement, if both parties are receptive to solving the problem.

- Recognize that it is hard to speak up, especially if you have never had to be assertive before. But it is very important to solve the problem before it grows and poisons the relationship.

- Most large medical centers have social workers and psychologists on staff to help families. One of their major duties is to serve as mediators between staff and parents. Ask their advice on problem solving.

- Monitor your own feelings of anger and fear. Be careful not to dump on staff inappropriately. On the other hand, do not let a physician or nurse behave unprofessionally towards you or your child. We all have bad days, but we should not take it out on each other.

- Do not fear reprisal for speaking up. It is possible to be assertive without aggression or argument. In *Having Leukemia Isn't So Bad,* Cynthia Krumme reports that one day her daughter Catherine arrived at the hospital at 11 A.M., but:

   It was not until after 9:00 that the much feared spinal tap was administered. We were totally unprepared for the delays and despite our best efforts to remain calm, we were upset... We expressed our impatience with the delay, but we were hesitant to complain out of concern that if we rocked the boat it would come back to haunt us. This is a common fear among parents.

- There are times when no resolution is possible, but expressing one's feelings can be a great release. One mother told the following story:

   My son and I waited in an exam room for over an hour for a painful procedure. When I went out to ask the receptionist what had caused the delay, she said that a parent had brought in a child without an appointment. This parent frequently failed to bring in her child for treatment, and consequently, whenever she appeared, the doctors dropped everything to take care of the child. When the doctor finally came in, one and one half hours later, my son was in tears. The doctor did not explain the delay or apologize, he just silently started the procedure. After it was finished, I went out of the room, found the doctor, and said, "This makes me so angry. You just left us in here for hours and traumatized my son. Our time is valuable, too." He told me that I should have more compassion for the other mother because her life was very difficult. I replied that he encouraged her to not make appointments by dropping everything whenever she appeared. I added that it wasn't fair to those parents who played by the rules; she was being rewarded for her irresponsibility. After we had each stated our position, we left without resolution.

Changing doctors

Changing doctors is not a step to be taken lightly, but it can be a great relief if the relationship has deteriorated beyond repair. It is a good policy to exhaust all possible remedies prior to separating, or the same problems may arise with the new doctor. Communication, verbally or in writing, and mediation, using social service staff, can sometimes resolve the issues and prevent the disruption of changing doctors.

Although there is a myriad of reasons for changing doctors, some of the most common are:

- Grave medical errors made.

- Inability to communicate or answer questions.

- Serious clash of philosophy, for example, a paternalistic doctor and a parent who wishes to be informed and share in the decision making.

It is one of life's great struggles to face cancer. If the family has a physician whom they trust, can rely on for the best medical treatment, feel comfortable with, communicate freely with, and can count on for advice and support, the struggle is greatly eased. If, on the other hand, the doctor adds to your discomfort rather than reducing it, change.

Do not change doctors because you're searching for a better diagnosis. If two reputable physicians, or a tumor board, have agreed on the diagnosis and treatment, it is best for the child to immediately begin treatment.

Many parents choose to continue with a physician in whom they have no confidence due to fears of reprisals. This simply doesn't happen at large centers of excellence. While there may be lingering bitterness or anger between parents and doctors, the child will continue to benefit from the best-known treatment. Children may actually suffer more from the additional family stress caused by a poor doctor/parent relationship than from changing doctors.

*In a small treatment center like Group Health, there are only two
pediatric oncologists. When parents change doctors, the situation becomes
very tense because the terminated doctor still cares for their child nights,
weekends, and when he is on call. I would not recommend changing
doctors if there are only two doctors in the clinic. It's probably better to
change treatment centers if possible.*

Once the decision is made, parents must be candid. Either verbally or in
writing, an explanation should be given for the change and a formal request
made to transfer records to the new physician. Physicians are legally
required to transfer all records upon written request.

Minna Nathanson, in a statement presented to the President's Commission
for the Study of Ethical Problems in Medicine and Biomedical and Behavioral Research, stated:

> *And, finally, I wish that professional care team members would all
> accept and allow questioning, so that parents would feel more com-
> fortable being participants in the decisions about their child's treat-
> ment and assistants in their child's care, and that there would be an
> understanding that parents who show symptoms of stress are react-
> ing normally, not pathologically. Every parent I have ever talked to
> about their child's illness and hospitalization—whether it be for
> childhood cancer, cystic fibrosis, spinal bifida, or even a one-shot
> surgery—has confirmed that most parents are experts on their own
> child and as extra eyes and ears can help to avoid mistakes in
> treatment and aid in keeping the child more comfortable and emo-
> tionally better prepared for treatment. If there are medical care
> staff who would say that this is the opposite of what they find, I
> would ask them to search deeply to see if they are treating parents
> as intruders in the decision-making and caretaking processes.*

Resources

Reading for adults

Center for Attitudinal Healing. *Advice to Doctors and Other Big People from
Kids.* Berkeley, CA: Celestial Arts, 1991. Book written by children with catastrophic illnesses offers suggestions and expresses feelings about health

care workers. Wise and poignant, it reminds us how perceptive and aware children of all ages are, and how absolutely necessary it is to involve them in medical decisions.

Cousins, Norman. *Head First: The Biology of Hope and the Healing Power of the Human Spirit*. New York: E.P. Dutton, 1989. After 25 years as editor of Saturday Review, Cousins spent a decade on the medical staff of UCLA researching the biological basis for hope. He presents the mounting volume of evidence that positive attitudes help combat disease. Also contains excellent information on enhancing the doctor/patient relationship.

Komp, Diane M., M.D. *A Child Shall Lead Them: Lessons in Hope from Children with Cancer.* Grand Rapids, MI: Zondervan Publishing House, 1993. Written by a Christian pediatric oncologist, this book describes her feelings for her patients and her warm and loving approach to caring for children with cancer.

Leff, Patricia Taner, and Elanie H. Walizer. *Building the Healing Partnership: Parents, Professionals & Children with Chronic Illnesses and Disabilities.* Brookline, MA: Brookline Books, 1992. This book uses parents' and caretakers' personal stories to explore the feelings of both families and members of the medical team. Empathetic and practical guide for caring to children with chronic illnesses or disabilities.

Rosenbaum, Edward E., M.D. *A Taste of My Own Medicine: When the Doctor Is the Patient.* New York: Random House, 1988. A physician explores his own feelings after his diagnosis and treatment for cancer.

Rosenfeld, Isadore, M.D. *Second Opinion: Your Comprehensive Guide to Treatment Alternatives.* New York: Simon and Schuster, 1981. Well-written explanations on when and how to obtain a second opinion, patient care versus doctor ego, and new options for cancer treatment.

Scully, Thomas, M.D., and Celia Scully. *Playing God: The World of Medical Choices.* New York: Simon and Schuster, 1987. Easy-to-read, practical guide for families making difficult medical decisions. Good chapters on decision making, doctor/patient relationships, patient rights, and making life and death decisions for your child.

Biographies

Reading biographies is an excellent way to get an in-depth look at how individual families develop relationships with their medical team, solve problems, and address issues. Here are a few that I highly recommend. The description includes whether the child survives, as each parent has a different time when he can read books which end in death.

Gaes, Geralyn, Craig Gaes, and Philip Bashe. *You Don't Have to Die: One Family's Guide to Surviving Childhood Cancer.* New York: Villard Books, 1992. Well written, comprehensive story of one child's triumph over cancer. Explores many issues such as changes in family life, feelings at diagnosis, dealing with medical personnel, and siblings. Excellent resource lists.

Kruckeberg, Carol. *What Was Good About Today.* Seattle, Wa: Madrona Publishers, 1984. Moving story written by a mother whose young daughter dies from AML. Although the treatments are outdated, the emotional issues are very much the same.

Krumme, Cynthia. *Having Leukemia Isn't So Bad. Of Course It Wouldn't Be My First Choice.* Winchester, MA: Sargasso Enterprises, 1993. 14 Wildwood St., Winchester, Ma 01890. (617) 729-9037. Well-written book about Catherine Krumme, diagnosed with ALL at age 4, relapsed at age 7, finished treatment at age 10. Catherine is now in college.

Lund, Doris. *Eric.* Philadelphia: J.B. Lippincott Co., 1974. Afterword copyright, 1989. Although the treatments are out of date, this is a classic. Eric's mother, a professional writer, vividly captures the experience of cancer treatment for a teenager and his whole family. Eric dies, but his spirit and the powerful images of this book will remain with every reader.

Miller, Dena. *Praying for a Miracle.* 1994. Chai Lifeline, 48 W. 25th St., New York, NY 10010. (212) 255-1160. Dovid Miller was diagnosed in 1985 at age 19 months with ALL, had three years of chemo, and was cured. Dovid's mother writes about the events and experiences of her son's treatment from the perspective of the Orthodox Jewish faith, a source of great strength to the family.

CHAPTER 7

Surviving Your Child's Hospitalization

Every day is a journey, and the journey itself is home.

—Matsuo Basho

THERE ARE FEW THINGS in life worse than arising from a lumpy, pullout couch to face another day of your child's hospitalization for leukemia. Hospitals are huge bureaucracies, noisy, impersonal, and running on a time schedule all their own. For a child, being hospitalized means being separated from parents, brothers, sisters, friends, pets, and the comfort and familiarity of home. A child's hospitalization can rob both parent and child of a sense of control, leaving them feeling helpless. There are ways, however, to wrest back some power, while adding a great deal of cheerfulness to the proceedings.

The room

Hospital rooms are usually painted a nauseating shade of gray or green, and somehow, most windows seem to look out over the power plant. Covering the walls with big, bright posters (Disney characters, sports figures, rock groups) can liven up the room immensely.

> *The first thing we put up in Meagan's room was a huge poster of the Little Engine That Could saying, "I think I can, I think I can."*

Display cards on the walls, hanging from strings like a mobile, or taped around the window sills. Put up pictures of the child engaged in her favorite activity, and add photos of friends, too. Most hospitals don't allow flowers on oncology floors, but it's fun to have bouquets of balloons bobbing in the corners. Younger children derive great comfort from having a favorite stuffed animal, blanket, or quilt on their bed. If it doesn't bother your child, make the room smell good with potpourri or aromatherapy oils.

To personalize the visit of each member of the medical staff, some parents bring a "guest" book to sign. Others put up a visitor sign-in poster, which must be signed before examinations begin or vital signs are taken. Another variation of the sign-in poster is to have each staff member outline her hand and write within the print.

> In my position as a parent consultant, I suggest that a journal (some titles are Book of Hope, Book of Sharing, My Cancer Experience, Friends Indeed) be kept in the child's room for any visitor, family member, or medical care giver to write in at any time. Leaving a message if the child is sleeping or out of the room for procedures can be a nice surprise. Later, a surviving child and her family, or the family of a child who has died, have a memory book of those who have touched their lives.

Bringing music will help block out some of the hospital noise as well as help everyone relax. A small cassette player, walkman with earphones, or CD boom box is portable and useful.

> My daughter's preschool teacher sent a care package. She made a felt board with dozens of cutout characters and designs that provided hours of quiet entertainment. She also included games, drawings from each classmate, coloring books, markers, get well cards, and a child's tape player with ear phones. Because we had run out of our house with just the clothes on our backs, all of these toys were very, very welcome.

Although many hospitals provide brightly colored smocks for the patients, most children and teens prefer to wear their own clothing if at all possible. This can pose a laundry problem, so check to see if the floor has washers available for families to use.

As soon as possible after admission, ask for a "floor tour." Find out if a microwave and refrigerator are available, learn what the approved parent sleeping arrangements are, and ask about showers and bathtubs for both patients and parents. Obtain a hospital handbook if one is available. These booklets often include information on billing, parking, discounts, and other helpful items.

Many children's hospitals have VCRs available. Sign up for a convenient time and bring in or rent a favorite or funny video. Humor helps. Bring in age appropriate games, puzzles, and books.

A friend brought in a bag from the local dime store. He included a water pistol (good for unwelcome visitors or unfriendly interns), play dough, slinky, checkers, dominos, bubbles, a book of corny jokes, and puzzles.

Food

Buying meals day after day in the hospital cafeteria is expensive. Check to see if the floor has a refrigerator for parent's food and stock it from home. Remember to put your name in a prominent place on your containers. Many hospitals have cooking facilities for families where they can cook or microwave favorite meals brought from home. Ask family and friends to bring food in when they visit, and consider ordering extra items to come up on your child's tray.

Just the smell of food nauseated my daughter. I'll never forget taking the tray out in the hall, and gobbling it down myself. I always felt so guilty, and thought that staff viewed me as that parent who ate her kid's food. But it saved money and prevented her meals from going to waste. I also did not want to leave her side for the few minutes it took to go to the cafeteria, although in hindsight, the walk would have done me some good.

Parking

Most parents of children with cancer have unpleasant memories of driving around in endless loops looking for a parking space while their child is throwing up in a bucket in the back seat (or even worse when the bucket was left at home). Learn about both long- and short-term parking arrangements. Ask other parents if parking passes are available or where the cheapest parking is located.

I had no idea that the hospital gave out free parking passes to their frequent customers. Now I tell every new parent to check as soon as possible to see if they can get a parking pass. It will save them lots of money that they would have spent on meters and parking tickets, and time they would have spent running out to move the car out of the emergency parking spot.

The endless waiting

Parents need to become experts in learning how to wait without losing their minds. They need to expect long waits for everything from blood draws to procedures. Many parents find themselves getting nervous or angry while waiting for the doctors to appear during "rounds" each morning (when the attendings, residents, and interns move from room to room in a large group); then feel let down when the visit lasts only a few moments. If you have questions to ask the doctors, write them down and tell the doctors when they come in that you would like a few moments to discuss concerns or ask questions.

It helps to come prepared for long waits each time that you go to the hospital. Some progressive (and well funded) institutions have VCRs and games available, but usually you need to bring your own things. Have your child pick out favorite card games, board games, computer games, drawing materials, and books. Remember to bring food and drinks.

Befriending the staff

Hospitals are staffed by many wonderful and some not so wonderful people. Many parents find that their heightened stress makes them less tolerant of inefficiency or confusion. As discussed in Chapter 6, *Forming a Partnership with the Medical Team*, working together, rather than becoming adversaries, will provide your child with a sense of security. Doing things like helping change soiled bedding, taking out food trays, and giving baths frees up overworked nurses to take care of medicines and IVs. Nurses really appreciate the help, and usually reciprocate by answering questions or negotiating with the doctors for you.

As soon as possible, learn about the shift changes on the oncology floor. If you need to leave during the day or night, don't leave a request with one nurse if another will be coming on duty soon. If you have a request or reminder, you can post it on the child's door, the wall above the bed, or on the chart.

> I always made a point of introducing myself to my daughter's nurse and resident for each shift. I told them my child's name and which room we were in. I told them that I would be there the whole time and I would help as much as I could. I tried to talk to them about non-hospital matters to give them a break from their routine, as well as get to know

them. I thanked them for any kindnesses and told them I appreciated how hard their job was. Although I wasn't angling for favors, I found that they soon came to like me and helped me out whenever any difficulty arose. Although there were a few that I didn't care for, on the whole I found the staff to be warm, caring, dedicated people.

Being an advocate for your child

Hospitals can be frightening places for children. Parents need to provide comfort, protection, and advocacy for their vulnerable child. To fulfill these roles parents need to be present.

Most pediatric hospitals are quite aware of how much better children do if a parent is allowed to sleep in the room. Sometimes small couches convert into beds, or parents can use a cot provided by the hospital. If hospital policy requires the parent to leave, insist on staying. Geralyn Gaes tells a story in *You Don't have to Die* about a confrontation at her local community hospital:

> *One night a nurse came into Jason's room and curtly informed me that I would have to leave, since it was past visiting hours. With my son pale and retching from chemotherapy, I was not about to go anywhere. Looking her in the eye, I said "You can send security after me if you like, but I'm not leaving here." No one disturbed me again.*

Of course, sometimes it isn't possible to stay with your child if you are a single parent or if both parents work full time. Many families have grandparents or close friends who stay with the hospitalized child when the parents cannot be present. Older children and teenagers may not want a parent in the room at night, but they need an advocate there during the day just as much as the preschoolers.

Whenever a family member cannot be present, children who are old enough should be taught to use the telephone. Tape a phone number nearby where a parent can be reached and have the child call if anyone tries to do procedures that are unexpected. The hospital staff should be informed that any changes in treatment need to be authorized by a parent.

> *Whenever my husband couldn't be at the hospital at bedtime, he would bring in homemade tapes of him reading bedtime stories. Our son would drift off to sleep hearing his daddy's voice.*

Hospitals strip children of control over their bodies. To help reverse this process, parents can take over most nursing care. Children prefer parents to help them to the bathroom or to clean up diarrhea or vomit. Making the bed, keeping the room tidy, changing dressings, and giving back rubs helps your child feel more comfortable and lightens the burden of the overworked nurses.

> I was embarrassed to have the nurse change the sheets when I had an accident in the bed. I couldn't help it when I was taking the cytoxan, but I was still embarrassed.

Parents can help their child regain some control by encouraging choices whenever possible. Older children should be actively involved in discussions about their treatment, while younger children can decide when to take a bath, which arm to use for an IV, what to order for meals, what position for procedures, what clothes to wear, and how to decorate the room. Some children request a hug or a handshake after all treatments or procedures.

Where do the kids play?

Children need to play, especially when hospitalized. Ask whether the hospital has a recreation therapy department (play therapy is discussed in Chapter 3, *Coping with Procedures*). Often, a large room is devoted to toys, books, dolls, and crafts, and is staffed by specialists who really know how to play with children. These rooms provide many therapeutic activities such as medical play with dolls, which help children to express fears or concerns about what is happening to them. By encouraging contact with other children in similar circumstances, recreation therapy helps children to feel less alone, less different from other children. The rooms are a cheerful change from lying in a hospital bed and are full of fun filled activities and smiling staff people. If the child is too ill or her counts are too low to go to the play area, arrangements can be made for a recreational therapist to bring a bundle of toys, games, and books to the room. This can give the parent time to go out to eat or take a walk.

> When I wanted to have a conference with the oncologist about Katy's protocol, I called recreation therapy and they sent two wonderful ladies to the clinic. The doctor and I were able to talk privately for an hour, and Katy had a great time making herself a gold crown and decorating her wheelchair with streamers and jewels.

Exercise is important, too. For kids strong enough to walk, exploring the hospital can be fun. Plan a daily excursion to the gift shop or the cafeteria. Go outside and walk the entire perimeter of the hospital if weather and the neighborhood permit. Don't feel limited by an IV pole; it can be pushed or pulled and will feel normal after a while. Many children have been seen standing on the base of the IV pole—hanging on for dear life—with a parent wildly pushing them down the hall at breakneck speed. Check to see if the hospital has a swimming pool (for you to swim in, your child probably can't use it).

Many neutropenic (low white count) children or teens feel refreshed by going up on the roof just to feel the wind ruffle their hair and the sun warm their skin. Some hospitals even grant "passes" to young patients whose white counts are high enough.

> Preston left the hospital several times on "passes." His IV was capped off and his arm was taped to a board resembling a cast. He attended a birthday party and went Christmas shopping on a pass.

Sometimes family members, friends, or classmates shave their heads as a sign of support. A youngster undergoing chemotherapy does not feel out of place in a room full of bald heads.

Any action that parents, family members, and friends take to support and advocate for the youngster with cancer buoys up the spirit. Courage is contagious.

Resources

Reading for adults

Child Life Council. *Preparing Your Child for Repeated or Extended Hospitalizations.* 1991. 11820 Parklawn Dr. #202, Rockville, MD 20852. (301) 881-7090. $11.50. Guidelines for self-education, using support services, working with hospital staff, and understanding the emotional and developmental needs of the child with special needs.

Kellerman, Johnathan. *Helping the Fearful Child.* New York: W.W. Norton, 1981. Although this book was written as a guide for everyday and problem anxieties, it is full of excellent advice for parents of children undergoing traumatic procedures. Chapters 7 "Going to the Doctor" and 8 "Coping with Hospitalization" are full of real life examples and methods to effectively help the child.

Reading for children

Child Life Council. *Going to the Hospital*. 1986. 11820 Parklawn Dr. #202, Rockville, MD, 20852. (301) 881-7090. $5.50. Booklet for children describing hospitalization. Provides simple, honest information illustrated by photographs of children.

Rogers, Fred. *Going to the Hospital*. New York: G. P. Putnam's Sons, 1988. With pictures and words, TV's beloved Mr. Rogers helps to make pre-schoolers less fearful of hospitals.

Choosing a Catheter

*No matter which catheter you ultimately choose, you go
through periods of wishing you had chosen the other.*

—A veteran parent

THE CHILD WITH LEUKEMIA requires intensive treatment including chemotherapy, intravenous (IV) fluids, IV antibiotics, blood and platelet transfusions, frequent blood sampling, and sometimes IV nutrition. Prior to the introduction of surgically implanted catheters, constant venipunctures (needle pokes) were the norm. Over time, children's tiny veins collapse, become scarred, and can be damaged by leakage of corrosive chemotherapy drugs into the surrounding tissues. Repeated venipunctures cause children physical and psychological distress.

Indwelling catheters have proved to be a very effective method for allowing entry into the large veins for intensive therapy. They eliminate the difficulty of finding veins for IVs and allow drugs to be put directly into a large vessel of the heart where they are rapidly diluted and spread throughout the body.

Other names for indwelling catheters are: venous access device, right atrial catheter, implanted catheter, central venous catheter, central line, Hickman, Broviac, or Port-a-cath.

The two types of indwelling catheters most commonly used in children are the external catheter and the subcutaneous port.

External catheter

The external catheter is a long, flexible tube with one end in the right atrium of the heart and the other end outside the skin of the chest. The tube tunnels under the skin of the right chest, enters a large vein (external or internal jugular) near the collar bone, and threads inside the vein to the heart (see Figure 1, External catheter). Because chemotherapy drugs, transfusions, and IV fluids are put in the end of the tube hanging outside the body, the child feels no pain. Blood for complete blood counts (CBC) or chemistry tests can also be drawn from the end of the catheter.

The main types of external catheters generally used are the Hickman or Broviac. With meticulous daily care, the external catheter can be left in place for years.

How it's implanted

External catheters can be implanted either with local anesthetic (only a small area numbed) or general anesthesia. Once the child is anesthetized, the surgeon makes two small incisions. One incision is near the right collarbone over the spot where the catheter will enter the vein, the other is the area on the chest where the catheter exits the body. To prevent the catheter from slipping out, it is stitched to the skin where it comes out of the chest (see Figure 1). There is a Dacron cuff around the catheter right above the exit site (under the skin) into which body tissue grows. This further anchors the catheter and helps prevent infection. After healing is complete, normal activities such as swimming and showers can resume.

Daily care

The external catheter requires careful maintenance to prevent infection or the formation of clots. The site where the catheter exits the body must be cleaned every other day and a fresh, sterile dressing needs to be applied and taped in place. The site should be checked for redness, swelling, or drainage. To prevent clots, parents or older patients are taught to flush the line every other day with a heparin solution. Nurses at the hospital instruct parents in catheter care, and plenty of practice should be provided until both parent and child are comfortable with the entire procedure.

> Kristin had her Broviac line for twenty-seven months with no infections. We were very careful to flush and change the bandages every other day.

Risks

The major complications of using the external catheter are infections—either in the blood or at the insertion site—and the formation of clots in the line. Rare complications are kinking of the catheter or the catheter's becoming dislodged from its proper position.

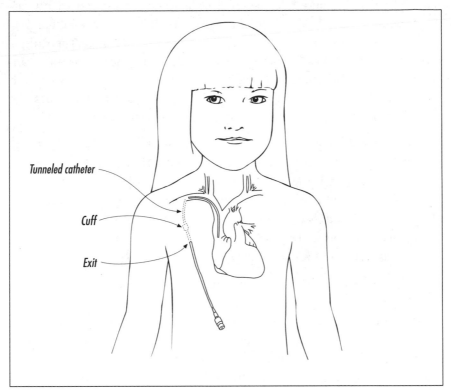

Figure 1. *External catheter*

Infections

Infections are common, occurring in 10 to 50 percent of all children with external lines. Children who are immunosuppressed (have low blood counts) for long periods of time are at risk for developing infections. The need for frequent flushing of the external line also increases the chance for bacteria to enter the catheter. Most infections are caused by a bacterium called staphylococcus epidermidis, although a host of other organisms may also cause infections.

If the child develops a fever over $101°$ F, redness or swelling at the insertion site, or pain in the catheter area, infection is suspected. To determine if bacteria are present, blood will be drawn from the catheter to culture (grow in a laboratory for 24 to 48 hours). Treatment with the antibiotic vancomycin, and sometimes other antibiotics, is usually effective. Treatment will start whenever there is a suspected infection and will end if the culture comes back negative. If the culture is positive, treatment usually continues for 10 to 14 days.

Some physicians require that the child be hospitalized for antibiotic treatment, while others allow the child to go home. It takes a committed parent(s) to deliver fourteen days worth of vancomycin at home. The drug is given through an infusion pump, one dose every eight hours. Because vancomycin can cause serious side effects, it must be given very slowly (each dose takes from one to two hours to deliver). If the infection does not respond to treatment, the catheter may have to be removed.

> When my daughter had a line infection, I wanted to use the antibiotic pump at home. It was hard, though. It took two hours per dose, three doses per day, for fourteen days. I would get up at 5 A.M. to hook her up, so that she would sleep through the first dose. The second dose I would give while she watched a tape in the early afternoon. Then I would hook her up at bedtime so she would sleep through it. I had to wait up to flush and disconnect, so I was very tired by the end of the two weeks.

During treatment with vancomycin, the physician will order peak and trough blood levels to adjust the dosage of this very strong antibiotic. A nurse will draw the trough blood sample from the line prior to the fourth dose of the drug and the peak blood sample one half-hour after the infusion of vancomycin is complete. The trough level should be below 10 to prevent possible damage to the kidneys. The peak level should be between 20 and 40. Levels above 40 can damage the child's hearing (this is very rare). Based on the lab results, the physician will raise or lower the dosage to keep the drug levels in the therapeutic range.

Clots

Even with excellent daily care, some external lines develop blockages and/or clots. If the catheter becomes blocked, it will be flushed with urokinase or streptokinase to dissolve the clot. If the line is blocked by a drug precipitate (usually only seen with the drug VM-26), dilute hydrochloric acid is often used to dissolve the blockage.

> We had no choice of catheter in 1985, and Judd received the Hickman line from Dr. Hickman himself. We had very little trouble with it until the last six months of the three-year protocol. It was found that Judd had a very large blood clot on the end of the line in his heart, possibly due to being too slow in flushing the line. With only one treatment to go, we had the line removed.

· · · · ·

Two months before the end of Kristin's treatment, her line plugged up. We tried several maneuvers at home unsuccessfully. We had to bring her in for the IV team to work on it. I think the bumpy ride to the hospital loosened it because they were able to dislodge the clot just by flushing it with saline.

Kinks

Rarely, a kink develops in the catheter due to a sharp angle where the catheter enters the neck vein. Some parents and nurses are able to work around this problem by experimenting with different positions for the child when the blood is drawn. Another method is to teach the child a Valsalva maneuver such as bearing down as if to have a bowel movement.

Breaks in the line do happen, but they are very rare. If the break or rupture of the line occurs when it is not in use, only heparin will leak into surrounding tissues. If the break occurs when corrosive chemotherapy drugs are flowing through the catheter, they may leak and cause damage to surrounding tissue. The risk of an internal line leaking is far lower than the chance of leakage from an IV in a vein of the hand or arm.

Other factors to consider

To use an external catheter successfully it takes a well-organized and motivated family. The site needs to be cleaned and dressed every other day, and heparin must be injected using sterile technique. Because the daily dressing must be secured to the skin with a very sticky large tape, if your child is very tape sensitive (cries whenever tape is removed or skin reddens and breaks out), the external line may not be a good choice.

The external line is a constant reminder of cancer treatment and causes changes in body image. Both parent and child need to be comfortable with the idea of seeing and handling a tube that emerges from the chest. It is noticeable under lightweight clothing and bathing suits. If there is a younger sibling(s) who might pull or yank on the catheter, the Hickman or Broviac might not be the appropriate choice.

On the other hand, the reason external lines are chosen so frequently is that there are no needles and no pain. This is a very important consideration for young children or any person who is frightened of needles and/or pain.

Subcutaneous port

Several different types of subcutaneous (under the skin) ports are used; the Port-a-cath is the most common. The subcutaneous port differs from the external catheter in that it is completely under the skin. A small metal chamber (1" x 1" x 1/2") with a rubber top, is implanted under the skin of the right chest. A catheter threads from the metal chamber (portal) under the skin to a large vein near the collarbone, then inside the vein to the right atrium of the heart (see Figure 2, Parts of the Port-a-cath). Whenever the catheter is needed for a blood draw or infusion of drugs or fluid, a needle is inserted by a nurse through the skin and into the rubber top of the portal.

Figure 2. Parts of the Port-a-cath

How it's implanted

The subcutaneous port is implanted under general anesthesia in the operating room in a procedure that generally takes less than an hour. The surgeon makes two small incisions: one in the right chest where the portal will be placed, and the other near the collarbone where the catheter will enter a vein (the external or internal jugular) in the lower part of the neck (see Figure 3, Subcutaneous port). First, one end of the catheter is placed in the large blood vessel of the neck and threaded into the right atrium of the heart. The other end of the catheter is tunneled under the skin where it is attached to the portal. Fluid is injected into the portal to ensure that the device works properly. The portal is then placed under the skin in the right chest, and stitched to the underlying muscle. Both incisions are then closed. The only evidence that a catheter has been implanted are two small scars and a bump under the skin where the portal rests.

> Before my child's surgery to have a port implanted, I saw other children being wheeled into the operating room screaming and trying to climb off the gurney to return to the parents. It broke my heart. When it was Jennifer's turn, I asked them to give her enough premedication so that she was relaxed and happy to go. I also insisted that I be in the recovery room when she awoke.

• • • • •

> Christine had her port surgery late at night. The resident gave her some premedication, then the chief resident ordered him to give her more. She felt so silly that she looked at me, giggled, and said "Mommy has a nose as long as an elephant's." I asked the surgeon if I could be in the recovery room before she awoke, and he said, "Sure." When I told the nurse that I had permission to go in recovery, she refused. When I persisted, she became angry. I told her that my child was expecting to wake up seeing my face, and I intended to be there. I added that if she didn't believe I had permission, she could just go in and ask the surgeon. She went in, came back out, and said, "I think this is ridiculous, but go on in."

How it works

Because the entire Port-a-cath is under the skin, the device must be accessed in order to use it. To access the catheter, the skin is thoroughly cleansed with antiseptic, then a special needle is inserted through the skin and the rubber top of the portal. The needle is attached to eight inches of tubing which hangs down the front of the chest. EMLA cream can be applied one hour prior to the needle poke to anesthetize the skin or ethyl chloride can be sprayed on right before the poke. Subcutaneous ports have a septum that is self-sealing after needle removal, and are designed to withstand years of needle insertions.

If the child is in a part of treatment where the line must be used every day, the nurse will attach the tubing to IV fluids or will close the end off with a sterile cap after flushing with saline solution. A transparent dressing will be put over the site where the needle enters the port. The port can remain accessed in this way for up to seven days. After that time, to avoid the risk of infection, the needle should be removed and the port reaccessed when necessary. If the needle and tubing are to be left in place, it is important to tape them securely to the chest to avoid accidents.

> *At the end of delayed intensification while getting cytoxan, Meagan (3 years old) got a line infection. Because she hated tape removal, we did not secure the IV tubing to her stomach or chest. On one of her many trips to the potty, we accidentally tugged on the tubing and caused a very small tear in the skin around the needle. It became infected. We did home antibiotics on the pump and felt very fortunate that we were able to clear the line with vancomycin and rifampin (two strong antibiotics). We were glad our doctor was not too quick to remove the line, but it did require at least two weeks off chemotherapy.*

If the port is only needed infrequently, e.g., during the maintenance phase, this will be the sequence of events: the site will be cleaned, needle put in, line rinsed with saline, drug given or blood drawn, line rinsed with saline, heparin added to line, needle withdrawn, and a Band-Aid placed over the site.

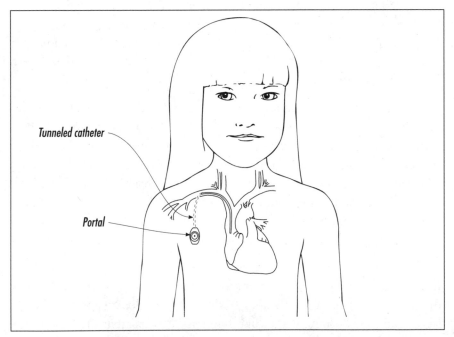

Figure 3. Subcutaneous port

Care of the subcutaneous port

The entire port and catheter are under the skin and therefore require no daily care. The skin over the port can be washed just like the rest of the body. Frequent visual inspections are needed to check for swelling, redness, or drainage.

The subcutaneous port must be accessed and flushed with saline and heparin at least once every thirty days, which usually coincides with the monthly clinic visit and blood checks. This procedure is done by a nurse or technician. The port system requires no maintenance by the parent or patient.

Risks

The risks for a subcutaneous port are similar to those for the external catheter: infection, clots, and rarely kinks or rupture. If the needle is not properly inserted through the rubber septum, fluids can leak into the tissue around the portal.

> Brent (8 years old) has had a Port-a-cath for thirty-three months with absolutely no problems. He uses EMLA to anesthetize it prior to accessing. He hates finger pokes so much that he has his port accessed every time he needs blood drawn.

· · · · ·

> We had a few unusual problems in the beginning with the catheter. It was a bit kinked as the catheter went under the clavicle (collar bone) and would not easily draw. This caused more stress than anything in the hospital because their middle-of-the-night blood draws were always an ordeal. They needed to wake her up and try multiple manipulations. Once we were familiar with its idiosyncrasies and were outpatient, we worked it out much better. Then about halfway through maintenance, her catheter broke at the kink and traveled into her heart. To make a long story short, it was retrieved by a cardiologist without major surgery, and she got a new one placed, this time with the catheter going down from her neck. It works like a dream.

Infection

Most studies show that the infection rate of subcutaneous ports is significantly lower than that of external catheters. This is an important consideration in making a choice of catheters. If the subcutaneous port does become infected, it is treated exactly the same as those in external catheters.

> Katy had two infections in her Port-a-cath during the twenty-seven months of her leukemia treatment. One occurred during reinduction when the tape loosened during a blood transfusion. She developed a fever the next day and required fourteen days of vancomycin. Eighteen months later, we went in for her monthly vincristine, and she became ill in the car on the way home. Her skin became white and clammy, and she felt faint and nauseated. She spiked a 102° temperature which only lasted for two hours. The blood culture both times grew staphylococcus epi.

Kinks, clots, ruptures

These events rarely occur with the subcutaneous port or the external catheter. If they do occur, they are treated as described in the external catheter section.

Choosing not to use a catheter

Some physicians do not recommend using implanted catheters in their pediatric patients with leukemia, while other physicians only use catheters in high-risk patients. If this occurs and you are at a major pediatric medical center, ask if it is a hospital policy to use no catheter (some fellows have opinions which differ from hospital policy). Ask the physician the reason for her recommendation, and request a second opinion if you think a catheter might be helpful to your child. (See Chapter 6, *Forming a Partnership with the Medical Team*, for methods to obtain second opinions.)

> Stephan (6 years old) has no catheter. Sometimes I wish he had one. It seems like it would be easier. We were told he didn't need it. He is running out of usable veins and it is getting harder and harder.

Some parents choose not to have a catheter implanted because they do not want to have to run to the hospital every time that their child has a fever. Blood cultures will be necessary if your child has a catheter implanted and develops a fever. Other parents feel that the risk of infection is a small price to pay for the benefit of years of trauma-free access to veins.

Our physician gave us the option of using a catheter for our six-year-old daughter with low-risk ALL, but he recommended against it. He said if she could stand the pokes it was better not to use it due to the chance of infections. She had several sessions with the staff psychologist to teach her visualization and imagery which she used successfully to deal with the two years of IVs.

To help you make the best decision for your particular situation, the table below, Comparison of Catheters, outlines the pros and cons for each catheter. There is no right or wrong choice; different options are available because each child, each parent, each family, is unique.

Comparison of Catheters

	External Catheter	Subcutaneous Port	No Catheter
Infection Rate	Higher	Lower	Very low
Maintenance	Daily	Monthly	None
Body Image	Changes: tube outside body	Minor: lump under skin	None
Pain	None	Needle poke to access (use EMLA)	High
Anxiety	Low	Low to high	High
Cost	More due to daily maintenance	Less; monthly maintenance	Low
Risk of drugs leaking into tissues	Lowest	Low	High

The decision: Which catheter for your child?

After reviewing the information presented and the comparison chart, discuss with your doctor his opinion as to the merits of each catheter. Talk over the pros and cons with your child if she is old enough. Then make the rounds of the cancer ward, asking both parents and children which type of catheter they chose and why. You will probably hear many strong opinions on the benefits and drawbacks for each catheter.

When we asked one of the young children on the ward which catheter she had, she pulled up her shirt with a big grin to show us her Hickman. She had a coil of white tubing neatly taped to her chest. My husband's face turned as white as her tubing.

*My four-year-old daughter loved ballet, and was extremely inter-
ested in her appearance. Her younger sister was very physical, and we
were worried that if we chose the Hickman she would grab and pull on
the tubing. We chose the port so that she could wear her tutus without
reminders of cancer and so that the children could play together without
mishap.*

• • • • •

*We chose the Hickman for Shawn because we didn't want any
needles coming at him. He spent almost the whole first year in the hospital, so it saved him from so many pokes. The line was a blessing. He went
three years and three months with no infections. We thought it was just a
beautiful thing.*

The nurses in the clinic and on the ward are another source of valuable
information. They will have seen dozens (or hundreds) of children with
catheters, and will be able to give excellent advice, given your family situation. There is no right or wrong choice, just different options for each
unique child.

Removal of indwelling catheters is explained in Chapter 18, *End of Treatment
and Beyond.*

Resources

Reading for children

Meeske, Kathy, and Susan Perry. *What Is a Right Atrial Catheter?* MCI/JJCCC
Educational Materials, Long Beach Memorial Medical Center, P.O. Box 1428,
Long Beach, CA. 90801-1428. Booklet for school-age children describing
right atrial catheters, their advantages, implantation, and home care.

Technical reading

Ingram, Joanne R.N., Sheila Weitzman, M.D., et al. "Complications of Indwelling Venous Access Lines in the Pediatric Hematology Patient: A Prospective Comparison of External Venous Catheters and Subcutaneous
Ports." *The American Journal of Pediatric Hematology/Oncology* 13(2) (1991):
130-136. Studied 144 patients with subcutaneous ports and 130 with
external catheters. Found children with the subcutaneous port had 0.6
infected lines and 0.7 infectious episodes per 1,000 patient days compared

to 2.9 infected lines and 4.3 infectious episodes per 1,000 patient days in those children with external catheters.

Korones, D. N., C. J. Buzzard, et al. "Right Atrial Thrombi in Children with Cancer and Indwelling Catheters." *Journal of Pediatrics* 128:6 (June 1996): 841-6. Examined 156 children with cancer and indwelling catheters to determine the prevalence of thrombi. Thirteen children (8.8%) developed right atrial thrombi: 6 had thrombi on the right atrial wall and 7 had a thrombus on the tip of the catheter. There was no association between the presence of a clot and how long the catheter had been in place.

Marcoux, Charlotte, and Sally Fisher. "Central Venous Access Devices in Children." *Pediatric Nursing* 16(2) (March-April 1990): 123-133; Discusses types of catheters and complications. Describes both nursing care and home care.

Ruble, K., C. Long, et al. "Pharmacologic Treatment of Catheter-related Thrombus in Pediatrics." *Pediatric Nursing* 20(6) (November-December 1994): 553-7. Explains the appropriate uses of thrombolytic therapy (streptokinase and urokinase) to restore function to catheters thereby saving the patient the cost and morbidity associated with removal and replacement of a dysfunctional catheter.

Shapiro, C.L. "Central Venous Access Catheter." *Surgical Oncology Clinics of North America* 4(3) (July 1995): 443-51. Discusses the indications and major complications of central venus catheters in adult and pediatric oncology patients.

Simmons, Jeane, MSII, Aman Buzdar, M.D., et al. "Complications Associated with Indwelling Catheters." *Medical and Pediatric Oncology* 20 (1992): 22-25. Studied 170 patients with indwelling catheters during the years 1983-1985. 56% of patients had no problems during treatment, 12% developed infections, 19% developed clots, and 7% had multiple complications.

Wiernikowski, John T., and Marilyn Rothney. "Evaluation of Home Intravenous Antibiotic Program in Pediatric Oncology." *American Journal of Pediatric Hematology/Oncology* 13(2) (1991): 144-147. Describes study of thirteen families who successfully participated in home treatment of twenty-two episodes of infection. Home care shown to be safe, effective, and cheaper than hospital care.

CHAPTER 9

Sources of Support

The effort to "put up a front" is draining, isolating, and counterproductive. Support groups can be a powerful way of letting down these fronts a bit at a time among people who understand and feel the same conflicting pressure—to act as though everything is all right when it is not.

—David Spiegel, M.D.
Living Beyond Limits

THE DIAGNOSIS OF CANCER can be a frightening and isolating experience. Every parent of a child with cancer has a story to tell of lost or strained friendships. Yet we are social creatures, reliant on a web of support from family, friends, neighbors, and church. We need the presence of people who not only care for us, but try hard to understand what we are feeling. Many parents experience deep loneliness after the first rush of visits, cards, and phone calls end, when the rest of the world goes back to normal life.

Members of families struck by childhood cancer—parents, child with cancer, and siblings—are turning increasingly to support groups and various other methods of psychological help. Families join support groups to dispel isolation, share suggestions for dealing with the illness and its side effects, and talk to others who are living through the same crisis. Individual and family counseling can help address shifting responsibilities within the family, explore methods to improve communication, and help find ways to channel strong new feelings constructively.

The various methods of support described in this chapter can help return to families a sense of control over their lives as well as provide a setting for making wonderful new friends.

Hospital social workers

While the need for skilled pediatric social workers is widely recognized, shrinking hospital budgets often prevent adequate staffing. If you bring your child to a children's hospital well-staffed with social workers, child life specialists, and psychologists, consider yourself lucky. Sadly, millions of dollars are spent on technology, while programs which help people cope emotionally are often the first to be discarded. If your pediatric center offers no support, explore the other methods described later in the chapter to get help in dealing with the pain of childhood cancer.

Pediatric social workers usually have a master's degree in social work, with additional training in oncology and pediatrics. They serve as guides through unfamiliar territory by mediating between doctors and families, helping with emotional or financial problems, locating resources, and easing the young patient back into school. Many social workers form close, long-lasting bonds with families, and continue to answer questions and provide support long after treatment ends.

> *On the day of Carl's diagnosis, we were introduced to a team whom we worked with for the next several years. The team included a primary nurse, a primary oncologist, a 1st-year resident, 2nd-year resident, 3rd-year resident, and our social worker. I remember that first day her telling us that she was there to help us with anything we needed such as hospital problems, billing, insurance, emotional issues, or behavior issues. She said her job was to be there for us, and she was, whenever we needed her.*

· · · · ·

> *We went to a children's hospital which was renowned in the pediatric cancer field. The medical treatment was excellent, but psychosocial support was nonexistent. The day after diagnosis, we were interviewed for twenty minutes by a psychiatric resident, and that was it. I never met a social worker, and the physicians were so busy, they never asked anything other than medical questions. If I started crying, they usually left the room. I didn't know Candlelighters existed; I didn't know that there was a local support group; I didn't know that there was a summer camp for the kids. I felt totally isolated.*

· · · · ·

> *The social worker was really good when we were in the intensive care unit (ICU). He seemed to always know when to be there and when to leave. He made phone calls for us and would call our priest when we needed him. To tell the truth, though, we got the most support from our doctors, nurses, friends, and family who faithfully visited us during hospital stays.*

· · · · ·

A social worker came to my room after my first bone marrow aspiration (I was 8 years old) and said, "I know how you feel." I knew he didn't have any idea, and it made me furious. I was feeling very violated. People were putting needles in me, and I had no idea what was going on. I'm in college now studying psychology so that I can help kids going through cancer treatment, and I will know exactly how they feel.

In addition to social workers, some hospitals have on-staff child life specialists, psychiatric nurses, psychiatrists, psychiatric residents, and psychologists who can help deal with problems while your child is an inpatient.

After Meagan's first bone marrow aspiration, which did not go well and was very painful for her, she stopped talking and she wouldn't even look at us. We couldn't comfort her in any of the normal ways; she didn't want to be held, read to, talked to, sung to. At the time it was more devastating than the leukemia. Anytime somebody would come to the door, she would start shaking. Days into this we asked, "Isn't there anybody here who helps kids who are feeling this way?" So they sent up a psychiatric nurse, who came once and really worked wonders. However, she never came back, so we made arrangements to see her occasionally on an outpatient basis. When we started getting Meagan anesthesia for her procedures, the withdrawal stopped, and she's a healthy and happy first grader now.

• • • • •

After I relapsed, I had a hard time with nausea, so I went to learn self-hypnosis. The doctor who taught the hypnosis also counseled me, and that was very helpful. He was somebody that I could relate to and talk to about what was going on. Talking about how I felt about having cancer, and how that affected my life, was very helpful to me.

• • • • •

We got the most support from our nurse Neva, who accessed Brent's port and gave him his chemo every three weeks. She was always cheerful, concerned, and supportive, not only with Brent, but with the whole family. She listened to us and made valuable suggestions. When she changed job locations, we asked our pediatrician to make arrangements so that we could continue to go to her. He did. She was so wonderful that Brent looked forward to his chemo days, just because he would see her. He's been off treatment for over a year, but we still drop by to visit, and he runs up to her, jumps into her arms, and they have a good, long hug.

Support groups for parents

We believe children with cancer are normal children with special needs. We believe a unique bond exists among families who are experiencing childhood cancer that allows for friendship and support through treatment, the uncertainties of daily life, the grief, and the triumphs. We believe in enjoying every day to its fullest and in providing a loving environment to all families facing childhood cancer.

—Seattle Candlelighters

Support groups fill the void left by the withdrawal or misunderstanding of family and friends. Parents in similar circumstances can share practical information learned through personal experience, provide emotional support, give hope for the future, and truly listen. Coping with life-threatening illness requires perspective—the ability to accept the gravity of the situation while not blowing it out of proportion. In support groups, many families find this frame of reference, for there are always those with more severe problems than yours as well as families whose children have completed treatment and are thriving. Just meeting people who have lived through the same situation is profoundly reassuring.

> *We hadn't lived here very long when Meagan was diagnosed so we didn't have many friends. So I found that most of my support came from the group. It was really helpful to meet other people who were facing the same problems.*

· · · · ·

> *The group was a real lifeline for us, especially when Justin was so sick. We looked forward to the meetings and were there for every one. It was a real escape; it was a place to go where people were rooting for us. People from the group would always swing by to see us whenever they were bringing their own kids in for treatment. They always stopped by to visit and chat. We amassed a tremendous library of children's books that the group members would drop off. The support was wonderful. But it came from the people more than it came from the group experience itself.*

· · · · ·

> *I felt like I was always putting up a front for my family and friends. I acted like I was strong and in control. This act was draining and counterproductive. With the other parents, though, I really felt free to laugh as well as cry. I felt like I could tell them how bad things were without*

causing them any pain. I just couldn't do that with my family. If I told them what was really going on, they just looked stricken, because they didn't know what to do. But the other parents did.

* * * * *

In the beginning, I was the only father who regularly attended the group. (After three years, I'm happy to report that more fathers now attend). It made me feel bad that the other fathers didn't come to group. I sometimes wonder how deep their love is for their child if they are not willing to come and learn. I think there are elements of both male pride and fear about sharing feelings that result in their lack of participation. They must think that because they can't protect their child from the cancer, there's nothing they can do. But there is.

* * * * *

Our Tuesday gatherings were an anchor for us. It was a time to meet with parents who truly understood what living with cancer meant. These parents had been in the trenches. They knew the midnight terrors, the frustrations of dealing with the medical establishment; after all, it was an alien world to most of us. They knew about chemo, hair loss, friend loss, and they knew the bittersweet side of cherishing a child more than one thought one could cherish anymore. We gathered to cry, to laugh, to whine, to comfort one another, to share shelter from a frightening world. It was a haven.

Many people find comfort in formal support groups, while others get support from informal groups, such as those in Ronald McDonald Houses. Cancer is a very isolating experience. The issues of all the other moms on the street are light years away from the mother of a kid with cancer. But the moms in the kitchen at Ronald McDonald can just look at a child on pred-nisone wolfing down a complete second dinner, and tell the new mom how fast the appetite goes when the prednisone is tapered. They understand each other's feelings and emotions because they are sharing the same experience. The understanding of a mother or father of a child with leukemia cuts across all social, economic, and racial barriers.

My two-year-old daughter was diagnosed one week after I gave birth to a new baby girl. I remember early in her treatment, I was sitting with Gina on my lap, and my husband sat next to me, holding the new baby. The doctor breezed in and said in a cheerful voice, "How are you feel-ing?" I burst into sobs and could not stop. He said just a minute and dashed out. A few minutes later a woman came in with her eight-year-old daughter who had finished treatment and looked great. She put her arms around me and talked to me. She told me that everyone feels horrible in the beginning, and it might be hard to believe, but treatment would soon become a way of life for us. She was a great comfort, and of course, she was right.

In addition to Candlelighters—the national support organization—there are dozens of different types of support groups ranging from those with hundreds of members and formal bylaws to three moms who meet for coffee once a week. Some groups deal only with the emotional aspects of the disease while others may focus on education, advocacy, social opportunities, or crisis intervention. Some groups are facilitated by trained mental health practitioners while others are "self-help" groups comprised of parents only. And, naturally, as older members drop out and new families join, the needs and interests of the group may shift.

We have found that it is hard to keep people coming to monthly meetings, even though we have a large membership. We have a 15-member board, which meets every month and plans parties and informational meetings with speakers. We have parties for Christmas, Easter, and Halloween, as well as trips to amusement parks and picnics. Our motto is, "If there's food, families will come." We are also lucky to have a full-time staff person who takes care of information, advertising our services, correspondence, and connecting parents with similar needs.

· · · · ·

Our group is very informal. We do have two social workers who are considered the facilitators, and are there as resource persons. We just talk about whatever anyone wants to discuss. Occasionally we have invited speakers in. I remember having a psychiatrist discuss stress management, and we also had a talk on therapeutic massage. We have formed close friendships from the group, and we still go twice a month even though our daughter is a year off treatment and doing great. I think our presence comforts the new families.

· · · · ·

I live in a rural area, over 100 miles from the group affiliated with the children's hospital. I started a parents' support group in my area for children with any life-threatening illness, and we had a good response initially, but it gradually fizzled out because our issues were just too varied.

But I did meet through that group a mother whose son had leukemia, and we have become fast friends. We have a support group of two. We talk on the phone several times a week, and try to go out to dinner or the movies occasionally, just to get a break. The local hospital gives out my name as the parent contact for newly diagnosed children, and I inform them of the local and national resources, and try to visit and answer questions.

Parents of the Jewish faith who are looking for support might want to contact:

Parents Caring and Sharing
c/o Chumie Bodek
109 Rutledge St.
Brooklyn, NY 11211
(718) 596-1542 or (718) 596-9002
(Call during business hours, Eastern Standard time.)

Parents Caring and Sharing provides outreach and a support network and writes a newsletter for Jewish Orthodox families with children with cancer. It holds monthly meetings and links families of children with similar diseases.

There are also telephone support services. Some of the organizations which provide them are listed in the "Resources" section at the end of this chapter.

Support groups for children with cancer

Many pediatric hospitals also have ongoing support groups for children with cancer. Often these are run by experienced pediatric social workers, who know how to balance fun with sharing feelings. For many children, these groups are the only place where they feel completely accepted, where most of the other kids are bald and have to take lots of medicine. The group is a place where children or adolescents can say how they really feel, without worrying that they are causing their parents more pain. Many children form wonderful and lasting friendships in peer groups.

I went to Junior Candlelighters, which was very helpful. The gal who facilitated the group was a survivor of osteosarcoma and had had her leg amputated. Yet, she skied, she drove, she did everything. I always thought, "If Patty can do it, I can, too. If she can live so well without a leg, I should be able to put up with having a cancer in my blood."

• • • • •

All four of my kids have been going to the support groups for over seven years now. We have one group for the kids with cancer which is run by a social worker. The sibs group is run by a woman who specializes in early childhood development. Both groups do a lot of art therapy, relaxation therapy, playing, and talking. They meet twice a month, and I will continue to take them until they ask to stop. I think it has really helped all of them. We also have two teen nights out a year. All of the teenagers with cancer get together for an activity such as watching a hockey game, or basketball game, or going bowling, to the movies, or out for pizza. They also see each other at our local camp for children surviving cancer (Camp Watcha-Wanna-Do) each year.

· · · · ·

Kristin goes to the kids' support group while my wife and I attend the parents' group downstairs. She doesn't talk much about what goes on, but the facilitator keeps the parents' apprised of how things are going. One very vocal nine-year-old boy has recently broken the ice with the kids. He really likes to talk about his feelings about having leukemia, and it has prompted the other children to begin to share their thoughts and reactions about the things that have happened to them. They also have lots of fun.

The Center for Attitudinal Healing in Tiburon, California, is a nonprofit, nonsectarian group founded by a child psychiatrist which sponsors a program for children with catastrophic or life-threatening diseases and their siblings. They use music and art in a loving, supportive program to help children ages 6 to 16 share their feelings about their situation. They sponsor local and national workshops and publish several excellent books. Should you desire further information, contact:

The Center for Attitudinal Healing
33 Buchanan Drive
Sausalito, CA 94965
(415) 331-6161

For children who are too ill or shy to join a group, there are alternatives. There are hundreds of kids who use computers to contact and chat with other kids in similar situations. Use Appendix 3 to access some of the available computer groups.

Another option for children to communicate with other children in similar circumstances is to contact:

Children's Hopes and Dreams Foundation
280 Rt. 46
Dover, NJ 07801
(201) 361-7348

This organization operates a free, worldwide pen pal program for children ages 5 to 17 with disabilities, chronic illnesses, or life-threatening illnesses. They will gladly send free enrollment cards to parents, social workers, teachers, nurses, or any other interested persons.

If you would like your child to receive letters and gifts to provide emotional support, contact:

Love Letters, Inc.
2105 Prentiss Drive E/107
Downers Grove, IL 60516
(708) 515-9501

Love Letters is a confidential, free service started by a mother whose son died of cancer. It is not a pen pal organization; confidentiality is guaranteed. It is run by a group of volunteers who wish to bring some happiness into the lives of catastrophically ill children by sending letters, cards, and gifts. They send out 4,000 pieces of mail monthly.

Support groups for siblings

Many hospitals have reacted to the growing awareness of siblings' natural concerns and worries by creating hospital visiting days for them. This allows not only one-on-one parent time for the siblings, but gives them the opportunity to explore and become familiar with the hospital environment. Sibling days allow interaction with staff, a time to have questions answered and concerns addressed. Some hospital staffs have expanded these one-day programs into ongoing support groups aimed not just at siblings who are having "problems," but also at improving communication, education, and support for all siblings.

> Both of Shawn's brothers went to the sib group for years. It seemed to really help them. I don't really know what they did in that room upstairs, but they always came down happy.

· · · · ·

Annie went to Club Goodtimes long after her brother stopped going and attended camp as many years as they would allow. She intends to be on the staff at camp next summer.

Parent-to-parent programs

Some pediatric hospitals, in conjunction with parent support groups such as Candlelighters, have developed parent-to-parent visitation programs. The purpose of these visits is for veteran parents to provide one-on-one support for newly diagnosed families. The services provided by the veteran parent can be informational, emotional, or logistical. The visiting parent can also:

• Empathize with the newly diagnosed parents.

• Help notify family and friends.

• Help overcome loneliness.

• Ease feelings of isolation.

• Provide hospital tours.

• Write down parents' questions for the medical team.

• Advise on sources of financial aid.

• Explain unfamiliar medical terms.

• Be available by phone for any problems that arise.

• Supply lots of smiles and hugs, but most of all, hope.

Newly diagnosed families can ask if the hospital has a parent-to-parent program. If not, ask to speak to the parent leader of the local support group. Often, this person will ask a veteran parent to visit you at the hospital. Many, many veteran parents are more than willing to visit, as they know only too well what those first weeks in the hospital are like. They are often accompanied by their child who has completed therapy, rosy-cheeked and full of energy, a living beacon of hope.

> *I am the parent consultant for our region. Among the services I provide are: meet with all newly diagnosed families; give a packet of information to each child or teen with cancer; continue to visit the families whenever they return to the hospital; educate families about the various local resources; provide moral support; stay with children during painful procedures if the parents can't; organize and present all of the school programs; liaison with schools for school reentry; organize and*

send out monthly reminders for Candlelighters meetings, child support group meetings, and sib group meetings; send out birthday cards to kids on treatment; serve as activities director at the summer camp; and generally try to help out each family in any way possible. My job is a part-time, paid position funded through the local independent agency, Cancer Services of Allen County, Inc.

For step-by-step suggestions on how to create, organize, recruit volunteers, and work with the hospital to create a parent-to-parent visitation program, obtain the booklet *Making Contact* from Candlelighters (see "Resources" at the end of this chapter.).

Clergy

Religion is a source of strength for many people. Many parents and children find that their faith is strengthened by the cancer ordeal, while some begin to question their beliefs. Others, who have not relied on religion in the past, sometimes turn to it now.

Most hospitals have staff chaplains who are available for counseling, religious services, prayer, and other types of spiritual guidance. Often, the chaplain visits families soon after diagnosis and is available on an on-call basis. As with any mental health encounter, some approaches that work well with one family are not welcome with others.

> *The day after my daughter was diagnosed, a chaplain started coming to the room every day. She was very nice, but I felt like she wanted me to talk about the cancer, and I just couldn't. I clearly remember feeling as if my body parts were being held together by the weakest of threads. I felt if I started talking, or even said the word leukemia, that those threads holding me together would break and I would fly apart into a million pieces. So we chatted about inconsequential things until one day I thanked her for coming but said I felt strong enough to start talking to my family and friends.*

· · · · ·

> *When Shawn was first diagnosed, Father Ron came in, and we all just really bonded with him. Shawn was in the hospital most of the first year, so we had a chance to become very close. Often Shawn would ask*

for Father Ron before he had to have a painful procedure. Father Ron would talk to him, give him a little stuffed animal and a big hug, and then Shawn would feel fine.

When Shawn was very ill, I began to worry about the fact that he had never been baptized, and I asked Father Ron to baptize him in the chapel. We ended up going to his own little church nearby, and we had a private service with just godparents and family because Shawn's counts were so low. It was a wonderful, special service; I'll never forget it.

Parents who were members of a church or synagogue prior to the diagnosis of their child's cancer derive great comfort from the clergy and members of their home church. Members of the congregation usually rally around the family, providing meals, baby sitting, prayers, and support. Regular visits from the priest, minister, or rabbi provide spiritual sustenance throughout the initial crisis and subsequent years of treatment.

We belong to a bible study group that has met weekly for eight years. In our group during that time there have been three cancer diagnoses and one of Multiple Sclerosis. We have all become an incredibly supportive family, and we share the burdens. I cannot begin to list the many wonderful things these people have done for us. They consistently put their lives on hold to help. They fill the freezer, clean the house, support us financially, parent our children. They do the laundry covered with vomit. They quietly appear, help, then disappear. I can call any one of them at 3 A.M. in the depths of despair and find comfort.

Individual and family counseling

Cancer is a crisis of major proportions for even the strongest of families. Parents do not need to face this crisis alone and unassisted. Many find it helpful to seek out sensitive, objective mental health care professionals to explore the difficult feelings—fear, anger, depression, anxiety, resentment, guilt—that cancer arouses. Family responsibilities and authority undergo profound changes when a child is diagnosed with leukemia. Sometimes members of the family have difficulty adjusting to the changes. While some families discuss the uncomfortable changes and feelings openly and agree on how to proceed, many need help.

Seeking professional counseling is a sign of strength, not failure. In dealing with children with cancer, problems often become too complex for families to deal with on their own. Seeking advice sends children a message that the parents care about what is happening to them and want to help face it together.

One of the first questions that arises is, "Who should we talk to?" There are a number of resource people in the community who can make referrals and valuable recommendations, including:

• Pediatrician.

• Oncologist.

• Nurse Practitioner.

• Clinic social worker.

• School psychologist or counselor.

• Health department social worker.

• Other parents who have sought counseling.

Ask each of the above for a short list of mental health care professionals who have experience working with your issues, for example, traumatized children, marital problems, stress reduction, or family therapy. Generally, the names of the most well-respected clinicians in the community will appear on several of the lists.

In making your decision, it helps to understand the different levels of training and education of the various types of mental health care professionals. You will be able to choose from individuals trained in one of these four related fields:

• **Psychology (Ed.D., M.A., Ph.D., Psy.D.)** Marriage and family psychotherapists have a master's degree, clinical and research psychologists have a doctorate (in some states, the use of the title "psychologist" may also be allowed for those with only a master's degree.)

• **Social work (M.S.W., D.S.W., Ph.D.)** Clinical social workers have either a master's degree or a doctorate in a clinically emphasized program.

• **Pastoral Care (M.A., M.Div., D.Min., Ph.D., D.Div.)** Laymen or members of the clergy who receive specialized training in counseling.

- **Medicine (M.D., R.N.)** Psychiatrists are medical doctors (and only they are able to prescribe medications). In addition, some nurses obtain post-graduate training in psychotherapy.

The designations L.C.S.W. (Licensed Clinical Social Worker), L.M.F.C.C. (Licensed Marriage and Family Child Counselor), L.P.C. (Licensed Professional Counselor), L.M.F.T. (Licensed Marriage and Family Therapist) refer to licensure by state professional boards, not academic degrees. These initials usually follow others that indicate an academic degree. If they don't, inquire about the therapist's academic training.

You may hear all of the above professionals referred to as "counselors" or "therapists." Currently, 37 states require licensure or certification in order for professionals to practice independently; unlicensed professionals are allowed to practice only under the supervision of a licensed professional (typically as an "intern" or "assistant" in a clinic or licensed professional's private practice).

When you are seeking a good counselor for yourself, ask the professional how long she has been in practice. A licensed marriage and family therapist who has been seeing patients for ten years may be a much finer clinician for your needs than a licensed psychologist or psychiatrist in their first year of practice.

Another method to find a suitable counselor is to call:

The American Association for Marriage and Family Therapy
1133 Fifteenth Street, N.W. Suite 300
Washington, DC 20005-2710
(202) 452-0109

This is a national professional organization of licensed/certified marriage and family therapists. It has more than 20,000 members in the U.S. and Canada, and its membership also includes licensed clinical social workers, pastoral counselors (who are M.F.C.C./L.M.F.T.s), psychologists, and psychiatrists.

To find a therapist, a good first step is to call two or three therapists who appear on several of your lists of recommendations. During your telephone interview, the following are some suggested questions to ask:

- Are you accepting new clients?
- Do you charge for an initial consultation?

- What training and experience do you have working with ill or traumatized children?

- How many years have you been working with families?

- What is your approach to resolving the problems children develop from trauma? Do you use a brief or long-term approach?

- What evaluation and assessment procedures will be used to define the problem?

- How and when will treatment goals be set?

- How will both parents be involved in treatment?

- What are your fees? Will the insurance company be billed directly?

The next step should be to make an appointment with one or two of the therapists who you think might be able to best address your needs. Be honest about the fact that you are interviewing several therapists prior to making a decision. The purpose of the introductory meeting is to see if you feel comfortable with the therapist. After all, credentials do not guarantee that a given therapist will work for you. Compatibility, trust, and a feeling of genuine caring are essential. It is worth the effort to continue your search until you find a good match.

> I called several therapists out of desperation about my daughter's withdrawal and violent tantrums. I made appointments with two. The first I just didn't feel comfortable with at all, but the second felt like an old friend after one hour. I have been to see her dozens of times over the years, and she has always helped me. I wasn't interested in theory; I wanted practical suggestions of how to deal with the behavior problems. My four-year-old daughter asked why I was going to see the therapist, and I said that Hilda was a doctor, but instead of taking care of my body, she helped care for my feelings. She asked to go to the "feelings" doctor, but was concerned about whether her conversations would be private. I asked the counselor to explain about the limits of confidentiality. So that began a very helpful course of therapy for my very traumatized daughter. To this day I don't know what was said, nor would I ever ask my daughter or Hilda. I do know that they did a lot of art therapy, and I know that it helped immensely.

• • • • •

We went to family counseling because I was concerned that my son seemed to be increasingly withdrawn and depressed. It was a disaster. The kids clammed up, I talked too much, and my husband was offended by some of the remarks that the counselor made. She was not a good choice for our family. It's a hard decision to change counselors when you know you need help, but it's better to make a move than to stay in an uncomfortable situation.

· · · · ·

I went to a psychologist the first year my son was in treatment. I had problems with anxiety and sleeplessness. We often talked about issues other than cancer that were bothering me. I just needed to learn how to cope and to face things that scared me. Once the psychologist asked me how my son coped, and I replied, "He just gets up each morning and it's a new day." He asked me if I thought that I could try to take his lead. So I try to face just one day at a time.

· · · · ·

We went into family therapy because every member of my family experienced misdirected anger. When they were angry they aimed it at me—the nice person who took care of them and loved them no matter what. But I was dissolving. I needed to learn to say "ouch," and they needed to learn other ways to handle their angry feelings.

Children need to be prepared for psychological intervention as for any unknown procedure. The following are several parents' suggestions on how to prepare your child:

- Explain who the therapist is, and what you hope to accomplish. For instance, you might be taking the whole family to improve communication or resolve conflicts. If you are bringing your child in for therapy, explain why you think talking to an objective person might benefit him.

- Older children should be involved in the process of choosing a counselor. Younger children's likes and dislikes should be respected. If your young child does not get along well with one counselor, change.

- Make the experience positive rather than threatening.

- Reassure young children that the visit is for talking, drawing, or playing games, not for anything that is physically painful.

- Ask the therapist to explain the rules of confidentiality to both you and your child. Do not quiz your child after a visit to the therapist.

- Make sure that your child does not think that she is being punished; instead assure her that therapists help both adults and children understand and deal with feelings.

- Go yourself for counseling or to support group meetings to model the fact that all ages and types of people need help from time to time.

> In the beginning of treatment, my son had terrible problems with going to sleep and then having nightmares, primarily about snakes. We took him to a counselor, who worked with him for several weeks and completely resolved the problem. The counselor had him befriend the snake, talk to it, and explain that it was keeping him awake. He would tell the snake, "I want you to stop bothering me because I need to go to sleep." The snake never returned.

In *Armfuls of Time*, Barbara Sourkes quotes Jonathan, a boy with cancer, who told her, "Thank you for giving me aliveness." She discusses the importance of psychotherapy for the child with a life-threatening illness:

> Even when life itself cannot be guaranteed, psychotherapy can at least "give aliveness" to the child for however long that life may last. Through the extraordinary challenges posed by life-threatening illness, a precocious inner wisdom of life and its fragility emerges. Yet even in the struggle for survival, the spirit of childhood shines through.

Camps

Summer camps for children with cancer, and often their siblings as well, are becoming increasingly popular. These camps provide an opportunity for children with cancer and their siblings to have fun, meet friends, and talk with others in the same situation. Counselors are typically cancer survivors and siblings of cancer victims, or sometimes oncology nurses and residents. Supervised by experts, children can have their concerns addressed without involving their parents. These camps provide a carefree time away from the sadness of the family or the all too frequent hospital visits.

> Of all the ways to get support, I think the camp really helps the most. You are all there together for enough time to break down the barriers. Although camp does not focus on cancer, many times we really got down to talking about how we really felt. I have been a counselor at the camp for eight summers now. Most of the campers know that I relapsed three times and I'm doing great many years later. They see the many

other long-term survivors who are counselors, and it gives them what they need the most—hope. The best support is meeting survivors, because nobody else truly understands.

· · · · ·

When we went to pick up seven-and-a-half-year-old Kristin from camp, she told us how wonderful it had been and exclaimed, "I want to come back every year until I am old enough to be a counselor." That said it all to me.

· · · · ·

Caitlin went to camp, and this was a dream come true for her. As we pulled into the parking lot she exhaled a deep breath and said, "I made it, I am finally normal!"

We are one family
        you and I—
Not by birth or legal joining
Not by choice, and definitely not by desire
        But by a commonality given to us by the unseen
                Seeking peace with uncertainty
                        Needing the support of another
                                who has known.

We are one family
        you and I—
We fight the beast hungry for our child
        and battle for their lives
Striving to plan for tomorrow
        explaining, educating, researching
Assertiveness and occasional aggression
To fight with
        and for
                Our child.

We are one family
        you and I—
With the same questions and fears
        Why my child? Did I do something to cause this horror?
        Am I weak because I still cry?
Will the beast return? When?

Am I missing an early sign?
What late effects of this battle will we see?
    How do we deal with them? Where do we get help?
What about my other children?
    Will the beast find them too?

We are one family
    you and I—
We share a bond that we wish did not exist
    and yet since it does exist
        we are glad it is there
We gather strength
    and rejoice in today
We accept the tears, acknowledge the fears
    love and are loved
We walk the road together
    not knowing where it leads
        on our common journey we are not alone,
          Thus we are blessed.

We are one family
    you and I—
Not by birth or legal joining
Not by choice, and definitely not by desire
    But by a commonality given to us by the unseen
        Seeking peace with uncertainty
          Needing the support of another
            who has known.

                    —Mary Riecke

Resources

Organizations

Cancer Care, Inc.
1180 Avenue of the Americas
New York, NY 10036
1-800-813-4673
(212) 302-2400
FAX: (212) 719-0263

Free telephone service that provides immediate psychological support to cancer patients and their families in Florida, Delaware, Pennsylvania, and New Jersey. The line is staffed by professional social workers who offer counseling, support, education, information, and referral. This organization also provides some funds to help with chemotherapy, transportation, or radiation.

Candlelighters Childhood Cancer Foundation Hot Line.
1-800-366-CCCF

Toll free hot line that provides answers on any pediatric cancer related question including help with finances, insurance, legal problems, technical questions, and referral to the nearest support group. For many parents of children with cancer, Candlelighters is their primary resource for any problem.

Reading for adults

American Psychological Association. *Finding Help: How to Choose a Psychologist.* To obtain free brochure, send self-addressed stamped envelope to *Finding Help* APA Public Affairs Office, 750 First St. NE, Washington, DC, 20002-4242. The brochure provides information about psychotherapy, the types of problems that people take into therapy, and how to choose a therapist.

Bogue, Erna-Lynne, A.C.S.W., and Barbara K. Chesney, M.P.H. *Making Contact: A Parent-to-parent Visitation Manual.* Bethesda, MD: The Candlelighters Childhood Cancer Foundation, 1987. To obtain, call 1-800-366-CCCF. Step-by-step guide on planning and running a parent-to-parent visitation program for parents of children with cancer. Includes guidelines for selection of parent visitors, training to improve parent-visitor contact, developing referral systems, and support resources.

Bruckner, Fredda, et al. *Making Therapy Work: Your Guide to Choosing, Using, and Ending Therapy.* New York: Harper & Row, 1988. Excellent book full of practical advice on how to find the right therapist, and get the most out of your sessions, and when to end therapy.

Chesler, Mark A., Ph.D. "Support Systems for Parents of Children with Cancer." *Candlelighters.* To obtain, call 1-800-366-CCCF. Dr. Chesler is a professor of sociology as well as the parent of a young adult who survived childhood cancer. This article describes the roles of family, friends, medical staff, community institutions, and self-help groups as support systems for the families of a child with cancer.

Chesler, Mark A., PH.D., and Barbara Chesney. *Cancer and Self-Help: Bridging the Troubled Waters of Childhood Illness.* Madison, WI: The University of Wisconsin Press, 1995. Written for and about the parents of children with cancer, this book provides explanations of how self-help groups are formed, how they function and recruit, and why they are effective. The authors explain how, through self-help groups, parents improve their coping abilities and become better advocates for their child in an increasingly complex health care system.

Goleman, Daniel, and Joel Gurin, eds. *Mind Body Medicine: How to Use Your Mind for Better Health.* Fairfield, OH: Consumer Reports Books, 1993. 9180 LeSaint Drive, Fairfield, OH 45014. This book explores the link between emotions and physical heath. Thirty-one experts discuss techniques such as meditation, biofeedback, and relaxation and their role in the treatment of disease.

Leukemia Society of America. *Emotional Aspects of Childhood Leukemia.* To obtain free copy, call 1-800-955-4LSA. 34-page booklet covers feelings of parents, ill child, and siblings from diagnosis through end of treatment or death. Includes many parent experiences.

Monaco, Grace Powers, J.D. "Parent Self-Help Groups for the Families of Children with Cancer." *Candlelighters.* To obtain a copy, call 1-800-366-CCCF. Short article which discusses the myriad benefits of participating in parent self-help groups.

Nathanson, Minna Newman. *Organizing and Maintaining Support Groups for Parents of Children with Chronic Illness and Handicapping Conditions.* Association for the Care of Children's Health. 7910 Woodmont Ave., Suite 300, Bethesda, MD 20814.. Outlines the benefits of support groups, activities, parent-professional relations, organization, structure, and group maintenance.

National Cancer Institute. *Taking Time: Support for People with Cancer and the People Who Care About Them*. NIH Publication No. 88-2059. To obtain free copy, call 1-800-4-CANCER. Sixty-one-page booklet includes sections on sharing feelings, coping within the family, and when you need assistance.

Sander, Seryl. *Vistas of Challenge: Profiles of Inspiring People and Their Courage*. New York: Mesorah Publications, 1996. 1-800-MESORAH or (721) 921-2000. Powerful stories of true life experiences of people who face adversity with joy, strength, and triumph. Jewish Orthodox perspective but not limited to that audience.

Spiegel, David, M.D. *Living Beyond Limits*. New York: Random House, 1993. Dr. Spiegel devised the landmark study which showed that support groups for women with breast cancer not only lowered rates of depression, but significantly increased life spans. This book is an excellent guide for coping with cancer, strengthening family relationships, controlling pain, dealing with doctors, and evaluating alternative medicine claims.

Sourkes, Barbara M., Ph.D. *Armfuls of Time: The Psychological Experience of the Child with a Life-Threatening Illness*. Pittsburgh: Univirsity of Pittsburgh Press, 1995. Written by a psychologist with over twenty years experience as the head psychologist at the Dana-Farber Cancer Institute and Children's Hospital in Boston, this eloquent book features the voices and artwork of children with cancer. *Armfuls of Time* clearly describes the devastating psychological effects of cancer on children as well as explains the power of the therapeutic process. Highly recommended for every parent of a child with a life-threatening illness.

Reading for clergy

R. A. Bloch Foundation. *Booklet for Clergy*. 4400 Main St., Kansas City, MO 64111. (816) 932-8435. This free booklet educates and assists members of the clergy in counseling cancer patients and survivors.

Technical reading

Bearison, David, and Raymond Mulhern. *Pediatric Psychooncology: Psychological Perspectives on Children with Cancer*. New York: Oxford University Press, 1994. Comprehensive, technical book on the many aspects of psychological impacts on children with cancer.

Video

National Institutes of Health. *Cancer Patient Education Videotape Directory.* NIH Publication No. 94-3105. To obtain a free copy, call 1-800-4-CAN-CER. 44-page directory which lists dozens of videotapes available to help educate patients and their families. General topics include introduction to cancer, living with cancer, diet, treatments, chemotherapy, radiation, bone marrow transplants, types of cancer, children and cancer, death and dying. This guide might help your support group focus on issues to discuss, as well as educate you on what videotapes are available, their cost, and how to order them.

Chemotherapy

Mommy, my arms look like pizza, and my legs look like worms.

—Five-year-old with ALL

THE WORD CHEMOTHERAPY is derived from the combination of "chemical" and "treatment." It means using drugs, singly or in combination, to destroy or disrupt the growth of cancer cells without permanently damaging normal cells.

This chapter describes the most common drugs that are used to kill cancer cells as well as drugs that prevent nausea and pain. Numerous stories are included that show the range of responses to different chemotherapy drugs.

Reading about potential side effects of chemotherapy can be disturbing. However it is important to be aware of the possibilities in order to recognize symptoms early and report them to the doctor so that swift action can be taken to make your child more comfortable. On rare occasions, side effects may be life-threatening and some can persist throughout life. However, most are merely unpleasant and subside soon after treatment ends. Remember that your child may experience several, a few, or none of the side effects discussed here.

How do chemotherapy drugs kill cancer cells?

Normal, healthy cells divide and grow in a well-established pattern. When normal cells divide, an identical copy is produced. The body only makes the number of normal cells that it needs at any given time.

Cancer cells, on the other hand, reproduce uncontrollably and grow in an unpredictable way. They invade surrounding tissue and can travel in blood or lymph to lodge in other parts of the body.

There are several groups of chemotherapy drugs that act on cancer cells in very different ways:

- **Alkylating agents.** All cells use building blocks (DNA and RNA) to make exact copies of themselves. Alkylating agents poison cancer cells by interacting with DNA to prevent cell reproduction.

- **Antimetabolites.** These drugs starve cancer cells by replacing essential cell nutrients.

- **Antibiotics.** This type of drug prevents cell growth by blocking reproduction.

- **Alkaloids.** These drugs, derived from plants, interrupt cell division.

- **Hormones.** These drugs create a hostile environment that slows cell growth.

- **Enzymes.** These interfere with cancer cells' ability to reproduce.

How are chemotherapy drugs given?

The four most common ways that drugs are given during treatment for leukemia are:

- **Intravenous (IV).** Medicine is delivered directly into the bloodstream via a right atrial catheter or IV needle in the arm or hand.

- **Oral.** Drugs, taken by mouth in liquid, capsule, or tablet form, are absorbed into the blood through the lining of the stomach and intestines.

- **Intramuscular.** Drugs that need to seep slowly into the bloodstream are injected into a large muscle such as the thigh or buttocks.

- **Intrathecal.** Doctors perform a spinal tap and inject the drug directly into the cerebrospinal fluid, circumventing the barrier between the blood and brain.

Dosages

Dosages vary among protocols; however, most are based on a term called m^2 (pronounced "meters squared"). Hospital personnel will measure your child's height and weight at the beginning of each visit, and then enter these figures into a computer that calculates your child's body surface area.

My daughter's m² ranged from .55 to .70 over the course of her treatment. During induction, the protocol required 60 mg/m² of prednisone on days 0 to 27. To determine her dose, the doctor calculated .55 x 60 = 33. He then wrote a prescription that she take 33 mg of prednisone a day in three doses of 11 mg each. So, I gave her one 10 mg tablet and one 1 mg tablet three times a day. You do not need to do the calculations, but you need to understand the dosage and how you should give it for each drug. Most families write the dosages on a calendar and cross them out when given to make sure they don't forget a drug.

Chemotherapy drugs and their possible side effects

The following drug information contains not only common and infrequent side effects, but also parent and survivor experiences and suggestions. You may be overwhelmed by reading all of the potential side effects of each drug. Please remember, each child is unique and will handle most drugs without any problems. Most side effects are unpleasant, not serious, and subside when the medication stops. Parent experiences are included to alert new parents to possibilities and provide comfort and suggestions should a child have an unusual side effect. Consult your child's pediatrician or oncologist should any concerns arise from the following information. The "Resources" section at the end of the chapter contains resources for obtaining information on drugs not covered here.

REMEMBER TO KEEP ALL CHEMOTHERAPY DRUGS IN A LOCKED CABINET AWAY FROM CHILDREN AND PETS!

Questions to ask the doctor

Prior to giving your child any drug, you should be given basic information including answers to the following:

- What is the dosage? How many times a day should it be given?
- What are the common, and the rare, side effects?
- What should I do if my child experiences any of the side effects?
- Will the drug interact with any over-the-counter drugs (e.g. Tylenol) or vitamins?

- Have teenage patients been given detailed counseling on avoiding risks such as drinking alcohol, smoking cigarettes or marijuana, and pregnancy?

- What should I do if I forget to give my child a dose?

- What are both the trade and generic names of the drug?

- Should I buy the generic version?

Guidelines for calling the doctor

Sometimes parents are reluctant to call their child's physician with questions or concerns. Here are general guidelines for when calling is necessary:

- Temperature above $101°$ F.

- Shaking or chills.

- Shortness of breath.

- Severe nausea or vomiting.

- Unusual bleeding, bruising or cuts that won't heal.

- Pain or swelling at chemotherapy injection site.

- Exposure to chicken pox or measles.

- Severe headache or blurred vision.

- Constipation lasting more than two days.

- Severe diarrhea.

- Painful urination or bowel movements.

- Blood in urine.

- Whenever child appears sick and parent is concerned.

Chemotherapy Drug List

Drugs used for chemotherapy are known by a variety of names. You may hear the same drug referred to by its generic name, abbreviation, or one of several brand names, depending on which doctor, nurse, or pharmacist you are talking to. The list below gives the most common names used for chemotherapy drugs, and tells you what name is used in this chapter so you can easily find it on the following pages of detailed information.

NAME	LOOK UNDER
Adriamycin	Doxorubicin
ARA-C	Cytarabine
Asp	L-Asparaginase
Cerubidine	Daunorubicin
Cyclophosphamide	Cyclophosphamide
Cytarabine	Cytarabine
Cytoxan	Cyclophosphamide
Cytosar	Cytarabine
Cytosine arabinoside	Cytarabine
Daunomycin	Daunorubicin
Daunorubicin	Daunorubicin
Decadron	Prednisone
Dexamethasone	Prednisone
DMR	Daunorubicin
DNR	Daunorubicin
Doxorubicin	Doxorubicin
Elspar	L-Asparaginase
Etoposide	Etoposide
Hydroxyurea	Hydroxyurea
Hydrea	Hydroxyurea
L-Asp	L-Asparaginase
L-Asparaginase	L-Asparaginase
Mercaptopurine	Mercaptopurine
Methotrexate	Methotrexate
Mexate	Methotrexate
MTX	Methotrexate
Oncovin	Vincristine
Prednisone	Prednisone
Purinethol	Mercaptopurine
Rubidomycin	Daunorubicin
VePresid	Etoposide
VCR	Vincristine
Vincristine	Vincristine
VP-16	Etoposide
6-MP	Mercaptopurine
6-TG	6-Thioguanine
6-Thioguanine	6-Thioguanine

L-Asparaginase (L-a-SPARE-a-gin-ase)

Also called: Asp, L-ASP, Elspar.

How given: Intramuscular injection.

How it works: This drug is an enzyme that blocks protein production in cancer cells to prevent them from reproducing.

Types: There are two types of L-asparaginase: E.Coli asparaginase and Erwinia asparaginase.

Precaution: Occasionally a child will have a severe allergic reaction to L-asparaginase. It is important that the drug be given by trained medical personnel who have emergency equipment available. The child should be monitored at the clinic for 20 to 30 minutes after receiving the drug in case a reaction occurs. If a child does have a reaction to E. Coli asparaginase, Erwinia asparaginase will be used for the next dose. If a reaction occurs again, asparaginase therapy is usually discontinued.

Common side effects:

- Loss of appetite and weight.
- Fatigue.
- Headache.
- Abdominal cramps.
- Nausea and vomiting.

Infrequent side effects:

- Allergic reaction including swelling, difficulty breathing, rash.
- Jaundice (yellow skin and eyes).
- Confusion or hallucinations.
- Convulsions.
- Swelling of feet or legs.
- Unusually frequent urination.
- High blood pressure.
- Kidney or liver damage.
- Stroke.
- Pancreatitis.

> *Meagan had no problem with the L-asparaginase other than the shots in her thigh were painful. This was before EMLA was available. I'd recommend that parents put EMLA on two hours before the shot to reduce the pain.*

Most children have no serious side effects from asparaginase. But for those who do, it can be both frightening and life-threatening.

> *A couple of hours after Preston's third dose of L-asparaginase his leg began to swell up around the injection site. His leg grew to three times its normal size. The doctors switched him to a different kind of L-asparaginase for all subsequent doses, and he had no further problems.*

• • • • •

> *A day after Brent received his last L-asparaginase dose, he began to have intense pain in his kidney area and began to pass blood in his urine. After his arrival at the hospital, his kidneys shut down and he stopped breathing. He was in the ICU on a ventilator and received kidney dialysis for a week. The doctors thought that he had a rare reaction to L-asparaginase which caused tiny blood clots in his kidneys. His kidneys function normally now, but he developed a seizure disorder as a result of the trauma to his brain.*

In *Having Leukemia Isn't So Bad*, Cynthia Krumme writes of her daughter's reaction to L-asparaginase:

> *Within thirty seconds of the administration of the drug, Catherine had a severe allergic reaction. It was a nightmare. Her body swelled up like a balloon. She began coughing, choking, complaining of pain in her stomach, and she developed chills and high blood pressure. The symptoms lasted for nearly two hours. Benadryl was administered by IV, an oxygen mask was applied, and she was wrapped in blankets.*

REMEMBER: The vast majority of children have NO reaction to L-asparaginase.

Cyclophosphamide (Sye-kloe-FOSS-fa-mide)

Also called: Cytoxan, Endoxan.

How given: Pills or IV injection.

How it works: An alkylating agent that disrupts DNA in cancer cells, preventing reproduction.

Precaution: The child should drink lots of water or be given large amounts of IV fluids while taking Cytoxan to prevent damage to the bladder. Antinausea drugs should be given before and for several hours after this drug is administered.

Common side effects:

- Immunosuppression (low blood cell counts).

- Nausea and vomiting (often prevented through the use of ondansetron, an effective antinausea drug).

- Loss of appetite.

- Mouth sores.

- Diarrhea.

- Hair loss.

Infrequent side effects:

- Hemorrhagic cystitis causing blood in the urine.

- Abdominal pain and diarrhea.

- Cough or shortness of breath.

- Dizziness and difficulty walking.

- Skin rash and itching.

- Menstrual periods in teenage girls may temporarily stop.

- Sterility (rare even for children who receive high doses).

> *Erica just could not tolerate the Cytoxan. She had continuous vomiting. At one point she had lost more than one third of her body weight. Our HMO wouldn't authorize using ondansetron (a very effective antinausea drug) because it was so expensive.*

· · · · ·

> *Christine breezed through the Cytoxan infusions. She would go to Children's in the afternoon, they would give her lots of IV fluids, and then ondansetron a half hour before the Cytoxan. She would sleep through the night with absolutely no nausea because they were so good about giving her the ondansetron all night and the next morning. It was harder on me*

because I had to wake up every two hours to change her diaper so that the nurse could weigh it to make sure she was passing enough urine.

• • • • •

Preston took Cytoxan in pill form, and it made him very ill. He even started to try to hide the pills. I tried to make him drink lots of water. He knew it was important, but it was very difficult.

Cytarabine (Sye-TARE-a-been)

Also called: ARA-C, Cytosar, cytosine arabinoside.

How given: IV, intrathecal, or subcutaneous.

How it works: Kills cancer cells by disrupting DNA.

Common side effects:

- Immunosuppression (low blood cell counts).
- Nausea and vomiting.
- Diarrhea.
- Loss of appetite.
- Hair loss.
- Mouth sores.
- Rash.

Infrequent side effects:

- Jaundice (yellow skin or eyes).
- Joint and bone pain.
- Fever or chills.
- Pneumonia.
- Numbing or tingling in fingers, toes, or face.
- Headache.
- Seizures.

I told my daughter's oncologist how happy I was that she had not had any severe nausea after her first few doses of ARA-C. His only reply was, "It's cumulative." Within an hour, on the long drive home, she was vomiting constantly. We became ensnared in a two-hour traffic jam. She ran out of clean clothes, so for two hours, I repeatedly carried her to the side of the road, a naked, bald, 25-lb. four-year-old with tubing hanging from her chest, and supported her as she dry heaved. The people in the cars around us were in tears, and kept asking if there was anything they could do to help. I just focused on comforting her, and getting her home to that vial of ondansetron in our fridge.

Daunorubicin (Daw-no-ROO-bi-sin)

Also called: Daunomycin, DMN, DNR, Cerubidine, Rubidomycin.

How given: IV injection or infusion over several days.

How it works: An antibiotic which prevents DNA from forming, thus preventing the cancer cell from multiplying.

Precaution: Daunorubicin is a red color, and may turn urine red for a day or two after each dose. This is normal.

Common side effects:

- Immunosuppression (low blood cell counts).

- Nausea and vomiting.

- Hair loss.

- Mouth sores.

- Diarrhea.

Infrequent side effects:

- Burning pain and swelling if any drug leaks into skin.

- Heart damage at high doses (dose exceeding 300mg/m² for children more than two years of age, and 10 mg/kg in children less than two years of age).

- Shortness of breath.

- Skin rash.

My son didn't have any problems, but I sure worried about heart damage. I went to a conference and learned that the cut-off dose was below what he had on the protocol. I requested an echocardiogram, and his heart function was normal.

Dexamethasone (Dex-a-METH-a-sone)

Refer to Prednisone for information.

Doxorubicin (Dox-o-ROO-bi-sin)

Also called: Adriamycin.

How given: IV injection or infusion.

How it works: An antibiotic that prevents DNA from forming, thus preventing cancer cells from multiplying.

Precaution: Doxorubicin is a red color, and may turn urine red for a day or two after each dose. This is normal.

Common side effects:

- Immunosuppression (low blood cell counts).
- Nausea and vomiting.
- Hair loss.
- Mouth sores.

Infrequent side effects:

- Loss of appetite.
- Diarrhea.
- Burning pain and swelling if any drug leaks into skin.
- Heart damage at high doses.
- Shortness of breath.
- Fever and chills.
- Abdominal pains.
- Dark or bloody stools.
- Darkening or ridging of nails.

> The Adriamycin just burned right through my son. He never got mouth sores, but he sure had problems at the other end. They had him lie on his stomach with the heat lamp on his bare bottom. His whole bottom was blistered so badly that it looked like he'd been in a fire. They used to mix up what they called "Magic Butt Paste," and I'll never forget the

recipe: 1 tube nystatin cream, one tube desitin, and nystatin powder. It was like spackle that they would just slather on. He had a lot of gastrointestinal bleeding, too, so he was continuously getting platelets. That's when they decided that he wouldn't have the delayed intensification phase.

· · · · ·

Other than red urine and the expected low counts, hair loss, and nausea, Christine had no problems from her many doses of Adriamycin.

Etoposide (E-TOE-poe-side)

Also called: VP-16, VePesid.

How given: IV injection.

How it works: Prevents DNA from reproducing, and also causes death of dividing cells.

Common side effects:

- Immunosuppression (low blood cell counts).

- Loss of appetite.

- Nausea and vomiting.

- Hair loss.

- Fatigue.

Infrequent side effects:

- Decreased blood pressure.

- Shortness of breath or wheezing.

- Difficulty in walking.

- Numbness or tingling in fingers or toes.

- Fever or chills.

- Rash.

Hydroxyurea (Hi-DROX-ee-yoo-REE-ah)

Also called: Hydrea.

How given: Pills by mouth.

How it works: Action is not well-understood, but it is thought to work by stopping DNA production.

Common side effects:

• Immunosuppression (low blood cell counts).

Infrequent side effects:

• Nausea and vomiting.

• Loss of appetite.

• Fever and chills.

• Rashes.

• Drowsiness.

• Diarrhea.

• Convulsions.

• Headache or dizziness.

• Stomach pain.

• Confusion or hallucinations.

Mercaptopurine (Mer-kap-toe-PYOOR-een)

Also called: 6-MP, Purinethol.

How given: Pills by mouth.

How it works: An antimetabolite which replaces nutrients in the cancer cell, causing cell death.

Common side effects:

• Immunosuppression (low blood cell counts).

• Loss of appetite.

Infrequent side effects:

• Nausea and vomiting.

• Skin rashes.

• Jaundice (yellow skin or eyes).

• Liver damage.

Christine had no problems with the 6-MP other than low counts. She needed blood work every two weeks and we were constantly cutting her doses in half or stopping the drugs altogether until her ANC recovered.

Methotrexate (Meth-o-TREX-ate)

Also called: Mexate, MTX.

How given: Pills by mouth, IV, or intrathecal injection.

How it works: An antimetabolite which replaces folic acid in cells, preventing them from dividing. Children should not be given extra folic acid in vitamins or the methotrexate will not be effective.

Common side effects:

- Immunosuppression (low blood cell counts).
- Sun sensitivity.
- Diarrhea.
- Fatigue.
- Skin rashes.
- Headache, backache, spinal cord irritation (when given intrathecally).

Infrequent side effects:

- Mouth sores.
- Hair loss.
- Nausea and vomiting.
- Loss of appetite.
- Dry cough caused by lung damage.
- Chills and fever.
- Dizziness.
- Jaundice (yellow skin and eyes).
- Shortness of breath.
- Neurotoxicity which can cause learning disabilities.

My daughter had serious problems with rashes during maintenance. The doctors thought that she had developed an allergy to the weekly methotrexate. She often would be covered with rashes which looked like small, red circles with tan, flaky skin inside. They were extremely itchy and unattractive. We spent hundreds of dollars at the dermatologist trying various prescription remedies. None worked. In desperation, I went to our local herbalist and asked if she had anything totally nontoxic, which would help the rash but not affect her chemotherapy. She sold me a small tub of salve made from olive oil, vitamin E oil, and calendula flowers. We checked with her oncologist before using it. It totally cured the rash after two days, and worked each time that the rash reappeared. What a relief!

. . . . .

Two years into maintenance, Shawn started throwing up every Friday night after receiving his methotrexate. We started giving him ondansetron before every dose and continued through the weekend.

. . . . .

Carl was on an experimental IV high-dose methotrexate protocol funded through the National Institutes of Health. Side effects ranged from nausea and vomiting to diarrhea, sore bones, mood swings, and disorientation.

. . . . .

My son developed learning disabilities from his high-dose methotrexate protocol. He received tutoring through high school and is doing extremely well in college.

Prednisone (PRED-ni-sone) and Dexamethasone (Dex-a-METH-a-sone)

These two steroids are grouped together because they are closely related chemically and have similar action and side effects. Dexamethasone is given in high doses as a chemotherapy drug and in low doses to prevent nausea. To see the side effects of dexamethasone when it is used as an antinausea drug, look under "Drugs Given to Prevent Nausea."

Also called: Dexamethasone is also called Decadron.

How given: Pills by mouth, liquid by mouth.

How they work: Hormones which kill lymphocytes.

Precaution: Every parent interviewed described problems that their children had while on prednisone. The side effects ranged from very mild to severe, but were universal. At high doses, prednisone creates major behavioral problems in children, which gradually subside after the drug is stopped.

Common side effects:

- Mood changes.

- Increased appetite.

- Food obsessions.

- Increased thirst.

- Indigestion.

- Weight gain.

- Fluid retention.

- Round face and protruding belly.

- Sleeplessness.

- Nightmares.

- Nervous, restless, hyperactive.

- Loss of potassium.

- Hypersensitive to lights, sound, motion.

- Extreme irritability.

Infrequent side effects:

- Decreased or blurred vision.

- Seeing halos around lights.

- Increased sweating.

- Weakness with loss of muscle mass.

- Muscle cramps or pain.

- Swelling of feet or lower legs.

- High blood pressure.

- High blood sugar.

- Hallucinations.

- Aseptic necrosis (destruction of blood supply to bones).

Judson was a hyper, high-strung child who became extremely hyperactive when he was on prednisone. My recommendation for other parents dealing with this difficult side effect is to run—don't walk—to your nearest library or bookstore and get some books on hyperactive behavior in children. It is important that parents understand this problem and learn to deal with it in a loving way. Remember, too, that this side effect will go away when the prednisone is out of the child's system. Judd would be hyperactive for the entire two weeks, desiring to eat every 15 minutes or so, making noises constantly, itching all over, sleeping less, having a terrible temper, and losing his fine motor and concentration skills.

During this time he would develop bad behavior because as parents we could not parent him the way we would normally. A few days after his prednisone ended, we would become very firm and structured in our parenting, and he would return to his normal behavior patterns. My son has been in remission ten years, has never exhibited abnormal hyperactivity since ending chemotherapy, and is a well-adjusted teen and an excellent student.

*   *   *   *   *

Meagan is very emotionally labile after only two doses of prednisone. She is very frustrated, quick to anger, hits, screams. For those five days we try to stay home, and this helps to decrease the stimulation. We plot it out on the calendar in advance so that we can plan accordingly. I think the kids deserve some tender, loving care while taking prednisone. Of course, I don't allow the hitting, but I do try hard not to aggravate the situation when she is on prednisone. I can see how she is uncomfortable being out of control, but she just can't help it.

*   *   *   *   *

Prednisone sends Stephan into a whirlwind of emotions. Sometimes he seems especially happy, and the rest of the time he is in tears at the drop of a hat. We explained to Stephan that the pill can make him feel this way, and it's OK to tell us, "I'm grumpy and I need to be alone for awhile." He gets physical side effects, too. He takes prednisone five days a month, and, like clockwork, on day 6 he gets itchy, on day 7 he aches all over, on day 8 he has severe back, chest, arm, and leg pain, and on day 9 he starts to feel better.

*   *   *   *   *

Preston didn't act out while on prednisone; instead he became depressed and too compliant. He spent most of his time moodily cooking himself food and eating. We bought a second wardrobe of sweat pants with elastic waists so that he would be comfortable.

· · · · ·

Rachel had a dual personality on prednisone. She would be fine one minute and then fly into a rage. One time, she literally had an argument with herself. She asked to watch a tape, and then for twenty minutes she argued with herself over whether she should watch the tape. It was painful to watch.

· · · · ·

Prednisone and dexamethasone were the worst drugs for Katy. When she was on for a month straight, she hallucinated horrible things. She'd scream that boys were chasing her or that her heart had stopped beating. She'd sob that I was melting and would disappear. She'd dig her fingers into my arm begging me to help her. She sometimes did this all night, and nothing consoled her. She slept very little while taking prednisone. She would eat an entire loaf of bread, and always asked to have "butter spread on it like icing on a cake." She has never once said that since ending treatment.

· · · · ·

Jeremy never slept well when he was on prednisone. He had nightmares of doctors chasing him through the hospital halls. He had a lot of night sweats, and was hungry all night and day. He slept with a loaf of bread, and when we would go places, he always carried a can of Campbell's chicken soup and a can opener. He desperately needed to make sure that he would never be without food.

· · · · ·

Carrie Beth was both hungry and irritable when taking dexamethasone. I remember once at the Ronald McDonald house a staff member whom she really liked simply said, "Hello, Carrie Beth," and she started to scream. She ended up on the floor kicking and yelling.

· · · · ·

Jody just seemed a little high when on prednisone. He was crazy for food but didn't have any behavior problems. He had lots of energy.

· · · · ·

Prednisone caused "moon" face, swollen stomach, dark circles under his eyes, and vomiting. Considering Carl was only two-and-a-half when he was going through this, it was difficult to explain the side effects to him. The best we could do was make him as comfortable as possible, stay with him, and make sure he had the blankets and stuffed animals he really loved.

• • • • •

John began prednisone when he was fourteen months old, and he began to swell immediately. His moods would swing quickly from happy to sad but he continued to sleep through the night, and he remained a happy child.

6-Thioguanine (Thigh-oh-GWAN-neen)

Also called: 6-TG.

How given: Pills taken by mouth.

How it works: Antimetabolite that interferes with DNA to prevent cancer cell division.

Common side effects:

• Immunosuppression (low blood cell counts).

• Nausea and vomiting.

Infrequent side effects:

• Jaundice (yellow skin or eyes).

• Stomach pain.

• Loss of appetite.

• Mouth sores.

Vincristine (Vin-CRIS-teen)

Also called: Oncovin, VCR.

How given: Intravenously (IV).

How it works: Vincristine is an alkyloid derived from the periwinkle plant. It causes cells to stop dividing.

Note: The side effects of vincristine are most pronounced during induction and consolidation when it is given weekly. It is generally better tolerated during maintenance when it is given monthly.

Common side effects:

- Constipation.
- Pain in jaw, face, back, joints, bones; may be severe.
- Foot drop (child has trouble lifting front part of foot).
- Numbness, tingling, or pain in fingers and toes.
- Extreme weakness and loss of muscle mass.
- Blurred or double vision, drooping eyelids.
- Hair loss.
- Pain and blisters if drug leaks during administration.

Infrequent side effects:

- Loss of appetite, sometimes nausea and vomiting.
- Weight loss.
- Headaches, dizziness, light-headedness.
- Convulsions.
- Difficulty urinating.
- Rashes.
- Difficulty sleeping.
- Itchiness.

Most parents interviewed stated that their children had no difficulties when given vincristine. But some children did develop severe problems.

> *Erica (diagnosed age 1) once had a vincristine burn on her arm at the IV site. It was red when we went home from the clinic, but by the second day it was badly burned. She developed a blister as big as a half dollar, which left a bad scar. It hurt and was sensitive for a long time. She also developed severe foot drop (she could not lift up the front part of her foot) and fell a lot.*

• • • • •

Preston (diagnosed age 10) had an awful time from vincristine. He would develop cramping in his lower legs, and would just curl up in bed, in great pain. It would start a couple of days after he received the vincristine, and would last a week. I would massage his legs, use hot packs, and give him Tylenol. I would have to carry him into the clinic because he couldn't walk. I did some research, and discovered that when the bilirubin is high, the child can't excrete the vincristine and therefore the toxicity is increased. We lowered his vincristine dose and got him into physical therapy.

· · · · ·

Stephan is a very tough boy who rarely complains, but he cries when he gets the vincristine because it gives him severe bone pain. I insisted that he get a strong pain killer, and we give him Tylenol with codeine when the pain starts. It usually only lasts a few days.

· · · · ·

Vincristine incapacitated Katy. She couldn't walk, lift her head, open one eyelid. She had trouble swallowing and stayed in bed for weeks during induction and consolidation. I read the package insert for vincristine and discovered that the manufacturer recommended that vincristine be given at least 12 to 24 hours before asparaginase to minimize toxicity. Katy's protocol required that both drugs be give at the same time. I negotiated with the doctors and had her schedule changed so that these two drugs were given on different days. She was soon back on her feet, but still, after a year off treatment, she has generalized muscle weakness and problems with balance.

· · · · ·

Carl received vincristine by IV. On two occasions (when residents were doing the procedure) they inserted the needle on the top of his hands. Both times the medicine leaked and caused a chemo burn. He required several weeks of physical therapy to regain use of his hand. The other hand has a small burn scar. But both marks are a constant reminder of a very unpleasant time.

Antinausea drugs used during chemotherapy

Antinausea drugs make chemotherapy treatments more bearable, but can potentially cause side effects. The following sections list both common and infrequent side effects of antinausea drugs.

Antinausea Drug List

As with chemotherapy drugs, several different names can be used to refer to each of the antinausea drugs. The list below will help you find detailed information about each drug on the following pages.

NAME	LOOK UNDER
Ativan	Lorazepam
Compazine	Prochlorperazine
Decadron	Dexamethasone
Dexamethasone	Dexamethasone
Hexadrol	Dexamethasone
Lorazepam	Lorazepam
Ondansetron	Ondansetron
Prochlorperazine	Prochlorperazine
Zofran	Ondansetron

Dexamethasone (dex-a-METH-a-sown)

Also called: Decadron, Hexadrol.

How given: IV injection, usually given in combination with other antinausea drugs.

Common side effects;

Side effects are different than those experienced when it is given in high doses for long periods of time. When dexamethasone is used to treat nausea, side effects may be:

• Euphoria.

• Restlessness.

• Confusion.

Lorazepam (lor-AZ-a-pam)

Also called: Ativan.

How given: Pills by mouth, IV injection, intramuscular injection.

When given: This is a tranquilizer, which is generally given in combination with other antinausea drugs.

Common side effects:

• Drowsiness or sleepiness.

• Forgetfulness.

• Unsteadiness.

• Low blood pressure.

Ondansetron (on-DAN-se-tron)

Ondansetron is the most effective antinausea drug currently in use. First used in 1991, it can usually prevent nausea and vomiting from even the most nausca-inducing drugs, with minimal to no side effects.

Also called: Zofran.

How given: IV injection, liquid by mouth, pill.

When given: Usually 30 minutes prior to chemotherapy drugs, and every 4 to 8 hours until nausea ends, or in a higher dose once a day.

Infrequent side effects:

• Mild headache.

• Constipation.

Prochlorperazine (pro-chlor-PAIR-a-zeen)

Also called: Compazine.

How given: Pills or long-acting capsule by mouth, rectal suppository, intramuscular injection, IV injection.

When given: Used alone if only mild nausea is expected.

Common side effects:

- Drowsiness.
- Low blood pressure.
- Nervousness and restlessness.
- Tightness in the muscles of the jaw and face.

Drugs used to relieve pain

As with other drugs, drugs used for pain relief can be given by various methods and can cause side effects.

EMLA cream

How given: Applied to the skin and covered with an airtight dressing 1 to 2 hours before procedures such as spinal tap, bone marrow aspiration, or injection.

How it works: Emulsion which contains two anesthetics, lidocaine and prilocaine.

Note: May take longer than an hour to achieve effective anesthesia in dark-skinned individuals.

> We use EMLA for everything: finger pokes, accessing port, shots, spinal taps and bone marrows. I even let her sister use it for shots because it lets her get a bit of attention, too. Both of my children have sensitive skin which turns red when they pull off tape, so I cover the EMLA with saran wrap held in place with paper tape. I also fold back the edge of each piece of tape to make a pull tab so the kids don't have to peel each edge back from their skin.

Morphine

How given: IV, pill by mouth.

How it works: Narcotic derived from the opium plant.

Common side effects:

- Euphoria.
- Nausea and vomiting.

- Drowsiness.
- Constipation.

Infrequent side effects:

- Reduction in body temperature.
- Respiratory depression.
- Allergic reactions, including hives.
- Seizures.

Demerol

Also called: Meperidine.

How given: IV, injection, liquid by mouth, pill by mouth.

How it works: Narcotic similar to morphine.

Common side effects:

- Sedation.
- Constipation.

Infrequent side effects:

- Dizziness.
- Nausea and vomiting.
- Sweating.
- Rashes.
- Respiratory depression.
- Decreased blood pressure.
- Seizures.
- Headaches.
- Visual disturbances.

Adjunctive treatments

In recent years there has been increasing research on mind-body medicine and its effect on coping with the side effects of illness. Adjunctive therapies are those that can be expected to add something beneficial to the ongoing treatment program. For example, the use of imagery and hypnosis are widely used in established treatment programs to help children and teens prepare for or cope with medical procedures. Other helpful adjunctive therapies are relaxation, biofeedback, massage, visualization, acupuncture, meditation, aromatherapy, and prayer. Chapter 3, *Coping with Procedures*, discusses adjunctive therapies and how to obtain information about them.

Alternative treatments

Alternative treatments can be defined as those that are used in place of conventional medical treatment or, if used in addition to treatment, may have unknown or adverse effects. Sometimes these therapies are illegal or unavailable in the United States, and patients travel to other countries to obtain them.

Alternative treatments are usually based on word-of-mouth endorsements called anecdotal evidence. Medical therapy is based on scientific studies using large groups of patients. In treating leukemia, these large clinical trials have resulted in increases in survival rates from near zero thirty years ago to over seventy percent in 1997. Given the excellent results of current leukemia treatments, it is best to give nothing to your child unless it has been proven to be safe and will not interfere with ongoing therapy.

Many alternative treatments can help parents and children feel that they are aiding the healing process. Even with a good prognosis for your child, it is difficult to ignore the advice of friends and relatives extolling the virtues of various alternative treatments. Parents just want to help their children in every way possible; they often feel helpless, and they agonize over the pain and misery that their child endures for years while on conventional therapy. Conventional treatment is brutal, but it is usually effective.

It is extremely important that any therapy that involves ingestion or injection into the body (herbs, vitamins, special diets, enemas) only be given with the oncologist's knowledge. The involvement of the physician is necessary to prevent giving something to your child that could lessen the effectiveness of the conventional chemotherapy. For instance, folic acid (a B vitamin) replaces methotrexate in cells and reduces or eliminates its effectiveness, allowing cancer cells to flourish. The oncologist will be much more knowledgeable about these potential conflicts than a parent, herbalist, or health food store salesperson.

Despite the effectiveness of leukemia treatment, you may wish to research one or more alternatives. Parents of children who have relapsed one or more times often are drawn to exploring alternative treatments. To help you evaluate claims made about alternative treatments, here are several ways to collect enough information to make an educated judgment:

- Go to or call your local American Cancer Society's division office and ask for their information on the therapy you are considering. They have compiled information on many therapies describing the treatment, its known risks, side effects, opinion of the medical establishment, and any lawsuits that have been filed. They are planning to add an online database with information about many alternative treatments.

- Check with the National Institutes of Health's Office of Alternative Medicine to see if any scientific evidence exists on the treatment that interests you.

  NIH Office of Alternative Medicine
  Bethesda, MD 20892
  (301) 443-3170

- Ask specifically what this treatment is expected to do for your child; ask what is in it; ask what tests will be done to ascertain whether your child needs it and whether your child is benefiting from it.

- Collect and study all available objective literature on the treatment. Ask the alternative treatment providers if they have treated other children with leukemia, what results have been achieved, how these results have been documented, and where they have reported their results. Ask for the reports so that your doctor can review them.

- Talk with other people who have gone through the treatment. Inquire about the training and experience of the person administering the treatment. Be sure to find out how much the therapy costs, as your insurance company may not pay for alternative treatments.

- Beware of any practitioner who will give your child the alternative therapy only if you stop taking the child in for conventional treatments.

Take all the information you have gathered to your child's oncologist to discuss any positive or negative impact that it may have on your child's current medical treatment. Do not give any alternative treatment or over-the-counter drugs to your child in secret. Some treatments negate the effectiveness of chemotherapy while other substances, such as those containing aspirin or related compounds, can cause uncontrollable bleeding in children with low platelet counts.

If, after thorough investigation, you feel strongly in favor of using an alternative treatment in addition to conventional treatment and your child's oncologist adamantly opposes it, listen to his objections, and then go get a second opinion. It is important not to give your child something harmful; it is also important to have a physician who you can talk with and who treats you respectfully. You may need to change to another board certified oncologist if you have trouble discussing treatment options with the one you have. But remember, the child is the most important person here. Don't give the treatment in secret or your child may be the loser.

Resources

Organizations

The Health Resource, Inc.
564 Locust St.
Conway, AR 72032.
(501) 329-5272.

Company that will research and prepare a report on any medical issue, treatment plan, or alternative treatment. Fees depend on the service you request and the complexity of the topic.

Planetree Health Information Service
2040 Webster St.,
San Francisco, CA 94115.
(415) 923-3680

A nonprofit consumer-oriented resource for health information, including relaxation and visualization techniques. Write or call for a catalog and price list.

Reading for adults

Baker, Lynn, M.D. *You and Leukemia: A Day at a Time*. Philadelphia: W.B. Saunders Co, 1988. The section on chemotherapy describes many commonly used drugs in clear, easy-to-understand terms.

Bruning, Nancy. *Coping with Chemotherapy*. rev.ed. New York: Ballantine Books, 1993. Practical and comprehensive guide to the physical and emotional aspects of chemotherapy.

Leukemia Society of America. *Directory of Prescription Drug Patient Assistance Programs*. To obtain free copy, call 1-800-955-4LSA. Directory lists companies that provide prescription drugs to eligible patients either free or at minimal cost.

Leukemia Society of America. *Understanding Chemotherapy*. To obtain a free copy, call 1-800-955-4LSA. 36-page guide includes general information on side effects of chemotherapy and detailed information on drugs used to treat leukemia, lymphoma, and multiple myeloma.

McKay, Judith, R.N., and Nancee Hirano, R.N., M.S.N. *The Chemotherapy Survival Guide*. Oakland, CA: New Harbinger Publications, 1993. A very comforting, user-friendly guide to all aspects of chemotherapy treatment.

National Institutes of Health. *Chemotherapy & You: A Guide to Self-Help During Treatment*. NIH Publication # 91-1136. To obtain a free copy, call 1-800-4-CANCER. 64-page booklet includes answers to commonly asked questions about chemotherapy, its side effects, emotions while on chemotherapy, and nutrition.

National Institutes of Health. *Young People with Cancer: A Handbook for Parents*. NIH Publication No. 92-2378. To obtain free copy, call 1-800-4-CANCER. 85-page booklet covers chemotherapy, common health issues, side effects, medical procedures, and coping with cancer.

Adjunctive and alternative treatments

Cousins, Norman. *Anatomy of an Illness as Perceived by the Patient: Reflections on Healing and Regeneration*. New York: W.W. Norton & Co., 1979. Describes one man's tenacious fight to battle a crippling disease, relying on the power of his mind as well as a close relationship with his physician. Powerful and full of hope.

Cousins, Norman. *Head First: The Biology of Hope and the Healing Power of the Human Spirit*. New York: E.P. Dutton, 1989. After 25 years as editor of Saturday Review, Cousins spent a decade on the medical staff of UCLA researching the biological basis for hope. He presents the mounting volume of evidence that positive attitudes help combat disease. Also contains excellent information on enhancing the doctor/patient relationship.

Lerner, Michael. *Choices in Healing: Integrating the Best of Conventional and Complementary Approaches to Medicine*. Cambridge, MA: The MIT Press, 1994. Written by one of the country's leading authorities on complementary cancer treatments, *Choices in Healing* gives a comprehensive overview of both conventional and complementary approaches to cancer treatment, including nutritional therapies, physical therapies, psychological and spiritual approaches, traditional medicines from around the world, and methods for living with cancer. Compassionate and objective.

Monaco, Grace, J.D., and Saul Green, Ph.D. "Recognizing Deception in the Promotion of Untested and Unproven Medical Treatments." *New York State Journal of Medicine* 93 (2) 88-91. Describes some of the claims made by promoters of unproven remedies, provides examples, gives clear instructions on how to evaluate such claims, includes resource lists for places to gather information, and contains an extensive bibliography.

Tyler, Varro, Ph.D. *The Honest Herbal: A Sensible Guide to the Use of Herbs and Related Remedies*. Binghamton, New York: Haworth Press, 1993. Clearly explains the scientific evidence on the benefits and/or harmfulness of most common herb remedies.

Weil, Andrew, M.D. *Spontaneous Healing: How to Discover and Enhance Your Body's Natural Ability to Maintain and Heal Itself*. New York: Alfred A. Knopf, 1995. Written by a physician, this book describes the body's mechanisms for healing and ways people can optimize the functioning of their own systems through nutrition, environment, exercise, vitamins, supplements, and herbs. Discusses several popular alternative therapies, but states that childhood leukemia is one of the types of cancer for which current chemotherapy and radiation treatment are effective.

Magazine

Alternative Therapies in Health and Medicine. Bimonthly publication, whose editorial board includes practitioners of both mainstream and unconventional medicine. The journal's focus is on the integrated use of alternative therapies with conventional medicines. Subscription is $48/year. Call 1-800-345-8112.

Technical reading

Close, P., E. Burkey, et al. "A Prospective, Controlled Evalutation of Home Chemotherapy for Children with Cancer." *Pediatrics* 95:6 (June 1995): 896-900. Billed charges, loss of wages, out-of-pocket expenses, medical outcome, and quality of life of fourteen patients were compared for one course of chemotherapy in the hospital with an identical course at home. The study found that administration of selected chemotherapy at home resulted in lower billed charges, reduced expenses, reduced loss of income for parents, and a more satisfying lifestyle for patients and parents.

Drigan, Rosemary; Anthony Spirito, and Richard Gelber. "Behavioral Effects of Corticosteroids in Children with Acute Lymphoblastic Leukemia." *Medical and Pediatric Oncology* 20 (1992): 13-21. Technical journal article details the results of a study on children's emotional and behavioral problems while taking prednisone.

USP DI, Volume II, *Advice for the Patient: Drug Information in Lay Language.* United States Pharmacopeial Convention, Inc., 1995. Contains detailed drug information in non-medical language. Available in most libraries.

Physicians' Desk Reference. Oradell, New Jersey: Medical Economics Data, 1996. Reference issued yearly lists authoritative information on all FDA approved drugs. Technical language. Available at reference desk in most libraries.

Zoubek, A., M. Kronberger, et al. "Ondensetron in the Control of Chemotherapy-induced and Radiotherapy-induced Emesis in Children with Malignancies." *Anticancer Drugs* 4 Suppl 2 (December 1993): 17-21. The management of chemotherapy-induced nausea and emesis presents a major problem in children with cancer. This article presents a literature review on the use of ondansetron in children and provides recommendations on its use during chemotherapy and radiotherapy in pediatric oncology.

CHAPTER 11

Common Side Effects of Chemotherapy

The first wealth is health.

—Ralph Waldo Emerson

CHEMOTHERAPY DRUGS interfere with cancer cells' ability to grow or reproduce. Because rapidly dividing cells are more susceptible to chemotherapy drugs, cancer cells are severely affected. Unfortunately, healthy cells that multiply rapidly can be damaged as well. These normal cells include those of the bone marrow, mouth, stomach, intestines, hair follicles, and skin. This chapter explains the most common side effects of chemotherapy drugs, and explores ways to effectively deal with them. Chemotherapy side effects that prevent good nutrition are discussed in Chapter 14, *Nutrition*.

Hair loss

Chemotherapy drugs destroy not only cancer cells, but also normal cells that are produced at a rapid rate. Because hair follicle cells reproduce quickly, chemotherapy causes some or all body hair to fall out. The hair on the scalp, eyebrows, eyelashes, underarms, and pubic area may slowly thin out or may fall out in big clumps.

Hair regrowth usually starts one to three months after maintenance starts or intensive chemotherapy ends. The color and texture may be different from the original hair. Straight hair may regrow curly; blond hair may be brown. Toward the end of maintenance, some children's hair begins to thin out again.

The following suggestions for dealing with hair loss come from parents:

- When hair is thin or breaking, use a brush with very soft bristles.

- Avoid bleaches, permanents, curlers, blow dryers, or hair spray, as these may cause additional damage.

- If hair is thin, use a mild shampoo specifically designed for overtreated or damaged hair.

- A flannel receiving blanket placed on the pillow at night will help collect hair that is falling out.

- Recognize that hair loss is traumatic for all but the youngest children. It is especially hard on teenagers.

- Emphasize to your child that the hair loss is temporary, and, indeed, is a sign that the drugs are doing the job of destroying all rapidly dividing cells. Remind your child that the hair will grow back.

- Try to have your child meet children in maintenance or off therapy, so that they can see for themselves that hair will regrow soon.

- Allow your child or teen to choose a collection of hats, scarves, or cotton turbans to wear. These are tax-deductible medical expenses, and may be covered by insurance.

- To order several styles of reversible all cotton headwear for girls 7 to 12 and women, contact:

  Just In Time
  P.O. Box 27693
  Philadelphia, PA
  (215) 247-8777

- If your child expresses an interest in wearing a wig, take pictures of her hairstyle prior to hair loss. Also cut snippets of hair to take in to allow a good match of original color and texture. The cost of the wig may be covered by insurance if the doctor writes a prescription for a "wig prosthesis." This should include the medical reason for the wig such as "Alopecia due to cancer chemotherapy." To find a wig retailer, look in the yellow pages of your phone book under "Hair Replacements, Goods, and Supplies." The American Cancer Society (1-800-ACS-2345) and some local cancer service organizations offer free wigs in some areas. Another source for a free wig is:

  Hair Club for Kids sponsored by
  Hair Club for Men
  345 Hudson Street 12th Floor
  New York, NY 10016
  (212) 462-1400 ext. 3085

- Advocate that school-age children be permitted to wear hats or other head coverings to school.

- Separate your feelings about baldness from your child's feelings. Many parents rush out to buy wigs and hats without discussing with their child how he wants to deal with his baldness.

- Allow your child to choose whether to wear head coverings or not. Let it be okay to be bald.

Hair loss is quite variable for children being treated for leukemia. Some only lose part of their hair, some have hair that thins out, and some quickly lose every hair on their head.

> Preston never completely lost his hair, but it became extremely thin and wispy. When he was first diagnosed, a friend bought him a fly-fishing tying kit, and he became very good at tying flies. He even began selling them at a local fishing shop. When his hair began to fall out, we would gather it up and put it in a plastic bag. He started tying flies out of his hair, and they were displayed in the shop window as "Preston's Human Hair Flies." He was only 11, but the shop owner hired him to help around the shop. He became very popular with the clientele, because everyone wanted to meet the boy who tied flies from his own hair. He really turned losing his hair into something positive.

· · · · ·

> Three-year-old Christine's hair started to fall out within three weeks of starting chemo. She had beautiful curly hair, but she never talked about losing it, and I thought it didn't bother her. Occasionally she would wear a hat or the hood of a sweatshirt, but most of the time she went bald. One day, I learned how she really felt. We were talking about the different colors of hair in our family, and she began shouting, "I DON'T have brown hair! I'm bald, just like a baby."

· · · · ·

> The chemo greatly affected Meagan's hair. During maintenance, it came back in lush and curly, then after a few months it began falling out again. This was very upsetting. She hasn't gone completely bald again, but it remains very thin and unhealthy hair, while others in the same stage of treatment have beautiful hair back again.

· · · · ·

> Jeremy, four years old, was great. Once he was watching his brother in a T-ball game when the members of the other team started to point and laugh. One started shouting, "Look at that kid, he's fat and bald."

Jeremy just walked right up to him and said, "Do you know why I look this way? Because I have cancer and the chemo made my hair fall out." We bought him hats but he never wore them.

Cynthia Krumme wrote of her daughter's wig in *Having Leukemia Isn't So Bad*:

> *From January of 1984 to the summer of 1985, Catherine had either no hair or almost no hair. For the most part this did not bother her, although she did have some problems with one classmate who teased her about wearing her wig. We approached the teacher for help and ended up with Catherine initiating a discussion with the girl and telling her a bit about what she was experiencing. While the girls did not become best friends, the teasing about hair ceased. She wore the wig to school and discarded it the minute she got home, usually by pulling it off at the kitchen door and letting it fly across the counter top where it would land in a heap.*

Nausea and vomiting

The effects of anticancer drugs vary from person to person and dose to dose. A drug that makes one child violently ill often has no effect on other children. Some drugs produce no nausea until several doses have been given, while others cause nausea after a single dose. Because the effects of chemotherapy are so wildly variable, each child's treatment must be tailored to her individual needs. There is no relationship between the amount of nausea and the effectiveness of the medicine.

The following is a list of suggestions for helping children and teenagers cope with nausea and vomiting:

- Give your child antiemetic (antinausea) medications as prescribed. Do not skip any doses.

- Your child should wear loose clothing because it is both more comfortable and easier to remove if soiled.

- Parents should always have at least one change of clothes for their child in the car.

- Carry a bucket, towels, and baby wipes in the car in case of vomiting.

- Try to keep your child in a quiet, well-ventilated room after chemotherapy.

- Smells can trigger nausea. Try not to cook in the house when your child feels ill. If possible, open windows to provide plenty of fresh air.

- If your child is nauseated by smells, use a covered cup with a straw for liquids.

- Do not serve hot foods, as the odor can aggravate nausea.

- Serve dry foods such as toast, pretzels, or crackers in the morning or whenever the child is feeling nauseated.

- Serve several small meals rather than three large ones.

- Have the child keep his head elevated after eating. Lying flat can induce nausea.

- Provide plenty of clear liquids such as water, juice, Gatorade, or ginger ale.

- Avoid giving sweet, fried, or very spicy food. Instead, serve bland foods such as potatoes, cottage cheese, soup, or toast.

- Watch for any signs of dehydration. These include dry skin and mouth, sunken eyes, dizziness, and decreased urination. Call the physician if your child appears dehydrated.

- Use distractions such as TV, videos, music, games, or reading aloud to divert attention from nausea.

- After the child vomits, rinse his mouth with water or a mixture of water and lemon juice to remove the taste.

- If your child develops a metallic taste in her mouth, chewing gum or sucking on popsicles may help.

> Meagan has always had problems in every phase of treatment with stomachaches, especially in the morning. She will often vomit once and then be over it. She is frequently soothed with just rubbing her tummy or laying a hot towel on it.

If the various antinausea medications do not work well for your child, investigate the Relief Band. This wrist band gives an electrical stimulation (too faint to feel) to an acupuncture point in the wrist that affects the portion of the brain which controls nausea. After ten years of study, the band has been approved by the FDA. Information can be obtained from Maven Laboratories, 1-800-469-1518.

Low blood counts

Bone marrow, the spongy material which fills the inside of the bones, produces red cells, white cells, and platelets. Chemotherapy drugs destroy the cells inside the bone marrow and dramatically lower the number of cells circulating in the blood. Frequent blood tests are crucial in determining whether the child needs transfusions. Almost all children treated for leukemia require many transfusions of red cells and platelets. Transfusions of white cells are not effective. Consequently, when the number of infection-fighting white cells is low, the child is in danger of developing serious infections.

What is an ANC? (also called AGC)

The activities of families of children with leukemia revolve around the sick child's white count, specifically the absolute neutrophil count (ANC). This is sometimes called an absolute granulocyte count (AGC). The ANC (or AGC) provides an indication of the child's ability to fight infection.

When a child has blood drawn for a complete blood count (CBC), one section of the lab report will state the total white count and a "differential." This means that each type of white cell will be listed as a percentage of the total. For example:

White Blood Cells (WBC) — 1500

Neutrophils — 49% (also called polys or segs)

Bands   — 1% (also called stabs)

Basophils — 1% (also called basos)

Eosinophils — 1% (also called eos)

Lymphocytes — 38% (also called lymphs)

Monocytes — 10% (also called monos)

To calculate the ANC, add the percentages of neutrophils and bands, and multiply by the total WBC. Using the example above, the ANC is 49% + 1% = 50%. 50% of 1500 (.50 x 1500) = 750. The ANC is 750.

Erica ran a fever whenever her counts were low, but nothing ever grew in her cultures. They would hospitalize her for 48 hours as a precaution. She was never on a full dose of medicine because of her chronically low counts. She's two years off treatment now and doing great.

How to protect the child with a low ANC

Generally, an ANC over 1000 provides the child enough protective neutrophils to fight off exposure to infection due to bacteria and fungi. With an ANC this high, you can allow your child to attend all normal functions such as school, athletics, and parties. However, it is wise to keep close track of the pattern of the rise and fall of your child's ANC. If you know that the ANC is 1000, but is on the way down, it will affect your decision on what activities are appropriate. The following are general guidelines for children with low ANCs:

ANC 500-1000: Keep your child away from large groups of people.

ANC 200-500: Keep your child at home. Visitors should be healthy and should wash their hands.

ANC 0-200: Keep your child at home. It is better to allow no visitors, as your child is very susceptible to infection.

The following are parent suggestions to prevent and detect infections:

- Insist on frequent, thorough hand washing for every member of the family. Use antibacterial soap and warm water, lather well, and rub all portions of the hands. Children and parents need to wash before preparing meals, before eating, after playing outdoors, and after using the bathroom.

    We always had antibacterial baby wipes in our car. We washed Justin's hands, and our own, after going to any public places such as parks, museums, or restaurants. They can also be used to wipe off tables or high chairs at restaurants.

- Keep your child's diaper area and skin creases clean and dry.

- Make sure that all medical personnel at the hospital or doctor's office wash their hands before touching your child.

- When your child's ANC is low, make arrangements with your pediatrician to use a back entrance to the office to avoid exposure to sick kids in the waiting room. It sometimes helps to make all appointments for early morning so that your child can be seen in a room that hasn't had several sick children in it.

- Whenever your child needs a needle stick, make sure that the technician cleans your child's skin thoroughly with both betadine and alcohol.

- Protect your child if she has a low ANC.

    I asked our fellow what steps she suggested to protect Katy from infection. Her advice was simple, "Keep her home and away from people until maintenance." This is not the conventional wisdom, but I did it (her counts were so low most of the time that we had no choice anyway). For eight months, we really didn't go anywhere except the hospital, doctor's office, and walking on a nearby deserted beach. My husband showered and changed at work before coming home. When her ANC was below 200, which was often (it went down to 0 several times), we wore masks in the house if we had a cold. She's the only kid I have ever heard of who was never hospitalized except for scheduled treatments. We were just lucky.

- If your child gets a small cut, wash with soap and water, rinse with hydrogen peroxide, and cover with a clean Band-Aid.

- Take your child's temperature every day at the same time. When your child is ill, take his temperature every two to three hours.

- Do not take the temperature rectally (in the anus) or use rectal suppositories, as this may cause anal tears.

- Do not use a humidifier as the stagnant water can become a reservoir for contamination.

- If you have plants or flowers in the house, change the water daily.

- Apply sunscreen whenever your child plays outdoors. Children taking methotrexate are sun sensitive, and a bad sunburn can easily become a site for infection.

- Your child should not be vaccinated while on chemotherapy.

- Siblings should not be vaccinated with live polio virus (OPV). They should get the killed polio virus (IPV). Verify that your pediatrician is using the appropriate vaccine for the siblings.

Katy was diagnosed just a week after her younger sister Alison had been give the live polio vaccine. Because there was a small risk that Alison could infect any immunosuppressed child with polio, we were not allowed to stay on the cancer floor of the hospital.

- If your child's ANC is low, an infected site may not become red or painful.

  My daughter kept getting ear infections while on chemo. They would find them during routine exams. I felt guilty because she never told me her ears were hurting. I told her doctor that I was worried because she didn't complain of pain, and he reassured me by telling me that she probably felt no pain because she didn't have enough white cells to cause swelling inside her ear.

  · · · · ·

  Shawn had continual ear infections while on treatment. He had two sets of tubes surgically implanted while on chemo.

- Never give aspirin for fever. It may interfere with blood clotting. If your child has a fever, call the doctor before giving any medication.

- Call the doctor if any of the following symptoms appear: fever above 101° F, chills, cough, shortness of breath, sore throat, severe diarrhea, bloody urine or stool, and pain or burning while urinating.

  Whenever my daughter (diagnosed when 1 year old) was on antibiotics (frequently), she developed a vaginal yeast infection. It was very painful for her and a nightmare for me.

  · · · · ·

  My son's big toes became large and red from ingrown toenails while on treatment. He had several surgeries to remove the corners of each nail to prevent infection. That was several years ago, and his toes look bad but are not painful.

Two common, but serious, infections that plague children during treatment for leukemia are pneumonia and chicken pox.

Pneumonia

Pneumonia is inflammation of the lungs caused primarily by bacteria or viruses. The symptoms of pneumonia are rapid breathing, chills, fever, chest pain, cough, and bloody sputum. Children with low blood counts can rapidly develop a fatal infection, and must be treated quickly and aggressively. The following are three experiences from veteran parents whose children survived pneumonia.

My son received his high-dose methotrexate and vincristine injection just days before he was scheduled to go to the American Cancer Society's camp. His ANC was 1200 and he looked so sick, but he begged to go and I let him. It was early in his treatment and I didn't realize the pattern of his blood counts. They called me from camp on Friday to say he had a temperature of 103° and needed to go to the hospital. He was very weak and feverish; his WBC was 140, and his ANC was 0. Both lungs were full of pneumonia. I was furious at the doctor for giving him permission to go to camp and at myself for not paying closer attention to how quickly his counts dropped. They started him on five different antibiotics, and his fever went up to 106° that night. We didn't know if he would live or die. He started to gradually improve the next morning and was completely recovered in a week.

• • • • •

At the beginning of interim maintenance, Justin developed a fever. His oncologist said to give him Tylenol and call if it didn't go down. The next day he was breathing faster and his little hands and feet were turning purple. We rushed him to the hospital, and the chest x-rays showed pneumonia in both lungs. He rapidly deteriorated over the next 48 hours, so they tried an experimental constant flow ventilator which had only been used on premature infants. It was the last-ditch effort to save his life. He gradually improved. He spent a total of five months in the hospital, four more months on a portable ventilator at home with full-time nursing care, and he breathed through his tracheostomy until he completed his treatment two years later. It was a miracle.

• • • • •

Erica complained that her back hurt for two days. Then she woke up in the night crying, and she couldn't move because it hurt her too badly. She was blazing with fever, and screamed if I touched her. Her x-ray showed that her left lung was half full of fluid. They put her on antibiotics, and within 24 hours she was on the mend.

Chicken pox

Chicken pox is a common childhood disease caused by a type of herpes virus called varicella zoster. The symptoms are headache, fever, and malaise, rapidly followed by eruptions of pimple-like red bumps. The bumps typically start on the stomach, chest, or back. They rapidly develop into blister-like sores which break open, then scab over in three to five days. Any contact with the sores can spread the disease.

Chicken pox can be a fatal disease for immunosuppressed children, so extreme care must be taken to prevent exposure. It will be necessary to educate all teachers and friends to be vigilant in reporting any outbreaks. The child can then be kept home from school or preschool until the outbreak is over.

If an immunosuppressed child is exposed to chicken pox, call the doctor immediately. If the doctor is able to administer a shot called VZIG (Varicella Zoster Immune Globin) within 72 hours of exposure, it may prevent the disease from occurring or minimize its effects.

> We knew when Jeremy was exposed, so he was able to get VZIG. He did get chicken pox, but only developed a few spots. He didn't get sick; he got bored. He spent two weeks in the hospital in isolation. We asked for a pass, and we were able to go outside for some fresh air between doses of acyclovir.

If a child develops chicken pox while on chemotherapy, the current treatment is a five-to-ten-day hospitalization or, if possible, home therapy for IV administration of acyclovir, a potent antiviral medication. This drug has dramatically lowered the complication rate of chicken pox.

> Kristin broke out with chicken pox on the 4th of July weekend. Our hospital room was the best seat in the house for watching the city fireworks. She did get covered with pox, though, from the soles of her feet to the very top of her scalp. We'd just give her gauze pads soaked in calamine lotion and let her hermetically seal herself. They kept her in the hospital for six days of IV acyclovir, then she was at home on the pump (a small computerized machine that will administer the drug in small amounts for several hours) for four more days of acyclovir. She had no complications.

A child who has already had chicken pox may develop herpes zoster (shingles). If your child develops eruptions of vesicles similar to chicken pox which are in lines (along nerves), call the doctor. The treatment for shingles is identical to that for chicken pox.

> Kristin also got a herpes zoster infection, this time on Thanksgiving. It looked like a mild case of chicken pox, limited to her upper right arm, her upper right chest, and her right leg. They kept her overnight on IV acyclovir and then let her go home for nine more days on the pump.

Chicken pox can be transmitted through the air or by touch. Exposure is considered to have occurred if a child is in direct contact or in a room for as little as ten minutes with an infected person. If your child has never had chicken pox, it is better to take him to beaches or parks rather than indoor play areas.

Untreated chicken pox or shingles can result in life-threatening complications including pneumonia, hepatitis, and encephalitis. Parents must make every effort to prevent exposure and be vigilant in watching for signs of the diseases while their child is on treatment.

An immunization for chicken pox has been developed and is likely to be given to children with leukemia in the near future.

Can pets transmit diseases?

If you already have a pet, several precautions need to be taken in order to prevent transmission of disease, worms, or infection to a child with a low ANC.

- Make sure that the animal is vaccinated against all possible diseases.
- Have pets checked for worms as soon as possible after your child is diagnosed, and then every year thereafter (more often for puppies).
- Do not let pets eat off plates, or lick your child's face.
- Keep children away from the cat litter box and any animal feces outdoors.
- Have children wash hands after playing with the pet.
- Make sure that your pet has no ticks or fleas.

- If you have a pet that bites or scratches, consider finding another home for it. On the other hand, if you have a gentle, well-loved pet, do not give it up.

> *I think parents should know that you should not automatically get rid of your dog because your child has a low ANC. We went through a small crisis trying to decide whether to give away our large but beloved mongrel. The doctors wouldn't really give us a straight answer, but a parent in the support group said, "DO NOT get rid of your dog. Your son will need that dog's love and company in the years ahead." She was right. The dog was a tremendous comfort to our son.*

If your child wants to buy a pet while undergoing treatment for leukemia, here are some suggestions:

- Do not get a puppy. All puppies bite while teething, increasing the chance that your child may contract an infection.

- Do not get a cat because of the danger of toxoplasmosis.

- Do not get a parrot or parakeet as these species can transmit psittacosis.

- Do not get a turtle as they sometimes carry salmonella.

- Avoid buying any animal that is likely to bite or scratch.

If you have any concerns or questions about pets you already own or are thinking of purchasing, ask your oncologist for advice.

Diarrhea

Chemotherapy destroys cancer cells, as well as any cells that are produced at a rapid rate such as those that line the mouth, stomach, and intestines. This damage can cause diarrhea, ranging from mild (frequent, soft stools) to severe (copious quantities of liquid stool). Diarrhea during chemotherapy can also be caused by some antinausea drugs or intestinal infections. After chemotherapy ends and immune function returns to normal, the lining of the digestive tract heals and the diarrhea ends.

The following suggestions for coping with diarrhea come from parents:

- Do not give any over-the-counter drug to your child without approval from the doctor. He may want to test your child's stool for infection prior to treating the diarrhea. Frequently recommended drugs for diarrhea are Kaopectate, Lomotil, or Immodium.

- It is very important that your child drinks plenty of liquids. This will not increase the diarrhea, but will replace the fluids lost.

   My three-year-old had stopped drinking from bottles months before her diagnosis. When she first began her intensive chemotherapy, she had uncontrollable, frequent diarrhea. Liquid would just gush out without warning. It was hard for her to drink from a cup, so one night she said in a small voice, "Mommy, would it be okay if I drank from a bottle again?" I said, "Of course, honey." It was a great comfort to her, and she took in a lot more fluids that way.

- Hot or cold liquids can increase intestinal contractions, so serve plenty of room-temperature clear liquids or mild juices such as water, Gatorade, ginger ale, peach juice, or apricot juice.

- Diarrhea depletes the body's supply of potassium. Provide foods high in potassium such as bananas, oranges, baked or mashed potatoes without the skin, broccoli, halibut, mushrooms, asparagus, tomato juice, and milk (if tolerated).

- Low potassium can cause irregular heartbeats and leg cramps. If these occur, call the doctor.

- Do not serve greasy, fatty, spicy, or sweet foods.

- Do not serve roughage such as bran, fruits (dried or fresh), nuts, beans, or raw vegetables.

- Do serve bland, low-fiber foods such as bananas, white rice, noodles, applesauce, unbuttered white toast, creamed cereals, cottage cheese, fish, and chicken or turkey without the skin.

   In the middle of maintenance, Brent had severe diarrhea for a week. He had large amounts of liquid stools twenty times a day. I felt so sorry for him. The doctor cultured a stool specimen, but they never identified a cause. It cleared up after a week of the BRAT diet (bananas, rice, applesauce, toast). He had a problem with diarrhea almost weekly throughout his treatment.

- Keep a record of the number of bowel movements and their volume to keep the doctor informed. Call the doctor if you notice any blood in the stool, or if your child has any signs of dehydration such as dry skin, dry mouth, sunken eyes, decreased urination, or dizziness.

- Keep the area around the anus clean and dry. Wash with warm water and mild soap after every bowel movement. Pat dry gently.

- If the anus is sore, check with the doctor before using any non-prescription medicine. She may recommend using Desitin or A&D ointment after each bowel movement.

> *While taking ARA-C my daughter had a terribly sore rectum, which was a big problem. It hurt to have bowel movements, she'd cry and have to squeeze our hands to go, then the urine would run back and burn. She was very itchy. We carried around bags with Q-tips and every known brand of rectal ointment-A&D, Preparation H, Desitin, Benadryl. Thank goodness this cleared up quickly on maintenance.*

Constipation

Constipation means a decrease in the normal number of bowel movements. There are many reasons that constipation occurs on chemotherapy. Some drugs, such as vincristine, slow the movement of the stool through the intestines resulting in constipation. Pain medication, decreased activity, decreased eating and drinking, and vomiting can all affect the normal rhythm of the intestine. When movement through the intestine slows, stools become hard and dry.

The following are parents' suggestions for preventing and helping constipation:

- To prevent constipation, encourage your child to be as physically active as possible.

- Encourage your child to drink 8 to 10 glasses of liquid a day. Prune juice is especially helpful.

- Prepare high-fiber foods such as raw vegetables, beans, bran, whole wheat breads, whole grain cereals, dried fruits (especially prunes, dates, and raisins), and nuts.

- Check with the doctor prior to using any medications for constipation. He may recommend a stool softener like colace. If the doctor suggests liquid ducosate, be aware that it tastes horrible. Metamucil or citrucel increase the volume of the stool which stimulates the intestine. Milk of magnesia or magnesium citrate help the stool to retain fluid and remain soft.

- Do not give enemas or rectal suppositories. These can cause anal tears which can be dangerous for a child with a weakened immune system.

- When your child feels the need to have a bowel movement, sipping a warm drink can help.

> My four-year-old daughter either had diarrhea or severe constipation for the entire eight months of intensive treatment. Her bowel habits returned to normal during maintenance. When constipated, she would just sob and try to hold it in. This made her stool even harder and more painful. One time she cried, "Why is my anus round and my poop square?" We ended up just putting her in a warm bathtub, gave her warm drinks, and let her go in the bathtub. We had to scrub the bathtub frequently, but it seemed much less painful for her.

Fatigue, weakness, and loss of coordination

Fatigue is a feeling of weariness, which is an almost universal side effect of treatment for cancer. General weakness and loss of coordination, while different from fatigue, are caused by many of the same things, and are treated the same way. Fatigue and weakness may be constant throughout therapy, or intermittent. They can be minor annoyances or totally debilitating. Many parents worry that if fatigue is present, so is the cancer, but this is not the case. Fatigue, weakness, and loss of coordination can be caused by one, or a combination, of the following things:

- Your child's body working overtime to heal tissues damaged by treatment and to rid itself of dead and dying cancer cells.

- Medications to treat nausea or pain.

- Mineral imbalances caused by chemotherapy, diarrhea, or vomiting.

- Infection.

- Emotional factors such as anxiety, fear, sadness, depression, or frustration.

- Malnutrition caused by nausea, vomiting, loss of appetite, or taste aversions.

- Anemia (low red cell count).

- Disruption of normal sleep patterns (common when hospitalized or when taking prednisone).

The following suggestions come from parents:

- Make sure that your child gets plenty of rest. Naps or quiet times spaced throughout the day help.

    Erica took a two-and-a-half hour nap every afternoon throughout therapy. She's four now and off treatment, but her endurance is low and she still tires easily.

- Limit visitors if your child is weak or fatigued.

    While in the hospital, my daughter was very weak. She had too many visitors, yet didn't want to hurt anyone's feelings. We worked out a signal that solved the problem. When she was too tired to continue a visit, she would place a damp washcloth on her forehead. I would then politely end the visit.

- Serve your child well-balanced meals and snacks.

- Parents and children should try to avoid physical or emotional stress.

- Encourage child to pursue hobbies or interests if able. For example, if your child is too weak to play on his athletic team, let him go to cheer the team on.

    My four-year-old daughter wanted desperately to be in the annual kid's parade in our town. She could barely stand, much less march in a parade. So I put her in a big red wagon lined with blankets, and pulled her the entire way. I think she got more cheers than the floats!

- Prioritize activities. Help your child make a list of what he wants to accomplish, with number one being the most important. If he feels strongly that he wants to attend a certain activity, and you think he may run out of energy, throw a wheelchair or stroller into the car and go.

- Encourage your child to attend a kid's support group, and go to the parent group yourself. Seeing that others have the same problems and talking about how you are feeling can lighten the load.

Many children breeze through the low- or average-risk protocols for leukemia without fatigue or weakness while other children are not so lucky. The following are two typical stories.

Before Brent was diagnosed at age six, he was exceptionally well coordinated and a very fast runner. During treatment, he slowed down to about average. He played soccer and T-ball throughout, and was very competitive.

· · · · ·

Jeremy has had some major, persistent problems with weakness and loss of coordination. When he was nine years old, a year off therapy, he still could not catch a ball. When he ran, he was like a robot, and the trunk of his body stayed straight. Some kids made fun of him, and he got very frustrated with himself. He had five years of physical therapy, and now, three years off chemo, his skills have improved, but he still has to work harder than the other kids. We put him into martial arts in hopes of further increasing his motor skills and his confidence.

Bed wetting

Bed wetting, although infrequent, can be a very upsetting side effect of chemotherapy. Some drugs increase thirst while others disrupt normal sleep patterns, both of which can make bed wetting more likely. When the bed wetting is caused by a specific drug, time will cure the problem. Once the drug is no longer necessary, the bed wetting will stop.

There are also psychological reasons for bed wetting during chemotherapy. The trauma of the treatment for cancer causes many children to regress to earlier behaviors such as thumb sucking, baby talk, temper tantrums, and bed wetting. Punishment for this type of bed wetting only adds to the child's trauma and rarely solves the problem. The following are veteran parents' suggestions:

- Double sheet the bed. Put down one plastic liner with fitted and flat sheet, then put on top another plastic liner with fitted and flat sheet. During the night, simply pull off the top sheets and plastic, and there are fresh sheets below.

- Keep a pile of extra-large or beach towels next to the bed. Cover the wet spot with towels, and save the bed change for the morning.

- Give the last drink two hours before bedtime, to allow the child's bladder to totally empty right before bed.

- Change sleeping arrangements.

Prednisone caused my child to have nightmares and frequent bed wetting. I felt if she could sleep through the night the bed wetting might stop. I told her she could sleep with me for the month that she was on prednisone, but that after that she would move back into her own bed. It calmed her to sleep with me. The nightmares and bed wetting decreased, and she moved back into her own bed without complaint when the time came.

- Adopt an attitude that lets the child know that bed wetting is "no big deal." There should be no shaming or punishment.

- If the child is extremely distressed by his bed wetting, ask him if he wants you to set the alarm for the middle of the night in order to help him get up to go the bathroom.

- Give extra love and reassurance.

When my daughter started bed wetting, I didn't think it was the drugs. I thought long and hard about any additional worries that she might have, and I realized that because her dad had emotionally with-drawn from her during her illness, she might be worried that I would do the same. So I told her one night, "You know, I just realized that every day I tell you how much I love you. But I've never told you that no matter how hard life gets and no matter how mad we get at each other I will always love you. I love you now as a child, I will love you as a teen-ager, and I will love you when you are all grown up." She started to sob and hugged and hugged me. Now I say every night, "I love you tonight and I'll love you forever." She has never wet the bed again.

· · · · ·

My teenaged son wet the bed whenever he was given antinausea medicine prior to high doses of chemotherapy. He was so embarrassed. I stayed with him every night at the hospital. He was so groggy that even if he woke up in time, I had to help him out of bed, and support him while he stood, half asleep, to use the urinal.

· · · · ·

My son wet the bed before, during, and after the three years of his treatment for ALL. We just kept him in diapers at night. He would abso-lutely flood the bed while on prednisone. After he completed treatment, they put him on a drug called DDAVP to help cure the bed wetting.

Dental problems

Both radiation and chemotherapy can cause changes in the mouth and teeth. Awareness of the potential problems coupled with good preventative care can help your child be more comfortable during treatment.

Some anticancer drugs and radiation can cause changes in children's ability to salivate. Plaque may build up rapidly on your child's teeth, increasing the chance for both cavities and gum infections. Take your child to the dentist for cleaning and check-up every three to four months, as long as his ANC is above $500/\text{mm}^3$ and platelet count above $20,000/\text{mm}^3$. If your child has a central venous catheter (Hickman or Port), he should be given antibiotics before and after each visit to the dentist. Ask your dentist to refer to the current issue of the *Pediatric Dentistry Reference Manual* to formulate a dental plan.

Get recommendations from your child's oncologist and dentist for advice on teeth care when counts are very low. Often parents are advised to use a sponge or damp gauze to gently wipe off their child's teeth after meals instead of brushing.

> *My daughter had problems with thick yellow saliva during the entire time she was treated. It coated her teeth and formed a lot of plaque. I brought her to an excellent pediatric dentist every three months to have the plaque removed. She took antibiotics half an hour before treatment and then again six hours afterward. He also put sealants on all of her molars and, even though there were many weeks when her teeth could not be brushed, she never got a cavity.*

Some parents also report delays in the arrival of their child's permanent teeth.

> *We delayed getting my son's braces until after he completed his treatment. His orthodontist pointed out that two of his upper teeth never descended and would have to be surgically uncovered. I would not let him take any x-rays, so he sent me to an oral surgeon. I asked the surgeon if he could locate the teeth without x-rays, and he said yes. The oral surgeon removed the skin covering the two teeth, and the orthodontist banded them and attached a wire. He was able to gradually pull the teeth back into their proper position.*

For additional information on dental problems, refer to Chapter 18, *End of Treatment and Beyond.*

Mouth and throat sores

The mouth and throat are lined with cells which divide rapidly and can be severely damaged by chemotherapy drugs. This is more common for children on very intensive protocols and those having bone marrow transplants. The sores are very painful and can prevent eating and drinking. Check your child's mouth periodically for sores, and if any are present ask advice from the oncologist. Some parent suggestions are:

• To prevent infection, the mouth needs to be kept as clean and free of bacteria as possible. After eating, have your child gently brush teeth, gums, and tongue with a soft, clean toothbrush.

• If your child is old enough, have her rinse her mouth several times a day with salt water rinse. Recipe: 1/2 teaspoon salt, 1/2 teaspoon baking soda, 1 cup warm sterile water (water that has been boiled then brought back to room temperature).

• Serve bland food, meals put through the blender, or baby food.

• Use a straw with drinks or blender-processed food.

> *Preston got bad mouth sores every time he was on high-dose methotrexate. He could not swallow, but we were supposed to be forcing fluids to flush the drugs out. The only thing that felt good on his throat was guava nectar. It was very expensive and hard to find, and he would drink several quarts a day. Unfortunately, my daughter and husband both developed a liking for it, too. At one point we cornered the market on guava nectar at three grocery stores in our neighborhood.*

• There are several prescription products available to treat mouth sores. One common product is called "Magic Mouthwash" containing equal parts of Benadryl, Nystatin, Maalox, and viscous Xylocaine. Some formulations add dexamethasone. If your child has painful mouth sores, ask the oncologist for a prescription.

> *Soon after my daughter's diagnosis, I noticed that one precious little boy across the hall seemed very ill. I asked one of the residents what was happening, and she said that he was on a morphine drip for pain from severe mouth sores. I asked her if my daughter would get similar sores, and she replied that some do and some don't. I said, "Is there anything that can prevent them?" She said they used nystatin mouth rinses after the kids got sores, but that some doctors thought that nystatin could be used to prevent them as well. I asked her to order some for us. I rinsed*

my daughter's mouth four times a day with it, she never developed a single sore, and she was on a high-risk protocol. It may have been coincidence, but it was one less problem for us to deal with.

Changes in taste and smell

Chemotherapy can cause changes in the tastebuds, altering the brain's perception of how food tastes. Meats often taste bitter, and sweets can taste unpleasant. Even foods that children crave taste bad. Coupled with altered taste, the sense of smell is also impacted by chemotherapy. The sense of smell can be heightened so that smells which other family members are unaware of can cause nausea in a child on chemotherapy.

Both the sense of smell and taste can take months to return to normal after chemotherapy ends.

> *Once Katy begged me to make her my special double chocolate sour cream cake. Surprisingly, it smelled really good to her as it baked. She took a big bite, spit it out all over the table, and ran back to her room sobbing. She cried for a long time. She told me later that it had tasted "bitter and horrible."*

Skin and nail problems

Minor skin problems are frequent while on chemotherapy. The most common problems are rashes, redness, itching, peeling, dry skin, and acne. The following are suggestions for preventing and treating skin problems:

- Avoid hot showers or baths as these can dry the skin.
- Use moisturizing soap such as Basic or Avena.
- Apply a water-based moisturizer after bathing.
- Avoid scratchy materials such as wool. Your child will feel more comfortable in loose, cotton clothing.
- Have your child use sunscreen with a sun protection factor of at least SPF15.
- If your child is bald, and especially if she has had cranial radiation, insist on head coverings or sunscreen every time she goes outdoors.
- Buy your child lip gloss with sunscreen.

- If your child has chemotherapy drugs injected into the veins (rather than a central catheter), you may notice a darkening along the vein. This will fade after chemotherapy ends.

- Skin and underlying tissues can be damaged or destroyed by drugs which leak out of a vein. If your child feels a stinging or burning sensation, or you notice swelling at the IV site, call a nurse immediately.

- Rubbing cornstarch on itchy skin is often soothing.

- Call the doctor anytime your child gets a severe rash or is very itchy. Scratching rashes can cause infections, so you need to get medications to control the itching.

Chemotherapy affects the growing portion of nails located under the cuticle. After chemotherapy, you may notice a white band or ridge across the nail as it grows out. These brittle bands are sometimes elevated and feel bumpy. As the white ridge grows out toward the end of the finger, the nail may break. Keeping your child's fingernails trimmed can help prevent breakage.

Learning disabilities

Some children who have been treated for leukemia are at risk of developing learning disabilities as a consequence of their treatment. Those at highest risk are: children under five years old who receive both cranial radiation and intrathecal methotrexate, children who were on a high-dose methotrexate protocol, and young children who are given significant dosages of intrathecal methotrexate. There is considerable research on the types of learning difficulties exhibited by these children. This information will be covered fully in Chapter 15, .

Eating problems

Most children have major nutritional problems while on chemotherapy. Chapter 14, *Nutrition*, is devoted to explaining eating problems such as anorexia (lack of appetite), food aversions, over-eating, and the myriad other problems induced by chemotherapy and radiation.

Resources

Reading for adults

Dodd, Marylin J., R.N. Ph.D. *Managing the Side Effects of Chemotherapy and Radiation Therapy: A Guide for Nurses and Patients.* New York: Prentice Hall Press, 1987. This book contains thorough explanations of possible side effects of chemotherapy and radiation and suggestions for managing them.

National Institutes of Health. *Chemotherapy and You.* To obtain free copy, call 1-800-4-CANCER and ask for Publication Number 92-1136.

McKay, Judith, R.N., and Nancee Hirano, R.N., M.S.N. *The Chemotherapy Survival Guide.* Oakland, CA: New Harbinger Publications, Inc. 1993. A very comforting, user friendly guide to all aspects of chemotherapy treatment.

Baker, Lynn S., M.D. *You and Leukemia: A Day at a Time.* Philadelphia, PA: W.B. Saunders Co. 1988. The section on chemotherapy and side effects describes many commonly used drugs in clear, easy-to-understand terms.

Technical reading

Berkowitz, Robert J., D.D.S., G. A. Feretti, D.D.S., and J. H. Berg, D.D.S. "Dental Management of Children with Cancer." *Pediatric Annals* 17:11 (November 1988). Discusses the effect of chemotherapeutic drugs and radiation on the mouth and teeth, infections, hemorrhage, and effects of bone marrow transplantation. Also contains a section on prevention of oral complications and long-term side effects of treatment.

Buda, K., and D. G. Tubergen. "The Frequency and Consequences of Varicella Exposure and Varicella Infection in Children Receiving Maintenance Therapy for Acute Lymphoblastic Leukemia." *Journal of Pediatric Oncology/Hematology* 18:2 (May 1996): 106-12. Retrospectively analyzed 472 children receiving maintenance therapy. Of these, 60 contracted varicella with medical costs averaging $7,450 per case. Article proposed using varicella vaccine after six months of maintenance therapy to save medical charges, prevent morbidity and mortality, prevent hospitalizations and work and school disruptions.

Cheatham, B. D., and R. J. Henry. "A Dental Complication Involving Pseudomonas During Chemotherapy for Acute Lymphoblastic Leukemia." *Journal of Clinical Pediatric Dentistry* 18:3 (Spring 1994): 215-7. This article describes the case of an eleven-year-old girl who developed endodontic failure and Pseudomonas infection during induction chemotherapy. These complications affected the child's medical management and demonstrate the importance of dental consultation for oncolgy patients.

Video

My Hair's Falling Out...Am I Still Pretty? 1992. 22 minutes. Distributed by Necessary Pictures, 7 West 20th St., Suite 2-F, New York, NY 10011. 1-800-221-3170, (212) 675-1809. Purchase: $25, families; $79, professionals. Moving film about two children with cancer who are hospital roommates. Using dance, animation, and music, the video explores the feelings of the patients, families, and friends while it sensitively informs and educates the viewers about the emotional and physical aspects of childhood cancer. The child with leukemia grows up to become a doctor, while her roommate with a tumor dies. For school-age children and their families.

Radiation

Radiation is used to kill blasts. It is very effective, and it kills blasts by the thousands. Radiation is used in the head (Doctors call the head a cranium) and the spinal cord. Radiation comes out of a big machine. It will travel right through the air and into the body. It makes the hair fall out.

—Matthew Krumme, ten years old
Having Leukemia Isn't So Bad.
Of Course It Wouldn't Be My First Choice.

FOR CERTAIN CHILDREN with high-risk leukemia, radiation is a life-saving therapy that has dramatically improved survival rates. However, radiation therapy to the brain, spine, or testes can cause mild, short-term side effects, and sometimes permanent damage that may not be evident until months or years after treatment. The benefits and risks of treatment with radiation must be carefully weighed by both doctors and parents.

This chapter will help parents understand what radiation is, when and how it is used, and what side effects could develop. It will dispel myths and alleviate concerns by clearly explaining what the parent and child can expect from radiation treatment.

What is radiation?

Radiation treatment, also called irradiation or radiotherapy, is the use of high-energy x-rays to kill cancer cells. A large machine called a linear accelerator directs x-rays to the precise portion of the body needing treatment. The treatment is usually given in small doses measured in units called centigrays or rads (short for radiation absorbed dose). Radiation is usually given every day for ten to sixteen days, excluding weekends. The daily doses allow smaller amounts of radiation to be used, lessening side effects and allowing any damaged normal cells to heal.

Children do not become radioactive from these treatments.

Who needs radiation treatment?

Because of the possibility of long-term side effects from treating children with radiation, only 10 to 12 percent of children with leukemia receive radiation. Some of the children for whom radiation is prescribed are:

- Children who have leukemia blasts in their central nervous system (CNS) at diagnosis.

- Children who are determined to be at high-risk of relapse in the central nervous system, for example, those with white counts above 100,000/mm^3 at diagnosis.

- Children who have relapsed in their central nervous system or testes.

- Children who will undergo a bone marrow transplant.

Treatment for childhood leukemia is constantly evolving. Even as this book is being written, several ongoing clinical trials are evaluating alternative methods for CNS prophylaxis. Perhaps in the near future, no child with leukemia will need radiation. But for the present, although there are possible side effects, radiation to the brain provides children with high-risk leukemia or CNS leukemia the best chance to be cured.

When is radiation treatment given?

Cranial radiation is most effective if given after remission is achieved, usually at the end of the induction phase. For children who have relapsed, cranial, spinal, and/or testicular radiation is prescribed at the time of relapse, regardless of the phase of treatment.

Questions to ask about radiation treatment

- Why does my child need radiation?
- What type of radiation does she need?
- What part of her body will be treated with radiation?
- What is the total dose of radiation that she will receive?
- How many treatments of radiation will be necessary?
- How much experience does this institution have in administering this type of radiation to children?
- How will he be positioned on the table?
- Will any restraints be used?

- Will anesthesia or sedation be used?

- How long will each treatment take?

- What are the possible short-term and long-term side effects?

- Could this type and dosage of radiation cause cancer later?

- What are the alternatives to radiation?

Where should your child go for radiation treatment?

To have optimal treatment, children should receive radiation therapy only at major medical centers with experience in treating children with cancer. Do not go to a local radiation center or the radiation department in your community hospital. All treatments should be supervised by physicians who are board-certified or equally experienced in radiation oncology. State-of-the-art equipment, expert personnel, and vast experience with pediatric cancers are what you should look for in choosing a center.

Who is a radiation oncologist?

A radiation oncologist is a medical doctor with years of specialized training in using radiation to treat disease. Other names for these specialists are radiotherapist, radiation therapist, or therapeutic radiologist. In partnership with the pediatric oncologist, the radiation oncologist develops a treatment plan tailored specifically for each individual child.

The radiation oncologist will explain to both child and parents what radiation is, how it will be administered, and any possible side effects. She will answer all questions regarding the proposed treatment. Parents will be given a consent form to take home and review prior to signing. Parents should not sign the consent form until they thoroughly understand all benefits, risks, and possible side effects of the radiation. The radiation oncologist will meet at least weekly with child and parents to discuss how the treatment is going and to address concerns or answer questions.

Who is a radiation therapist?

The radiation therapist is a specially trained technologist who operates the machine that delivers the dose of radiation prescribed by the radiation oncologist. This member of the medical team will give the child a tour of the radiation room, explain about the equipment, and position the child for treatment. The technologist will operate the x-ray machine, and will monitor the child via closed-circuit TV and a two-way intercom.

When three-year-old Katy was being given the tour of the radiation room by her technologist, Brian, he was just wonderful with her. He gave her a white, stuffed bear which he used to demonstrate the machine. He immobilized the bear on the table using Katy's mask (device to hold the head still during treatment), then moved the machine all around it so that she could hear the sounds made by the equipment. He then took a Polaroid picture of the bear on the table, in the mask, for Katy to take home with her.

What is a mask?

To immobilize very young children, a mask of the youngster's face is made to hold the head perfectly still during the cranial radiation treatment. Great care should be taken to ensure that making the mask is not traumatic. This can often be accomplished by utilizing play therapy to demonstrate the procedure.

Masks are made from a lightweight, porous, mesh material. First, the technologist should explain and demonstrate the entire mask-making process to the child. The child then lies down on a table. The technologist places a sheet of the mask material in warm water to soften it. This warm mesh sheet is placed over the child's face and quickly molded to her features. The child can breathe the entire time through the mesh material but must hold still for several minutes as the mask hardens. The mask is lifted off the child's face, and the technologist cuts holes in it for the eyes, nostrils, and mouth.

The cancer center staff had scheduled two hours for mask making for my three-year-old daughter. I asked them to very quietly explain every step in the process. I told her that I would be holding her hand, and I promised that it would not hurt, but it would feel warm. I asked her to choose a story for me to recite as they molded the warm material to her face to make the time go faster. She picked "Curious George Goes to the Hospital." She held perfectly still; I recited the story; the staff were gentle and quick; and the entire procedure took less than twenty minutes.

• • • • •

Shawn (2 years old) needed to be sedated for his ten doses of radiation. They also made his mask while he was anesthetized.

What other immobilization devices are used?

Different institutions use a variety of devices to immobilize children to ensure that the radiation beam is directed with precision. Some of the products used are custom-made plaster of paris casts, thermal plastic devices, vacuum-molded thermoplastics, and polyurethane foam forms. Custom fitting the forms on a child who has already undergone numerous painful procedures requires skill and patience. Immobilization devices can be fitted on well-prepared, calm children or sedated children. The following are parent suggestions for preparing a child for the fitting of her immobilization device:

• Give the child a tour of the room where the fitting will take place.

• Explain in clear language each step in the process.

• Be honest in describing any discomfort the child may experience.

• For small children, fit the device onto a mannikin or stuffed animal to demonstrate the process.

• For older children or teenagers, show a video or read a booklet describing the procedure.

> Seventeen-month-old Rachel was fitted with two immobilization devices. They made a mask to hold her head in position, as well as a body mold from her neck to her thighs.

The more time spent on preparation, the less time will be spent on fitting a device. If the fitting goes well, it establishes trust and good feelings that will help make the actual radiation treatments proceed smoothly.

> After relapsing while on treatment, Stephan (7 years old) needed cranial and spinal radiation. I took him on a tour and explained in detail what would happen. All of his questions were answered. He would go in, have the black marks put on, and lie face down on a bed. There was a thing for his forehead to rest on, but he didn't require any other supports. He would just hold perfectly still. We kept a bucket next to the bed, because he was on high dose ARA-C, and after his radiation session, he would often need to lean over and vomit.

> He was so wonderful about it. He would go up to all of the older patients who were awaiting treatment and chat. He really reached out to them, and their eyes would just sparkle.

Why are some children sedated?

All infants, most preschoolers, and some school-age children require sedation or anesthesia to ensure that they will remain perfectly still during the radiation treatment. Most radiation facilities use a combination of anesthetics that are effective, yet allow the child to recover quickly so that he does not need to go to a recovery room.

Each radiation facility should give parents written instructions concerning pediatric anesthesia. Generally, the child must not eat for eight hours prior to his appointment. Clear liquids are usually allowed four hours prior to anesthesia. Children can eat and drink immediately after treatment.

The anesthetic is given through the child's catheter or IV while the parent is holding or comforting him. The child will go to sleep in the parent's arms, and then the parent leaves the room while the treatment takes place. The anesthesiologist will bring the child to the parent in the waiting room when the child is partly awake. Once the child is easily aroused, the child and parents can leave. The entire procedure takes from 30 to 60 minutes. Nausea and vomiting are occasional side effects of anesthesia.

> Shawn was almost three years old when he needed his cranial radiation. He is an extremely active child, and we agreed with the medical team that he would have to be sedated. His appointment was always at 1 P.M., and we were told that he could have apple juice or Jell-O at 6 A.M. but nothing to eat or drink after that. Every single morning he would drink the juice and then throw up. At the radiation room, I would hold him while he was anesthetized, then wait in the waiting room. They would bring him out to me in 30 to 45 minutes.

During a course of radiotherapy, the dose, drugs, and methods to sedate or anesthetize the child may need to be changed because some children develop a tolerance to certain drugs. Good communication between parent and members of the treatment team should prevent unnecessary anxiety about increased dosages or the use of a different drug.

> Most of the young children at our facility were sedated, but it was not necessary for Rachel (17 months old). She had just spent nine weeks in the hospital and was very weak. She just laid there under her mask and didn't move. The first day she whimpered and cried a bit, but after that it didn't seem to bother her.

What is a radiation simulation?

Prior to actually receiving any therapy, many measurements and technical x-rays are taken to map the precise area to be treated. This preparation for therapy is called the "simulation." The simulation will generally take longer than any other appointment, from thirty minutes up to two hours. Because simulation is not a treatment with high-dose radiation, parents are often allowed to remain in the treatment room to help and comfort their child. As discussed previously, some children will need to be sedated for the simulation.

During simulation, the radiation oncologist and technologist use a specialized x-ray machine to outline the treatment area. They will adjust the table that the child lies on, the angle of the machine, and the width of the x-ray beam needed to give the exact dosage in the proper place. In addition, the oncologist or technologist will put small ink marks on the skin to pinpoint the area to be treated. These marks should not be scrubbed in the bath or shower. They do fade with time, so the technologist may need to add more ink at some point in the child's treatment.

Children who wear masks during treatment will have these ink marks put on the mask, not their skin. At some institutions, children who require spinal radiation may have tiny black dots permanently tattooed on their skin. These tattoos are made by putting a drop of India ink on the skin, then pricking with a pin. They look like tiny black freckles.

After the simulation is completed, the child can go home while the radiation oncologist carefully evaluates the developed x-ray film and measurements to design the treatment field.

Description of a cranial radiation treatment

To receive cranial radiation, children are given appointments for ten weekdays, the same time each day. They usually have the weekend off. At some institutions, children go twice a day for ten days. When the parent and child arrive, they must check in at the front desk. The technologist comes out to take the child into the treatment room. Often, the parent accompanies her young child into the room. If the child requires anesthesia, it will take place in the treatment room.

For conscious children, the technologist will secure them in position with either the mask (which is screwed down to the table on either side of the head) or other device. The technologist will take measurements to verify that the child's body is perfectly positioned. Frequently, the technologist will shine a light on the area to be irradiated to ensure that the machine is properly aligned. The technologist and parents will leave the room, closing the door behind them.

At some institutions, parents are allowed to stay and watch the TV monitor and talk to their child via the speaker system. If this is the case, the parent should be careful not to distract the technologist as he administers the radiation. At other institutions, parents must wait in the waiting room. The treatment takes only five to ten minutes, and can be stopped at any time if the child experiences any difficulty. When the treatment is finished, the technologist turns off the machine, removes the immobilization device, and parents and child can go home. There is no pain at all when receiving x-ray treatment.

> I desperately wanted my three-year-old to be able to receive the radiation without anesthesia. I asked the center staff what I could do to make her comfortable. They said, "Anything, as long as you leave the room during the treatment." So, I explained to my daughter that we had to find ways for her to hold very still for a short time. I said, "It's such a short time, that if I played your Snow White tape, the treatment would be over before Snow White met the dwarves." Katy agreed that was a short time, and asked that I bring the tape for her to listen to. She also wanted a sticker (a different one every day) stuck on the machine for her to look at. I brought her pink blanket to wrap her in because the table was hard and the room cold. Each day, she chose a different comfort animal or doll to hold during treatment. So we'd arrive every day with tapes, blanket, stickers, and animals. She felt safe, and all treatments went extremely well.

· · · · ·

> There was something about the radiation or the anesthesia that frightened Shawn terribly. He would scream in the car all the way to the hospital. It was a scream as if he was in pain. He had nightmares while he was undergoing radiation and every night after it was over. We decided a month after radiation ended to bring a box of candy to the staff who had been so nice. Shawn asked, "Do I have to go in that room?"

When I explained that it was over and he didn't need to go in the room anymore, he asked if he could go in to look at it once more. He stood for a long time and just looked and looked at the equipment. Somehow he made his peace with it, because he never had any more nightmares.

If your child is receiving spinal radiation, the back of the heart may be affected. A baseline EKG and echocardiogram should be performed prior to treatment and on a regular basis thereafter. Spinal radiation may also damage the thyroid gland which is located behind the Adam's apple. The oncologist should evaluate the functioning of this gland if spinal radiation has been given.

Description of a testicular radiation treatment

For boys or teens with leukemic cells in the testes, radiation is included in the treatment plan. At the present time, most protocols require 2400 rads, given in 200 rad doses, once a day for 12 days. Radiation treatment is usually only given Monday to Friday, with weekends off. Treatment plans will vary among protocols and institutions.

Prior to your son's radiation to the testes, the technologist or child life worker will give a tour of the facility, describe the machines, and explain exactly how the radiation sessions will be done. Usually, only older boys require radiation to the testes, so anesthesia is rarely needed. Instead, the boy or teen will lie on the table, the technologist will support the testicles on a small piece of lead, and the penis will be taped up to keep it out of the radiation field. Each treatment will last less that five minutes, during which time the boy must hold perfectly still. As with cranial radiation, the technologist will be watching your son through a window and will be in verbal contact through a two-way intercom system.

For all sexually mature males, sperm banking should be discussed with the oncologist prior to treatment. Sperm can be kept viable for 10-15 years, and this may allow some teens the opportunity to become fathers later in life.

Description of a total body radiation (TBI) treatment

Total body radiation is given prior to bone marrow transplantation. There are numerous protocols, each with a different treatment schedule. Two examples are: 200 rads are given twice a day for three days, or 120 rads given three times a day for four days. The treatments are usually five to six hours apart. Prior to treatment, the child will be measured by the radiation therapist using tape measures and calipers. The therapist will give the family a tour and will show the two cobalt machines on either side of the stretcher in the middle of the room.

On the first day of treatment, the child will be brought to the room (at some institutions small kids will ride a trike or are pulled in a wagon), and may choose to watch TV or a movie, or to listen to a tape or radio. He will lay on the stretcher between the two cobolt machines, and the therapist will position him on his side or on his back. These positions will alternate each treatment, once on the back, then on the side. It doesn't matter which side, so if a child has a sore left side, he can always lay on his right. The child can move a bit, for example, scratch his nose or cross his ankles, but cannot get off the stretcher. The therapist will remove all metal from the child or his clothing—watches, zippers, rings, clamps. Anything with tight elastic— diapers or tight socks—will be loosened or removed. Treatment time lasts from 18 to 35 minutes, depending on the size of the child or teen.

Antinausea drugs are given to prevent vomiting, and these often make the child drowsy enough to doze through the treatment. Some small or extremely active children are sedated.

> The radiation was easy. When I wasn't sleeping, I watched TV or listened to the radio. I threw up once, but they gave me benadryl and I never was sick again from the radiation. The room was neat, it was painted lots of bright colors and had two big blue machines on each side of me.

Possible short-term side effects

Generally, radiation given to children with leukemia lasts less than two weeks. Many children suffer no short-term side effects at all. If side effects do occur, it is often hard to differentiate those caused by radiation and those caused by the high-dose chemotherapy that is being given at the same time. Possible short-term side effects are:

- Loss of appetite.
- Nausea and vomiting.
- Fatigue.
- Slightly reddened or itchy skin.
- Hair loss.

- Low blood counts.

- Changes in taste and smell.

- Sleepiness (Somnolence Syndrome)—from cranial radiation.

- Swollen parotid (salivary) glands—from TBI.

Methods of coping with most of the above side effects are contained in Chapter 11, *Common Side Effects of Chemotherapy*. Somnolence syndrome is uniquely associated with cranial radiation and is characterized by drowsiness, prolonged periods of sleep (up to twenty hours a day), low-grade fever, headaches, nausea, vomiting, irritability, difficulty swallowing, and difficulty speaking. It can occur anywhere from three to twelve weeks after radiation treatment ends, and can last from a few days to several weeks.

Nine weeks after ending her cranial radiation, my daughter started complaining of severe headaches. She would hold her head and just sob with pain. She also vomited several times. Then she became very sleepy, and dozed on the couch most of the day. She developed a low fever and choked when she tried to swallow liquids or solid food. This lasted for about a week, and I was worried sick. I called her oncologist, her radiation oncologist, and her pediatrician, and they all said they didn't think that it was related to the radiation or chemotherapy. I went to the medical library and discovered somnolence syndrome.

• • • • •

Stephan (8 years old) had no side effects from the cranial and spinal radiation other than sleepiness, but he was very affected by it. First, he just started taking naps and generally slowing down. Then the naps got longer, and he was awake less. Finally, he only woke up to eat. Luckily, that part coincided with Christmas vacation so he didn't miss much school. Altogether, it lasted about six weeks.

• • • • •

Ryan (14 years old) had his radiation during consolidation when he was very ill from the chemotherapy. He would develop severe headaches and vomiting an hour after each radiation treatment. As a matter of fact, he became so sick that they decreased the number of his treatments.

• • • • •

Three weeks after her radiation ended, Rachel (18 months old) slept for three days. We tried to wake her to eat, but she literally would fall asleep with her face in her food. After three days, she gradually became more alert, with the whole episode lasting only a week and a half. Oddly enough, the oncology people warned me about the possibility of sleepiness, but the radiation staff insisted that it wasn't related to the radiation.

Possible long-term side effects

While short-term effects appear and subside, long-term side effects may not become apparent for months or years after treatment ends. The effects of radiation on cognitive functioning, growth, and puberty range from no late effects to severe, life-long impacts. The possible long-term side effects of total body radiation are covered in Chapter 20, *Bone Marrow Transplantation.*

Cognitive problems

Intrathecal and intravenous methotrexate and/or radiation to the brain can sometimes cause damage to the central nervous system. Some children develop learning disabilities which can start immediately or several years after treatment. Typically, poor performance is noted in mathematics, spatial relationships, problem solving, attention span, and concentration skills. Here are the stories of three parents:

My daughter is a year off treatment and three years past radiation and seems to have no cognitive problems at all. She is doing well in kindergarten. She reads and writes, and has taught herself to add and subtract all of the combinations up to twenty. I was worried while she was on chemotherapy that her comprehension was slow. She continually asked me to reread portions of books and didn't seem to understand without constant repetition. But that faded away after the chemotherapy ended, and now she's quick to understand stories read aloud. She does, however, have significant social problems which may be related to the radiation.

· · · · ·

My son turned three years old while receiving his cranial radiation. He is now five years old and has major cognitive problems. He can't count, and so far he hasn't been able to learn the alphabet. He is in a preschool for the developmentally disabled, and the teacher feels that he has just hit a brick wall. I gave her the Candlelighters book, "Educating the Child with Cancer," and several articles. She is trying different techniques with him. He is a super kid, though, with a great attitude, and we hope for the best.

· · · · ·

Rachel received 1800 rads of cranial radiation when she was seventeen months old. She's six now, in kindergarten. She has multiple cognitive problems, including problems with letter and number recognition and short-term memory. She is a child who will need extra help in school, including phonics and drilling while learning to read. It is challenging for her to sit quietly in class and listen to the teacher. After much observation, I truly think that these kids have a quirky organizational system for their brain. They seem to have a different way of inputting and outputting information. She will frequently say something completely out of the blue during a conversation that is totally unrelated to what is being discussed. My husband and I both realize that school may be a struggle for her, but we intend to get her all of the help available to persons who are traumatically brain injured. Her self-esteem is high, she is a very bright, verbal child, and we will work with each of her teachers to ensure that she gets the best education possible.

It is important to remember that doctors cannot predict which children will develop cognitive problems. Children at greatest risk for cognitive problems are those treated when less than five years of age, with those under two at the highest risk. Chapter 15, , discusses in great detail the types of educational problems some children face, and how to deal effectively with them.

Problems with growth

The brain contains the hypothalamus and the pituitary gland, which control many body processes including growth and reproduction. At the initial dosages of radiation given to most children with leukemia (1800 rads to the cranium), growth is usually not affected except in younger, female patients. Effects on growth usually begin to be seen in those children who received 2400 rads or more. If the child requires additional cranial radiation or radiation to the spine, growth can be slowed or stopped. The growth of children who receive cranial radiation or craniospinal radiation should be followed closely. Children should be measured (sitting and standing) at every follow-up visit and their growth plotted on a chart to measure velocity.

If your child is one of the rare individuals who experiences premature puberty (before the age of eight for girls and ten for boys), growth may also be affected. These children may be given daily growth hormone injections to support their growth until they reach their final height.

Children who receive total body radiation prior to bone marrow transplant also may exhibit delayed growth, especially if they had cranial and/or spinal radiation previously. These children should be under the care of a pediatric endocrinologist who is experienced in follow-up care for bone marrow transplant patients.

Early or delayed puberty

Some young children who receive radiation to the brain do not experience puberty at the appropriate age. A very small percentage of children enter precocious puberty, which means that puberty begins several years earlier than normal. This is most common in children who also have impaired growth. Conversely, puberty in some children is significantly delayed. Teenage girls who do not show signs of puberty—pubic and underarm hair, breast development—should be evaluated by a pediatric endocrinologist. Similarly, teenage boys who show no signs of puberty—growth of body hair, deepening voice—should also consult a specialist.

Secondary cancers

Children who receive cranial radiation do have an increased risk of malignancy (cancer) years after treatment. The risk is reported to range from 1 to 5 percent.

Despite the possibility of potential late effects from radiation treatment, parents and survivors must focus on the benefits and keep the risks in perspective. The reality is that radiation saves the lives of many children with high-risk disease, and the majority go on to live healthy, happy, and productive lives.

Resources

Reading for adults

Dodd, Marylin J., R.N. Ph.D. *Managing the Side Effects of Chemotherapy and Radiation Therapy: A Guide for Nurses and Patients.* New York: Prentice Hall Press, 1987. Contains thorough explanations of possible side effects of chemotherapy and radiation and suggestions for managing them.

National Cancer Institute. *Radiation Therapy and You: A Guide to Self-help During Treatment.* To order a free copy, call 1-800-4-CANCER. 51-page booklet clearly defines radiation, explains what to expect, describes possible side effects, and discusses follow-up care.

O'Connell, Avice, M.D., and Norma Leone. *Your Child and X-Rays: A Parents' Guide to Radiation, X-Rays and Other Imaging Procedures.* Rochester, NY: Lion Press, 1988. 89-page book explains all types of x-ray treatments in easy-to-understand language.

Technical reading

Bucholtz, Jennifer D. "Issues Concerning the Sedation of Children for Radiation Therapy." *Oncology Nursing Forum* 19(4) (1992): 649-55. Discusses the need for sedation and/or anesthesia for some pediatric patients during a course of radiation therapy. Issues concerning the use of sedation, the drugs used, and the nurse's role both medically and as a liaison to the family.

Butler, Robert W., and Donna R. Copeland. "Neuropsychological Effects of Central Nervous System Prophylactic Treatment in Childhood Leukemia: Methodological Considerations." *Journal of Pediatric Psychology* 18(3) (1993): 319-338. Reviews 53 studies on the effects of CNS prophylactic treatment on children. Recommends methods to improve research on late effects of radiation and/or chemotherapy to the brain.

Cherlow, J. M., H. Sather, et al. "Craniospinal Irradiation for Acute Lymphoblastic Leukemia with Central Nervous System Disease at Diagnosis: A Report from the Children's Cancer Group." *International Journal of Radiation Oncology/Biology/Physics* 36(1) (1996): 19-27. Study attempted to determine if CNS disease at diagnosis is a poor prognostic factor for children with ALL and whether 6 Gy of spinal radiation is an adequate dose for these patients. For patients receiving systemic chemotherapy with an intensive consolidation phase, event-free survival was similar to those without CNS involvement at diagnosis. For those children receiving intensive chemotherapy, 6 Gy dose of spinal radiation is sufficient.

Fletcher, Jack M., and Donna R. Copeland. "Neurobehavioral Effects of Central Nervous System Prophylactic Treatment of Cancer in Children." *Journal of Clinical and Experimental Neuropsychology* 10(4) (1988): 495-538. Reviews 41 studies on the effects of CNS prophylactic treatment in children.

Green, Daniel M., M.D., and Giulio J. D'Angio, M.D., eds. *Late Effects of Treatment for Childhood Cancer.* New York: Wiley-Liss, 1992. Anthology of articles by experts in the field of late effects resulting from treatment for cancer. Some of the chapters explain neuropsychological functioning after cranial radiation, effects of irradiation on growth and development, precocious and delayed puberty following cranial radiation for ALL, and other topics.

Halperin, Edward C., Louis S. Constine, Larry E. Kun, et al. *Pediatric Radiation Oncology.* 2nd ed. New York: Raven Press; 1994. Excellent technical text with chapters on radiation treatment for acute leukemia, late effects of cancer treatment, secondary tumors, pediatric anesthesia, and stabilization devices.

Mandell, Lynda R., M.D., Ph.D., Russell W. Walker, et al. "Reduced Incidence of the Somnolence Syndrome in Leukemic Children with Steroid Coverage During Prophylactic Cranial Radiation Therapy." *Cancer* 63 (1989): 1975-78. Defines somnolence syndrome and a pilot study using steroids during radiation. In the study, the incidence of somnolence syndrome decreased in those children on steroids.

Rim, I.J., F.C. Li, et al. "Brain Tumors After Cranial Irradiation for Childhood Acute Lymphoblastic Leukemia." *Cancer* 59 (1987): 1506-8. Literature review of cases of brain tumors in children with ALL who were treated with 2400 rads of CNS radiation. Most tumors occurred within ten years. Further study is needed to see if the increased incidence of brain tumors is due to treatment or genetic predisposition.

Sklar, C., A. Mertens, et al. "Final Height After Treatment for Childhood Acute Lymphoblastic Leukemia: A Comparison of No Cranial Irradiation with 1800 and 2400 Centigrays of Cranial Radiation." *Journal of Pediatrics* 123:1 (July 1993): 59-64. Analyzed growth and final heights in 127 patients with ALL. Study found a modest impact on height for patients who had no cranial irradiation, a greater loss in height for those treated with 1800 cGy, and the greatest loss for those treated with 2400 cGy. Both younger age and female sex were associated with a greater decrease in final height for patients who received cranial irradiation.

Record Keeping and Finances

Better known as: How musch shall I organize these piles?

A veteran parent

KEEPING TRACK OF THE voluminous paper work—both medical and financial—is a trial for every parent of a child with cancer. It is a necessary evil, however, because accurate records prevent medical errors and insurance over-billings. Poor record keeping can allow changes in lab results to go unnoticed and untreated. Poor organization of bills often results in parents being hounded by collection companies. This chapter will suggest simple systems for keeping both medical and financial records.

Keeping medical records

Think of yourself as someone with two sets of books, the hospital's and yours. If the hospital loses your child's chart or misplaces lab results, you will still have yours. If your child's chart becomes a foot thick, you will still have your simple system that makes it easy to spot trends and retrieve dosage information. Good doctors appreciate organized parents.

The following are suggestions of the information that parents should record:

• Dates and results of all lab work.

• Dates of chemotherapy, drugs given, and dose.

• All changes in dosages of medicine.

• Any side effects from drugs.

• Any fevers or illnesses.

• Dates for all medical appointments and name of the doctor seen.

• Dates for any procedures done.

• Child's sleeping patterns, appetite, and emotions.

Keeping daily records on your child's health for two or three years is hard work. But remember that your child will be seen by pediatricians, oncologists, residents, radiation therapists, lab techs, nutritionists, psychologists, and social workers. Your records will keep it all straight and help pull all information together. They will help you remember questions to ask, prevent mistakes, notice trends. They will help busy doctors remember what happened the last time your child was given a certain drug. Your records will help the entire team provide your child with the best possible care.

There are as many good ways to record the above information as there are parents. Some of the methods used by veteran parents follow.

Journal

Keeping a notebook works extremely well for people who like to write. Parents make entries every day about all pertinent medical information and often include personal information such as their own feelings or memorable things that their child has said. Journals are easy to carry back and forth to the clinic, and can be written in while waiting for appointments. They also have the advantage of having unlimited space. One disadvantage is that they can be misplaced.

In *You Don't Have To Die*, Geralyn Gaes writes of the value of keeping a journal:

> Some days my entries consisted of only a few words: "Good day. No problems." Other times I had so many notes and questions to jot down that my handwriting spilled over into the next day's space. I must confess that I probably went overboard, documenting every minute detail of Jason's life down to what he ate for each meal. If he gets over this disease, I thought, maybe this information will be useful for cancer research.
>
> I'm not so sure I was wrong. Jason went two years without a blood transfusion, unusual for a child receiving such aggressive chemotherapy. Studying my journal, one of his physicians remarked, "This kid eats more oatmeal than anybody I've ever seen." Which was true. Jason wolfed it down for breakfast, after school, and before bedtime. The doctor speculated, "Maybe that's why Jason's blood is so rich in iron and builds back up so fast."

· · · · ·

Stephan's oncologist is kind of hard to communicate with. I learned early on to keep a journal of Stephan's appointments, drugs given, side effects, and blood counts. That way if I ever had to call the doctor I would have it right in front of me. I also recorded his temperature when his counts were low to keep track of infections.

· · · · ·

RECORD KEEPING. Very important! My father came to the hospital soon after diagnosis and brought a three-ring binder and three-hole punch. I would punch lab reports, protocols, consent forms, drug information sheets etc. and keep them in my binder. A mother at the clinic showed me her weekly calendar book, and I adopted her idea for recording blood counts and medications. Frequently the clinic's records disagreed with mine as to meds and where we were on the protocol. I was very glad that I kept good records.

Calendar

Many parents reported great success with the calendar system. They buy a new calendar each year and hang it in a convenient place such as next to the telephone. Parents can record counts on the calendar while talking to the nurse or lab technician on the phone and take it with them to all appointments.

Each year I purchase a new calendar with large spaces on it. I write all lab results, any symptoms or side effects, colds, fevers, and anything else that happens. I bring it with me to the clinic each visit, as it helps immensely when trying to relate some events or watch trends. I also use it like a mini journal, recording our activities and quotes from Meagan. Now that she's off treatment, I'm superstitious enough to still bring it to our monthly checkups.

· · · · ·

I wrote the counts on a calendar or on little pieces of paper which got lost. But, to be honest, I didn't keep the medical records very well. I'm upset with myself when I think of it now.

· · · · ·

For a long time I was unorganized, which is very unlike the way I usually am. I found that my usual excellent memory just wasn't working well. It all seemed to run together, and I began to forget if I had given her

all of her pills. Then I began using a calendar for both counts and medi-
cations. I wrote every med on the correct days, then checked them off as I
gave them.

Blood count charts

Many hospitals supply folders containing xeroxed sheets for record keeping. The one used by the hospital that my daughter went to contained four sheets with thirty lines per page. Each line had a space for the date, WBCs, ANC, Hct (hematocrit), platelets, chemotherapy given, and side effects. By the end of treatment I had to xerox more pages.

> *My record-keeping system was given to me by the hospital on the*
> *first day. We were given a notebook with information about the illness*
> *and treatment. Also included were charts that we could use to keep all*
> *the information about the child's blood work, progress, reactions to drugs,*
> *etc. While we were at the hospital we were able to get the information off*
> *one of the computers on our floor each afternoon. My notebook holds*
> *records and notes for three years. Perhaps I was being compulsive with*
> *my record keeping, but it made me feel that I was part of the team*
> *working on bringing my boy back to health.*

Appendix B, *Blood Counts and What They Mean*, contains examples of actual lab sheets, and a record-keeping sheet that you can use to keep track of your child's blood counts.

Tape recorder

For parents who keep track of more information than a calendar can hold and who find writing a journal too time consuming, using a tape recorder works well. Small machines are very inexpensive, and can be carried in a pocket.

> *I started keeping a journal in the hospital, but I was just too upset*
> *and exhausted to write in it faithfully. A good friend who was a writer by*
> *profession told me to use a tape recorder. It was a great idea and saved a*
> *lot of time. I could say everything that had happened in just a few*
> *minutes every day. I kept a separate notebook just for blood counts so*
> *that I could check them at a glance.*

Computer

For the computer literate, keeping all medical records on the computer is an attractive option. Parents can print out bar graphs of the blood counts in relation to chemotherapy and quickly spot trends.

Keeping financial records

You will not need a calendar or journal for financial records, just a big, well-organized file cabinet. It is essential to keep track of bills and payments. Dealing with financial records is a major headache for many parents, but keeping good records can prevent financial catastrophe.

The following are ideas on how to organize financial records:

- Set up a file cabinet just for medical records.

- Have hanging files for hospital bills, doctor bills, all other medical bills, insurance explanations of benefits (EOB), prescription receipts, tax deductible receipts (tolls, parking, motels, meals), and correspondence.

- Whenever you open an envelope, file the contents immediately. Don't lay it on the desk or throw it in a drawer.

- Keep a notebook with a running log of all tax deductible medical expenses, including the service, charge, bill paid, date paid, and check number.

- Don't pay a bill unless you have checked over each item listed to make sure that it is correct.

- Start new files every year.

I bought an accordion-style file folder each year to hold everything to do with Stephan. It had a slot each for hospital bill printouts, insurance explanation of benefits, receipts for all prescriptions, all Candlelighter newsletters, pediatrician bills, laboratory bills, and Leukemia Society information.

• • • • •

To be honest, the paper trail really gets me down. I can only deal with the stacks every few months. I open things and make sure that the insurance company is doing their part, and then I try to sort through and pay our part.

• • • • •

I started out organized, and I'm glad I did because the hospital billing was confusing and full of errors. I cleared out a file cabinet and put in folders for each type of bill and insurance papers. I filed each bill chronologically so I could always find the one I needed. I made copies of all letters sent to the insurance company and hospital billing department. I wrote on the back of each EOB (estimate of benefits) any phone calls that I had to make about that bill. I wrote down the date of the call, the person's name that I spoke to, and what she said. It saved me a lot of grief.

What are deductible medical expenses?

It is estimated that families of children with cancer spend 25 percent or more of their income on items not covered by insurance. Examples of these expenses are gas, car repairs, motels, food away from home, health insurance deductibles, prescriptions, and dental work. Many of these items can be deducted on federal income tax. Often parents are too fatigued to go through stacks of bills at the end of the year to calculate their deductions. If a monthly total is kept in a notebook, then all that needs to be done at tax time is adding up the monthly totals. It is well worth it.

Medical expenses that could be deducted for 1996 were: acupuncture, ambulance, artificial limb, artificial teeth, expenses to modify your home to provide medical care for your child, crutches, dental treatment, HMO fees, hearing aids, hospital services, insurance premiums, laboratory fees, special school or tutor for child with learning disabilities, lodging costs for family when child is hospitalized, meals at hospital, physician's services, medicines, nursing care, operations, osteopath, oxygen, psychiatric care, psychological care, therapy, transplants, transportation to obtain medical care, wheelchair, and x-rays.

To find out what can be legally deducted for the years your child is undergoing cancer treatment, get IRS publication 502. This booklet is available at libraries and IRS offices or by calling 1-800-TAX-FORM (1-800-829-3676) from 8 A.M. to 5 P.M. weekdays and 9 A.M. to 3 P.M. Saturdays.

If you do keep a calendar, an easy way to keep track of tax-deductible items is to glue an envelope to the inside cover. Whenever you incur an expense that is tax deductible, put the receipt in the envelope, and file it when you get home.

Dealing with hospital billing

Unfortunately, problems with billing are the norm rather than the exception for parents of children with leukemia. Here are two typical experiences:

> *Insurance was an absolute nightmare. It almost gave me a nervous breakdown. After all we go through with our children to have to deal with the messed-up hospital billing was just too much—it was the worst part of the whole experience.*

> *We would stack the bills up and try to go through them every two or three months. Our insurance was supposed to pay 100 percent, but the billing was so confusing that they refused to cover some things because it wasn't clear what they were being billed for. The hospital frequently double billed, especially for prescriptions. We just stopped getting our prescriptions there.*

> *We would call them to try to get the mess straightened out, but the billing department was just as confused as we were. They kept sending our account to collections. We did everything in our power to get it straight, but we never did.*

· · · · ·

> *We had two distinctly different experiences at the two institutions that we dealt with. The University hospital where my daughter received her radiation gave me a folder the first day. It included, among other things, a sheet from a financial counselor giving all the information needed for preventing and solving billing problems. I never needed to call her because the hospital billing was clear, prompt, and organized.*

> *The children's hospital where she was a frequent inpatient and clinic patient was another story altogether. They billed from three different departments, put charges from the same visit on different bills, frequently over-billed, continuously made errors, and constantly threatened to send the account to collections. I never spoke to the same billing clerk twice. It was a never ending grind and a constant frustration.*

It is impossible to prevent billing errors, but it is necessary to deal with them. Here are step-by-step suggestions on solving billing problems:

- Keep all records filed in an organized fashion.

- Check every bill from the hospital to make sure there are no charges for treatments not given or errors such as double billing.

The hospital changed billing systems halfway through Carl's treat-ment. For some reason, they were unable to retrieve the records for charges already billed. They lost several hundreds of dollars of charges. I kept calling to get it resolved, but they assured me that the new bills were correct. I gave up trying to pay what we owed, but it was a very ineffi-cient billing system.

· · · · ·

During maintenance, my daughter went to the clinic every three months. She had identical treatment every visit—port accessed, vincris-tine given, physical exam, and intrathecal methotrexate given via spinal tap. Each bill was different, ranging from $329 to $740, for identical visits! There were errors on each bill, including numerous charges for IV benedryl that she never received. I would get the errors removed, then they would reappear on the next bill.

- Check to see if the hospital has financial counselors. If so, make contact early in your child's hospitalization. Counselors provide services in many areas, including help with understanding the hospital's billing system, billing insurance carriers, understanding explanations of bene-fits, hospital/insurance correspondence, dealing with Medicaid, working out a payment plan, designing a ledger system for tracking insurance claims, and resolving disputes.

- If you find any billing error, call the hospital immediately. Write down the date, the name of the person you talk to, and the plan of action.

I often couldn't even get through to the billing representative, I was just put on hold forever. Then I tried to discuss the problems with the director of billing, but she was never in. After about twenty phone calls, I finally said to her secretary, "You know, I have a desperately sick child here, and I have more important things to do than call your boss every day. I've been as patient and polite as I can. What else can I do?" She said, "Honey, get irate. It works every time." I told her to put me through to somebody, anybody, and I would. She connected me to the person who mediates disputes, I got irate, and we went through all the bills line by line.

- If the error is not corrected on your next bill, call and talk to the billing supervisor. Explain politely the steps you have already taken and how you would like the problem fixed.

The hospital billing was so bad, and I had to call so often, that I developed a telephone relationship with the supervisor. I always tried to be upbeat, we laughed a lot, and it worked out. She stopped investigating every problem and would just delete the charge from the computer.

- If the problem is still not corrected, write a brief letter to the billing supervisor explaining the steps you have taken and requesting immediate action. Keep a copy of each letter that you write.

- Every time you receive an explanation of benefits (EOB) from your insurance company, compare it to the hospital bill. Track down discrepancies.

- If you are inundated with a constant stream of bills and there are major discrepancies between the hospital charges and what is being paid for by your insurance, ask both the hospital billing department and your insurance company, in writing, to audit the account. Insist on a line-by-line explanation for each charge.

Within five months of my daughter's diagnosis, the billing was so messed up that I despaired of ever getting it straight. When the hospital threatened to send the account to a collection agency, I took action. I wrote letters to the hospital and the insurance company demanding an audit. When both audits arrived, they were $9,000 apart. I met with our insurance representative, and she called the hospital, and we had a three-way showdown. We straightened it out that time, but every bill that I received for the duration of treatment had one or more errors, always in the hospital's favor.

• • • • •

Our bills were so botched up that we always asked for audits. Very often we would never hear from the hospital again about those charges. It seemed to me that they just canceled them whenever we asked for an audit.

- If you are too tired or overwhelmed to deal with the bills, ask a family member or friend to help. He could come every other week, open and file all bills and insurance papers, make phone calls and write all necessary letters. Some friends might even enter all your records on a computer for storage.

- Don't let billing problems accumulate. Your account may end up at a collection agency, which can quickly become a nightmare.

Our insurance was constantly months behind in paying our bills to the Children's hospital. The hospital sent our account to collections, despite my assurances that I was doing everything I could to get the insurance to pay. We were hounded on the phone constantly by the collection people, often until we were in tears. We finally just took out a second mortgage and paid off the hospital, but now I don't know if we will be reimbursed by insurance.

Not all stories are so grim. People who are in managed health care systems or on public assistance never even see bills. Many people with insurance encounter no problems throughout their child's treatment.

Our insurance paid 80 percent of everything, no questions asked and always paid us within a month. People shouldn't have to worry about finances or their insurance program at a difficult time like this.

•   •   •   •   •

We have a low income, so we are on the state plan. They give us coupons for each child, and we just hand over a coupon at each visit. I have never seen a bill.

Coping with insurance

Finding one's way through the insurance maze can be a difficult task. Understanding the benefits and claims procedures can help parents get the bills paid without undue stress. The following are some steps to help prevent problems with insurance.

Understand your policy

As soon as possible after diagnosis, read your entire insurance manual. Make a list of any questions you have on terms or benefits. Learn who the "participating providers" are under the plan, for, in today's managed health care climate, there may be a limited network of providers and hefty penalties or no benefits if the patient goes outside the network. Find out what your "deductible" is. Find out if there is a point where coverage increases to 100 percent. Determine if there is a lifetime limit on benefits. Find out when a second opinion is required. Learn when you have to notify the company about hospitalizations—many firms require pre-notification except in the case of emergency.

> *I realized that my daughter had been treated for over four months and I had never called the insurance company. When I read the manual, I was horrified to find out that I had not pre-notified them about three scheduled hospitalizations. There was a $200 penalty for each lapse. I called in tears, and they only charged me for one mistake, not all three.*

Get a copy of every form that you may need to submit, for example, claim forms for inpatient care, outpatient care, or prescriptions. You can cut down on paperwork by filling in all the subscriber information on one of each type of form (except date and signature) and then making many copies. You will have a form ready to send in with each bill.

It may be helpful to determine whether your policy has benefits for counseling. If so, find out how many visits are covered and the level of training required (sometimes only counseling by persons with an M.A. or Ph.D. degree is covered). Is there a home nursing benefit? How many visits?

> *We changed to a new pediatrician, and he asked me if I thought it would be easier on my son to have visiting nurses come to our home to do the chemotherapy injections and some blood work. Since he had very low counts, it made a lot of sense not to have to go out. It also lessened his fears to be able to stay at home and have the same nurse come to do the procedures. It was a pleasant surprise to find these services covered by our insurance.*

Find a contact person

As soon as possible after diagnosis, call your insurance company and ask who will be handling your claims. Explain that there will be years of bills with frequent hospitalizations, and it would be helpful to always deal with the same person. Insurers may be able to offer parents a contact person for claim review or special needs. Ask the contact person to answer any questions that you have on benefits. Try to develop a cooperative relationship with your contact person because she can really make your life easier. Also, the employer may have a benefits person who can operate as a liaison with the insurer.

> *My employee benefits representative was Bobbi. She was just wonderful. The hospital would send her copies of the bills at the same time as they sent mine. Since I found so many errors, she would hold the bills a week until I called to tell her that they were correct before she paid them. She was very pleasant to deal with.*

Negotiate

Don't be afraid to negotiate with the insurance company over benefits. Often, your contact person may be able to redefine a service that your child needs to allow it to be covered.

> Our insurance company covered 100 percent of maintenance drugs only if the patient needed them for the rest of their lives. Christine's drugs were only needed for two years but were extremely expensive. I asked my contact person for help, and she petitioned the decision-making board. They granted us an exemption and covered the entire cost of all her maintenance drugs.

· · · · ·

> My husband works for a small city that contracts out health insurance. A year into our child's treatment, the contract was being renegotiated. He brought home a copy of the proposed contract, and I was horrified to see that they had halved the benefit for transplants, from $200,000 to $100,000. I called the members of the committee negotiating the contract, the union representative, the city insurance liaison, and the city attorney. I was very polite, but I told them that if my child needed a bone marrow transplant, the new contract would bankrupt us. We would lose our home and have to sell all of our belongings to pay our part of the procedure. Then I called two transplant centers, and had them fax me the estimated cost of a routine bone marrow transplant (about $220,000). I sent copies of the fax to everyone that I could think of, and followed it up with phone calls. They changed the new contract back to $200,000. One person can make a big difference.

Challenging a claim

The key to obtaining the maximum benefit from your insurance policy is to keep accurate records and to challenge any denied claims. Some tips on good record-keeping are:

* Make photocopies of everything you send to your insurance company, including claims, letters, and bills.

* Pay bills by check, and keep all of your canceled checks.

* Keep all correspondence you receive from billing companies and insurance.

- Write down the date, name of person contacted, and conversation of all phone calls concerning insurance.

- Keep accurate records of all medical expenses and claims submitted.

Policyholders have the right to appeal a claim denial by their insurance company. The following are suggested steps to contest a claim:

- Keep original documents in your files, and send photocopies to the insurance company with a letter outlining why you think the claim should be covered. Demand a written reply.

- If the insurance company is refusing coverage because they claim the procedure is "investigational" or "experimental" and therefore not covered, contact the Childhood Cancer Ombudsman Program by calling (703) 492-0045. This organization offers a free ombudsman program to help families maximize benefits or resolve disputes.

- Contact your elected representative to the U.S. Congress. All Senators and members of the House of Representatives have staff who help constituents with problems.

- If all of the above steps do not resolve the dispute, take your claim to small claims court, or hire an attorney skilled in insurance matters to sue the insurance company.

Above all, don't be afraid to ask questions, and be persistent!

Sources of financial assistance

Sources of financial assistance vary from state to state and town to town. To begin to track down possible sources, ask the hospital social worker for assistance. In addition, some hospitals have community outreach nurses or case workers who may point out potential sources of assistance.

Hospital policy

If you find yourself unable to pay your hospital bills, don't sell your house or let your account go to collections. Ask the social worker to set up an appointment for you with the appropriate person to discuss the hospital policy on financial assistance. Many hospitals write off a percentage of the cost of care if the patient is uninsured or underinsured.

SSI (Supplemental Security Income)

SSI is a program administered by Social Security, and is an entitlement based on family income. Recipients must be ill, blind, or disabled, with a low family income. Children with cancer qualify as disabled for this program, making some of them eligible for monthly aid if the family income is low enough. To find out if your child qualifies, look in the phone book under "United States Government" for the "Social Security Administration." Ask to speak to someone regarding eligibility for SSI. In cases of hardship, the caseworker will take your application over the phone and will tell you if you qualify.

Medicaid

Medicaid is administered by the state government, with the federal government providing a portion of the entitlement. Rules on eligibility vary, but families with private insurance sometimes are eligible if huge hospital bills are only partially covered. Call your local or county social service department to obtain the number for the Medicaid office in your area.

In addition to helping pay some or all hospital bills, Medicaid sometimes also pays transportation and prescription costs. Some states cover children under the age of 21 if they are hospitalized for more than 30 days, regardless of parental income. Ask for a detailed list of benefits available in your state.

If you are having difficulty applying for or obtaining government benefits, contact the Childhood Cancer Ombudsman Program (703-492-0045) for free help. They have expert medical and vocational volunteers who can help you through the maze of government benefit programs.

Free medicine programs

Many drug companies have programs to provide free medicines (including chemotherapy) to needy patients. Eligibility requirements vary, but most are available to those not covered by private or public insurance programs. Ask your physician to request, on letterhead, a free copy of the Directory of Pharmaceutical Indigent Programs from:

Pharmaceutical Manufacturers Association
1100 15th St. NW
Washington DC 20005
Toll-free hot line for physicians: 1-800-PMA-INFO
World Wide Web: *http://www.oncolink.com/specialty/chemo/indigent_drugs.html*

Service organizations

There are numerous service organizations that can help families in need. They provide all kinds of aid: transportation, wigs, special wheelchairs, and food. Often, all a family has to do is describe their plight, and good Samaritans appear. Some organizations that may exist in your community are: American Legion; Elks Club; fraternal organizations such as the Masons, Jaycees, Kiwanis Club, Knights of Columbus, Lions, Rotary; United Way; Veterans of Foreign Wars; and churches of all denominations. In addition, local philanthropic organizations exist in many communities. To locate them, call your local Health Department, speak to the social worker, and ask for help.

Organized fund raising

Many communities rally around a child with cancer by organizing a fund. Help is given in various ways, ranging from mason jars in local stores to an organized drive using all of the local media. There are many pitfalls to avoid in fund raising, and great care must be exercised to protect the privacy of the sick child as much as possible. If you are contemplating starting a fund, read Sheila Peterson's, *A Special Way to Care* (listed in the "Resources" section). This guide gives detailed, step-by-step advice on determining the needs of the family, finding benefits, using publicity, generating community support, and managing the fund.

Resources

Organizations

The Sparrow Foundation
1155 N. 130th, Suite 310
Seattle WA 98104
(206) 745-5403

This nonprofit charitable and educational organization was started by the family of a child who needed a bone marrow transplant, for which their insurance carrier refused to pay (described in the book *One Small Sparrow*, listed in the "Resources" section). The foundation provides seed money to schools, youth organizations, service clubs, and churches which help persons with medical needs.

Steven Greenwood Childhood Cancer Foundation
1555 Wilson Blvd., Suite 300
Arlington, VA 22209
(703) 875-8627

Provides financial aid for non-medical expenses of patients diagnosed with cancer prior to age twenty-one.

Cancer Fund of America
2901 Breezewood Lane
Knoxville, TN 37921
1-800-578-5284
FAX: (615) 938-2968

Helps defray cancer-related expenses not covered by insurance.

The Leukemia Society of America

Refer to the information in Chapter 1, *Diagnosis,* on The Leukemia Society of America's financial assistance program. This organization can provide up to $750 worth of assistance.

Reading for adults

Blum, Laurie. *Free Money for Heart Disease and Cancer Care.* New York: Simon & Schuster, 1992. Book containing a state-by-state listing of associations, foundations, businesses, and agencies which give grants to eligible people or employees.

Leeland, Jeff. *One Small Sparrow: The Remarkable Real-Life Drama of One Community's Compassionate Response to a Little Boy's Life.* Sisters, OR: Multnomah Books, 1995. Written by the father of a baby with leukemia, this heartwarming true story describes how a community raised the entire cost of a successful bone marrow transplant. Contains numerous ideas for methods to raise funds. Christian perspective.

National Information Center for Children and Youth with Disabilities. *Meeting the Medical Bills.* To order call 1-800-695- 0285. Written by the mother of a chronically ill child, this booklet reviews options for meeting medical bills. Includes tips, bibliography, associations, state insurance commissions, and state Medicaid associations.

Peterson, Sheila, and Jane Dove. *A Special Way to Care.* Friends of Karen, Box 217, Croton Falls, NY 10519. A free 187-page guide for neighbors, friends, and community members in their efforts to provide financial and emotional support for terminally and catastrophically ill children. Highly recommended for those who are starting a fund.

Technical reading

Lansky, Shirley B. "High Cost of Cancer." *American Journal of Pediatric Hematology/Oncology* 9(1) (Spring 1987): 89-91.

Mental Health Law Project. *SSI: New Opportunities for Children with Disabilities.* 1101 15th St. NW, Washington, DC 20005. Explains Supplemental Security Income (SSI), a Social Security benefit, to parents. Answers eligibility questions and how to appeal a denial of claims.

CHAPTER 14

Nutrition

Let your food be your medicine and your medicine be your food.

—Hippocrates (fifth century B.C.)

THE EATING HABITS of children with leukemia go haywire. Parents know that eating the right types of food will help their child heal faster, feel better, and continue to grow. Moreover, cancer treatment itself increases the need for balanced nutrition. The child's body works hard to repair the damage to healthy cells caused by chemotherapy, and to break down and excrete the cancer cells killed by treatment. Just metabolizing the numerous chemotherapy drugs given stresses children's systems.

Despite knowing that children need to eat nutritious meals, the reality is that sick children often do not want to eat. This chapter discusses eating problems, explains good nutrition, suggests ways to pack extra calories into small servings, and offers tips on how to make food more appealing to children.

Treatment side effects and eating

Eating is tremendously impacted by most types of chemotherapy. Listed below are several common side effects of treatment which conspire to prevent good eating. Other common side effects, including nausea, vomiting, diarrhea, constipation, and mouth and throat sores, are covered in detail in Chapter 11, *Common Side Effects of Chemotherapy*.

Loss of appetite

Anorexia, or loss of appetite, is one of the most common problems associated with the treatment of cancer. Children suffering from nausea and vomiting, diarrhea or constipation, altered sense of smell and taste, mouth sores, and other unpleasant side effects understandably do not feel hungry. Loss of appetite is most pronounced during the intensive periods of treatment, such as induction, consolidation or delayed intensification. If your child loses more than 10 to 15 percent of her body weight, she may need to be fed intravenously or by tube. Sometimes this can be avoided by parents learning how to increase calories in small amounts of food.

> *My son looked like a skeleton several months into his protocol for high-risk ALL. I used to dress him in "camouflage" clothes—several layers thick. This kept him warm and prevented stares.*

In addition to simple loss of appetite, your child may experience a side effect of chemotherapy called early filling. This means that the child has a sense of being full after only a few bites of food. If the child is suffering from early filling and only eats when hungry, she may begin losing weight and become malnourished. This chapter will provide dozens of creative ways to encourage your child to eat more.

Increased appetite and weight gain

When children are given high doses of steroids such as prednisone or dexamethasone, they develop voracious appetites. They are hungry all the time, develop food obsessions, and frequently wake parents up during the night begging for another meal.

> *Early in her treatment when Carrie Beth was taking dexamethasone, she would start hitting me in the face in the middle of the night demanding food. I learned to have a bag of snacks and a bottle sitting next to the bed, so I could just hand them over and go back to sleep.*

Most parents become very concerned as their child consumes huge quantities of food and gains weight. A moon face with chubby cheeks and a rotund belly are classic features of a child on high-dose steroids. Much of the extra weight is fluid which steroids cause the body to retain. There are two important points for parents to remember about treatment with steroids: when the steroids stop, the extra fluid is excreted and weight drops, and the child's appetite usually goes from voracious to poor.

Do not put your child on a diet when he is taking steroids. Instead, try to make the most of this brief time of good appetite to encourage consumption of a variety of nutritious foods. A well-balanced diet now will help your child withstand the rigors of treatment ahead.

If you are concerned about the weight gain, consult your child's oncologist. If the fluid retention is extreme, the doctor may have you restrict your child's salt intake, and in some cases children are given drugs called diuretics to rid the body of excess fluid.

Lactose intolerance

Lactose intolerance is when the body can't absorb the sugar (lactose) contained in milk and other dairy products. Both antibiotics and chemotherapy can cause lactose intolerance in some individuals. The part of children's intestines that breaks down lactose stops functioning properly resulting in gas, abdominal pain, bloating, cramping, and diarrhea. If your child develops this problem, it is important to talk to a nutritionist to learn about low-lactose diets and alternate sources of protein. The following are suggestions for parents of lactose-intolerant children:

- Adding enzyme tablets or drops to dairy products makes them digestible for some children. Some of these are over-the-counter additives, while others require a prescription. Discuss these additives with the oncologist prior to using.

- Replace milk with cheese, nonfat yogurt, buttermilk, or sour cream.

- Replace milk with acidophilus milk or soy milk, which are easier to digest.

- Remember that milk is a common ingredient in other foods, even bread. Read ingredient lists carefully.

- If no dairy products are tolerated, supply calcium by serving canned salmon, sardines, or calcium-fortified fruit juices. Consult your child's oncologist and nutritionist about calcium supplements.

Diet and Nutrition and *Eating Hints* are free booklets listed in the "Resources" section at the end of this chapter. They both contain recipes and suggestions for lactose-restricted diets.

Altered taste and smell

One common reason why children do not eat is because food has no taste, or tastes bad. If the problem is food having no taste, try serving highly seasoned food (e.g., Italian, Mexican, or curried foods). If foods taste bitter or metallic, avoid using metal pots, pans, and utensils. Serve the child's food with plastic knives, forks, and spoons. Replace red meat with tofu, chicken or turkey, eggs, and dairy products.

Some children's taste returns to normal when maintenance starts, some after treatment ends, and for a few children, it takes years before some foods taste pleasant again.

What is a balanced diet?

A good diet includes sufficient calories to ensure a normal rate of growth, fuels the body's efforts to repair and replace damaged normal cells, and provides the energy the body needs to break down the various chemotherapy drugs given and excrete their by-products. Research has shown that a well-nourished body will:

- Tolerate more treatment.

- Tend to have fewer side effects.

- Maintain weight.

- Recover faster from treatment.

When the body becomes malnourished, body fat and muscle decrease. This leads to:

- Weakness, lack of energy, weight loss.

- Decreased ability to digest food.

- Limited ability to heal and fight infection.

To keep your child's body well-nourished, foods from all of the five basic food groups are needed. The five groups are breads and cereals, fruits, vegetables, dairy products, and meats and meat substitutes. The groups and recommended daily servings are shown in Figure 4, Food Guide Pyramid.

Below are examples of foods contained in each group, with a small child's serving size in parentheses beside each food. Consult a nutritionist to determine the serving size appropriate for your child.

Meat and Meat Substitutes (2 or 3 servings per day)

Meat (1 ounce)	Eggs (1)
Fish (1 ounce)	Peanut butter (2 Tbsp.)
Poultry (1 ounce)	Dried beans, cooked (1/2 cup)
Cheese (1 ounce)	Dried peas, cooked (1/2 cup)

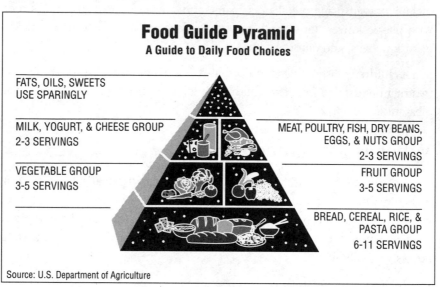

Food Guide Pyramid
A Guide to Daily Food Choices

FATS, OILS, SWEETS
USE SPARINGLY

MILK, YOGURT, & CHEESE GROUP
2-3 SERVINGS

MEAT, POULTRY, FISH, DRY BEANS,
EGGS, & NUTS GROUP
2-3 SERVINGS

VEGETABLE GROUP
3-5 SERVINGS

FRUIT GROUP
3-5 SERVINGS

BREAD, CEREAL, RICE, &
PASTA GROUP
6-11 SERVINGS

Source: U.S. Department of Agriculture

Figure 4. Food Guide Pyramid

These foods provide protein, which helps build and maintain body tissues, supply energy, and help form enzymes, hormones, and antibodies. Some typical one-ounce servings of meat and meat substitutes are: a meatball one inch in diameter, a one-inch cube of meat, one slice of bologna, a one-inch cube of cheese or one slice of processed cheese. As you can see, two to three meatballs a day provide all the protein needed by a school-aged child.

Dairy Products *(2 or 3 servings per day)*

Milk (1/2 cup)   Tofu (1/2 cup)
Cheese (1 ounce)   Custard (1/2 cup)
Ice cream (1/2 cup)   Yogurt (1/2 cup)

These foods provide calcium, vitamin D, and protein.

Breads and Cereals *(6 to 11 servings per day)*

Bread (1/2 slice)   Dry cereal (1/2 cup)
Oatmeal (1/2 cup)   Granola (1/2 cup)
Cream of wheat (1/2 cup)   Cooked pasta (1/2 cup)
Graham crackers (1 square)   Saltines (3 squares)
Rice (1/2 cup)   Potatoes (1 baked)

These foods supply vitamins, minerals, fiber, and carbohydrates. Try to use only products made with whole wheat flour and limited sugar to get more nutrients per serving. One sandwich made with two slices of bread provides 4 servings of this food group.

Fruits (2 to 4 servings per day)

Fresh fruit (1 medium piece)   Dried fruits (1/4 cup)
Canned fruit (1/4 cup)   Fruit juice (1/4 cup)

Fruits provide many vitamins, minerals, and fiber. Add dried fruits to cookie and muffin recipes. Fruits can be camouflaged by pureeing them with ice cream in the blender to make a tasty milk shake.

Vegetables (3 to 5 servings per day)

Raw vegetables (1/4 cup)   Cooked vegetables (1/4 cup)

Vegetables, like fruit, are excellent sources of vitamins, minerals, and fiber. If your child does not want vegetables, they can be grated or pureed and added to soups or spaghetti sauce. If you own a juicer, add a vegetable to fruits being juiced.

Fats (several servings a day)

Butter or margarine   Cheese
Mayonnaise   Whipped cream
Peanut butter (or nuts)   Avocado
Meat fat (in gravy)   Olives
Ice cream   Chocolate

Although the food pyramid calls for fats to be used sparingly, higher consumption of fats is needed for children being treated for cancer. Experiment to find the fats that your child enjoys eating, and serve them frequently.

Are vitamin supplements necessary?

Yes, vitamin supplements are usually necessary. The nutritional needs of kids with cancer are higher than other children's, yet kids on treatment eat less food. Most children with cancer are unable or unwilling to eat the variety of foods necessary for good health. In addition, damage to children's digestive systems from chemotherapy alters the body's ability to absorb the nutrients contained in the food they do manage to eat.

Vitamin supplementation should only be done in consultation with your child's oncologist. Oversupplementation of some vitamins, folic acid for example, can make your child's chemotherapy less effective. But providing other vitamins can make the difference between a child with dull hair, no energy, and dry peeling skin to one with stronger hair, clear skin, and a better attitude. Vitamin supplements should be individually tailored for your child in consultation with the oncologist and nutritionist.

> *Halfway through maintenance, my daughter just looked awful. Her new hair began to thin out and break easily and her skin felt papery. I had been giving her a multivitamin and mineral tablet every day because her appetite was so poor, but it didn't seem to be enough. I talked to her doctor, then began to give her more of the anti-oxidant vitamins: betacarotene, E, and C. I bought the C in powder form which effervesced when mixed with juice. She really liked her "bubble drinks." The betacarotene and E she swallowed along with the rest of her pills. Within a few weeks her hair stopped falling out, her skin stopped peeling, and she felt better.*

· · · · ·

> *I gave my teenaged daughter supplements of vitamins and some minerals. I also increased her vitamin intake by using the juicer every day. She always drank a big glass of fruit or vegetable juice, and I really think it helped her do as well as she has.*

Making eating fun and nutritious

In some homes, mealtimes turn into battlegrounds, with worried parents resorting to threats or bribery to get their child to eat. After such scenes, parents, the ill child, and siblings are exhausted, and nutritious food still has not been consumed. The next several sections are full of methods used successfully by many veteran parents to make mealtimes both fun and nutritious.

How to make food more appealing

Many children are finicky eaters at the best of times. Cancer and its treatment can make eating especially difficult. Here are some general suggestions to make eating more enjoyable for your child:

• Give small portions throughout the day rather than three large meals. Feed your child whenever she is hungry.

- Remember that your child knows best which foods he can tolerate.

> *In the beginning of treatment, we decided that my son had to eat what the rest of the family was having. If he didn't eat that, he got no more food. He usually just didn't eat. Some mornings, I had trouble waking him up. He was limp, and would have his eyes rolled back in his head. He was tested, and diagnosed with hypoglycemia (low blood sugar). The doctor told us to make sure he ate something right before bed, even if it was ice cream or cookies and milk. Since he has been off chemo, he has not had any problems.*

- Explain clearly to your child the importance of eating a balanced diet.

- Make mealtimes pleasant and leisurely.

- Rearrange eating schedules to serve the main meal at the time of day when your child feels best. If she wakes up feeling well most days, make a high-protein, high-calorie breakfast.

- Praise and encourage eating well.

- Don't punish the child for not eating.

- Set a good example by eating a large variety of nutritious foods.

- Have nutritious snacks available at all times. Carry them in the car, to all appointments, and packed in knapsacks for school.

- Serve fluids between meals rather than with meals to keep your child from feeling full after only a few bites of food.

- Limit the amount of less desirable foods in the house. Potato chips, corn chips, soda pop, and sweets with large amounts of sugar may fill your child up with empty calories.

- If your child is interested, include him in making a grocery list, shopping for favorite foods, and food preparation.

Make mealtime fun

Here are some suggestions on how to make mealtime more fun:

- Try to take the emphasis off eating food because it's good for you and focus instead on setting a mood of enjoying each other's company while sharing a meal. Encourage good conversation, tell stories and jokes, perhaps light some candles.

- Make one night a week restaurant night. Use a nice tablecloth, candles, allow the children to order from a menu, and pretend the family is out for a night on the town.

- Since any change in setting can encourage eating, consider having a picnic on the floor occasionally. Order pizza or other takeout, spread a tablecloth on the floor, and have an in-home picnic. Some parents even send lunch out to the treehouse for a lark.

> My son enjoyed eating in different places around the house and seemed to eat more when he was having fun. I sometimes fed the kids on their own picnic table outdoors in good weather, and at the same picnic table in the garage during the winter. They were thrilled to wear their coats and hats to eat. Occasionally I would let them eat off TV trays while watching a favorite program or tape.

- Some families have theme meals, such as Mexican, Hawaiian, Chinese. They use decorations, wear costumes, and cook foods with exotic spices.

- Some children seem to eat better if food is attractively arranged on the plate or is decorated in humorous ways. Preschoolers enjoy putting a smiling face on a casserole using strips of cheese, nuts, or raisins. Sandwiches can be cut into funny shapes using knives or cookie cutters.

> My daughter liked to have food decorated. For example, we would make pancakes look like a clown face by using blueberries for eyes, strawberry for a nose, orange slices for ears, etc. She also enjoyed eating brightly colored food, so we would add a drop of food coloring to applesauce, yogurt, or whatever appealed to her.

How to serve more protein

Since many children cannot tolerate eating meat while on chemotherapy, here are some suggestions for increasing protein consumption:

- Add one cup of dried milk powder to a quart of whole milk, then blend and chill. Use this extra-strength milk for drinking and cooking.

- Use extra-strength milk (above), whole milk, evaporated milk, or cream instead of water to make hot cereal, cocoa, soup, gravy, custards, or puddings.

- Add powdered milk to casseroles, meat loaf, cream soups, custards, and puddings.

- Add chopped meat to scrambled eggs, soups, and vegetables.

- Add chopped, hard-cooked eggs to soups, salads, sauces, and casseroles.

- Stir an extra egg into eggnogs, milk shakes, puddings, mashed potatoes, pancake mix, and custards.

- Add grated cheese to pizza, vegetables, salads, sauces, omelets, mashed potatoes, meat loaf, and casseroles.

- Serve bagels, English muffins, hamburgers, or hot dogs with a slice of cheese melted on top.

- Spread peanut butter on toast, crackers, and sandwiches. Dip fruit or raw vegetables into peanut butter for a quick snack.

- Spread peanut butter or cream cheese onto celery sticks or carrots.

- Serve nuts for snacks, and mix nuts into salads and soups.

- Serve yogurt and granola bars for extra protein. Top pie, Jell-O, pudding, or fruit with ice cream or whipped cream.

- Use dried beans and peas to make soups, dips, and casseroles.

- Use tofu (bean curd) in stir-fried vegetable dishes.

- Add wheat germ to hamburgers, meat loaf, breads, muffins, pancakes, waffles, vegetables, and as a topping for casseroles.

Guidelines for boosting calories

Parents need to alter their perceptions of what constitutes healthy food when they are struggling to feed a child on chemotherapy. Many parents have ingrained habits of low-fat cooking and food preparation. That habit must be replaced by methods to constantly find ways to add calories to their child's food.

- Add butter or margarine to hot cereal, eggs, pasta, rice, cooked vegetables, mashed potatoes, and soups.

- Use melted butter as a dip for raw vegetables and cooked seafood such as shrimp, crab, and lobster.

- Use sour cream to top meats, baked potatoes, and soups.

- Use mayonnaise instead of salad dressing on salads, sandwiches, and hard-cooked eggs.

- Add mayonnaise or sour cream when making hamburgers or meat loaf.

- Use cream instead of milk over cereal, puddings, Jell-O, and fruit.
- Make milkshakes, puddings, and custards with cream instead of milk.
- Serve your child whole milk to drink instead of 2 percent milk.
- Saute vegetables in butter.
- Serve bread hot so it will absorb more butter.
- Spread bagels, muffins, or crackers with cream cheese and jelly or honey.
- Make hot chocolate with cream, and add marshmallows.
- Add granola to cookie, bread and muffin batters. Sprinkle granola on ice cream, pudding, and yogurt.
- Serve meat and vegetables with sauces made with cream and pan drippings.
- Combine cooked vegetables with dried fruit.
- Add dried fruits to recipes for cookies, breads, muffins.
- Add honey to cereal, milkshakes, yogurt.
- Glaze chicken with honey when cooking.

Nutritious snacks

Try to get into the habit of always bringing a bag of nutritious snacks whenever you leave home with your child. This allows you to feed her whenever she is hungry and avoids stopping for non-nutritious junk food. Here are some examples of healthful snacks:

- Apples or applesauce.
- Baby foods.
- Burritos made from beans or meat.
- Buttered popcorn.
- Celery sticks stuffed with cheese or peanut butter.
- Cookies made with wheat germ, oat meal, granola, fruits, nuts.
- Cereal.
- Cheese.
- Cheesecake.
- Chocolate milk.

- Cottage cheese.

- Crackers with cheese, peanut butter, tuna salad.

- Custards made with extra eggs and cream.

- Dips made with cheese, avocado, butter, beans, or sour cream.

- Dried fruit such as apples, raisins, apricots, or prunes.

- Fresh fruit.

- Granola mixed with dried fruit and nuts.

- Hard-cooked and deviled eggs.

- Ice cream (the kind made with real cream).

- Juice (made from 100% fruit).

- Milkshakes made with whole milk or cream.

- Muffins.

- Nuts.

- Peanut butter on crackers or whole wheat bread.

- Pizza.

- Puddings.

- Sandwiches (with real mayonnaise or butter).

- Vegetables like carrot sticks or broccoli florets.

- Yogurt, regular or frozen.

Ask for help

It is very helpful to consult the hospital nutritionist to obtain more information and ideas on how to add more protein and calories to your child's diet.

> I had two quite different experiences with hospital nutritionists. At the children's hospital, I couldn't get the doctors concerned about my daughter's dramatic weight loss. She was so weak she couldn't stand, and her muscles seemed to be wasting away. I finally asked the receptionist to please send in a nutritionist. A very young woman came in and talked to me about the major food groups. I felt my cheeks begin to flush, and my eyes glistened as I said, "I know what she is SUPPOSED to eat, I need to know how I can make her want to eat." I must have sounded a bit crazy, because she just handed me a booklet and backed out the door.

> *The next week when my daughter began her radiation, the radiation nurse took one look at her and called the nutritionist right down. This nutritionist was very warm and caring. She helped me to understand that I needed to think fat, protein, and calories, and she gave me lots of practical suggestions on how to boost calories. I think that she probably saved my daughter from tube feedings.*

Another resource is the American Institute for Cancer Research Nutrition Hotline, 1-800-843-8114, Monday through Friday, 9 AM to 5 PM EST. A registered nutritionist will answer your questions about your child's nutrition.

What kids really eat

The previous part of the chapter listed ideas for increasing calories and making food more appealing. What follows are accounts of what several kids really ate while on chemotherapy. You'll notice how varied the list is, so experiment to see what your child finds palatable. Remember also that children's tastes and aversions change as time passes while on treatment.

> *Judd craved chicken chow mein and fried rice take out from a Chinese restaurant. He also loved spaghettios and hot dogs.*

· · · · ·

> *I let Preston eat whatever tasted good to him which was usually lots of potatoes and eggs. He liked spicy food (especially Mexican) while on prednisone.*

· · · · ·

> *Katy typically only ate one food for days or weeks at a stretch. One time, she ate pesto sauce (made from olive oil, garlic, Parmesan cheese, and basil leaves) on pasta every meal for weeks. She also went through a spicy barbecue sauce phase, in which she wouldn't eat any food unless it was completely immersed in sauce. She ate no fruits, vegetables (except potatoes), or meat for the entire period of treatment. She ate mostly cereal and beans when she was feeling well, and mostly pureed baby food when she was really sick.*

· · · · ·

In the beginning when Meagan lost so much weight, we snuck Polycose (a powdered nutritional supplement) into everything. She finally got stuck on cans of mixed nuts. They are high calorie, and were instrumental in putting back on the weight. She also craved capers, and would eat them by the tablespoonful.

· · · · ·

All Brent asks for are "peanut butter and jelly sandwiches, cut in fours, no crusts, with Fritos." The only fruit he has eaten for three years is an occasional banana, and he eats no vegetables. He always ate everything before his diagnosis at age 6.

· · · · ·

The doctor told me to keep Kim on a low-salt, low-folic-acid diet. She wouldn't eat anything, so he eventually said he didn't care what she ate, as long as she ate. She liked spaghettios, chick-fil-a nuggets, chick-fil-a soup, and McDonald's sausage and pancakes.

· · · · ·

All that Carl ate was dry cereal, dry waffles, oatmeal, and bacon. He ate no other meat or vegetables throughout treatment, but did drink milk. I thought that he would never be healthy, but he's 15 now (diagnosed when 2), eats little junk food, never gets sick, and looks great.

· · · · ·

While on prednisone I felt like I could never get out of the kitchen because Shawn ate nonstop. The rest of the time he ate almost nothing. He survived on bagels, dry cereal, french fries, popcorn, and burritos.

· · · · ·

Stephan's appetite went back to normal on maintenance. But after he relapsed and had cranial and spinal radiation, things have never been the same. He only wants junk food such as hot dogs and chicken nuggets. Most meats make him sick, and he's having problems with smells making food unappetizing.

· · · · ·

John (14 months old) craved creamed corn and pork and beans. I would just sit him on a potty chair at the table and let him eat, and it would go in one end and out the other. When on prednisone, he would sit at the table almost all day. He also drank a gallon of apple juice a day. He rarely eats meat to this day (2 years off treatment).

• • • • •

On prednisone, Rachel ate only hot dogs, bologna, scrambled eggs with cheese, and potato chips. She would eat until she literally threw up. Now, two years off treatment, she is gradually expanding her repertoire. She only drinks milk (no water, juice, or soda), eats no sweets, and prefers all salty foods. I really have no idea whether it is learned behavior or is a result of the cancer treatment.

• • • • •

I guess Carrie Beth is the exception that proves the rule. She is on maintenance and has an excellent appetite. She eats fruits, vegetables, and lots of meat.

Parent advice

Several veteran parents whose children have completed therapy offer the following suggestions on how to handle the inevitable eating problems of children on therapy:

- Doctors sometimes reassure parents by saying, "His appetite will return to normal on maintenance." Don't be surprised if this does not happen.

- Let the child control what type of food and how much he wants. In the beginning, any food is good food.

- Buy a juicer, and use it every day. This was the only way we got any fruits or vegetables into our daughter. Make apple juice and sneak in a carrot. Sometimes we would make the juice, then blend it in the blender with ice cubes to make an iced drink, which we would serve with a straw.

- I solved my daughter's salt cravings by buying sea salt and letting her dip french fries in it once a week. For some reason, that satisfied her and stopped her from begging for regular table salt at every meal.

- Try not to worry about your child's future eating habits. During treatment, you just have to let go of normal requirements and feed him whatever he wants, whenever he is hungry.

- When your child is on prednisone, don't try to restrict his food intake. It can be hard to watch these rotund little ones just shovel the food in, but once they get off the prednisone, they stop eating and quickly lose the weight. Then you have the opposite problem: how to get them to eat anything!

- Try to work around their taste problems. For example, my son wouldn't drink milk, so I made his oatmeal and cream of wheat with milk instead of water.

- If you only keep good food in the house, and don't buy junk food, your child will eat more nutritious food.

- Take good care of yourself by eating well. We are all under tremendous stress and need good nutrition. I gave my daughter healthy foods and glasses of juiced fresh fruits and vegetables while I was living on lattes (a coffee drink). I now have breast cancer and wish that I had eaten well during my daughter's treatment.

- There is reason for hope. My daughter ate almost nothing while on treatment. After treatment ended, she ate more food but still no variety. She didn't turn the corner until a year off treatment, but now she is gradually trying new foods, including fruits and vegetables again. I'm glad I never made an issue of it.

Commercial nutritional supplements

Many children cannot tolerate solid food or can only eat small amounts each day. Liquid supplements can help provide the necessary calories. The following is a sampling of the variety of supplements that can be purchased at pharmacies or grocery stores. If you are unable to locate a particular brand, your pharmacist may be able to order it for you.

- **Sustacal.** Lactose-free liquid. Flavors are chocolate, vanilla, eggnog, and strawberry. Also comes in a high-protein or extra-fiber formula. 240 calories and 15 grams protein per 8 oz. can (Mead Johnson).

- **Sustacal Pudding.** Like Sustacal in pudding form. Flavors are chocolate, vanilla, and butterscotch. 240 calories and 6.8 grams protein per 5 oz. can (Mead Johnson).

- **Sustacal HC.** Concentrated liquid. Vanilla, chocolate, strawberry, eggnog. 360 calories and 14 grams protein per 8 oz. can (Mead Johnson).

- **Ensure.** Lactose-free liquid. Chocolate, vanilla, black walnut, coffee, butter pecan, banana, and strawberry. Other formulas are high protein or extra fiber. 250 calories and 9 grams protein per 8 oz. can (Ross Laboratories).

- **Ensure Plus.** Concentrated liquid. 355 calories and 13 grams protein per 8 oz. can (Ross Laboratories).

- **Isocal.** Lactose-free liquid. Vanilla. 250 calories and 8 grams protein per 8 oz. can (Mead Johnson).

- **Enrich.** Liquid with fiber. Lactose free. 260 calories and 9 grams protein per 8 oz. can (Ross Laboratories).

- **Instant Breakfast.** Powder, which is added to milk. Variety of flavors. When mixed with 8 oz. whole milk provides 280 calories and 15 grams protein (Carnation Co.).

- **Citrotein.** Powder to add to water or juice. Orange flavor. 127 calories and 8 grams protein per 1/4 cup (Doyle Pharmaceutical).

- **Polycose.** Liquid or powder. Adds carbohydrates for extra calories. Add to milk, juice, gravy, soups. One tablespoon adds 30 calories.

Feeding by tube and IV

Although feeding by tube and IV may require additional hospitalization, parents need to understand the benefits clearly. If a child with cancer becomes malnourished, events are set in motion that can have grim consequences. As appetite and weight decrease, the child's ability to repair cellular damage caused by treatment is impaired. The child becomes progressively weaker and resistance to infection decreases. Infections and weakness may require interruptions in treatment. This scenario needs to be prevented. Most protocols require tube or IV feeding after a certain percentage of body weight is lost. The two types of supplemental feeding are:

Total parenteral nutrition (TPN)

Total parenteral nutrition, also known as hyperalimentation, is a form of intravenous feeding used to prevent malnutrition in those children who cannot eat or eat enough to meet basic nutritional needs. Some of the many reasons why your child may require TPN are severe mouth and throat sores which prevent swallowing, severe nausea, vomiting, and diarrhea, or a loss of more than 10 percent of body weight. TPN ensures that the child receives all of the protein, carbohydrates, fats, vitamins, and minerals she needs. The TPN is administered through the central or IV line, but children receiving TPN can also eat solids and drink fluids.

Enteral nutrition

If a child requires supplemental feeding and the bowel and intestines are still functioning well, enteral nutrition may be recommended. Enteral nutrition is feeding via a tube placed through the nose, mouth, or directly into the stomach through the abdominal wall. Nutritionally complete liquid formulas are fed through the tube. The appropriate formula will be decided by the oncologist and nutritionist. Infrequent side effects of enteral nutrition are irritated throat, nausea, or constipation.

One parent shared her thoughts on her son's chemotherapy-induced eating problems with these words:

> *I feel good nutrition is very important to good health but the reality of the situation with our child was that he hated anything nutritious when he was on chemotherapy. I could doctor it up, add the best toppings, make it look terrific, season it just right, and it would still be rejected. So I decided since my son wasn't allowed to make any decisions in regards to the pills, treatments, tests, or hospital stays, he wouldn't be forced to eat everything nutritious if he didn't want to. Whether this was a right or wrong decision, I don't know. I just know that I served him a lot of processed foods during those years and he's a healthy and happy boy ten years later. After he was finished with chemotherapy, however, we did require that he eat healthier foods.*

Resources

Reading for adults

Margie, Joyce Daly, and Abby S. Bloch. *Nutrition and the Cancer Patient.* Radnor, PA: Chilton Books, 1983. Self-help book shows patients how to take an active role in their treatment. Includes chapter on caring for children with cancer. Lists more than 300 easy, nutritious recipes.

National Cancer Institute. *Diet and Nutrition: A Resource for Parents of Children with Cancer.* To obtain free copy, call 1-800-4-CANCER. NIH Publication No. 82-2038. 57-page booklet that explains good nutrition, treatment side effects that affect eating, ways to encourage your child to eat, and several pull-out sections on special diets. An excellent resource.

National Cancer Institute. *Managing Your Child's Eating Problems During Cancer Treatment.* To obtain, call 1-800-4-CANCER. NIH Publication No. 92-2038. 32-page booklet which covers how cancer treatments affect eating, how to cope with side effects, and how to serve more protein and calories.

National Cancer Institute. *Eating Hints: Tips and Recipes for Better Nutrition During Cancer Treatment.* To obtain, call 1-800-4-CANCER. NIH Publication No. 91-2079. 96-page booklet covers eating well during cancer treatment, managing eating problems, special diets, family resources, and recipes.

Ramstack, Janet, and Ernest H. Rosenbaum. *Nutrition for Chemotherapy Patients.* Palo Alto, CA: Bull Publishing, 1990.

Wilson, J. Randy. *Non-Chew Cookbook.* Glenwood Springs, CO: Wilson Publishing, Inc., 1986. P.O. Box 2190, 81602. (303) 945-5600. Contains recipes for patients unable to chew due to the side effects of chemotherapy and/or radiation.

General nutrition

Barnard, Neal, M.D. *Food for Life: How the New Four Food Groups Can Save Your Life.* New York: Random House, 1993. Written by a doctor, this book espouses a vegetarian diet to prevent cancer, control weight, and improve vitality. I included this book in resources because of the chapter on cancer and also because half the book is comprised of appealing, tasty recipes that may entice your child to eat.

Chase, Leah, and Johnny Rivers. *Down Home Healthy.* National Cancer Institute, 1994. To obtain free copy, call 1-800-4-CANCER ask for Publication No. 94-3408. Family recipes of black American chefs updated to lower fat and salt without compromising taste. Contains very good recipes with beautiful photographs of the meals.

Goodwin, Mary T., and Gerry Pollen. *Creative Food Experiences for Children.* Available from the Center for Science in the Public Interest, 1875 Connecticut Avenue, NW, Suite 300, Washington, DC, 20009.

Moloney, Kathleen. *Parent's Guide to Feeding Your Kids Right.* New York: Prentice Hall Press, 1989. This is a good, basic, easy-to-read text on children's nutritional needs. It has sections on food and the body, the nutritional needs of children, and food and behavior.

U.S. Department Of Agriculture/ U.S. Department of Health and Human Services. *Nutrition and Your Health: Dietary Guidelines for Americans.* For free copy, write Consumer Information Center, Department 514-X, Pueblo, CO. 81009, and request HG-232.

Winick, Myron, M.D. *Growing Up Healthy: A Parent's Guide to Good Nutrition.* New York: William Morrow & Co. Inc, 1982. Dr. Winick, one of the world's most prominent authorities on good nutrition, has written an informative book full of practical advice on feeding from birth through adolescence, including a chapter on sick children.

Technical reading

Copeman, M. C. "Use of Total Parenteral Nutrition in Children With Cancer: A Review and Some Recommendations." *Pediatric Hematology/Oncology* 11(5) (Sept-Oct 1994): 463-70. TPN is a standard component of supportive treatment in many pediatric oncology units for patients undergoing intensive therapy. TPN incurs many risks and significant costs, however, that may not always be balanced by major benefits. TPN is associated with infections and numerous metabolic problems, and may also enhance tumor growth. Recommendations for TPN use in pediatric oncology include using TPN formulas which include glutamine and timing TPN cycles to be given just before chemotherapy.

Lerner, Michael. *Choices in Healing: Integrating the Best of Conventional and Complementary Approaches to Medicine.* Cambridge, MA: The MIT Press, 1994. Written by one of the country's leading authorities on complementary cancer treatments, *Choices in Healing* gives a comprehensive overview of both conventional and complementary approaches to cancer treatment, including chapters on mainstream nutritional science, vitamins and minerals, and unconventional nutritional cancer therapies.

CHAPTER 15

School

Most of us had two feelings at the same time: wanting to go back to school and being scared of going back. We didn't like feeling different. We also felt dumb because we missed so much school and we thought we would never catch up.

—Eleven children with cancer
There Is a Rainbow Behind Every Dark Cloud

CHILDREN WITH LEUKEMIA often experience disruptions in their education due to repeated hospitalizations, side effects from chemotherapy, or generally not feeling well enough to fully participate in daily school life. As their health improves and treatment allows, returning to school can be either a relief or a major challenge for children with cancer. For many children, school is a refuge from the world of hospitals and procedures, a place for fun, friendship, and learning. Because school is the defining structure of every child's daily life, returning to school signals normalcy; indeed, expectations of school attendance impart a clear and reassuring message that there is a future.

Other children, especially teens, may dread returning to school because of altered appearance or concerns that prolonged absences may have changed their social standing with their friends. Additionally, school can become a major source of frustration for those children who develop learning disabilities as a result of treatment. These learning differences, if handled in an insensitive or uninformed manner, can seriously affect a child's confidence and self-esteem.

The issues of educating children with cancer are complex, but most can be successfully managed through planning and good communication. In this chapter, many veteran parents share advice and experiences to help you meet the educational needs of your child.

Keeping the school informed about treatment

Communicating with the school often does not enter a parent's mind during the nightmarish days after diagnosis. Keeping the school informed, however, lays the foundation for years of collaboration as the child goes through the rigors of treatment for leukemia. Parents need to forge a strong alliance with the school professionals to ensure that their child, who may be emotionally and/or physically fragile, continues to be welcomed and nurtured at school.

The first step in ensuring a good relationship is choosing an advocate to be the liaison among hospital, family, and school. The advocate will work to keep information flowing between the hospital and school, and will help pave the way for a successful school reentry for the sick child. Often the advocate is the hospital social worker, but it can also be the school nurse, psychologist, principal, or other motivated individual. The most important qualifications for this role are good communication skills, knowledge of educational programs and procedures, comfort in dealing with school issues, and organizational skills. It must be someone you trust to fairly act on your child's behalf.

The advocate should locate a contact person at the school (or hospital) and should provide frequent updates about the child's medical condition, treatment, emotional state, and tentative reentry date. The advocate should encourage questions, and address staff concerns about having a seriously ill child in school.

> We had absolutely no problem keeping the school informed as we lived directly behind it. The teacher would frequently stop by on her way home to drop off homework assignments and cards or messages from Stephan's classmates. The school nurse, psychologist, and teacher were at my beck and call. Whenever I felt that we needed to talk, I'd call and they would set up a meeting within 24 hours. I gave them the Candle-lighters' book "Educating the Child with Cancer" and they even attended a Candlelighters meeting. They have been wonderful.

Keeping teacher and classmates involved

While your child is hospitalized, it is vital to his well being to stay connected with his teacher and classmates. The teacher should be getting updates through the advocate, but the parent can help by calling the teacher periodically, and bringing notes or taped messages to the classroom. Other suggestions are:

- Give the teacher copies of *Educating the Child with Cancer* and *Back to School: A Handbook for Teachers of Children with Cancer* (listed in the "Resources" section at the end of the chapter).

- Have the nurse or social worker come to class to give a presentation about what is happening to their classmate and how he will look and feel when he returns. This should include a question and answer session to clear up misconceptions and allay fears. Teenagers should be involved in any decision on what information should be given to classmates.

- Encourage classmates to keep in touch by sending notes, calling on phone, sending class pictures, or making a banner.

Call the American Cancer Society (1-800-ACS-2345) to ask for the *School Health Education Resources Catalog*. This will provide a comprehensive listing of the printed materials and outreach programs available for teachers and parents.

Keeping up with schoolwork

Whenever your child is able, keeping up with schoolwork should be a priority. Learning can continue despite school absences. Parents should communicate with the teacher to keep abreast of the subjects being covered in school. Often, the teacher will send assignments and materials home with siblings, or arrangements can be made for pick-up. Friends or relatives can volunteer to be tutors, providing a much needed link to the school as well as a welcome break for parents.

Joanne Holt, a high school Director of Special Education, suggests:

> If children are having difficulty remaining interested in school work due to fatigue and not feeling well, it may be useful to consider alternative learning activities. In such circumstances, a parent and child might identify an area of special interest or curiosity (e.g., dinosaurs, space,

*animals, nature, the Wild West, etc.). Children may find it more interest-
ing to develop reading skills, learn math concepts, develop writing skills,
and learn research and study principles in the context of a high-interest
area while still learning and maintaining the concepts being introduced in
school. Play is a significant part of such activities and can often spark
imaginative activities. It is important that the school be aware of and
supportive of such an approach; most often they are and, in fact, may be
valuable resources for ideas and activities. The goal is to encourage confidence and prepare the child for the least disruptive reentry to school routines.*

• • • • •

*Stephan really wanted to keep up in school, so he did his homework
whenever he was feeling well enough. Even after he relapsed and was so
sleepy from the radiation, whenever he woke up, the first thing he wanted
to do was his homework. His teacher stopped by every day after school to
drop off and pick up his homework.*

Siblings need help, too

The diagnosis of cancer catastrophically affects all members of the family.
Siblings can be overlooked in the early months when the parents are spending most of their time caring for the ill child at the hospital, clinic, or in the
home. Many siblings keep their feelings bottled up inside to prevent placing
additional burdens on their distraught parents. Often, the place where siblings act out the most is at school. It is very common for siblings to withdraw or become disruptive in the classroom, cry easily, become frustrated,
fall behind in classwork, bring home failing grades, cut classes, become
rebellious towards authority, or have fistfights with classmates. Siblings, like
parents, are overwhelmed by feelings, and generally have fewer coping
skills.

*Lindsey was in kindergarten when Jesse was first diagnosed. Because
we heard nothing from the kindergarten teacher, we assumed that things
were going well. At the end of the year, the teacher told us that Lindsey
frequently spent part of each day hiding under her desk. When I asked
why we had never been told, the teacher said she thought that we already
had enough to worry about dealing with Jesse's illness and treatment. She
was wrong to make decisions for us, but I wish we had been more atten-
tive. Lindsey needed help.*

Remember to include the siblings' teachers in all conferences at school. They need to be aware of the stresses facing the family, and understand that feelings may bubble to the surface in their classroom. It is essential that parents advocate for the healthy child's emotional and educational needs as well as their sick child's. Chapter 16, *Siblings*, deals exclusively with the problems, feelings, and burdens of the siblings, and contains suggestions for coping.

Returning to school

Although it is normal that parents don't think about school during the early efforts to save their child's life, hospital personnel should reinforce the importance of an early return to school. Going to school helps children regain a sense of normalcy and provides a lifeline of hope for the future.

Preparation is the key to a successful reentry to school. The parent should ask the physician or primary nurse to prepare a letter for the school staff containing the following information:

- The student's health status and its probable affect on attendance.

- Whether she will attend full or half days.

- Whether he can attend general physical education classes, general P.E. with restrictions (e.g., no running), or Adaptive Physical Education for disabled children.

- How much recess is allowed.

- A description of any changes in her physical appearance.

- Her feelings about returning to school.

- Any anticipated behavioral changes resulting from medication or treatment.

- The possible effect of medications on her academic performance.

- If any medications or other health services need to be given at school.

- Reminder to never give any medication, especially aspirin, which can cause uncontrollable bleeding, without parental permission.

- Any special considerations such as extra snacks, rest periods, or extra time to get from class to class.

- Concerns about exposure to communicable disease.

- List of signs and symptoms requiring parent notification, e.g., fever, nausea, pain, swelling, bruising, or nosebleeds.

- Stress that the teachers job is to teach, and the parent and nurse will take care of all medical issues.

Once faculty have had a chance to read the letter, request a meeting that includes faculty, administrators, school nurse, school counselor or psychologist, and special education personnel. At this meeting, answer any questions about the information contained in the letter, pass out booklets on children with cancer in the classroom, formulate a communicable disease notification strategy (if necessary), discuss the ongoing need for appropriate discipline, and do your best to establish a rapport with the entire staff. Take this opportunity to express appreciation for the school's help and your hopes for a close collaboration in the future to create a supportive climate for your child.

> I still feel unbelievable gratitude when I think of the school principal and my daughter's kindergarten teacher that first year. The principal's eyes filled with tears when I told her what was happening, and she said, "You tell us what you need and I'll move the earth to get it for you." She hand-picked a wonderful teacher for her, made sure that a chicken pox notification plan was in place, and kept in touch with me for feedback. She recently retired, and I sent her a glowing letter which I copied to the school superintendent and school board. Words can't express how wonderful they were.

· · · · ·

> Jeremy's kindergarten teacher was the pits. He was on chemo, and she told Jeremy not to wash his hands, as it took too long. I was disappointed that even after the nurse came to class and gave a presentation, the kids still teased my son. They would say things like "You've got Jeremy germs, you are going to catch cancer" and "You can't get rid of cancer, you always die." During his kindergarten year, Jeremy needed to have heart surgery. I called the teacher to let her know, but he did not hear from anyone in his class, not one card or phone call even from the teacher. She didn't even tell the class why Jeremy was absent.

The following are additional parent suggestions on how to prevent problems through preparation and communication:

- Keep the school informed and involved from the beginning. This fosters a spirit that "we're all in this together."
- Reassure the staff that even if the child looks frail, he really needs to be in school.

The school librarian had a bed set up in the library for ailing students to use. I found out that sometimes Preston would spend the whole day there, because he was just too exhausted to attend class. It was very important to him and his sense of well-being to be at school. He would just drag himself in there in order to be with the other kids. Fortunately, all of his classmates were always nice to him.

• • • • •

There was a beanbag chair in the back of Brent's class, and he just curled up in it and went to sleep when he needed to.

- Bring the nurse back into the class to talk about cancer and answer questions whenever necessary. This should also be done at the beginning of each new year to prepare the new classmates.

- Ask the school to bend some rules and policies if you think it will help your youngster. For example, wearing a hat can sometimes eliminate teasing.

  My sixteen-year-old son was allowed to leave each textbook in his various classrooms. This prevented him from having to carry a heavy backpack all day. They also let him out of class a few minutes early because he was slower moving from room to room.

- For elementary school children, enlist the aid of the hospital advocate or school counselor to help select the teacher for the upcoming year. Although this violates the policy at some schools, it can go a long way toward preventing problems.

  Because my son has had such a hard third-grade year, I have really researched the fourth-grade teachers. I sat in and observed three teachers. I sent a letter to the principal, outlining the issues, and requested a specific teacher. The principal called me and was very upset. He said, "You can't just request who you want. What would happen if all the parents did that? You'll have to give me three choices just like everybody else." I said, "My son has had three years of chemotherapy, has a seizure disorder, behavior problems, and learning disabilities. Can you think of a child who has greater need for special consideration?" My husband and I then requested a meeting with him, and at the meeting he finally agreed to honor our teacher request.

- Prepare both teacher and student for the upcoming year.

I asked for a spring conference with the teacher selected for the next fall and explained what my child was going through, what his learning style was, and what type of classroom situation seemed to work best. Then, I brought my son in to meet the teacher several times, and let him explore the classroom where he would be the next year. This helped my son and the future teacher adjust to one another.

- Get professional help.

    My daughter went to a counselor for the years of treatment. It provided a safe haven for frank discussions of what was happening, and also provided a place to practice social skills, which was a big problem for her at school.

- Realize that teachers and other school staff can be frightened, overwhelmed, and discouraged by a child with a life-threatening illness in their classroom. Accurate information and words of appreciation can provide much needed support.

Avoiding communicable diseases

The dangers of communicable diseases to immunosuppressed children were discussed in Chapter 11, *Common Side Effects of Chemotherapy*. To prevent exposure, parents need to work closely with the school to develop a chicken pox, shingles, and measles outbreak plan. Parents need to be notified immediately if their child has been exposed to chicken pox or shingles so that the child can receive the varicella zoster immune globulin (VZIG) injection within 72 hours of exposure.

There are several methods used to ensure prompt reporting of outbreaks. Some parents notify all the classmates' parents by letter to ask for help. If the parent has a good rapport with the teacher, she can have the teacher report any cases.

My daughter's preschool was very concerned and organized about the chicken pox reporting. They noted on each child's folder whether he or she had already contracted chicken pox. They told each parent individually about the dangers to Katy, and then frequently reminded everyone in the monthly newsletters. The parents were absolutely great, and we always had time to keep her out of school until there were no new cases. With the help of these parents, teachers, our neighbors, and friends, Katy dodged exposure for almost three years. She caught

chicken pox seven months after treatment ended and had a perfectly
normal case.

Other parents enlist the help of the office workers who answer the phone calls from parents of absent children.

> *We asked the two ladies in the office to write down the illness of any*
> *child in Mrs. Williams' class. That way the teacher could check daily and*
> *call me if any of the kids in her class came down with chicken pox.*

What about preschoolers?

A large proportion of children diagnosed with leukemia are preschoolers. Parents face the dilemma of continuing preschool through treatment, risking exposure to all the usual childhood viruses and diseases, or holding their child out, which denies them the opportunity for social growth and development. The decision is a purely personal one made after considering such issues as:

- Has the child already had chicken pox?
- Is the child already enrolled and comfortable in a preschool program?
- Are social needs being met by siblings and/or neighbors?
- Is preschool an option given medical considerations?

> *We put Carl in preschool while he was on treatment because we*
> *really felt that he needed to socialize. He would scream when I dropped*
> *him off, and it took him a while to adjust. He was shy and very quiet and*
> *did not mingle with the other kids very much. He was not the type to*
> *protest when someone took a toy away from him. Now, in high school, he*
> *is more outgoing, involved in a lot of activities, and mixes well with his*
> *age group.*

$$\bullet \quad \bullet \quad \bullet \quad \bullet \quad \bullet$$

> *My daughter was three years old when diagnosed and she missed*
> *two years of preschool. She was still on her protocol when she would have*
> *gone to kindergarten, but we decided to enroll her in a small preschool*
> *(twelve five- and six-year-olds in her class) with two very skilled teach-*
> *ers. She was a very traumatized child, who would not make eye contact*
> *or talk to anyone outside of the family. That year did wonders for her.*
> *She began to look at people and trust some adults again. By the next year*
> *she was emotionally able to handle kindergarten.*

$$\bullet \quad \bullet \quad \bullet \quad \bullet \quad \bullet$$

Kristin was five years old, attending day care, when she was diag-nosed. Our doctor initially told us that "Daycares are a cesspool for infec-tion," so we kept her at home when she wasn't in the hospital. She had been attending the same day care since she was two months old, and both children and staff were very attached to her. Some of the children were very upset that Kristin seemed to have just disappeared. So my wife and I had a nurse and social worker give the kids a presentation about leuke-mia, and answered all of their questions. The nurse talked to the doctor, and they changed their minds about the value of the day care for Kristin. So she went back and was very happy. Whenever Kristin was having a bad day, the director would take her into her office and take care of her personally. The next year we enrolled her in a private kindergarten which had one full-time teacher and a full-time aide with fourteen children in the class. It's been great for her.

The terminally ill child and school

In the sad event that the child's health continues to deteriorate and all possi-ble treatments have been exhausted, it is time for the students and staff to discuss ways to be supportive during his final days. Classmates need timely information about their ill classmate, so that they can deal with his declining health and prepare for his death. The possibility of death from leukemia should have been sensitively raised in the initial class presentation prior to the student's return to school, but additional information is needed if the student's health declines. The following are suggestions on how to prepare for the death of a classmate:

- The entire school staff needs to be in continuous communication with parents and hospital. They need to be reassured that death will not sud-denly occur at school, that the child will either die at home or in the hospital.

- Staff needs to be aware that participation at school is vital to a sick child's well-being. They should welcome and support the child's need to attend school as long as possible.

- Staff can design flexible programs for the ill student, for example, part-time school attendance and/or part-time home tutoring (if appropriate) for a child too weak to attend school all day.

Jody was lucky because he went to a private school, and there were only sixteen children in his class. Whenever he could come to school, they made him welcome. Because children worked at their own pace, he never had the feeling that he was getting behind in his classwork. He really felt like he belonged there. Sometimes he could only manage to stay an hour, but he loved to go. Toward the end when he was in a wheelchair, the kids would fight over whose turn it was to push him. The teacher was wonderful, and the kids really helped him and supported him until the end.

- Staff can designate a "safe person" and "safe haven" in the school building so that the student can retreat if physically or emotionally overwhelmed.

- The hospital advocate should meet with school personnel and the student's class to answer questions about the student's health status and to address fears and misconceptions about death.

- It is helpful to provide reading materials on death and dying for the ill child's classmates, siblings' classmates, teachers, and staff.

- Extraordinary efforts should be made to keep in touch once the child can no longer attend school. Cards, banners, tapes, telephone calls, or conference calls (on the principal's speaker phone) from the entire class are good ways to share thoughts and best wishes.

- Visits to the hospital or child's home should be made, if appropriate. If the child is too sick to entertain visitors, the class could come wave at the front window and drop off cards or gifts.

- The class can send a book of jokes, a walkman and tapes, or a basket of small gifts to the hospital.

- The class can decorate the family's front door, mailbox, and yard when the child is returning home from the hospital.

All of the above activities encourage empathy and concern in classmates, as well as help them adjust to the decline and imminent death of their friend.

When the child dies, a memorial service at school gives students a chance to grieve. School counselors or psychologists should talk to the classmates to allow them to express their feelings.

Parents appreciate receiving stories or poems about their departed child from classmates, and attending the funeral also supports the grieving family.

Identifying cognitive late effects

State-of-the-art treatment for childhood leukemia has increasingly resulted in greater numbers of long-term survivors, but not without cost. Some survivors suffer neurotoxic effects, which cause changes in their learning style as well as social behavior. Those with the highest risk of cognitive problems are young children who receive cranial radiation or high-dose systemic methotrexate, but children given high-dose intrathecal methotrexate can also gradually develop subtle learning difficulties. In some cases, significant intellectual loss can occur. It is important that parents and educators remain vigilant for potential learning problems to allow for quick intervention. The signs of possible learning disabilities are problems with:

- Handwriting.

- Spelling.

- Reading or reading comprehension.

- Understanding math concepts, remembering math facts, comprehending math symbols, sequencing, and working with columns and graphs.

- Auditory or visual language processing. These children have trouble with vocabulary, blending sounds, and syntax.

- Attention deficits. Some children become either inattentive or hyperactive or both. These behaviors are indicative of neurologically-based deficits in attention, which can cause children to be more impulsive and distractible than their peers.

- Short-term memory and information retrieval.

- Planning and organizational skills.

- Social maturity and social skills.

You should also suspect learning difficulties if:

- Your child was an A student prior to leukemia, and she is working just as hard and getting Cs.

- Your child reads a story and then has trouble explaining the plot.

- Your child frequently comes home frustrated from school, saying he just doesn't understand things as well as the other kids.

- Your child's teacher complains that she "just doesn't pay attention" or "just needs to work harder."

If any of the above situations are occurring, take action to begin the evaluation process before your child's self-esteem plummets. It is often hard to take this first step because children affected by radiation and/or chemotherapy can reason well and think clearly and may be above average academically in several areas. They tend to fall behind their classmates, however, on tasks that require fast processing skills, short-term memory, sequential operations, and organizational ability. Once identified, these differences can be addressed by strategies such as tutoring in memory enhancement, eliminating timed tests, improving organizational skills, and providing extra help in mathematics, spelling, and reading.

> When she entered adolescence, my daughter became very angry about her learning disabilities. She used to be gifted, and now does very well, but it is a struggle for her. We honestly explained that the choices were life with the possibility of some academic problems versus death, and we chose life.

· · · · ·

> My son was on a high-dose methotrexate protocol and developed learning disabilities. He was having problems with concentration, organization, and mathematics. At that time, medical personnel were not aware of the potential for learning problems as a result of treatment. He really didn't get help until high school when the learning specialist on the staff tested him for short-term memory and ability to concentrate. She decided to treat him just like a head injury patient. She reprogrammed him to be able to concentrate for longer periods of time. His schedule was redesigned so that it was comprised of fifteen-minute blocks. She taught him numerous tricks like word associations to improve his short-term memory. She was the first person who really got through to him, even though he had had tutors before. She was the first to say, "Yes, you have a problem, and this is what I can do to help." It worked. He is at a well-known university now, carrying a full load, and doing well.

· · · · ·

> Judd was on a high-dose methotrexate protocol from age three to six. He entered preschool while on therapy, and we enrolled him in a private kindergarten because of the small classes. He transitioned to public school in second grade with no problems. He is now fifteen, an A student who excels in math. He has had no cognitive after effects from his years of treatment.

· · · · ·

My son was two years old when he was diagnosed and put on a high-dose methotrexate protocol. In fourth grade his teacher believed he had short-term memory problems; he sometimes needed information repeated several times before he grasped it. He was extremely hard on himself because he believed he had to get all A's. We took him in for a battery of developmental tests geared to his age level, and the results showed his potential in the average to above average range. We had a long discussion with the psychologist, who explained to him what this meant in terms of work effort and grades. Before each school year we alerted teachers to ensure he got the extra attention he needed.

Your legal rights

The cornerstone of all federal special education legislation is Public Law 94-142, the Individuals with Disabilities Education Act (IDEA). The major provisions of this legislation are the following:

- All children, regardless of disability, will be served.

- Children will receive fair testing to determine if they need special education services.

- Schools are required to provide a free and appropriate public education through an individually designed program for every eligible child. An amendment to 94-142, called Public Law 99-457, requires early intervention programs for at risk infants and toddlers.

- Children with disabilities will be educated in the least restrictive environment, usually with children who are not disabled.

- The decisions of the school system can be challenged by parents, with disputes being resolved by an impartial third party.

- Parents of children with disabilities participate in the planning and decision making for their child's special education.

Of course, each school district has different interpretations of the requirements of the law, and implementation varies, so you should contact the school superintendent, director of special education, or special education advisory committee to obtain a copy of the school system's procedures and regulations for special education. Depending on the district, this document may range from two to several hundred pages. Also write to your state Superintendent of Public Instruction to obtain a copy of the state rules governing special education. To get the address, ask the school principal, a reference librarian, or refer to the resource section of *Negotiating the Special Education Maze* listed in this chapter's "Resources" section.

Armed with this information, you will be prepared to be an advocate for your child as he goes through the several steps necessary to determine the best possible education available to him. The steps that will be taken are referral, evaluation, eligibility, developing an individual education plan (IEP), and annual review.

> *My son had problems as soon as he entered kindergarten while on treatment. He couldn't hold a pencil, and he developed difficulties with math and reading. By second grade, I was asking the school for extra help, and they tested him. They did an IEP, and gave him special attention in small remedial groups. The school system also provided weekly physical therapy, which really helped him.*

Parents or teachers can make a referral by writing the school principal, requesting special education testing. Some school districts automatically will set up an IEP for any child who has had cranial radiation as part of his therapy, while other school districts are extremely reluctant to even evaluate struggling children for possible learning disabilities. Therefore, it is best for the parent or physician to send a written request to the principal, stating that the child is "health impaired" due to treatment for cancer, list his problems, and request assessments and an IEP meeting.

Once the referral is made, an evaluation is necessary to find out if the school district agrees that the child needs additional help, and if so, what types of help would be most beneficial. Usually a multidisciplinary team consisting of at least the teacher, school nurse, district psychologist, medical advocate (whoever is serving as the hospital liaison with the school), and social worker meet to administer and evaluate the testing. Areas usually included in the evaluation process are educational, medical, social, psychological, and others.

Children with a history of chemotherapy and/or radiation to the brain usually require thorough neuropsychological testing, which is best administered by psychologists experienced in testing pediatric patients. Most large children's hospitals have such personnel, but it sometimes takes very assertive parents to get the school system to use these experts. Your written consent is required prior to your child's evaluation, and you have the right to obtain an independent evaluation if you believe that the school's evaluation is biased or flawed in any way. However, you are responsible for this cost unless the district agrees or you follow the appeal procedures.

After the evaluation, a conference is usually held to discuss the results and reach conclusions about what actions will be necessary in the future. Make sure that in all written correspondence with the school, you clearly express a wish to be present at all meetings and discussions concerning your child's special education needs. You know him best, and you have the right to be there.

Parents need to be aware that children of very high intelligence unfortunately can fall into a gap where services will not be offered. This is because they may continue to perform "adequately," according to the school district standards (e.g., achievement scores within two grade levels of the child's age). Gifted children may receive good enough grades (As, Bs, Cs) even though their potential is of an A+ student. This discrepancy can frustrate them significantly. In this case, parents should be strong advocates, and continue to seek special services through the school or private tutoring if they can afford to pay out of pocket for it.

Individual Education Plan (IEP)

The Individual Education Plan describes the special education program and any other related services specifically designed to meet the individual needs of your child with learning differences. It is developed as a collaboration between parents and professional educators to determine what the student will be taught, and how and when the school will teach it. Students with learning disabilities need to learn the same things as other students: reading, writing, mathematics, history, and other preparation for college or vocational training. The difference is that, with an IEP in place, many specialized services, such as small classes, home schooling (usually five hours per week), speech therapy, physical therapy, counseling, and instruction by special education teachers, are used.

The IEP has five parts:

1. **A description of the child.** Includes present level of social, behavioral, and physical functioning, academic performance, and learning style.

2. **Goals and objectives.** Lists skills and behaviors that your child can be expected to master in a specific period of time. These should not be vague like "John will learn to cooperate," but rather, "John will prepare and present an oral book report with two regular education students by May 1." Each goal should answer the following questions: Who? What? How? Where? When? How often? When will the service start and end?

3. **Related services.** There are many specialized services that might be mandated by the IEP which will be provided at no cost to the family. These can include hearing or speech therapy, counseling by social workers, medical services, occupational therapy, parent counseling and training, physical therapy, transportation, and psychological services. For these services, the IEP should list the frequency and duration, e.g. "Jane will receive physical therapy from 9:00 to 10:00 A.M. on Tuesday and Thursday from September until December, when her needs will be reevaluated."

4. **Placement.** Describes the least restrictive setting in which the above goals and objectives can be met. For example, one student would be in the regular classroom all day with an aide present, while another might leave the classroom for part of each day to receive specialized instruction in the resource room or physical therapy. The IEP should state the percent of time the child will be in the regular education program.

5. **Evaluating the IEP.** At least once a year, and more frequently if requested by a parent or teacher, a meeting is held to review the progress towards meeting the short- and long-term goals and objectives of the IEP.

It is best to create a positive relationship with the school so that you are able to work together to promote your child's well-being. If, for whatever reason, communication deteriorates and you feel that your child's IEP is inadequate or not being followed, there are several facts that you need to know:

- Changes to the IEP cannot be made without parental consent.

- If parents disagree about the content of the IEP, they can withdraw consent and request (in writing) a meeting to draft a new IEP.

- Parents can request to have the disagreement settled by an independent hearing officer.

Many children with learning disabilities benefit greatly by using a computer during their school years. If the IEP calls for a computer, the school has to provide it. If you desire to obtain one yourself, IBM has a program to help disabled persons purchase a discounted computer and software, for rehabilitative or therapeutic purposes. For referral to an agency handling this program, call 1-800-426-4832.

> This year (3rd grade) has been a nightmare. My son has an IEP that focuses on problems with short-term memory, concentration, writing, and reading comprehension. The teacher, even though she is special ed qualified, has been rigid and used lots of timed tests. She told me in one conference that she thought my son's behavior problems were because he was "spoiled." We asked her at the beginning of the year to please send a note home with my son if he has a seizure, and she has never done it. She even questions him when he tells her that he had a seizure at recess. I began communicating directly with the principal, and I finally received a written notice that he had a seizure. I learned that the IEP is only as valuable as the teacher who is applying it.

• • • • •

> Initially, the school was reluctant to test Gina because they thought she was too young (6 years old). But she had been getting occupational therapy at the hospital for two years, and I wanted the school to take over. I brought in articles from Candlelighters Childhood Cancer Foundation, and spoke to the teacher, principal, nurse, and counselor. She had a dynamite teacher who really listened, and she helped get permission to have Gina tested. Her tests showed her to be very strong in some areas, and very weak in others. Together, we put together an IEP which we have updated every spring. Originally, she received weekly occupational therapy and daily help from the special ed teacher. She's now in fourth grade and is doing so well that she no longer needs occupational therapy, and she only gets extra help during study hall. They even recommended her for the student council, which has been a tremendous boost for her self-confidence.

Services for infants and preschoolers

Federal law also mandates early intervention services for disabled infants and toddlers, and in some cases, children at risk of having developmental delays. Infants, toddlers, or preschoolers with cancer may be eligible for these services in order to avoid developmental delays caused by cancer treatments. These services are administered either by the school system or the state health department. You can find out which agency to contact by asking the hospital social worker or by calling the special education director for your school district.

The law requires services not only for the infant or preschooler, but for the family as well. Therefore, instead of an IEP, an Individualized Family Service Plan (IFSP) is developed. This plan includes:

1. Description of child's physical, cognitive, language, speech, psychosocial, and other developmental levels.

2. Goals and objectives for family and child.

3. Description, frequency, and delivery of sevices needed, such as:
   • Speech, occupational, and physical therapy.
   • Health and medical services.
   • Family training and counseling.

4. A caseworker who locates and coordinates all necessary services.

5. Steps to support transition to other programs and services.

> We have had an excellent experience with the school district throughout preschool and now in kindergarten. We went to them with the first neuropsych results, which were dismal. They retested him, and suggested a special developmental preschool and occupational therapy. Both helped him enormously. He had an IEP done, and now has a full-time aide in kindergarten. He is getting the help he needs.

Record keeping

Other than medical record keeping, no records are more important to keep than those concerning your child's special education. Many parents recommend that you keep a yearly file that includes the name of the teacher, principal, and district psychologist, copy of the IEP, all test results, all correspondence, a current copy of the local and state regulations, and all of your child's report cards. You should also include in the file a list of the medications taken by your child during the year. The thought of this may seem overwhelming, but try to think of it this way: appropriate schooling is what will enable your child to overcome the cancer experience and become a productive adult. And your child needs your help to secure that future.

On accepting disabilities

Many of the disabilities of survivors of childhood leukemia are invisible. To help children and teens reach their true potential, changes in intellectual functioning must be diagnosed early and addressed. Students whose style of learning has changed as a result of treatment need their parents and teachers to explore the many excellent methods to enhance their ability to learn.

It is also important to remember that higher cognitive functioning usually remains intact, it is just getting the information in ("processing") that is impaired. Children who were gifted usually remains so; children with average abilities retain them. Their performance may be slower; they may require tutoring in memory enhancement and organizational skills, but they can still achieve to their potential. There are thousands of survivors in their late teens and twenties who are successfully attending college, or who have graduated and are pursuing professional careers. A disabled cancer survivor wrote:

> These children are not going to have their rights protected, or be eligible (presuming they are eligible) for various services, benefits, programs, and affirmative action unless they say they are disabled. As far as the civil rights laws are concerned, they will be considered disabled from diagnosis till death, even if they are as healthy as the average person. Furthermore, the limited civil rights protection that applies to their parents, siblings, spouses, and partners won't apply unless they say they are disabled.
>
> I do not think that there is anything shameful or stigmatizing about saying you are disabled. I think the efforts some parents have gone to so they can avoid this word are similar to the old days, when black children wore their hair like white children, and other families changed their last names and stopped speaking their native tongues for fear of "not fitting in." I think if disability is correctly explained to children, they will understand and accept. When I was a child, I was told I wasn't disabled (that was for people who were deaf, retarded, or in a wheelchair), I was merely "very sick" most of the time. It is better to make the effort to teach and have the children enjoy friendships with both non-disabled and disabled children. Otherwise, you end up with adults who feel isolated from even their own siblings.

> *Not to panic you, but some of the saddest phone calls I have received are from parents of ALL/AML survivors who are now in their 20s and living at home because they can't hold a job or manage their own affairs. After testing and referrals, the parents find out the extent of their impairments, but this could have been avoided if the late effects had been accepted, followed, and accommodated.*

Armed with the information from this chapter, and material from the "Resources" section, you will be prepared to effectively work with the school to ensure the very best education possible for your child, the survivor.

The following was written by Brigit Tuxen and is reprinted from Candlelighters Youth Newsletter, Fall 1994, Vol. XVI No. 4. Brigit was diagnosed in 1981, and is now a junior at Carnegie Mellon University in Pennsylvania.

> *My diagnosis of high-risk ALL gave me a 50 percent chance of survival. Cranial radiation and three years of blood tests, IV, chemotherapy, bone marrows, and spinal taps were my prescription. A positive outlook pushed me through the bad times. Somehow I understood that all the hurt was for a good reason, and that it would make me well.*
>
> *Call it a miracle, luck, or determination to live—I survived! But I would soon realize that I would never be like all the other kids. The radiation which destroyed cancer cells also harmed some of my brain cells. For the past five years, I have had slight difficulty with math and science courses at school, but, with the help of a tutor, I've managed to pull through challenging honors classes with As and Bs. However, I am often the last to finish class assignments or tests. It is very frustrating and often embarrassing. The SAT has become my ultimate challenge. Despite this minor disability, I continue to set high standards for myself. I feel extremely lucky to have beaten this disease, and I want to do anything I can to help those who are fighting cancer or some other hardship.*

Resources

Reading for adults

American Cancer Society. *Back to School: A Handbook for Parents of Children with Cancer.* To obtain a free copy, call 1-800-ACS-1234, ask for 88-20M-No. 4462-PS. 16-page introductory booklet covers school reentry, classroom presentations, the importance of advocates, legal issues, IEPs, and special needs.

Anderson, Winifred, Stephen Chitwood, and Deidre Hayden. *Negotiating the Special Education Maze: A Guide for Parents and Teachers.* Bethesda, MD: Woodbine House, 1990. (2nd ed. due June 1997) Excellent, well-organized text which clearly explains the step-by-step process necessary to obtain help for your child. Has up to date resource list and a comprehensive bibliography. Essential reading for parents of children with special educational needs. If you only read one book, this should be the one.

Barkley, Russell, Ph.D. *Taking Charge of ADHD: The Complete Authoritative Guide for Parents.* New York: The Guilford Press, 1995. Dr. Barkley is one of the original clinical researchers in the field of attention deficits. This is his current book, which thoroughly explains ADHD from both a medical and a psychological perspective. Most importantly, he offers specific guidelines for parents to help children manage their behaviors.

Cutler, Barbara Coyne. *You, Your Child, and 'Special' Education: A Guide to Making the System Work.* Baltimore, MD: Brookes Publishing Co., 1993. Excellent guide for parents includes chapters on understanding the local school system, legal rights, IEPs, confrontation, and advocacy and contains many parent stories and sample letters. Also includes appendices on resources, how to file a complaint, and the law.

Deasy-Spinetta, Patricia, and Elisabeth Irvin. *Educating the Child With Cancer.* Candlelighters Childhood Cancer Foundation. Single copies free to families of children with cancer, all others $7.50 per copy. Call, 1-800-366-CCCF for an order form. A must read for parents. This 137-page book discusses all aspects of educating the child with cancer including educational issues, peer relationships, school reentry, liaison programs, classroom presentations, cognitive late effects, preparing for college, college alternatives, legal aspects, siblings, and a bibliography.

Peterson's Guides. *Peterson's Guides to Colleges with Programs for Learning Disabled Students.* 4th ed. Princeton, NJ: Peterson's Guides, 1994. Excellent reference, available at most large libraries.

Scheiber, Barbara, and Jean Talpers. *Unlocking Potential: College and Other Choices for Learning Disabled People: A Step-by-Step Guide.* Maryland: Adler & Adler, 1985. Essential guide if your child is nearing college age. Includes very clear information on diagnosis, making choices, accommodations, study skills, getting help, and resources.

Silver, Larry, M.D. *The Misunderstood Child: A Guide for Parents of Children with Learning Disabilities.* 2nd ed. Blue Ridge Summit, PA: Tab Books, 1992. Comprehensive discussion of positive treatment strategies that can be implemented at home and in the school to help children with learning disabilities. Excellent chapters on psychological, social, and emotional development, evaluation, and treatment.

Tuttle, Cheryl Gerson, and Penny Paquette. *Parenting a Child with a Learning Disability: A Practical, Empathetic Guide.* New York: Doubleday, 1993. Extremely informative, easy-to-read guide to identifying learning disabilities and suggestions for dealing with the problems both at school and in the home. Practical and empathetic.

Tuttle, Cheryl Gerson, and Penny Paquette. *Thinking Games to Play with Your Child: Easy Ways to Develop Creative and Critical Thinking Skills.* Los Angeles: Lowell House, 1991. A book full of fun games to help preschoolers to third graders understand concepts that will help them learn to read, write, and do math. Great for using while waiting at the doctors, while in the car, or when in the hospital.

Reading for teachers

American Cancer Society. *Back To School: A Handbook for Teachers of Children with Cancer.* To obtain free copy, call 1-800-ACS-2345, ask for 88-20M-No. 2640-LE. 28-page booklet designed to aid teachers in effectively educating children with cancer. Covers communication, school reentry, IEPs, special needs, terminally ill students, classroom presentations, common questions, and emotional support.

Candlelighters Childhood Cancer Foundation Canada. *School Reentry Resource Manual.* 1992. Write to: CCCFC, 10 Alcorn Ave., Suite 200, Toronto, Ontario M4V 3B1, Canada. Sections for parents, educators, and health care professionals regarding siblings, adolescence, survivor's quality of life, programs, bereavement, and grief.

Chai Lifeline. *Back to School: A Handbook for Educators of Children with Life-threatening Diseases in the Yeshiva/Day School System.* 1995. Write to: 48 West 25th St. New York, NY 10010 or call (212) 255-1160. Covers diagnosis, planning for school reentry, infection control in schools, needs of junior and senior high school students, children with special educational needs, saying good-bye when a child dies, bibliography, and resources.

Peckham, Virginia. "Children with Cancer in the Classroom." *Teaching Exceptional Children* 26(1) (1993): 26-32. Contains a lesson plan for grades 1-6 which includes numerous questions and answers explaining cancer and how it is and will affect the students' classmate with cancer. Also has suggestions on how to handle the issue of death.

Grief in the Classroom

The Compassionate Friends. *Suggestions for Teachers and School Counselors.* P.O. Box 3696, Oak Brook, IL 60522. (708) 990-0010.

Fox, Sandra. *Good Grief: Helping Groups of Children When a Friend Dies.* 1988. NEAEYC, 35 Pilgrim Rd., Boston, MA 02215. Excellent resource contains chapters on tasks for bereaved children, how adults can help, ideas in action, and extensive resource list including books, films, and articles.

Gliko-Braden, Majel. *Grief Comes to Class: A Teacher's Guide.* Centering Corporation, 1531 N. Saddle Creek Rd., Omaha, NE 68104. (402) 553-1200. Comprehensive guide to grief in the classroom. Includes chapters on grief responses, the bereaved student, teen grief, developmental changes, sample letter to parents, sample teacher/parent conference, and suggestions for do's and don'ts.

Reading for children

Levine, Mel, M.D. *All Kinds of Minds.* Cambridge, MA: Educator's Publishing Service, Inc., 1993. Highly readable books about different learning styles. Written for grade-school-aged children, but parents benefit from reading them, too.

Levine, Mel, M.D. *Keeping a Head in School: A Student's Book About Learning Abilities and Learning Disorders.* Cambridge, MA: Educator's Publishing Service, Inc., 1990. Book about different learning styles for junior high and high school students.

Video

Hairballs on my Pillow. CARTI. P.O. Box 5210, Little Rock, AR 72215. 1-800-482-8561 or (501)660-7630. Videotape interviews children with cancer and their friends about friendship and returning to school. $35 for video and newsletters for students, exercises and activities for students, and a teachers notebook of information about cancer and its treatment, dealing with returning students, and additional resources.

Leukemia Society of America. *I'm Still Me*. 1989. To obtain a free copy, call 1-800-955-4LSA. 18-minute video program about children with leukemia, with accompanying handbook for medical personnel, teacher, and parents. Susan Linn and her puppets deal with successful reentry into the classroom covering topics such as hair loss, guilt, worry, teasing, physical changes, and feelings.

Siblings

Why was his hair falling out? Why was he going to the hospital all the time?
Why was he getting bone marrows all the time? It never occurred to me that he
might die. What was happening? I didn't get to go to the hospital to see him.
What was leukemia? Why was he getting so many presents???

—Chet Stevens

Straight from the Siblings:
Another Look at the Rainbow

CHILDHOOD CANCER touches all members of the family, with especially long-lasting effects on siblings. The diagnosis creates an array of conflicting emotions in siblings; not only are the siblings concerned about their ill brother or sister, but they usually resent the turmoil that the family has been thrown into. They feel jealous of the gifts and attention showered on the sick child, yet feel guilty for having these emotions. Their lives have been ripped from their mooring; the parents are physically absent or mentally distracted; financial problems loom large; and daily routines no longer exist. The days, months, and years after diagnosis are difficult, indeed, for the sibling of a child with leukemia.

Of all the topics covered in this book, parents expressed the most regret and guilt over how they handled the pain and worry of their "healthy" children. They will share with you their experiences, in the hope that it will help you to find the time to listen to and love the frequently overlooked brothers and sisters.

Emotional responses of the siblings

Brothers and sisters are shaken to the very core by leukemia in the family. Their parents, the leaders of the family clan, are immobile for a while, with empty eyes. There is no time, and little energy, to focus on the siblings. During this major crisis for the siblings—this time when their beings are flooded with anger and concern, jealousy and love, when they are in conflict as never before—they often have no one to turn to for help. They may feel utterly alone, abandoned, desolate in their pain. If you recognize these strong, ever-changing emotions of siblings as normal, not pathological, you will be better able to help your child talk about and cope with his overpowering feelings.

Concern for sick brother or sister

Children really worry about their sick brother or sister. It is hard for them to watch someone they love be hurt by needles, sickened by medicines, lose weight, and be bald. It is hard to feel so healthy and full of energy when the brother or sister has to stay indoors because of weakness or low blood counts. The siblings may also be old enough to understand that death is a possibility. There are plenty of reasons for concern.

> Christine's younger sister has really developed the nurturing side of her personality as a result of the leukemia. She frequently puts her arm around her sister, comforts her with soothing words or touches, and seems to feel her pain.

Fear

It is very common for siblings of children with cancer to think that the disease is contagious, that they can "catch it." Many also worry that one or both parents may get cancer. The diagnosis of cancer changes all of the children's view that the world is a safe place. They feel vulnerable, and they are afraid. Depending on their age, siblings worry that their brother or sister may get sicker, or may die. Some siblings develop symptoms of illness in an attempt to regain attention from the parents.

Fears of things other than cancer may emerge: fear of being hit by a car, fear of dogs, fear of strangers. Many fears can be quieted by accurate and age-appropriate explanations from the parents or medical staff.

> My three-year-old daughter vacillated between fear of catching cancer ("I don't ever want those pokes") to wishing she was ill so that she would get the gifts and attention ("I want to get sick and go to the hospital with mommy"). She developed many fears and had frequent nightmares. We did lots of medical play which seemed to help her. I let her direct the action, using puppets or dolls, and I discovered that she thought there was lots of violence during her sister's treatments. She continues to ask questions, and we are still explaining things to her, four years later.

Jealousy

Despite feeling concern for the ill brother or sister, almost all siblings also feel jealous. Presents and cards flood in for the sick child, mom and dad stay at the hospital with the sick child, and most conversations revolve around the sick child. When the siblings go out to play, the neighbors ask about the sick child. At school, teachers are concerned about the sick child. Is it any wonder that they feel jealous?

The siblings' lives are in turmoil, and, being human, they feel a need to blame someone. It's natural for them to think that if their brother didn't get sick, life would be back to normal.

> Our nine-year-old son seemed to be dealing with things so well until one evening as I was tucking him in he confided that he had tried to break his leg at school by jumping out of the swing. He began to cry and told me he doesn't want his brother to be sick anymore; that he needs some attention, too. As parents, we were always so concerned with our sick child that we didn't realize how much our healthy child was suffering, too.

Guilt

Young children are egocentric; they feel that the world revolves around them. It is logical to them to feel that since their sister has cancer, they caused it. They may have said in anger, "I hope you get sick and die," and then their brother got sick.

It is vital that this notion be dispelled right after diagnosis. Children really need to be told, many times, that cancer just happens, and no one in the family caused it. They need to understand that just because you think something or say something, it doesn't make it happen.

Beyond feeling guilt for causing the cancer, virtually every sibling feels guilt for their normal responses to cancer like anger and jealousy. They think, "How can I feel this way about my brother when he's so sick?" Assure them that the many conflicting feelings they are experiencing are normal and expected. As a parent, share some of your conflicting feelings (anger at the behavior of a child on prednisone, guilt about being angry).

Some children even feel guilt for being healthy! They think, "Why should I feel great when she's so frail and sick?"

Abandonment

Parental attention revolves around the sick child, causing siblings to feel isolated and resentful. Even when parents make a conscious effort not to be so preoccupied with the ill child, siblings still perceive that they are not getting their fair share of attention, and may be left feeling rejected.

> One day when my four-year-old son was in day care, we had to unexpectedly bring Erica in for emergency surgery on a septic hip. (It turned out to be a life-threatening surgery, and she ended up staying in for weeks). I called the day care and said that I couldn't pick up Daniel by closing time and the teacher said, "No problem, I live right across the street and I'll take him home for dinner." We went to get Daniel that evening, and he was very withdrawn. Later, he exclaimed, "All the mommies came. Then teacher turned out the lights, and you didn't come to get me." Then he burst into tears. In hindsight, one of us should have gone to bring him to the hospital to just sit with us. It was tense there, but at least he would have been with us, included as part of the family.

Sadness

Siblings have many very good reasons to be sad. They miss their parents and the time they used to spend together. They miss the life they used to have, the one they were comfortable with. They worry that their brother or sister may die. Some children show their sadness by crying often; others withdraw and become depressed. Often children confide in relatives or friends that they think their parents don't love them anymore.

> When Jeremy was very sick and hospitalized, we sent his older brother Jason to his grandparents for long periods of time. We thought that he understood the reasons, but a year after Jeremy finished treatment, Jason (9 years old) said, "Of course, I know that you love Jeremy more than me anyway. You were always sending me away so that you could spend time with him." It just broke my heart that every time he made that long drive over the mountains with his grandparents, he was thinking that he was being sent away.

· · · · ·

Months after his four-year-old sister's treatment ended, my six-year-old son confided to his grandmother that his parents loved her more than him. He still has never told his father or me, but he does sometimes ask if his sister is going to die. When I say no, he looks sort of disappointed.

Anger

Children's lives are totally disrupted by the diagnosis of a sister or brother with cancer, and it can make siblings very angry. Questions such as "Why did this happen to us?" or "Why can't things be the way they used to be?" are common. Children's anger may be directed at their sick brother, their parents, relatives, friends, or doctor. Children's anger may have a variety of causes, for instance, being left with baby-sitters so often, unequal application of family rules, or additional responsibilities at home. Because each member of the family may have frayed nerves, explosions of temper can occur.

As we were driving home from school one day, Annie was talking, and I was only half listening. All of a sudden I realized that she was yelling at me. She screamed, "See, this is what I mean. You never listen, your mind is always on Preston." I pulled the car over, stopped, and said, "You're right. I was thinking about Preston." I told her that from now on I would try to give her my full attention. I realized that I would really have to make an effort to focus on what she was saying and not be so distracted. This conversation helped to clear the air for a while. I tried to take her out frequently for coffee or ice cream to just sit, listen, and concentrate on what she was saying.

Worry about what happens at the hospital

Children have vivid imaginations, and when they are fueled by disrupted households and whispered conversations between teary parents, children can imagine truly horrible things. Seeing how their ill sister looks upon returning from a hospital stay can reinforce their fears that awful things happen at the clinic or hospital. Age-appropriate, verbal explanations can help children be more realistic in what they think happens at the hospital, but nothing is as powerful as a visit. Of course the effectiveness of a visit depends on your child's age and temperament, but many parents said bringing the siblings along helped everyone. The sibling gained an accurate understanding of hospital procedures, the sick child is comforted by the presence of the sibling, and the parent gets to spend time with both (or more) children.

Another method to minimize worry is to read age-appropriate books together. Many children's hospitals have coloring books for preschoolers that explain hospital procedures with pictures and clear language. School-age children benefit from reading *You and Leukemia: A Day at a Time* with a parent (see the "Resources" section). Adolescents might be helped by seeing videos on the subject or joining a sibling support group.

Veteran parents suggested that another way to reduce siblings' worries is to allow even the youngest children to help the family in some way. As long as children have clear explanations of the situation, and concrete jobs to do that will benefit the family, they tend to rise to the occasion. Make them feel that they are a necessary and integral part of the family's effort to face leukemia together.

Concern about parents

Exhausted parents often are not aware of the strong feelings of their healthy children. They sometimes assume that children understand that they are loved, and would be getting the same attention if they were the one who had cancer. But siblings frequently do not share their powerful feelings of anger, jealousy, or worry because they love their parents and do not want to place additional burdens on them. It is all too common to hear siblings say, "I have to be the strong one. I don't want to cause my parents any more pain." But burdens are lighter if shared, and parents need to try to encourage all of their children to talk about how they are feeling.

Sibling experiences

Siblings feel a terrible isolation, as if they are in a lifeboat in the middle of the ocean, alone. They feel bereft of the life that they knew, that they want, that they feel they deserve.

Simply understanding the depth of the pain and fears of your "healthy" children eases their path. Being available to listen, to say, "I hear how painful this is for you," or, "You sound scared. I am, too," makes siblings feel that they are still valued members of the family; that even though their brother or sister is absorbing the lion's share of parents' time and care, they are still cherished. Even if parents do not have time to spend with them, siblings need to hear that what they feel matters. If parents understand that these overwhelming emotions are normal, expected, healthy, they can provide solace.

In the hope that telling their stories will illuminate the massive difficulties faced by the siblings, brothers and sisters of children with leukemia shared the following.

Silent Hurting Heart

Dayna Erickson, 13 years old. One of Dayna's brothers died of a brain tumor, and her other brother is in remission from ALL. This poem was published in *Bereavement* magazine (see the "Resources" section in Chapter 21, *Death and Bereavement*).

> *"Oh, nothing's wrong," she smiled,*
> *grinning from ear to ear.*
> *The frown that just was on her face*
> *just seemed to disappear.*
>
> *But deep down where secrets are kept,*
> *the pain began to swell.*
> *All the hurt inside of her*
> *just seemed to stay and dwell.*
>
> *All the pain in her heart*
> *was too much for her to take.*
> *Pretending everything's OK*
> *is much too hard to fake.*
>
> *She'd duck into the bathrooms*
> *and hide inside the stalls*
> *Because no one could see her tears,*
> *behind those dirty walls.*
>
> *She was sick and tired of losing*
> *and things never turning out right.*
> *She had no hope left in her.*
> *She was ready to give up the fight.*

But she wiped away the teardrops,
put a smile back on her face,
pulled herself together and
walked out of that place.

Life went on and things got better.
She thought that was a start.
But still, no one could see inside
her silent hurting heart.

· · · · ·

Alana's Story

Alana Friedman, 11 years old.

My sister was in fifth grade, and had been sick for the last week or so. Laura always seemed to be my hero, although we got into arguments, all siblings get into fights, so I didn't worry. I didn't know what was about to happen, but neither did anyone else.

I don't quite remember how my parents told me she had cancer, but I do remember a lot of tears.

As time progressed my life changed. I lived with my best friend and her parents, Catherine and Bill, but that changed too. Kelsie (my friend) and I got into a lot of arguments, but we still do. I don't know if that is why my Grandmother and Grandfather moved up to live in our house so that they could take care of me. Living with them was different. My Grandmother had different expectations of me than my mother did.

My parents would each take turns staying at the hospital. Some nights I would live with my mom, grammy, and grandpy; and the next it would be with my dad and them.

Of course going through this dilemma I felt left out. Here I was living with my grandparents, and my sister got to live with our parents. She got lots of flowers, cards, and gifts and all I got was the feeling of love from my relatives. I know that love is better than material things, but when you are six years old, you don't think so.

Things stayed the same for a long time. Then my sister went into remission and started living at home. I had to get used to my parents again and missed my grandparents.

My sister was spoiled at home too. They bought her a water bed, so she wouldn't get cold. What did I get? A heating blanket; a used heating blanket.

A few months after she came home, her remission ended. She went back to live in the hospital, and my grandparents moved up to live with me.

Things went downhill from there. My life was turned around again. My sister went into a coma, and didn't really have much of a chance of coming out of it. Soon it would be her best friend's birthday, and Laura had to miss it. She was taken to heaven that day. Taken out of her misery and leaving us with a feeling of shock.

The day my sister died I had no idea what was happening. Kelsie's mom took care of me and everything was going great. To me that is, but when her mom took me back home, I remember my dad at the door talking to her. I headed in the other direction, but my father stopped me. My dad went into my parents' bedroom with me, and there I found my mom, lying on the bed helplessly, and to this day I still remember what she said to me, "It's over." Those words didn't make a lot of sense to me, I didn't know if the earth was going to explode. And then those two words sunk into my heart and I knew; my sister had died.

· · · · ·

Having a Sister With Leukemia

Alison Leake, 6 years old.

I think having a sister with leukemia is not fun. My mom paid more attention to Kathryn my sister. I had to stay with daddy! Mommy picked Kathryn up and not me! I wanted my sister's PJ's. Guess what? I did not get them! Although my mommy wanted to stay with me she did not want to leave my sister alone. Sometimes I felt like I was going to throw up. But now it has been five years since she has stopped having medicine and she is completely better. To celebrate that my sister and me were such good sports when my sister had leukemia we are going to Disneyland. The End.

· · · · ·

Siblings: The "Forgotten Children" in Childhood Cancer

Allison Ellis, 20 years old. Allison is now a graduate of Smith College and counselor at camp for victims of childhood cancer and their siblings.

I remember walking into my sister's room one morning and seeing large clumps of blond hair on her pillow. "Mommy, why is Lisa's hair falling out?" I asked.

"She's sick," was the only reply possible from my mother; she had no time for lengthy explanations to a three year old. So I was left to solve the mystery for myself. I went with Lisa and my mother several times a week to the hospital where Lisa would get finger "pokies" and sometimes "bone marrows" (which I thought of as "bone arrows" because the procedure entailed being punctured in the back by a large needle). Lisa would always cry afterward—the kind of childhood cry that seems to go on for hours at a deafening pitch. She lost all of her hair, so she wore bonnets that my grandmother made for her until her hair grew back. Sometimes she would get sick and throw up, and sometimes she stayed overnight at the hospital. I remember not understanding at all what was happening to my sister and not receiving any explanations. I remember the toys, gifts, and candy that were given in surplus to Lisa in a futile attempt to ease her pain. I felt jealous, neglected, and isolated because of Lisa's illness and the subsequent attention that was given to her and taken from me. I spent a lot of time with baby-sitters and television and less with my parents and the relatives who visited only to see Lisa. It seemed as though she was the only one people cared about. In this, I was the typical sibling of a victim of childhood cancer.

Lisa was diagnosed with leukemia in 1973 when she was just two years old and I was three. It was not expected that Lisa would live; in fact, all diagnoses of leukemia before 1970 were terminal. My parents were told not to talk about the disease with anyone; a child dying of cancer was just too frightening. Lisa underwent radiation therapy as well as chemotherapy to rid her body of the cancer-causing cells.

Yet, the result of this trauma was that I, as a sibling, received no attention relative to the rest of my family, and I felt extremely left out. I remember having a baby-sitter who stayed with me and my newborn baby sister during Lisa's treatment who seemed to understand how I was feeling. She would say, "Allison, I bet you're feeling a little bit left out with all the fuss over your sisters." (The youngest was given a lot of attention because everyone pays attention to newborn babies.)

I would always utter a modest, "Yeah, I guess so" while really thinking, "Yes, nobody pays attention to me. All I do is watch Sesame Street and watch Lisa play with her new toys that she got because she is sick and she won't share them with me. You bet I feel left out!"

I remember going places with my mother and being totally ignored by the people we would meet. People would say to my mother, "How is your daughter?" I would always say, "Fine," but they were never referring to me.

"Not you," they would say, "The other one," rendering my health and condition completely unimportant. I felt like a nonentity.

I began to taunt my sister, and we would fight frequently over sharing toys or clothes, which for the most part could be attributed to normal sibling rivalries, yet a lot of my hostilities ran deeper than a few pulled hairs. Lisa was the favored member of the family, and she received deferential and preferential treatment. When she came home crying after school, which was frequently the case in the first few years after her treatment was completed, she was always met with solace and understanding, whereas if I was ever upset, I was left to work things out for myself.

Today I understand better why I had the feelings that I did regarding my sister's cancer. For many years I resented her for something she had no control over and was angry at my parents for treating her differently than me. I now realize that no parent is superhuman and that they were doing what they thought was best under the unfortunate circumstances. Yet I know there are certain things I cannot change, such as being the first born. Whereas cancer made my sister vulnerable and my parents more protective, being the sibling of a cancer patient made me more independent. I was forced to find other sources of comfort at an early age, which usually meant that it had to come from within myself. Being at camp made me realize that I wasn't the only one who had experienced such a difficult role, however, and that there are many others who have been affected by childhood cancer much more deeply than me.

In conclusion, I wish to offer some advice. Siblings: please tell your parents in any way you can how you are feeling. Remember that you are not alone and you need not be forgotten, but try to understand where your parents are coming from. Parents: listen to your children. Recognize that siblings have different needs from cancer patients and try to even out attention-giving. Don't be surprised if your sibling child is angry at you. Professionals and neighbors: sometimes you are the only hope for a neglected sibling, yet you also have the potential to make things worse. Don't forget the sibling.

• • • • •

My Brother's a Legend

Erin Hall, 18 years old.

I'm really proud of my brother Judson for handling everything so well. During those years there were times when I was jealous of him, not only for the attention he received, but for his courage as well. This little boy was going through so much and I still cowered at getting my finger pricked. As I look back, I wonder if I would have been able to make it through, not only physically, but emotionally as well.

According to some people a person needs to be dead in order to be a legend, or to have been famous, or well liked. A legend to me though, is someone who has accomplished something incredible, enduring many hardships and pains, and still comes out of it smiling.

Judd is a legend to me because he didn't give up in a time that he might have. He is a legend because he survived an illness that many do not. Now I look at him after being in remission for almost five years, and I hope that someday if I am ever faced with a challenge like his, I will have the same strength and courage he had.

• • • • •

My Brother Has Leukemia

Amanda Moodie, 8 years old.

Sometimes having a brother with leukemia is fun, like when my family goes on the Fantasy Flight to the North Pole, and going to the special summer camp, and getting special privileges at Disney World.

But other times, it can be really hard, especially when William gets put in the hospital. Right now, he can't leave his room in the hospital, and the doctors wear masks when they come in. I HATE seeing that. And he stays in for very long periods of time. The first time, he was there for almost three weeks! It comes so suddenly. He has stayed out for five months, then BAM! He's back in. And the worst of it is, people are always pitying us. "Poor little boy." "Poor William." I guess they like pitying us.

So, leukemia has ups and downs like everything else, but to me it's mostly downs.

• • • • •

For Brothers and Sisters

Ellen Zimmerman. Reprinted with permission from *Candlelighters Youth Newsletter* Summer 1994, Vol. XVI No. 3.

I am the first of four children and the only girl. When I was diagnosed with ALL at the age of fourteen, it affected all our lives. My brother Wes was thirteen, Matthew was four, and Erik was two. They and my parents were my support system.

When I was first diagnosed and in the hospital, Dr. Plunkett asked if I wanted anyone besides my parents present when he gave us the diagnosis. I told him I wanted Wes with me. Wes is only fourteen months younger than I am, and we have always been very close. He took it all in, and we all decided that we would face this thing, and beat it, as a family. Then he and I sent our parents off so we could have some private time together.

Wes was my support at school and at home. He stuck up for me and kept an eye on me. I lost some of my "friends" after I was diagnosed because of my illness and their fear of it. Wes was always there for me. That's not to say we didn't have our fights. Poor Wes—I could hit him but he couldn't hurt me physically because of my low blood counts. Sometimes I took advantage of that.

Matt and Erik were also a great source of comfort and support. They would accompany my mom and me to treatments and hold my hand when I got stuck. If one of them wasn't with me when I went in, the nurses would ask me where they were. These little boys made it easier for me to be brave.

I hope my brothers know how much I appreciate, too, the extra time they gave me with our parents during my illness. My parents were very good about splitting time between me and my brothers. If one was with me at treatment or the hospital, then the other was spending time with the boys. Family and friends were also a big help.

I've been out of treatment for ten years now. I teach second grade and spend a week of my summer as a counselor at a camp for kids with cancer. I am the proud sister of three Eagle Scouts. Wes is married now and lives in another state. I realize how much he meant to me during that trying time and how much he means to me now.

If you are a sibling to someone with cancer and wonder if you make a difference to your sick brother or sister, I would like to tell you that *you make a very big difference.*

· · · · ·

When My Brother Got Cancer

Annie Walls, 15 years old.

One experience in my life that was in no way comfortable for my family or myself and caused me a lot of confusion and grief was when my brother had Leukemia. Along with the disruption of this event, it also caused me to grow tremendously as a person. The Thanksgiving of my third-grade year, Preston, my brother, became very ill and was diagnosed a few weeks later with having cancer.

This event helped me to grow to become a better person in many ways. When my brother had very little hair or was puffed out from certain drugs I learned to respect people's differences and to stick up for them when they're made fun of. Also, when Preston was in the hospital I was taught to deal with a great amount of jealousy that I had. He received many gifts, cards, flowers, candy, games, and so many other material things that I envied. Most of all though, he received all the attention and care of my mother, father, relatives, and friends. This is what I was jealous of the most. As I look back now, I can't believe that I was that insensitive and self-centered to be mad at my brother at a time like that.

The thing that made this a "graced" experience was the fact that it enabled me to be very close to my brother as we grew up. My brother and I are now good friends and are able to talk and share our experiences with each other. I don't think that we would have this same relationship if he never had Leukemia and I think that has been a very positive outcome. Another thing that has been a positive outcome of this event is the people I've been able to meet. Through all the support groups, camps, and events for children with cancer and their siblings, I have met some people with more courage and more heart than anyone could imagine. In no way am I saying that I'm glad my brother had cancer, but I will say I'm very glad with some of the outcomes from it.

• • • • •

My Sister Had Cancer

Jeff Pasowicz, 11 years old. Reprinted from CCCF Canada CONTACT newsletter Vol. XVI No. 2 Spring 1994.

My sister Jamie got cancer when she was 23 months old. I was eight, and my two other sisters were six and four.

My sisters and I were scared that my sister was going to die. We weren't able to go to public places and also weren't allowed to have friends in my house. We missed a lot of school when there was chicken pox in our school. I got teased in school sometimes because my sister had no hair. Once an older kid called my sister a freak. My mom was sad most of the time. It was very hard.

We are all pleased that Jamie is doing well, and our lives are getting back to normal. It was an experience I'll never forget, and I hope it has made me a stronger person.

• • • • •

From a Sibling

Sara McDonnall, 15 years old. Sara's essay won first prize in the 1995 Candlelighters Creative Arts Contest.

Childhood cancer—a topic most teens don't think much about. I know I didn't until it invaded our home.

Childhood cancer totally disrupts lives, not only of the patient, but also of those closest to him/her, including the siblings. First, I was numbed with unbelieving shock. "This can't be happening to me and my family." Along with this came a whole dictionary full of incomprehensible words and a total restructuring of our (up to that time) fairly normal life-style.

One day in July 1988, I was waiting for my parents to pick me up from summer camp and anticipating the start of our family vacation to Canada. When they arrived, they informed me that my older brother Danny was very sick, and we wouldn't be taking that trip after all. The following day the call came that confirmed the diagnosis. Instead of packing for vacation, we packed our bags and headed for Children's Hospital in Denver, 200 miles away, where Danny was scheduled for surgery and chemotherapy.

I developed my own disease (perhaps from fear I would "catch" what Danny had), with symptoms similar to my brother's:

- Sympathy pains. I asked, "Why him?" when he came home from the hospital, exhausted from throwing up a life-saving drug for three days.

- Fear. "How much sicker is Danny going to get before he gets well? He is going to get well, isn't he?"

- Resentment. My parents seemed so worried about him all the time. They didn't seem to have time for me anymore.

- Confusion. Why couldn't Danny and I wrestle around like we used to? Why couldn't I slug him when he made me mad?

- Jealousy. I felt insignificant when I was holding down the fort at home.

The parts I hated the most were: not understanding what was being done to him; answering endless worried phone calls; and hearing the answers to my own questions when my parents talked to other people.

I was helped to sort out these feelings and identify with other siblings when I attended a program held just for teens who had siblings with cancer. We got together, tried to learn how to cross-country ski, and talked about our siblings and ourselves.

Perhaps you remember this story: "U.S. [speed skating] star Dan Jansen, 22, carrying a winning time into the back straightaway of the 1000 meter race, inexplicably fell. Two days earlier, after receiving word that his older sister, Jane, had died of leukemia, Dan crashed in the 500 meter" (Life Magazine). Having a sibling with cancer can immobilize even an Olympic athlete. Dan was expected to bring home two gold medals, but cancer in a sibling intervened. He became, instead, the most famous cancer sibling of all time. He shared his grief before a television audience of two billion people. Dan later went on to win the World Cup in Norway and Germany, and capture the gold at the Olympics. He is the first to tell you the real champions can be found in the oncology wards of children's hospitals across our nation, and the siblings who are fighting the battle right along beside them.

· · · · ·

Siblings: Having Our Say

Naomi Chesler.

Twelve young people aged 7 to 29 met at the 25th Anniversary Candlelighters Conference to talk about what it is like having a sibling with cancer in the family. We talked about our families, our anger, jealousy, worries, and fears, and thought about what we wanted to tell others about our experiences. In fact, we made lists of things we wanted other people to know: one for parents, one for other children or young adults in our position, and one for the child who has been diagnosed with cancer.

Some parts of these lists reflect anger and bitterness, but that was not the overriding feeling in the session. I hope it isn't the only message you take away. If nothing else, the issues raised here may provide you with a good starting point for discussions in your own family.

To Parents:

- We know you are burdened and trying to be fair. But try harder.

- Give us equal time.

- Be tough on disciplining the child with cancer. No free rides.

- Put yourself in our shoes once in a while.

- If you are away from home a lot, at least call and tell us, "I love you."

- Tell us what is going on. Don't just sit us in front of a video (about cancer); talk with us about it.

- Keep special time with us like lunch once a week or something. Time for just us. And if you can't be with us, find someone who can.

- When you talk to family members, say how everyone is doing—what we are doing is important, too.

- Ask how we are feeling. Don't assume you know.

To siblings of newly diagnosed kids:

- Keep a diary if you don't want to talk to your parents.

- Expect to not get as much attention.

- Expect that your parents are going to be extra cautious about what your brother/sister does, who he/she hangs out with, etc.

- Hang in there. You're all you've got for now.

- Don't feel like you have to think about the illness all the time.

- Be understanding of your parents and stay involved.

- Tell someone how you are feeling—don't bottle it up.

- Go to the hospital to visit when you can.

- Make as many friends as possible at school.

To our siblings who struggled or are struggling with cancer:

- The world does not revolve around you.

- Stop feeling sorry for yourself.

- Not everything is related to cancer. Stop using that as an excuse for everything.

- I'm jealous of you sometimes, but I'm not mad. I know it sometimes seems like I'm mad, but I'm not.

- Don't take advantage of all the extra attention you get.

- Tell mom and dad to pay attention to me sometimes, too.

- Now that you are feeling better, where's the gratitude for all those chores that I did?

- I really admire your strength and courage. I wouldn't have gotten through your illness without you.

Helping siblings cope

The following are the experiences and advice from several families on things that help the brothers and sisters cope.

- Make sure that you explain leukemia and its treatment to the siblings in terms that they understand. Create a climate of openness, so that they can ask questions and know that they will get answers. If you don't know the answer to a question, write it on your list to ask the doctor at the next appointment, or ask your child if he would like to go to the appointment with you and ask the question himself.

   We drew a lot of pictures of red cells, white cells, and platelets. We showed each doing its job: red cells carrying oxygen around, white cells gobbling up cold germs as well as leukemia blasts, and platelets clumping up to form scabs. Drawing opened the floodgates of questions, and I was always amazed at how each child understood some things so clearly, and really was confused and frightened by other things.

· · · · ·

We always, always explained everything that was happening to Brent's older brother Zac (8 years old). He never asked questions, but always listened intently. He would say, "OK. I understand. Everything's all right." We tried to get him to talk about it, but through all these years, he just never has. So we just kept explaining things at a level that he could understand, and he has done very well through the whole ordeal. The times that he seemed sad, we would take him out of school, and let him stay at the Ronald McDonald House for a few days, and that seemed to help him.

- Make sure that all the children clearly understand that cancer is not contagious. They cannot catch it, nor can their ill brother give it to anyone else. Impress upon them that nothing the parents or brothers and sisters did caused the cancer.

- Bring home a picture of the brother or sister in the hospital, and carry a tape recorder back and forth to relay songs and messages.

- It is very hard for mothers and babies or toddlers to be separated. Some families leave out family photo albums for the caregiver to show the toddler whenever she gets sad.

My daughter was eighteen months old when her three-year-old sister was diagnosed. Each member of the family flew in to stay at the house for two-week shifts, so she had a lot of caregivers. A friend of mine gave her a big key chain which held eight pictures. We put a picture of each member of the family (including pets) on her key chain, and she carried it around whenever we were away. It seemed to comfort her.

- Try to spend time individually with each sibling.

We began a tradition during chemotherapy that really helped each member of our family. Every Saturday each parent would take one child for a two-hour special time. We scheduled it ahead of time to allow excitement and anticipation to grow. Each child picked what to do on their special day—such as going to the park, eating lunch at a restaurant, riding bikes. We tried to put aside our worries, have fun, and really listen.

• • • • •

Kim's hospitalizations were very hard on five-year-old Kelly. My parents kept Kelly during the week, so this helped a lot. Dennis would pick her up after work. I remember being at the hospital all week long, then Dennis would come on the weekends, and I would go home and do things with Kelly. We would go out to eat, or roller skating, etc. I really missed her, and it was just so hard on everyone. I remember being so tired, but I feel that you need to spend time with all of your children because they need you also.

- If people only comment on the sick child, try to bring the conversation back to include the sibling. For example, if someone exclaims, "Oh look how good Lisa looks," you could say, "Yes, and Martha has an attractive new haircut, too. Don't you like it?"

- Share your feelings about the illness and its impact on the family. Say, "I'm sad that I have to bring your sister to the hospital a lot. I miss you when I'm gone." This allows the sibling an opportunity to tell you how she is feeling. Try to make the illness a family project by expressing how the family will stick together to beat it.

  I never kept my feelings secret from Shawn's two older brothers (5 and 7 years old). If I was scared, I talked about it. Once when we thought he was relapsing, my stomach was so knotted up that I could barely walk. Kevin said, "Mom, I'm really worried about Shawn." I told him that I was, too, and then we both just hugged and cried together. They really opened up when we didn't hide our feelings.

- Include siblings in decision making, such as giving choices on how extra chores will be done or devising a schedule for parent time with the healthy children.

  We always gave the boys choices about where they would stay when Shawn had to be in the hospital. I felt like it gave them a sense of control to choose baby-sitters. They usually stayed at a close neighbor's house where there were younger children. It allowed them to ride the same bus to school and play with their neighborhood friends. Their lives were not too disrupted. They also really pitched in and helped with the younger kids. I think it helped them to help others.

- Allow siblings to be involved in the medical aspects of their brother's illness, if they wish it. Often the reality of clinic visits and overnight stays are easier than what siblings imagine. Many siblings are a true comfort when they hold their brother's hand during spinal taps or bone marrows.

- Give lots of hugs and kisses.

We assumed everything was fine with Erin because she had her grandma, who adored her, staying with her. We made a conscious decision to spend lots of time with her and include her in everything. But, we realized later that she felt very left out. My advice is to give triple the affection that you think they need, including lots of physical affection such as hugs and kisses. For years, Erin felt jealous. She thought her brother got more of everything: material things, time with parents, opportunities to do things she was not allowed to do. She finally worked it out while she was in college.

- Be sure to alert teachers of siblings about the tremendous stress at home. Many children respond to the worries about cancer by developing behavior or academic problems at school. Teachers should be vigilant for the warning signals, and provide extra support or tutoring for the stressed child or teen. Continue to communicate frequently with the teachers of the siblings to make sure you are aware of any developing problems.

- Expect your other children to have some behavior problems as part of living with cancer in the family. This is a "normal," not pathological, response.

When my four-year-old "healthy" child screams and sobs over a minor skinned knee, she gets as much sympathy as my child with leukemia does during a bone marrow aspiration. I put a bandage on the knee, rock her, sing a song, and get her an ice pack. The injuries are not equal, but the needs of each child are. They both need to be loved and cared for; they both need to know that mom will help, regardless of the severity of the problem. I even let the sib use EMLA for routine shots. My pediatrician laughs at me, but I just tell him, "Sibs need perks, too."

- The child with cancer receives many toys and gifts resulting in hurt feelings or jealousy in the siblings. Provide gifts and tokens of appreciation to the siblings for helping out during hard times, and encourage your sick child to share.

- Encourage a close relationship between an adult relative or neighbor and your other children. Having a "someone special" when the parents are frequently absent can help prevent problems and help your child to feel cared for and loved.

- Take advantage of any workshops, support groups, or camps for siblings. These can be of tremendous value for siblings, providing fun and friendships with others who truly understand their feelings.

Positive outcomes for the siblings

After stating all of the above potential troubles that your children might experience, it is important to note that many siblings evade the negative possibilities and exhibit great warmth and active caretaking while their brother or sister is being treated for leukemia. Their empathy and compassion seem to grow with the crisis. Some brothers and sisters of children with cancer feel that they have benefited from the stressful experience in many ways, such as: increased knowledge about disease, increased empathy for the sick or disabled, increased sense of responsibility, enhanced self-esteem, greater maturity and coping ability, and increased family closeness. Many of these siblings mature into adults interested in the caring professions, such as medicine, social work, or teaching. Character can grow from confronting personal crisis, and many parents speak of the siblings with admiration and pride.

I don't think it matters how old the siblings are—it's a reality that the healthy ones will not get their fair share for a while. From what I've been able to observe in my own and other families, the siblings do eventually take it in stride and even seem to benefit from the opportunity to learn compassion, selflessness, and responsibility. As they get older, they even take comfort in the realization that, had they been the sick one, THEY would have received all the necessary attention and that their parent(s) can cope (somehow) with whatever comes around. Libby added to her observations that she noted carefully how I reacted to Casey's illness at first (fell apart!) but that the next day I could gather my strength and do what had to be done. She likes to think she would also react similarly should the occasion arise (although, at her age, every blip in her universe is a catastrophe).

Resources

Reading for adults

Faber, Adele, and Elaine Mazlish. *Siblings Without Rivalry: How to Help Your Children Live Together So You Can Live Too.* New York: Avon Books, 1987. Required reading for parents with fighting siblings. Offers dozens of astonishingly simple yet effective methods to reduce conflict and foster a cooperative spirit.

Leukemia Society of America. *Emotional Aspects of Childhood Leukemia.* To obtain free copy, call 1-800-955-8484. 32-page booklet deals with the gamut of emotions experienced by all members of the family, including siblings.

Murray, Gloria, and Gerald Jamplosky, eds. *Straight from the Siblings: Another Look at the Rainbow.* Millbrae, CA: Celestial Arts, 1982. Written by 16 children who have brothers and sisters with a life-threatening illness who met at the Center for Attitudinal Healing. A must read for both parents and siblings. Contains beautiful artwork by the children as well as wise words from the heart about reactions to the news, feelings, facing death, making choices, being part of a group, and thoughts for other siblings in a similar situation.

Reading for siblings

American Cancer Society. *When Your Brother or Sister Has Cancer.* To obtain free copy, call 1-800-ACS-2345. 16-page booklet which describes the emotions felt by siblings of a child with cancer.

Baker, Lynn, M.D. *You and Leukemia: A Day at a Time.* Philadelphia, PA: W.B. Saunders Company, 1988. This book may help siblings understand what leukemia is and why some of the drugs and procedures are necessary.

National Cancer Institute. *When Someone in Your Family Has Cancer.* To obtain free copy, call 1-800-4-CANCER. Booklet helps young people understand more about cancer, its treatment, and their feelings and concerns.

Technical reading

Chesler, Mark, Ph.D., Jennifer Allswede, et al. "Voices from the Margin of the Family: Siblings of Children with Cancer." *Journal of Psychosocial Oncology* 9(4) (1991): 19-41. Interviews explore the views and experiences of siblings: worry about ill brother or sister; lack of attention; concern about other family members.

Craft, Martha J., and John L. Craft. "Perceived Changes in Siblings of Hospitalized Children: A Comparison of Sibling and Parent Reports." *Children's Health Care: Journal of the Association for the Care of Children's Health* 18(1) (1989). Study examined parental perceptions of sibling problems and sibling perceptions. Results show that siblings feel a far greater number of problems resulting from their sister or brother being hospitalized than the parents were aware of.

Heiney, Sue P., Karen Goon-Johnson, et al. "The Effects of Group Therapy on Siblings of Pediatric Oncology Patients." *Journal of Pediatric Oncology Nursing* 7(3) (July 1990): 95-100. Study tested the coping abilities of 9 to 15 year olds. Concludes that peer support groups provide siblings with the opportunity to decrease their sense of isolation, ventilate negative feelings, and learn from each other.

Leonard, Barbara J. "Siblings of Chronically Ill Children: A Question of Vulnerability Versus Resilience." *Pediatric Annals* 20(9) (September 1991): 501-506. Stresses the importance of focusing on the strengths of siblings rather than their weaknesses.

Video

Siblings of Children with Cancer. 30-minute videotape. Available from: Biomedical Communications, University of Arizona Health Sciences Center, Tucson, AZ. 85724. (602) 626-7343. $275 to buy, $50 weekly rental. Interviews with four preadolescent and adolescent siblings discuss how they learned of sibling's illness, what they understood, positive and negative effects on their sibling relationship, response to sibling death, advice to parents, other siblings, and health care team. Includes a discussion leader's guide.

Feelings, Communication, and Behavior

When I approach a child, he inspires in me two sentiments:
tenderness for what he is, and respect for what he may become.

—Louis Pasteur

UNDER THE BEST OF circumstances, child rearing is a daunting task. When parenting is complicated by an overwhelming crisis such as leukemia, communication within the family may suffer. Prior to the diagnosis, children know the family rules and understand the limits for their behavior. Afterwards, normal family life is disrupted, and all sorts of confusing and distressing feelings appear. Parenting must change in response to the frequently shifting needs of the ill child and affected siblings. This chapter examines some emotional and behavioral changes in both children and parents, and presents suggestions on how to maintain effective communication and appropriate behavior within the family.

Feelings

In Chapter 1, *Diagnosis*, there was an extensive list of feelings that parents may experience after the diagnosis of leukemia in their child. It is important to remember that children, both siblings and the ill child, are also overwhelmed by strong feelings, and they generally have fewer coping skills than do adults. At varying times and to varying degrees, children and teens may feel fearful, angry, resentful, powerless, violated, lonely, weird, inferior, incompetent, betrayed. All of these powerful feelings, if unresolved, create massive stress. Children have to learn ways to deal with these strong feelings to prevent "acting out" behaviors (behavioral problems) or "acting in" behaviors (depression, withdrawal). Good communication is the first step toward helping your family cope with the strong feelings and changes brought about by a leukemia diagnosis.

Communication

Treatment is very hard and rigorous. You sometimes feel like you don't want to live anymore. I was really delirious. I changed moods every five minutes. I couldn't concentrate on anything, not even reading. I didn't know what I wanted out of life or why I wanted it. It was really hard for my parents and brother. I had horrible temper tantrums and said things that I didn't mean.

—Noah Wolfson
Advice to Doctors and Other Big People

Honesty

Above all else, children need to be able to trust their parents. They can face almost anything, as long as they know that their parents will be at their side. Trust requires honesty. For your ill child and his brothers and sisters to feel secure, they must always know that they can depend on you to tell them the truth, be it good news or bad.

We were always very honest. We felt that if she couldn't trust us to tell her the truth how scary that would be. I've seen a few incidents in the clinic of people with totally different styles who don't tell their kids the truth. I have run into the bathroom at the clinic crying after overhearing a mother who had deceived her child into coming to the clinic. Then he found out he needed a back poke and completely lost it. It makes me cringe. Children just have to be prepared. If they can't trust their parents, who can they trust?

Listening

Just trying to get through each day consumes most parents' time, attention, and energy. Consequently, one of the greatest gifts we can give our children is our time. A special time when we really focus on what they are saying, when we listen to not only the words, but the feelings that generate them. A time we stop to think before we speak. Many behavior problems can be prevented if our children think that we understand, if they feel that no matter how leaky the boat is, we are all in it together.

After my relapse at age thirteen, the chemotherapy was much more difficult to tolerate. My appearance changed dramatically due to hair loss and rapid weight gain from prednisone. The L-asparaginase made my legs stiff and sore so that it was difficult to walk. After a two month-

absence, when I returned to school, the treatment I received from the other students was unbearable. I finally refused to go to school. I felt so strongly about not going to school that once, on the way there, I jumped out of the car at an intersection. This helped mom and dad make the decision to send me to a private school. The kids and staff at the new school knew my situation and were very compassionate. The decision to change schools was one of the best things my parents ever did for me.

· · · · ·

When my daughter was seven, three years after her treatment ended, I realized how important it was to keep listening. She was complaining about a hang nail and I told her that I would cut it for her. She started to yell that I would hurt her. I asked her, "When have I ever hurt you?" and she said, "In the hospital." I sat down with her in my arms, rocked her, and explained what had happened in the hospital during her treatment, why we had to bring her, and how we felt about it. I told her that I cried along with her when she was hurt by procedures. I asked her to tell me her feelings about being there. We cleared the air that day, and I expect we will need to talk about it many more times in the future. Then she held out her hand so that I could cut off her hang nail.

Talking

If you are not in the habit of talking to your children about how you are feeling, it is hard to start in a crisis. But now, more than ever, it's important to try. Parents can provide an opening for discussion by simply stating how much they miss their other children, for example, "I really miss you when I have to take your sister to the hospital. I'll call you every night just so I can hear your voice," or, "Sometimes I really get mad at the cancer. I wish the family didn't have to be separated so much." It is also helpful to tell your child with leukemia how the illness is affecting her siblings, for example, "It is very hard for Jim to stay at home with a baby-sitter when I bring you to the hospital. Let's try to think of something nice to do for him." These statements not only reassure children of your continued love for them and distress about being separated from them, but creates an opportunity for them to share with you how they feel about what is happening to the family.

My daughter, diagnosed when one year old and now entering fifth grade, has three older siblings, so we have been through many developmental stages as far as communication goes. I try to answer their ques-

tions honestly, but only tell them what I think they can understand without overwhelming them with information. I remember one of my boys, soon after her diagnosis, asked me if she was going to die, and I said "no" emphatically. I regretted it immediately, and realized that I would have to deal with my fears about the possibility of her dying, then go back and tell him the truth. So, later, I told him that I hadn't given an accurate answer because I was scared; that we didn't know if she was going to die, we hoped not, but we would have to wait and see.

I have found that as their understanding deepens, they come back with more questions, needing more detailed answers. So, my motto is, be honest but don't scare them. If you say everything is okay but you are crying, they know something is wrong, and that they can't trust you for the truth.

Common behavioral changes of children

Discipline under the best of circumstances can be difficult. But when one child has leukemia, parents are stressed, siblings are angry, and the situation may become unmanageable. The first step is to decide whether the ill child is going to be treated as if she only has a few months to live, or as if she will survive and need training in self-control and temper management. Step two is to examine your own behavior to see if you are modeling the conduct that you expect from your children. Step three is to develop a consistent method to externally control the angry or destructive child, then systematically teach the child to learn to control her own impulses.

Barbara Sourkes, an experienced child psychologist, wrote in her book *Armfuls of Time: The Psychological Experience of the Child with a Life-Threatening Illness:*

> *While loss of control extends over emotional issues, and ultimately over life itself, its emergence is most vivid in the child's day-to-day experience of the illness, in the barrage of intrusive, uncomfortable or painful procedures that he or she must endure. The child strives desperately to regain a measure of control, often expressed through resistant, noncompliant behavior or aggressive outbursts. Too often, the source of the anger—the loss of control—goes unrecognized by parents and caregivers. However, once its meaning is acknowledged, an explicit distinction may be drawn for the child between what he or she can or cannot dictate. In order to maximize the child's sense of control, the environment can be*

structured to allow for as much choice as is feasible. Even options that appear small or inconsequential serve as an antidote to loss, and their impact is often reflected in dramatic improvements in behavior.

In the following sections, parents share how they handled various behaviors of their ill child.

Anger

Parents respond to the diagnosis of leukemia with anger, and so do children. Not only is the child angry at the disease, but also at the parents for bringing her in to be hurt, at having to take medicine that makes her feel terrible, at losing her hair, at losing her friends, and on and on. Children with cancer have good reasons to be angry. Our job is to allow them to vent their feelings in appropriate ways.

I think that much anger can be avoided by giving choices and letting kids have some control. Parents need to clearly explain that there are some things that simply have to be done (spinal taps) but that the child or teen is in control of positions, people present, music, even timing. For example, if your teen gets bad headaches after spinals, help him negotiate the date and time when the spinal will be done so that sports or social life will not be impacted.

· · · · ·

Justin has extreme bursts of anger sometimes. I don't know if it's related to the leukemia, or if it's just personality or normal development. He starts yelling, and I feel like I have a tasmanian devil loose in my house. But I just use time-outs ("You go sit on your bed until you are over this") or loss of privileges ("You do this now or you won't be able to watch a movie later.")

· · · · ·

We have a case of the halo or the horns. Our son is either very defiant or an absolute angel. He argues about every single thing. I really think that it is because he has had so little control in his life. I have very clear rules, am very firm, and put my foot down. But I also try to choose my battles wisely, so that we can have good times, too. My husband reminds me when I get aggravated, that if he wasn't this type of tough kid, he wouldn't have made it through so many setbacks. Then I am just glad to still have him with us.

Tantrums

Healthy children have tantrums when they are overwhelmed by strong feelings, and so do children with leukemia. In some cases, tantrums can be predicted by parents paying close attention to what triggers the outburst. This knowledge helps parents to prevent tantrums by avoiding situations that create overload for their child. In other cases, there is no warning of the impending tantrum.

> *We never knew what would set off three-year-old Rachel, and to tell the truth, she didn't know what the problem was herself. She was very verbal and aware in many ways, but she had no idea what was bothering her and causing the anger. I would just hold her with her blanket, hug her, and rock until she calmed down. Later she would say, "I was out of control," but she still didn't know why.*

Often parents wonder whether the frequent tantrums are the result of the medication or are a psychological response to the stress of being ill. The parents interviewed for this book thought that regardless of what caused the tantrums, the reaction should be the same. Some of the methods used were: ignore the tantrum, use a time-out in the room until the child calmed down, or hold the child.

> *At one point Caitlin had overeaten her beloved french fries and had a "worse than agony case of gas" as she described it. She spent the evening howling and really created a stir on the pediatric floor. She had a classic tantrum. I went in to take a shower, and when I returned to her room there was a note taped to her door apologizing to all the people on the floor for her screaming attack.*

Of course, if the child begins to be destructive, he must be restrained. For a child who is frequently destructive, professional counseling is necessary. *The Misunderstood Child* by Larry Silver (listed in the "Resources" section at the end of the chapter) has a chapter that explains in detail how parents can initiate a behavior modification program at home.

> *My son had frequent, violent rages which sometimes caused damage (toys thrown at the walls, books ripped up). He was small, but strong. I talked to him when he was calm about how the tantrums would be handled. Tantrums with no damage would be ignored; afterwards we would cuddle and talk about what prompted the anger and others ways for him to handle the anger. If he began to break things or hurt people, I would*

wrap him in a blanket and rock him until he relaxed. I would tell him, "I need to hold you because you are out of control. Soon, you will learn how to control yourself." All of the tantrums ended after he went off treatment, but, dealing with his destructive anger was one of the hardest things that I have ever experienced.

Withdrawal

Some children withdraw rather than blow up in anger. Like denial, withdrawal can be temporarily helpful as a way to come to grips with strong feelings. However, too much withdrawal is not good for children. It can also be a sign of the kind of depression which some children suffer. Parents or counselors need to find ways to gently allow withdrawn children to express how they are feeling.

My daughter became very depressed and withdrawn as treatment continued. She started to talk only about a fantasy world that she created in her imagination. She seemed to be less and less in the real world. She didn't ever talk to her therapist about her feelings, but they did lots of art work together. At the beginning, she only drew pictures of herself with her body filling the whole page. After EMLA became available, and she was less terrified of being hurt, she began to draw her body more normal sized. As she got better, she began to draw the family again. When she drew a beautiful sun shining on the family, I cried. She just couldn't talk about it, but she worked so much out through her art.

Comfort objects

Many parents worry when, after diagnosis, children regress to using a special comfort object. Many young children ask to return to using a bottle, or cling to a favorite toy or blanket. It is reasonable to allow your child to use whatever he can to find comfort against the terrible realities of treatment. The behaviors usually stop either when the child starts feeling better or when treatment ends.

My daughter was a hair twirler. Whenever she was nervous, she would twirl a bit of her hair around her finger. As her hair fell out, she kept grabbing at her head to find a wisp to curl. I told her that she could twirl mine until hers grew back. She spent a lot of time next to me or in my lap with her hand in my hair. It was annoying for me sometimes, but it had a great calming effect on her. When hers grew back, I would gently

*remind her that she had her own hair to twirl. She also went back to a
bottle although we did limit the bottle use to home or hospital. Both
behaviors, hair twirling and drinking from a bottle, disappeared within
six months of the end of treatment, when she was six years old.*

Talking about death

Part of effective parenting is allowing children to talk about topics that make
us uncomfortable. In our culture, the subject of death has become taboo.
Children are generally protected from talk about death or dying. A diagnosis
of cancer forces both parents and children to acknowledge that death is a
very real possibility. Even children as young as three years old think about
death and what it means.

*Eighteen months into treatment, five-year-old Katy said, "Mommy,
sometimes I think about my spirit leaving my body. I think my spirit is
here (gesturing to the back of her head) and my body is here (pointing to
her bellybutton). I just wanted you to know that I think about it sometimes."*

· · · · ·

*After my first relapse at age 13, my parents always kept the focus on
the future. On the way to every procedure, we would plan the wonderful
things that we were going to do afterwards. They never discussed death.
But when I asked if leukemia could kill people, my father was honest and
he told me, "Yes, some kids die." I appreciated him being straight with
me, and I went right back to being optimistic.*

*After my third relapse, my nurse said something to me about death
and dying. I clearly remember my reaction. I told her, "I know kids die
from this, but I'm not going to!"*

Trusting your child

Sometimes, if we listen to our children, they will tell us what they need to
do to persevere. It may not be the way we cope; it may make us nervous.
But, it is their way to make peace with the day-to-day reality of cancer.

*Early one summer morning, twelve-year-old Preston and I left the
hospital after a week-long stay for his high-dose methotrexate infusion.
He had been heavily sedated, and was groggy and shaky on his feet. My
husband and daughter were getting ready to go on a boat trip, and I felt*

Preston was too sick to go. We sadly saw them off, then returned to the car. Preston said, "Mom, I really need to go fishing. I know you don't understand, but I really need to do this."

It made me very uncomfortable, but we went home to get his equipment. We then drove up to the mountains to a very deserted spot on the river, and Preston said that he needed to be out of my sight. So, I watched him put on his waders, walk into the swift river and disappear around a bend upstream. I went out into the river and sat on a rock. I waited for two hours before Preston came back. He said, "That's what I needed; I feel much better now."

There is a fine line between providing adequate protection for our children or teens and becoming overly controlling due to worry about the disease. You might ask yourself, "If she didn't have cancer would I let her do this?"

Some kids have good coping skills

Some children, due to both temperament and the environments in which they have lived, are blessed with good coping abilities. They understand what is required, and they do it. Many parents expressed great admiration for their child's strength and grace in the face of adversity.

Stephan has not had any behavior problems while being treated for his initial diagnosis (age 5) or his relapse (age 7). He has never complained about going to the hospital and views the medical staff as his friends. He has never argued or fought about painful treatments. Unlike many of the parents in the support group, we've never had to deal with any emotional issues. We are fortunate that he has that confident personality. He just says, "We've got to do it, so let's just get it done."

Common behavioral changes of parents

The best upbringing that children can receive is to observe their parents taking excellent care of themselves—mind, body, spirit. Children, being the world's greatest mimics, naturally and automatically model their parents' behavior.

—Benjamin Spock

It's impossible to talk about children's behavior without discussing parental behavior. Parents are under enormous physical, emotional, financial, and existential stress. Our worries are endless. The crisis can cause us to behave in ways of which we are not always proud. Some of the problem behaviors mentioned by veteran parents were:

Dishonesty

As stated earlier, children feel safe when their parents are honest with them. If the parents start to keep secrets from the child or "protect" her from bad news, the child feels isolated and fearful. She thinks, "If mom and dad won't tell me, it must be really bad," or, "Mom won't talk about it. I guess there's nobody that I can tell about how scared I am."

Denial is a type of "unconscious" dishonesty. This occurs when parents say things to children, such as, "Everything will be just fine" or "It won't hurt a bit." This type of pretending just increases the distance between child and parent, leaving children with no support. However horrible the truth, it seldom is as terrifying to a child as a half truth upon which his imagination builds.

Depression

Depression among parents of children with life-threatening illnesses is common. If you are consistently experiencing any of the following symptoms, get professional help immediately: changes in sleeping patterns (sleeping too much, waking up frequently during the night, early morning awakening), appetite disturbances (eating too little or too much), loss of sex drive, fatigue, panic attacks, inability to experience pleasure, feelings of sadness and despair, poor concentration, social withdrawal, feelings of worthlessness, suicidal thoughts, drug or alcohol abuse. If a parent becomes depressed, children are neglected. Depression is very common, very treatable, and should be dealt with early.

Not showing any emotion or sharing too much emotion

Either one of these extremes can frighten children.

> I am a very controlled person and tended to do most of my crying in the shower. I think that my daughter needed me to show that I was very upset, too. One day I brought her to the lab for yet another poke. She started screaming, fighting, just went wild that day. I held her and told her that she could scream, but she couldn't kick me or the technician. It was horrible. She yelled at me all the way out to the car, saying, "You just

want them to hurt me, You don't love me, Why do you take me to get hurt?" I sat in the car in the parking lot and burst into tears. I told her that having to bring her for procedures and pokes was the hardest thing that I'd ever done in my life. That I wished it was me instead of her. That I loved her so much and wanted to protect her from hurt, but I couldn't. I told her that I wanted her to get better, and we just had to get through the treatment. Oh, I really cried. She looked at me, all of four years old, patted me on the arm, and said, "It's okay now, Mom, let's just go home."

• • • • •

My husband is very tender-hearted and cries easily. It has caused many problems during treatment because he just can't bear the thought of his daughter being hurt. So he has never gone to a procedure. His eyes even fill up with tears when I tell her it's her day for a finger poke. It seems to have made her very angry. She stopped talking to him and clung to me. I think it would have been better if he had found a way to deal with his emotions so he could have been there when she needed him. She would have felt safer.

Losing your temper excessively

All parents lose their temper sometimes. They lose their tempers with spouses, healthy children, pets, even strangers. But it is especially painful when the target of the anger is a very sick child. Abuse of spouses and children increases at times when either or both spouses feel incompetent and powerless. If you find yourself unable to control your temper, seek professional counseling.

I had my share of temper tantrums. The worst was when he was having his radiation. I tried to make him eat because it would be so many hours before he could have any more food. He always threw up all over himself and me, several times, every morning. It seemed like we changed clothing at least three times before we even got out of the house each day. I remember one day just screaming at him, "Can't you even learn how to throw up? Can't you just bend over to barf?" I really flunked mother of the year that day. I can't believe that I was screaming at this sick little kid, who I love so much.

• • • • •

In the beginning, my two-year-old daughter was incredibly angry. She would have massive temper tantrums, and I would just hold her and tell her that I wouldn't let her hurt anybody. I would continue to hold her until she changed from angry to sad. When she was on the dexamethasone, she would either be hugging me or pinching, biting, or sucking my neck. It drove me crazy. Now, on maintenance, she's not having as many fits, but she still pushes her sisters off swings or the trampoline. She has a general lack of control. Sometimes, when I can't stand it anymore, I swat her on the bottom, and then I feel really bad.

. . . . .

I had always taught my children that feeling anger was okay, but we had to make good choices about what to do with it. Hitting other people or breaking things was a bad choice; hitting pillows, running around outside, or listening to music were good choices. But, as with everything else, they learned the most from watching how I handled my anger, and during the hard months of treatment my temper was short. When I found myself thinking of hitting them, I'd say, in a very loud voice, "I'm afraid I'm going to hurt somebody so I'm going in my room for a time-out." If my husband was home, I'd take a warm shower to calm down; if he wasn't, I'd just sit on the bed and take as many deep breaths as it took to stop feeling homicidal.

Unequal application of household rules

You will guarantee family problems if the ill child enjoys favored status while the siblings must do extra chores. Granted, it is hard to know when is the right time to insist that your ill child must resume making his bed or setting the table, but it must be done. Siblings need to know from the very beginning that any child in the family, if sick, will be excused from chores, but will have do them again as soon as he is physically able.

I spoiled my sick daughter and tried to enforce the rules for my son. That didn't work, so I gave up on him and spoiled them both. He was really acting out at school. What he needed was structure and more attention, but what he got was more and more things. They both ended up thinking the whole world revolved around them, and it was my fault.

Overindulgence of the ill child

Overindulgence is a very common behavior of parents of children with cancer.

> I bought my daughter everything that I saw that was pretty and lovely. I kept thinking that if she died she would die happy because she'd be surrounded by all these beautiful things. Even when I couldn't really afford it, I kept buying. I realize now that I was doing it to make me feel better, not her. She needed cuddling and loving, not clothes and dolls.

• • • • •

> Someone asked me once if I didn't want to spoil him rotten or baby him because he might not survive. I said, "No, because what would I do if he does survive? I'd have a raging brat." So we just try to be normal and discipline like we would if he didn't have leukemia. We don't let him get away with murder. We don't believe in hitting, but we do use time-outs, loss of privileges, and loss of opportunities to do things he enjoys.

One aspect of overindulgence that is quite common is the parent's reluctance to teach the sick child life skills. After years of dealing with a physically weak and sometimes emotionally demanding child, parents forget to expect age-appropriate skills.

> I realized that I had formed a habit of treating my child as if she was still young and sick. I was still treating her like a three year old, and she was seven. One day, when I was pouring her juice, I thought, "Why am I doing this? She's seven. She needs to learn to make her own sandwiches and pour her own drinks. She needs to be encouraged to grow up." Boy, it has been hard. But I've stuck to my guns, and made other extended family members do it, too. I want her to grow up to be an independent adult, not a demanding, overgrown kid.

Overprotection of sick child

For a child to feel normal, he needs to be treated as if he is normal. Ask the doctor what changes in physical activity are necessary for safety, and do not impose any additional restrictions that go beyond this on your child. Let the child be involved in sports or neighborhood play, and even though it is hard, stop yourself from constant reminders to "be careful."

Not spending enough time with the sibling(s)

While acknowledging that there are only so many hours in a day, the parents interviewed for this book felt the most guilt about the effect of the leukemia on the siblings. They wished that they had asked family and friends to stay with the sick child more often, allowing them to use more of their precious time with the siblings. Many expressed pain that they didn't know how severely affected the sibs had been.

> We didn't have problems with our child with cancer, but his brother (6 years old) really suffered. He would get the flu and sob all night. He would scream that he would have to go to the hospital and that he would die. He also had behavior problems at school. I ended up quitting work because my son with leukemia was having trouble making it through the entire school day, and his brother needed some loving attention. Many of the sibling problems cleared up with lots of one-on-one attention.

Using substance abuse to cope

Many parents find themselves turning to alcohol or drugs to help them cope. Not only illegal drugs are abused; overuse of over-the-counter sleeping pills or other medications also occurs. If you find yourself drinking so that your behavior is affected or using drugs to get through the day or night, seek professional help.

Some parents have good coping skills

Some parents have no major problems adjusting to the diagnosis and treatment of their child with cancer. They find unexpected reserves of strength and are able to ask for help from their friends and family when they need it. They realize that different needs arise when there is a great stress to the family, and they alter their expectations and parenting accordingly. These families usually had strong and effective communication prior to the illness, and pull together as a unit to deal with it.

The majority of families, however, have periods of calmness and other times when nerves are frayed and tempers short. But usually families survive intact and are often strengthened by the years of dealing with cancer.

Improving communication and discipline

Parents suggest the following ways to keep the family on a more even keel;

* Make sure that the family rules are clearly understood by all of the children. Stressed children feel safe in homes that are very structured with regular, predictable routines.

    After yet another rage by my daughter with leukemia, we held a family meeting to clarify the rules and consequences for breaking them. We asked the kids (both preschoolers) to dictate a list of what they thought the rules were. The following was the result, and we posted copies of the list all over the house (which created much merriment among our friends):

    1. No peeing on rug

    2. No jumping on bed

    3. No hitting or pinching

    4. No name calling

    5. No breaking things

    6. No writing on walls

    7. No being alone in room

    If they broke a rule, we would gently lead them to the list and remind them of the house rules. It really helped.

* Have all caretakers consistently enforce the family rules.

    We kept the same household rules. I was determined that we needed to start with the expectation that Rachel was going to survive. I never wanted her to be treated like a "poor little sick kid" because I was afraid she would become one. We had to be careful about baby-sitters because we didn't want anyone to feel sorry for her or treat her differently. I do feel that we avoided many long-term behavior problems by adopting this attitude early.

* Give all the kids some power by offering choices and letting them completely control some aspects of their lives, as appropriate.

    For a few months we ignored Shawn's two brothers as we struggled to get a handle on the situation. We just shuttled them around with no consideration for their feelings. When we realized how unfair we were being, we made a list of places to stay, and let them choose each time we had to go off to the hospital. We worked it out together, and things went much smoother.

• • • • •

My bald, angry, four-year-old daughter asked me for some scissors one day. I asked what she was going to do, and she said cut off all her Barbies' hair. I told her those were her dolls and she could cut off their hair if she chose. I asked her to consider leaving one or two with hair, because when she had long hair again, she might want dolls that looked like her then, too. But I said it was up to her. She cut most completely off, and left some intact. It really seemed to make her feel better.

- Take control of the incoming gifts. Too many gifts make the ill child worry excessively ("If I'm getting all of these great presents, things must be really bad") and makes the siblings jealous. Be specific if you want people not to bring gifts, or if you want gifts for each child, not just the sick one.

- Recognize that some problems are caused solely by the drugs (see the prednisone section of Chapter 10, *Chemotherapy*). It helps to remember that these children are not naturally defiant or destructive. They are feeling sick, powerless, and altered by massive doses of toxic drugs, and we need to try to help by sympathizing, yet setting limits. Remember, when they get off the drugs, their real personalities will return.

- Even though many oncologists tell parents that during the maintenance phase of treatment life will return to "normal," it usually does not. It is better than the intensive parts of treatment, but often, emotional and behavioral difficulties arise when the child regains his strength during maintenance. Be glad if your child's difficulties subside during maintenance, but expect them not to.

- If your child likes to draw, paint, knit, do collages, or other art work, encourage it. Art is both soothing and therapeutic and it allows the child a positive outlet for feelings and creativity. Making something beautiful really helps raise children's spirits.

When Jody was in the laminar airflow (isolation) room for weeks after his bone marrow transplant, he passed the time by doing many collages. I kept him well-supplied with all sorts of materials, and he created beautiful things.

- If your child does art work or writing, recognize that powerful emotions may surface for both child and parents.

  At my daughter's preschool, once a week each child would tell the teacher a story, which the teacher wrote down for the child to take home. Most of my daughter's stories were like this: "There was a rhinoceros. He lived in the jungle. Then he went in the pool. Then he decided to take a walk. And then he ate some strawberries. Then he visited his friend." But the week before or after a painful procedure, she would dictate frightening stories (and this from a kid who wasn't allowed to watch TV). Two examples are: "Once there were some bees and they stung someone and this someone was allergic to them and then they got hurt by some monkeybars and the monkeybars had needles on them and the lightning came and hit the bees," and, "Once upon a time there were six stars and they twinkled at night and then the sun started to come up. And then they had a serious problem. They shot their heads and they had blood dripping down."

- Allow your child to be totally in charge of his art. Do not make suggestions or criticize (e.g., "stay inside the lines" or "skies need to be blue not orange"). Rather, encourage them and praise their efforts. Display the artwork in your home. Listen carefully if your child offers an explanation of the art, but do not pry if it is private. Above all, do not interpret it yourself or disagree with your child on what the art represents. Being supportive will allow your child to explore ways to soothe himself and clarify strong feelings.

  Jody was continually making "projects." We kept him supplied with a fishing box full of materials, and he glued and taped and constructed all sorts of sculptures. He did beautiful drawings full of color, and every person he drew always had hands shaped like hearts. If we asked him what he was making, he always answered, "I'll show you when I'm done."

- Come up with acceptable ways for your child to physically release anger. Some options are: ride a bike, run around the house, swing, play basketball or soccer, pound nails into wood, mold clay, punch pillows, yell, take a shower or bath, or draw angry pictures. In addition, teach your child to use words to express his anger, for example, "It makes me furious when you do that" or "I am so mad I feel like hitting you." Releasing anger physically and expressing anger verbally are both valuable life skills to master.

Shawn was very, very angry many times. We had clear rules that it was okay to be angry, but he couldn't hit people. We bought a punching bag which he really pounded sometimes. Play dough helped, too. We had a machine to make play dough shapes which took a lot of effort. He would hit it, pound it, push it, roll it. Then he would press it through the machine and keep turning that handle. It seemed to really help him with his aggression.

• • • • •

Our therapist recommended that we have our five-year-old daughter make an "angry sheet." She should be encouraged to draw or write what she felt like doing when she was angry, and encouraged to get it all out. It was pretty scary, because she drew pictures of stamping people, gouging their eyes out, shooting them, etc. It was amazing how much better she felt afterwards. Then we went through the pictures together and discussed which ones she could really do, and which ones she could only think about doing because really doing it would hurt someone.

- Treat the ill child as normally as possible.

When Justin was in the hospital, I could never stand to see him in those little hospital gowns. I asked if we could dress him in his own out-fits, and they said yes. So even when he was in the ICU with all the tubes coming out of his body, we dressed him every day in something cute. It just felt better to see him in his clothes. Several months later my mother said that she had really admired us for doing that because we were sending the message to Justin that everything was going to be okay. That even though he couldn't breathe on his own, he was still going to get up every day and get dressed. Now I think it probably did communicate to him that things were going to be normal again.

- Get professional help whenever you are concerned or run out of ideas on how to handle emotional problems. Mental health care professionals (see Chapter 9, *Sources of Support*) have spent years learning how to help resolve these kinds of problems, so let them help you.

My daughter and I both went to a wonderful therapist throughout most of her treatment for ALL. My daughter was a very sensitive, easily overwhelmed child, who withdrew more and more into a world of fantasy as cancer treatment progressed. The therapist was skilled at drawing out her feelings through art work and play. She also helped me with very spe-cific suggestions on parenting. For instance, when I told the therapist that my daughter thought that treatment would never end (a reasonable assumption for a preschooler), she suggested that I put two jars on my daughter's desk. One was labeled "ALL DONE," and the other was labeled "TO DO." We put a rock for every procedure and treatment already completed in the ALL-DONE jar, and one rock for every one yet to do in the TO-DO jar. (Only recommended if the child is more than half-way through treatment) Then, each time that we came home, my daughter would move a rock into the ALL-DONE jar. It gave her a concrete way to visualize the approach of the end of treatment. She could see the dwindling number of pebbles left. On the last day of treatment, when she moved the last pebble over and the TO-DO jar was empty, I cried, but she danced.

- Most emotional problems that children develop as a result of treatment for cancer can be resolved by professional counseling. However, some children may also need medications to get them through particularly rough times.

  My daughter was doing really well throughout treatment until a combination of events occurred that was more than she could handle. Her grandmother died from cancer during the summer, one of her friends with cancer died on December 27, then another friend relapsed for the second time. She was fine during the day, but at night she constantly woke up stressed and upset. She had dreams about trapdoors, witches brewing potions to give to little children, and saw people coming into her room to take her away. She would wake up smelling smoke. She was awake three or four hours in the middle of the night, every night. Her doctor put her on sleeping pills and antianxiety medications, and the social worker came out to the house twice a month.

- Try to determine if cancer treatment is making a preexisting problem of any kind worse. If so, treat the problem, not the symptoms.

  My daughter had been hypersensitive since birth. She had trouble wearing clothes because they never felt good, she had sensitive hearing and would frequently scream and cover her ears, she would flinch at any motion or bright lights, etc. She was a child who was totally overwhelmed, and that was before leukemia! Afterwards, she was either violent or withdrawn. It was frightening to think that we might beat the disease, but she seemed to be losing her mind. I heard about Auditory Integration Training which claimed to be able to desensitize the hearing of kids with hyperacute hearing. We went for twenty sessions, and my daughter changed from a child who was asocial and terrified to one who is able to ride the bus to school, makes friends, and is generally more socially competent and comfortable. It changed her life.

- Teach children relaxation or visualization skills to help them cope better with strong feelings. (See "Resources" in Chapter 3, *Coping with Procedures,* for books on such skills.)

- Have reasonable expectations. If you are expecting a sick four-year-old to act like a healthy six-year-old, or a teenager to act like an adult, you are setting your child up to fail.

  It seemed like we spent most of the years of treatment waiting to see a doctor who was running hours behind schedule. Since my child had trouble sitting still and was always hungry, I came well prepared. I always carried a large bag containing an assortment of things to eat and drink, toys to play with, coloring books and markers, books to read aloud, and play dough. He stayed occupied and we avoided many problems. I saw too many parents in the waiting room expecting their bored children to sit still and be quiet for long periods of time.

- As often as possible, try to end the day on a positive note. If your child is being disruptive, or if your feelings toward your child are very negative, the following is an exercise that can end the day in a pleasant way. At bedtime, parent and child each tell one another something they did that day that made them proud of themselves, something they like about themselves, and something they are looking forward to the next day. Then a hug and a sincere "I love you" bring the day to a calm and loving close.

Checklist for parenting stressed children

A group of veteran parents compiled the following checklist to help you parent your stressed child.

- Model the type of behavior you desire. If you talk respectfully and take time-outs when angry, you are teaching your children to do so. If you scream and hit, that is how your children will handle their anger.

- Seek professional help for any behaviors that trouble you.

- Teach your children to talk about their feelings.

- Listen to your children with understanding and empathy.

- Be honest and admit your mistakes.

- Help your children to examine why they are behaving as they are.

- Distinguish between feelings (always okay) and acting on strong feelings in destructive or hurtful ways (not okay).

- Have clear rules and consequences for violations.

- Teach children to recognize when they are losing control.

- Discuss acceptable outlets for anger.

- Give frequent reassurances of your love.

- Provide plenty of hugs and physical affection.

- Notice and compliment your child for good behavior.

- Recognize that the disturbing behaviors result from stress, pain, and drugs.

- Remember that with lots of structure, love, and time the problems will become more manageable.

Our children look to us to learn how to handle adversity. They learn how to cope from us. Although it is extremely difficult to live through your child's diagnosis and treatment for cancer, it must be done. So we each need to reach deep into our hearts and minds to help our children endure and grow.

Children Learn What They Live

> *If a child lives with criticism, he learns to condemn.*
> *If a child lives with hostility, he learns to fight.*
> *If a child lives with ridicule, he learns to be shy.*
> *If a child lives with shame, he learns to feel guilty.*
> *If a child lives with tolerance, he learns to be patient.*
> *If a child lives with encouragement, he learns confidence.*
> *If a child lives with praise, he learns to appreciate.*
> *If a child lives with fairness, he learns justice.*
> *If a child lives with security, he learns to have faith.*
> *If a child lives with approval, he learns to like himself.*
> *If a child lives with acceptance and friendship,*
> *He learns to find love in the world.*

—Dorothy Law Nolte

Resources

Reading for adults

Balter, Lawrence, Ph.D. *Who's In Control? Dr. Balter's Guide to Discipline Without Combat*. New York: Simon & Schuster, 1988. Dr. Balter explains sensible and easy-to-understand guidelines for disciplining children. For each age group from infant to teen, he explains what the child is capable of developmentally, what discipline goals are appropriate, and what techniques are effective for that age group.

Berard, Guy, M.D. *Hearing Equals Behavior*. New Canaan, CT: Keats, 1993. Written by the French physician who developed auditory integration training (AIT), it explains the treatment clearly and describes the disorders which can be positively impacted by AIT.

Briggs, Dorothy. *Your Child's Self-Esteem: The Key to His Life*. Garden City, NY: Doubleday, 1975. The classic, and still the best, book on ways to enhance your child's self-esteem.

Center for Attitudinal Healing. *Advice to Doctors and Other Big People from Kids*. Berkeley, CA: Celestial Arts, 1991. Book written by children with catastrophic illnesses offers suggestions and expresses feelings about health care workers. Wise and poignant, it reminds us how perceptive and aware children of all ages are, and of the absolute need to involve them in medical decisions.

Crary, Elizabeth. *Without Spanking or Spoiling: A Practical Approach to Toddler and Preschool Guidance*. 2nd ed. Seattle: Parenting Press, 1993. Teaches the basics of parenting like how to use time-outs, active listening, giving consequences, positive reinforcement, praise, I-messages, and more. Contains very helpful examples and exercises.

Faber, Adele, and Elaine Mazlish. *How to Talk So Kids Will Listen...and Listen So Kids Will Talk*. New York: Rawson, Wade Publishers, 1980. The classic book on developing new, more effective ways to communicate with your children, based on respect and understanding. Highly recommended.

Faber, Adele, and Elaine Mazlish. *Siblings Without Rivalry: How to Help Your Children Live Together So You Can Live Too*. New York: Avon Books, 1987. Required reading for parents with fighting siblings. Offers dozens of astonishingly simple yet effective methods to reduce conflict and foster a cooperative spirit.

Kurcinka, Mary Sheedy. *Raising Your Spirited Child: A Guide for Parents Whose Child Is More Intense, Sensitive, Perceptive and Energetic.* New York: Harper Collins, 1992. Reassuring guide for how to effectively parent children who are more intense, sensitive, perceptive, persistent, energetic, or uncomfortable with change than average children. Many of the strategies are very effective for children stressed by cancer treatment.

Leukemia Society of America. *Emotional Aspects of Childhood Leukemia.* To obtain a free copy, call 1-800-955-4LSA. 32-page booklet which describes behaviors of seriously ill children, hospitalization, going home, school, and brothers and sisters.

Nelsen, Jane. *Positive Discipline.* rev. ed. New York: Ballantine Books, 1996. Written by a psychologist, educator, and mother of seven, this book teaches parents how to promote self-discipline and personal responsibility through kindness, encouragement, and mutual respect.

Pizzo, Philip, and David Poplack. *Principles and Practice of Pediatric Oncology.* Philadelphia: Lippincott-Raven, 1996. Chapter 48, "The Other Side of the Bed," by F. Leonard Johnson discusses the feelings of patients and their families while undergoing treatment for cancer, and how medical caregivers can provide support.

Saunders, Antoinette, Ph.D., and Bonnie Remsberg. *The Stress-Proof Child: A Loving Parent's Guide.* New York: Holt, Rinehart and Winston, 1984. Written by a child psychologist who was a pioneer in the field of stress reduction for children, this book gives basic advice on how to help children handle stress.

Silver, Larry, M.D. *The Misunderstood Child: A Guide for Parents of Children with Learning Disabilities.* 2nd ed. Blue Ridge Summit, PA: Tab Books, 1992. Comprehensive discussion of positive treatment strategies that can be implemented at home and in the school to help children with learning difficulties. Chapter 15 outlines a behavior modification program that could be a valuable tool in helping children whose behavior has been disrupted by years of painful cancer treatment.

Stehli, Annabelle. *Sound of a Miracle.* New York: Doubleday, 1991. Written by a mother of two small children, one with leukemia and one diagnosed as severely autistic. Describes the heartbreak of one daughter's treatment for and death from ALL, and the miracle of the second daughter's cure from autism by auditory integration therapy.

Reading for children

Crary, Elizabeth. *Dealing With Feelings*. I'm Frustrated; I'm Mad; I'm Sad Series. Seattle: Parenting Press, 1992. Fun, game-like books to teach pre-school and early elementary children how to handle feelings and solve problems.

Erickson, Karen, and Maureen Roffey. *I Was So Mad*. New York: Viking Kestrel, 1967. Young children learn that it's okay to get mad as long as they do not hurt others.

Kaufman, Gershen, and Lev Raphael. *Stick Up for Yourself!: Every Kid's Guide to Personal Power and Positive Self-Esteem*. Minneapolis: Free Spirit Publishers, 1990. Preteens and teens learn methods to be strong and in control without destructive aggression.

Nessim, Susan, and Barbara Wyman. *Draw Me a Picture*. A fun coloring book for children with cancer (ages 3-6). Marty Bunny talks about how it was when he was in the hospital for cancer and invites readers to draw about their experiences. Send $7.45 check to Cancervive, 6500 Wilshire Blvd., #500, Los Angeles, CA 90048.

Schmidt, Fran, and Alice Friedman. *Fighting Fair for Families*. Miami: Peace Press, 1989. School-aged children and parents learn how to solve problems cooperatively. A poster of Rules for Fighting can serve as a reminder to help put anger-control skills into practice. Write to: Peace Education Foundation, Inc., P.O. Box 191153, Miami Beach, FL 33119.

Simon, Norma. *I Was So Mad!* Chicago: Albert Whitman & Co., 1974. This story identifies things that trigger anger, such as frustration, anxiety, and loss of control. Helps younger boys and girls understand that anger is normal.

Watson, Janet, and Robert Switzer. *Sometimes I Get Angry*. Topeka, KS: Meninger Press, 1986. A simple, expressive story that helps children understand that anger is normal. Helps parents understand that anger is often the only way young children with limited communication skills can express strong feelings.

CHAPTER 18

End of Treatment and Beyond

The best formula for longevity: Have a chronic disease, and cure it.

—Oliver Wendell Holmes

THE LAST DAY OF TREATMENT is a time for both celebration and fear. Most families are thrilled that the days of pills and procedures have ended, but fear a future without drugs to keep the disease away. Concerns about relapse are an almost universal parental response, but for the majority of families, the months and years roll by without recurrence of leukemia. Many children and teens quickly return to excellent physical and mental health, while others have lingering or permanent effects from the treatment. This chapter covers the emotional and physical aspects of ending treatment, as well as medical follow-up and possible long-term side effects.

Emotional issues

Many parents describe ending treatment as almost as wrenching an experience as diagnosis. Families begin to experience the gamut of emotions—from elation to terror—months before the final day.

> *I had a lot of anticipatory worry—it started about six months before ending treatment. By the last day of treatment I had been worrying for months, so it was just a relief to quit.*

· · · · ·

> *I expected to feel a profound sense of relief when treatment ended. The six months prior to ending treatment I felt almost euphoric. But when she was finally finished, I began to be unexpectedly fearful. I just started to worry. I didn't really relax until she was a year off treatment. Now weeks go by without me thinking of relapse, although I still think of the years of leukemia treatment frequently.*

· · · · ·

The last day was traumatic. It just wasn't a celebration because it felt exactly like every other day that we had to drive for hours, wait for hours, then have painful treatments. When it was over, he was just as physically exhausted and emotionally drained as on other clinic days. I just felt numb. But then, over time, there was a gradual awakening that it was really over.

• • • • •

We were thrilled when treatment ended. I knew many people who felt that celebrating would jinx them; they just didn't feel safe. Well, I felt that we had won a big battle—getting through treatment—and we were going to celebrate that. If, heaven forbid, in the future we had another battle to fight, we'd deal with it. But on the last day of treatment, we were delighted.

Parents should anticipate that after years spent watching their child go through the rigors of treatment, they will have lost the feeling of a "normal" life. They will experience relapse scares, and they may need to call the doctor to describe the symptoms and be reassured.

Several months after my son ended treatment, I was driving down the street, and I started to worry that he seemed excessively tired lately. I started to feel my throat constricting, and tears sprang to my eyes. I had to pull over because I literally couldn't breathe. I had to force myself to calm down, breath slowly, and realize that I was just having a normal attack of being petrified that he would relapse.

• • • • •

We live in a cool climate, but went back East during a summer heat wave to visit relatives. My daughter was a year off treatment and doing extremely well. After a few days of 100 degree weather, she started waking up in a bed soaked with sweat. I was terrified because she had done that at diagnosis. All of those horrible feelings washed over me, and I had to stand in the shower and sob. I called my doctor who was 3,000 miles away, and listed all the normal things: good appetite, good color, good energy level, no behavior problems, no bruising, but my voice shook when I described the sweats in an air-conditioned house. He reassured me that it was almost certainly the hot weather. He said if I was too worried to enjoy my visit, he would arrange for her to get a CBC, but otherwise, just bring her by when we got back. I relaxed, didn't get the CBC, and the night sweats stopped when we got home.

With diagnosis came the awareness that life can be cruel and unpredictable, and when treatment ends parents must find a way to live with uncertainty, to find a balance between hope and reasonable worry.

Last day of treatment

Although individual cases vary, generally on the last day of treatment a child in remission from leukemia has a diagnostic spinal tap, a bone marrow aspiration, a complete blood count and chemistry screen, a thorough physical exam, and a discussion with the oncologist. The oncologist should review the treatment, outline the schedule for blood tests and exams for the future, and sensitively inform the family of the potential for long-term side effects. After the procedures, the family will usually wait to hear the preliminary report on the bone marrow aspiration, as true relief does not come until they hear that no leukemic blasts are present. One group of parents presented to physicians at a major children's hospital the following list of suggestions for the last day of treatment:

- Schedule enough time to have a conversation.

- Bring a sense of closure to the active phase of treatment.

- Express happiness that all has gone well.

- Be realistic but hopeful about the future.

- Praise the child for handling a very difficult time in her life with grace (or courage, or whatever word is appropriate).

- Praise the parents for all of their hard work.

- Allow time for the parents to give the physician feedback and thanks.

- Give a certificate of accomplishment to the child.

- Be aware that families are relieved but fearful of the future.

> Our last day of treatment was horrible. The fellow was angry at me because I had arranged to have my daughter sedated. The fellow was signing the necessary forms muttering over and over, "This is ridiculous." When I asked her what was bothering her, she said that she was going on a business trip, which I was delaying, and her son had chicken pox and she was worried about it. She said another doctor was going to do the procedures because she was in a hurry. When I asked if I should wait for the results of the bone marrow, she said, "End of treatment bone marrows are at the bottom of the pathologist's priority list, emergencies come first,

he'll get to it when he can, and the report won't be written for days." I
thought that she was being heartless and cruel, but I didn't want to fight
in front of my daughter. So, I marched across the hall and asked the
director of the clinic if she would please call me that afternoon with the
results of the bone marrow. She replied, "Absolutely." She called, told me
it was clear, and we felt jubilant and relieved.

• • • • •

The nurses at our clinic really made a big deal on the last day of
treatment. They brought out a cake and balloons, and sang "Going off
Chemo" to the tune of "Happy Birthday to You." They made Gina a
banner and bought her a present. I sat in a corner and cried, because I
was scared to death of the future. A nurse came over, hugged me, and
said, "This must be so hard, we're taking away your security blanket."
She was exactly right.

Catheter removal

Children usually cannot wait for the catheter to be removed, as it symbol-izes that treatment has truly ended. Physicians differ a great deal on when is the best time to remove the catheter. Some remove it when the child is sedated for the last bone marrow aspiration, while others want to wait until several weeks or months have passed. Ask the doctor for her reasons for the recommended delay, and discuss it fully if you or your child has strong feel-ings about waiting.

Removal of the external catheter (Hickman or Broviac) is an outpatient pro-cedure. The child is given a mild sedative, then the oncologist braces one hand against the child's chest and pulls the catheter out of the child's body with the other hand.

Kristin's Broviac removal wasn't too bad. They gave her fentanyl
ahead of time, so she was fairly relaxed. I wished that they had offered
me a sedative as well. One of the nurses had her hand on Kristin's shoul-
der and quietly talked to her to try to keep her focused elsewhere. I held
her legs, and my wife held her hand. The doctor put one hand on her
chest, and pulled on the tubing with the other. It only took about two
seconds to come out. There was little blood; they just put a Band-Aid on
the site and sent us home.

Implanted catheters such as the Port-a-cath are removed surgically in the operating room. Children are generally given general anesthesia, and the operation takes less than half an hour. Only one incision is made, usually just above the port at the same place as the scar from the implantation surgery. The sutures holding the port to the underlying muscle are cut, and the port with tubing is pulled out. The small incision is then stitched and bandaged. When the child begins to awaken, he is brought out to the parent(s). The family then waits until the surgeon has approved their departure. Often, the wait is short for as soon as the child is awake enough to take a small drink or eat a popsicle, he is released. If your child becomes nauseated from the anesthesia, the wait can be several hours until he is feeling better.

> Brent had a very easy time with his port removal surgery. We scheduled him to be the first patient early in the morning, so there was no delay getting in. Then the anesthesiologist asked him what flavor gas he wanted, which he liked. They brought him out to us while he was still groggy, and he woke up feeling goofy and happy. We went home soon thereafter. It felt more like the ending then than on the last day of treatment.

Ceremonies

Some families greatly benefit from having ceremonies to celebrate the end of cancer treatment. Especially for younger children who have spent much of their lives taking pills and having procedures, ceremonies can help them grasp that it is truly over. Here are ideas from many families on how to commemorate this important occasion:

- Take "good-bye" pictures of the hospital and staff.
- Take a picture of your child taking his last pill.
- Give trophies to your child and siblings.

> We had a big party during which my husband Scott stood up and called for everyone's attention. He gave a talk about how proud we were of Jeremy and handed him a big trophy. It had the victory angel on top and was engraved with "Jeremy, we are so proud of you and your victory. Love, Mom and Dad." We gave a plaque to his brother Jason for being the world's most supportive brother.

- Ask the clinic to present your child with a certificate.

- Let your child throw away or flush down the toilet all of the leftover pills.

> We waited for six months to celebrate, because we just didn't feel safe until then. But on his six-month anniversary we had a "toilet flushing party." Shawn threw every pill, and poured the liquid meds, saline, and mineral oil down the toilet, and just flushed and laughed. It was such a howl, I really wished we had videotaped it.

- Let your child tear or cut up the calendar used to record dates for procedures (not a good idea if any records are on it).

- Throw a big party.

> Erica ended treatment in December, and we threw a big party at the church. We called it a "Celebration of Life." We invited all of the families that we had become so close to through the support group. We especially wanted the families who had lost their children to cancer, and they all came. My normally even-tempered husband gave a talk about Club Goodtimes (the support group) and how it was a club that no one ever wanted to join. When he talked about the many wonderful people we met there, his voice shook with emotion. Then the preacher prayed for the children who weren't with us. We ate a huge cake, and the children were entertained by a clown. It was both moving and fun.

- If your child has been seeing a counselor, schedule a visit to talk about the accomplishment.

- Have friends and family send congratulations cards.

- Ask the surgeon to give your child her port or hickman line.

> I know that this may sound odd, but my six-year-old daughter hated her port and talked incessantly about getting it out. She even told me that she was going to slice it out herself with a knife. I told her it would be better to wait until the doctors put her to sleep, but I promised her that she could have it after the operation to do with as she wished. That idea brought a smile to her face. She came out of the recovery room clutching a baggie with the port inside. Once we were home, she carried it around for weeks, jumped on it, hit it with a hammer, and finally cut it to pieces. That port really symbolized all of the painful things that had happened to her, and it made her feel better to hurt it back.

- If consistent with your beliefs, have a religious ceremony of thanksgiving.

I preached the sermon at church after Kristin ended treatment. It was the first Sunday of Lent, and I related our experience to that. Other than that, we didn't celebrate, because it's still not over. We still have to go every month for blood work and need to be vigilant. Ending treatment was a big milestone, but it paled in comparison to having the line pulled. We all have so much more freedom: no more lines to flush, changing bandages, or wrapping up for baths and swimming.

· · · · ·

We're very much of the belief that there was a healing process from God when Justin was in the hospital. We had a ceremony at Mass after he finished treatment. I got up and told the story about how he had had leukemia and almost died from pneumonia, and how he had started his slow recovery after being anointed in the hospital with the Sacrament of the Sick. I asked them for their prayers for his future good health and gave thanks to our friends, family, and especially to God, for all of their help. Then we had a reception at our house.

- Go on a trip or vacation to celebrate.

All of the parents of children with leukemia in our community have become very close. When nine-year-old Brent finished his treatment, I called to congratulate him. He was so excited telling me about it, but then his voice started to shake and he cried when he told me, "My two aunts gave me a card with money inside to go to a motel with a pool for the weekend. They gave it to me because I had leukemia. Can you believe that?"

Some parents do not feel comfortable celebrating the end of treatment. One mother described her feelings this way:

We did nothing because we knew so many kids who relapsed. I didn't even throw away the pills for a year because I didn't trust that we were really done.

As you have read so often in this book, every child, parent, and relative reacts differently to every phase of treatment; what is important is not our differences, but the fact that we all are free to express and act on our own feelings, whatever they may be. You may be joyful, relieved, fearful or terrified, but end of treatment is emotionally charged for each of us.

What is normal?

After years of the treatment and trauma of leukemia, families grapple with the idea of returning to normal. Unfortunately, most parents don't really know what "normal" is any longer. Parents realize that returning to the care-free pre-cancer days is unrealistic, that life has changed. The constant inter-action with medical personnel is ending, and support from family and friends recedes. While it is true that the blissful ignorance of the days prior to cancer are gone forever, families do enter a period of calm in which rou-tines do not revolve around caring for a sick child, giving medicines, and keeping clinic appointments. Each family needs to carve out a new defini-tion of "normal."

> I listened to several parents in our support group discuss "returning to normal" after treatment ended. I felt that, in a sense, they were wishing for a magic carpet ride back in time. However, I think that life is a series of evolutions. Even if we hadn't endured our oncology odyssey, our life would be different now than it was three years ago. I think that parents need to set goals, decide which direction they want to go after treatment ends, and make an effort to get there.

· · · · ·

> It's been six months, and I feel worse. I felt like when she was on treatment I was actively doing something to keep it away. Now I'm not and I just worry. I'm a basket case.

· · · · ·

> It just seems like I can't leave it behind. If he gets diarrhea, I worry that it's a tumor. He has a bad skin rash now, and I keep thinking that it's cancer related. My husband has terrible skin, so I know it's genetic, but there's a little part of my mind that keeps trying to connect it to leukemia. He's been going to the playground; he's getting strong; he has rosy cheeks; he's just beautiful. When he has bruises on his legs, I automatically think his platelets are down. But when I look at the other kids, I realize that it's normal for active kids to have bruises on their knees. It's really hard to get used to. I still wake up at night, and the irrational side comes out. I'm just having a hard time letting go of it. I mean, I panicked when his feet were hurting, only to discover that his shoes were too small.

· · · · ·

We're a year off treatment, and I really don't think about relapse very often. I do occasionally find myself studying her to see if she looks pale, or I worry when she seems tired or her behavior is bad. Usually, I'm feeling safer. But honestly, I don't think any of us will ever go back to the days when we just assumed that our kids would grow up, that the parents would die first; that sense of security is probably gone forever.

· · · · ·

Shawn's six months off treatment, and he's just like a flower beginning to bloom. He's so happy and I try to be happy with him. I try very hard to put worries about the future out of my mind, because I feel that those thoughts will rob me of just being able to enjoy Shawn.

· · · · ·

My mother still calls my daughter "the fragile child" and says other things, such as, "She's been affected, she will never be the same. She'll be lucky to live to adulthood." However, I have left cancer thoughts behind me and feel that life is normal for us again.

Not only are parents and children experiencing a myriad of emotions, but children are undergoing physical changes as well, as their bodies excrete accumulated toxins and adjust to life without drugs.

For the month after treatment ended, Christine (6 years old) drank water constantly. It was amazing how much she drank. I guess it was her body's way of flushing itself. She also threw some grand-scale temper tantrums for a month or two.

· · · · ·

For two months after ending treatment, Meagan was worried about everything that went in her mouth. She'd say, "Is this okay to eat? Will this hurt me? Am I safe? Am I going to get hurt doing this?" This paranoid phase just faded away.

· · · · ·

These first two months off treatment, I've noticed Kristin steadily gaining in self-confidence and composure.

Many parents and children resolve their complicated feelings by giving back to the cancer community in some way. Helping others, for many people, is a satisfying way to reach out or bring closure to the active phase of cancer treatment. Helping others can create something enormously meaningful out of personal tragedy. Some examples of reaching out are:

- We started a Boy Scout project to keep the toy box full at the clinic.

- My children are counselors at the camp for kids with cancer.

- After my son died, I gave up my parish to begin work as a hospice chaplain.

- We organized a walk to raise funds for the Ronald McDonald House.

- We (a group of parents of children with leukemia) requested and were granted a conference with the oncology staff to share our thoughts on ways to improve pain management and communication between parents and staff. It was very well-received.

- We circulated a petition among parents to request increased hospital funding for psychosocial support staff. We presented it to the Director of the Hematology/Oncology service.

- I started a Candlelighters group and organized meetings, conferences, and picnics, and write a quarterly newsletter.

- I requested that the clinic and local pediatricians refer newly diagnosed families to me if the parents wanted someone to talk to. I remembered how impossible it was to go to meetings in the first few months, and how desperately I needed to talk to someone who had already traveled the same road.

- We held a bone marrow donor drive.

- I give platelets and blood regularly.

- I took all of our leftover Hickman line supplies to camp and gave them to a family who needed them.

- The family of one child started a nonprofit company which produces beauty products. All proceeds, no strings attached, go to the local children's hospital for cancer research.

- Grace Monaco, whose four-year-old daughter died in 1970 from ALL, started a support group, which has grown into the world renowned Candlelighters Childhood Cancer Foundation. Ms. Monaco has nurtured the growth of CCCF with wit and wisdom over the 25 years of its existence. She's devoted a quarter of a century to helping those of us who followed her down the hard road of helping our children live with or die from leukemia.

The possibilities are endless. Parents use whatever talents they have, from designing head coverings, to writing newsletters, to going online on their computer to dispense advice to newly diagnosed families, to help others.

An equally healthy response to ending treatment for cancer is to put it behind you. Many families, after years of struggles, just want to enjoy a new-found sense of normalcy. They don't want constant reminders of cancer, and feel that it's not good for children to be continually reminded of those hard times.

> I realized that it was time to put it behind us when I watched my two children playing house one day. There was only one adult and one child in the family. I asked what happened to the rest of the family and they both said, "Cancer, they died." I didn't want them to have any more cancer in their lives. They had had enough. I know people who worry all the time about the leukemia returning, and it is not healthy for them or their children. I decided to get out of the cancer mode, and back to being my usual upbeat self. I feel that we are finally back to normal, and it's a good place to be.

Parents and children need to talk to one another, examine their emotions, decide what course they want to chart, and work together towards a healthy life after cancer.

One year after treatment

After a year has passed since the end of treatment, parents have a different perspective. For some, the thoughts of cancer have receded, and life has resumed its predictable pattern. For others, fear is still a constant companion. The following are a sampling of comments from parents one year after the end of their child's treatment for leukemia:

> He still eats like a bird.

· · · · ·

> She went back to eating a balanced diet a couple of months after treatment ended.

· · · · ·

Her appetite has vastly improved, but she still has taste aversions, and only eats a few types of food.

. . . . .

It's been a year since treatment ended, and I don't think I'm obsessed with worry anymore, but in my quiet moments, I still get nauseated when she coughs (she had pneumonia at diagnosis).

. . . . .

I had to learn to stop referencing everything to the illness all of the time. For instance, I found myself saying things like, "Before you were sick" or "While you were sick." My six-year-old daughter finally pointed it out to me and asked me to stop. Now I use her age as a reference point.

. . . . .

I still worry and think in terms of the illness. For instance, he had to have some teeth pulled, and my first thought was to go get his counts checked to make sure that his platelets were high enough. Then I told myself that I was being ridiculous. I let him go in like a normal kid, and it was fine.

. . . . .

I feel worse off therapy, as if I have something hanging over my head. I still get very worried and fretful whenever he gets a fever, but going to the clinic for checkups no longer bothers me. But I still do things like calling the doctor in an absolute panic when he has a red stool, only to find out that my husband fed him beets for lunch.

. . . . .

I feel that the leukemia was almost a gift. We could have been like any other couple seeking the "American Dream" with both of us working and John in day care. But our priorities changed. I stay home, my husband began a home business, and we live every day to the fullest. Our time is spent loving and appreciating each other and every moment we have. I take nothing for granted—every smile, every hug, every "I love you" gets my undivided attention.

. . . . .

Shawn is a year off treatment and I find myself letting go of the bad memories more and more. They are just fading away. What I am left with is awe, admiration, and amazement that my son handled all of the hard-

ships of treatment and survived. He's very determined and strong-willed, and I'm so proud of him. When people say to me, "Oh, you were so strong to make it through that," I respond, "All I did was drive him to the appointments, he did the rest."

This experience has really changed me and my entire family. My marriage is much better, my other sons are stronger and closer to us, and Shawn has shown us all how tough a little kid can be. We take each precious day, one at a time, and try to get the most out of it. I so appreciate life and my family.

Possible long-term side effects

Vigilance is essential if the blossoms of success in pediatric oncology are not to bear bitter fruit. Cure is not enough.

—Giulio J. D'Angio, M.D.

At diagnosis, parents do not know what price their child will ultimately pay for reprieve from leukemia. For the majority of children with low or intermediate ALL, the price is low. Short-term effects are discomfort, a bald head, and occasional school absences. Long-term effects—sometimes none. For children with high-risk ALL, AML, CML, or those who have relapsed and require more intensive treatment, the price for life may be higher: subtle or pronounced learning disabilities, impaired endocrine system, growth difficulties, and many other possible consequences. One mother summed up her feelings by saying, "I hope for the best, and I'll deal with the rest."

Female fertility

Younger girls are more resistant to damage to the ovaries from chemotherapy than are older teenagers. There have, however, been rare cases of ovarian failure in young girls who have been given high doses of cyclophosphamide as part of their treatment for leukemia. Additionally, one study discovered damaged ovaries in a percentage of girls who received craniospinal radiation. In the vast majority of cases, prepubertal girls who have been treated for leukemia exhibit normal growth, sexual development, and fertility.

Most teenagers who are treated after puberty for leukemia retain normal ovarian function. If teenagers do not resume having periods after treatment ends, or if they develop symptoms such as hot flashes or breast discharge, a pediatric endocrinologist should be consulted.

After treatment for leukemia, the chances of becoming pregnant and having a normal pregnancy and birth are good. Preliminary data from the National Cancer Institute shows that offspring born to cancer survivors have the same risk of birth defects as the general population. However, all women treated with chemotherapy drugs which can cause cardiovascular damage (doxorubicin, daunomycin, cyclophosphamide) or who had x-rays to the chest or spine, should be monitored closely during pregnancy and delivery.

Fertility issues for children or adolescents who have undergone bone marrow transplants are covered in Chapter 20, *Bone Marrow Transplantation*. Precocious and delayed puberty are covered in Chapter 12, *Radiation*.

Male fertility

Use of methotrexate, vincristine, cytoxan (cyclophosphamide), and prednisone causes a rapid decrease in sperm count in teens or men who have passed puberty. Normal sperm production and motility generally return in the second year of maintenance.

After treatment for leukemia, males rarely have difficulty going through puberty. This does not mean that males are fertile. Males have cells that produce testosterone and cells that produce sperm. Therefore, a male could have normal testosterone-producing cells but abnormal sperm-producing cells. Patients who received cyclophosphamide or radiation to the testes should have testosterone levels and sperm count checked.

For all sexually mature males, sperm banking should be discussed with the oncologist prior to treatment. Sperm can be kept viable for 10 to 15 years, and this may allow some teens the opportunity to become fathers later in life.

Fertility issues for children or adolescents who have undergone a bone marrow transplant are covered in Chapter 20, *Bone Marrow Transplantation*.

Cardiovascular disorders

Heart problems may occur months or decades after treatment with anthracyclines (adriamycin, idarubicin, or daunomycin), high-dose cyclophosphamide, or chest irradiation. Symptoms include shortness of breath, fatigue, poor exercise tolerance, rapid heartbeat, and irregular heartbeat.

The heart damage is usually related to the cumulative dose of anthracyclines, and can range from mild electrocardiogram changes to sudden death from cardiac failure (very rare). For adults, the dose at which incidence of heart failure begins to increase is 550 mg/m^2, but there is growing evidence that for children who have received multiple chemotherapeutic agents including cyclophosphamide, the critical total anthracycline dose may be 350 to 400 mg/m^2 or lower.

Any child whose total dosage of doxorubicin and daunomycin exceeds 350 mg/m^2, who had chest radiation (not routine diagnostic x-rays), or who received high-dose cyclophosphamide prior to bone marrow transplantation, is at risk for future cardiovascular problems. Because early diagnosis and prompt treatment are crucial, most authorities now recommend that any child who has received potentially cardiotoxic therapies should undergo an annual exam, including a physical examination, thorough history, chest x-ray, 12-lead electrocardiogram, and echocardiogram.

In addition, for those children whose cardiac monitoring the first year off treatment is normal, the Children's Cancer Group recommends an EKG and echocardiogram every two to three years. They also recommend a radioneuclide angiocardiogram and 24-hour continuous-taped EKG every five years post therapy. Any pregnant woman with a history of anthracycline treatment should have her cardiac function followed closely throughout the pregnancy.

There is also a controversy regarding whether persons who were treated with high doses of anthracyclines should engage in isometric exercise (weight lifting, wrestling, football, rock climbing). Consult with your oncologist if your child or teen wishes to engage in these activities.

> My daughter's high-risk protocol required an echocardiogram before treatment began, and periodically during treatment. When I asked why she never had one after the baseline, I was told by the fellow that she needed the drugs so it didn't really matter if she had cardiac changes. When I asked at end of treatment about the echocardiogram, I was told that since she only received a total of 175 mg/m^2, an echocardiogram would only be given if symptoms developed. When I pulled out the Children's Cancer Group's recommendations on the subject and handed them over to my hometown pediatrician, he ordered an echocardiogram for her.

Dental abnormalities

Although it is not commonly discussed, dental abnormalities are a frequent side effect of treatment for leukemia, especially for children who are treated with cranial radiation. The most common problems are failure of the teeth to develop (agenesis), arrested root development, microdontia (unusually small teeth), and enamel abnormalities. Several parents report difficulties in insurance covering dental or orthodontic problems caused by radiation and/ or chemotherapy. If you are a member of this group, collect articles on the studies which show that a relationship exists between treatment for leukemia and dentofacial development, and bring them to your child's oncologist. Ask the oncologist to write a letter to the insurance company using the research to support his position that the dental work is cancer-treatment related. The journal articles on this topic in the "Resources" section at the end of the chapter have dozens of such articles listed in their bibliographies.

> Jeremy has had many dental problems. He lost his gums in front of his lower front teeth. To correct this, they took skin from the roof of his mouth, and did a skin graft. He also had an eyetooth that just broke off at the root and fell out.

· · · · ·

> Gina needed oral surgery to expose one of her molars. She also needed extensive work on her bite and wore braces and appliances. Another molar has a hook on the root and the braces could not budge it, so that will require more surgery. This will be followed by another round of extensive orthodontic work. My other three children had minimal orthodontic work for cosmetic reasons only.

Persistent weakness

Although the literature abounds with articles describing acute neuromuscular problems during treatment, very few studies have been published on the problem of persistent muscle weakness. Most children are remarkably resilient, and after treatment ends they resume normal activities at age-appropriate levels. But there are some children, particularly those who received cranial radiation, who have chronic problems with strength and coordination. As the population of leukemia survivors grows, it is hoped more attention will be focused on studying persistent weakness and investigating ways to prevent or overcome it.

When my daughter Christine ended treatment at age six, she was very weak, and had trouble with balance and coordination. For instance, she couldn't walk a balance beam holding an adult's hand, she couldn't skip or play hopscotch. I took her for a physical therapy consult, and it made her very angry. Even though they recommended therapy, I decided that she had had enough done to her body. It was time for her to learn to work with her body and have fun. She decided to take ballet and gymnastics, and we took her for many long walks and bike rides (with training wheels) to help her regain her strength. We made physical activities fun. I talked to her school gym teacher, her ballet instructor, and gymnastics teachers, and asked them to be supportive and encouraging. It's been a year since she ended treatment, and although she still has training wheels on her bike, she walks a balance beam with grace and assurance, can dribble a basketball, and is able to do almost all of the movements for ballet.

• • • • •

Judd finished his treatment at age six and had some muscular weakness. He tried organized sports, but preferred individual sports like skiing. Over several years, he gradually regained his strength and coordination so that his athletic ability was average.

• • • • •

We had Justin tested through the school district, and the district is giving him his physical therapy. He's weak in the hips and walks with his feet turned out. He's resistant to taking physical risks; for instance he sits down and slides off things rather than jumping off. He just loves to go to physical therapy.

• • • • •

John was diagnosed at 14 months, and his treatment was stopped a year early due to severe ataxia, an inability for him to perceive center. For instance, when he tried to walk through a door, he bumped into the side because he couldn't find the center of the opening. He had trouble with skills requiring balance and drooled continually. Some days he had no troubles; then other days he was severely affected. We took him to many doctors who had no suggestions to help him. Two years after his treatment ended, one doctor suggested we cut all caffeine from his diet *(he thought it might be blood vessel constriction in his cerebellum), and it improved overnight. His drooling has stopped, and his balance is continuing to improve.*

· · · · ·

Rachel is two years off treatment and starting kindergarten. She has trouble skipping and galloping, and cannot hop on one foot. I worry about competitiveness during gym classes.

Learning disabilities, delayed growth, and premature or delayed puberty are most commonly associated with cranial radiation and are covered in Chapter 12, *Radiation*. Coping strategies for dealing with learning disabilities are explored in Chapter 15, .

The above information is about infrequent long-term effects from cancer treatment. Certain groups of children and teenagers are more, or less, at risk for side effects than others. The risk for your child depends on many factors, including the type of leukemia, total dosage of individual drugs, combinations of different types of chemotherapy, location and dose of radiation, and age at diagnosis. As with all the information contained in this book, please consult with your oncologist if you have any questions or concerns. The field of cancer treatment is constantly evolving and improving, and the experts in the field are years ahead of the published material. They can explain to you the reasons for their recommendations, and should show you the books or articles that support their position if you ask to see them.

Follow-up care

Life is a hollow gift unless cancer survivors emerge from treatment as competent and worthy individuals, able to obtain insurance, equipped to earn a living, and prepared to participate in a medical surveillance program to "keep" the life they have won.

—Grace Powers Monaco

In the past, survivors of cancer were on their own after treatment ended. With increasing numbers of long-term survivors, it became apparent that these young men and women often faced complex medical and psychosocial effects from their years of treatment. As a result, many institutions began late-effects clinics to provide a multidisciplinary team to monitor and support survivors. The nucleus of the team is usually comprised of a nursing coordinator, pediatric oncologist, pediatric nurse practitioner, radiation oncologist, endocrinologist, school liaison, social worker, and psychologist.

The follow-up programs usually include a review of treatments received, counseling regarding potential health risks (or lack thereof), and case-specific diagnostic tests such as cardiac evaluations, hormonal studies, or testing for learning disabilities. These follow-up clinics not only provide comprehensive care for long-term survivors, but participate in research projects that track the effectiveness and side effects from various clinical trials. In addition, the follow-up clinic acts as an advocate for survivors with schools, insurance agencies, and employers. To obtain an up-to-date list of follow-up clinics in the U.S., call Candlelighters at 1-800-366-CCCF.

If your institution does not provide long-term follow-up care, there are several issues that should be addressed at the end of treatment. A discussion of some of these follows.

Follow-up schedule

Protocols for clinical trials require specific follow-up schedules. For instance, after treatment for average-risk ALL, your child may require monthly physical exams and a monthly CBC for the first year off treatment, and a less frequent schedule for the following years. Find out from the oncologist what the required schedule will be, and where the appointments will be. Make sure that your child understands that after treatment ends doctor appointments and blood draws will still be an occasional necessity.

Immunizations

If your child was diagnosed prior to receiving all of her immunizations, ask the oncologist when you should resume the regular schedule for immunizations.

> *My doctor said to wait a year before beginning to catch up on shots.*
> *It was nice for her to get a long break before any more pokes.*

Risks of smoking

Teens need continuing counseling on problems associated with smoking or engaging in other high-risk behaviors. Any child or teen who received anthracycline therapy (adriamycin, daunomycin, or idarubicin) is at risk for damage to the muscle of the heart. Smoking not only impacts the lungs, but it makes blood vessels hard, further decreasing the heart's ability to pump. The combination of heart damage from chemotherapy and smoking vastly increases the chance of heart disease, heart attack, congestive heart failure, or death from sudden cardiac failure. An article on survivors and smoking contained in the Candlelighters Winter 1994 youth newsletter ends with these words:

> If you've had cancer and your friends haven't, they don't face the same risks from smoking that you do. You've fought hard for your life. Don't put it out in an ashtray.

Safe sex

Every teen and young adult who has survived cancer should be counseled about safe sexual practices. Despite the prevalence of sexual messages in our culture, most teens are woefully underinformed about the facts. Many survivors think, erroneously, that if they are infertile, they do not have to be concerned about the use of condoms. However, all sorts of diseases, some potentially fatal (hepatitis C, AIDS), and some not (genital herpes, genital warts, gonorrhea), can be transmitted through sexual intercourse.

One nurse practitioner at a large follow-up clinic stated:

> I tell every teenager who comes through the door, regardless of their medical background, that I think that he or she is too young to have sex, and I explain why. But then I say, in the event that you do choose to become sexually active, you ALWAYS need to use a condom, and not just any condom. I tell them to only use a latex condom with a spermicide, which is the most barrier protective. I explain that no sex is the only guarantee to avoid the many diseases out there, but a latex condom with spermicide offers the next best protection. And I really stress that this should be done whoever the partner is, and for whatever type of sex. So many teenagers think that diseases only happen to other kinds of kids.

Keeping the doctor informed

For a variety of reasons, many children and young adults are no longer cared for by pediatric oncologists who are familiar with their history. Additionally, when treatment ends, many patients and parents are not adequately informed on the risks of developing physical difficulties months, years, or decades after treatment ends. The risks of such delayed effects are real. Moreover, many primary care physicians—pediatricians, family practice doctors, internists, gynecologists—are not fully aware of all the different treatments used for the multitude of childhood cancers and their late effects.

It is imperative that survivors be informed advocates in their own health care. They need to be educated, in a supportive and responsible way, of the risk for future physical adversities, so that if a problem does arise, it will be recognized early and receive prompt attention. Young adults who have survived childhood cancer need to be fully cognizant of their unique medical history and able to share this information with all future doctors who will care for them.

Figures 5 and 6 chart the possible late effects of treatment for ALL and ANLL and the methods used to screen for them. Survivors of the chronic leukemias require frequent follow-up from their bone marrow transplant center. If your child is not being followed in a late-effects clinic, you may wish to photocopy this information to share with your child's current doctor or to send to your child if she is already living away from home. These charts are reprinted from *Survivors of Childhood Cancer*.

Other important information that should be in your child's health history information includes:

- Name of disease.
- Date of diagnosis and relapse, if any.
- Place of treatment.
- Dates of treatment.
- Names of attending oncologist and primary nurse.
- Names and dosages of chemotherapeutic agents used.
- Type, areas treated, and amount of radiation used.
- Name of radiation center.
- Date(s) radiation received.
- Number of rads and to what location, e.g., whole body, cranial, testicular.
- Dates and types of any surgeries.
- Date and type of bone marrow transplant, if any.
- Any major treatment complications.
- Any persistent side effects of treatment.
- Recommended medical follow-up.

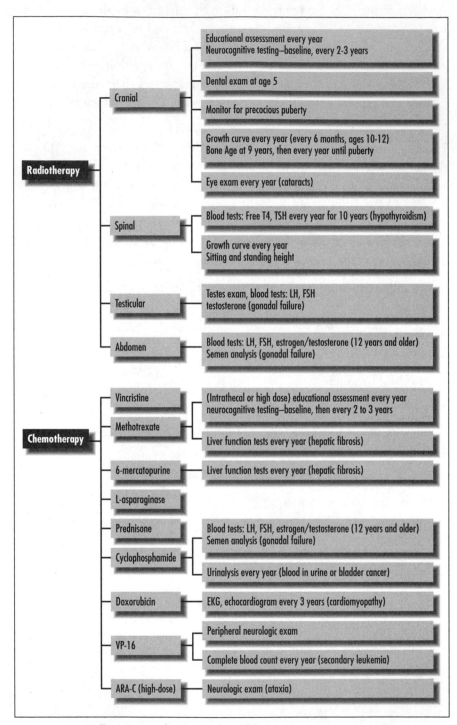

Figure 5. ALL: Follow-up tests for possible late effects

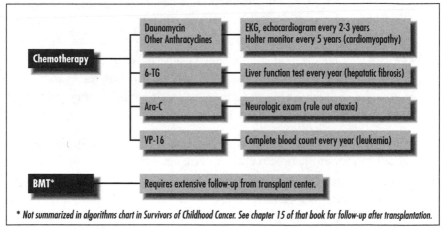

Chemotherapy	Daunomycin Other Anthracyclines	EKG, echocardiogram every 2-3 years Holter monitor every 5 years (cardiomyopathy)
	6-TG	Liver function test every year (hepatatic fibrosis)
	Ara-C	Neurologic exam (rule out ataxia)
	VP-16	Complete blood count every year (leukemia)
BMT*		Requires extensive follow-up from transplant center.

* Not summarized in algorithms chart in Survivors of Childhood Cancer. See chapter 15 of that book for follow-up after transplantation.

Figure 6. ANLL: Follow-up tests for possible late effects

If your child will not be periodically examined at a long-term follow-up clinic, write down this information, and make sure that your child has a copy to give to any future doctor who will be treating him.

Employment

Up to a point a man's life is shaped by environment, heredity, and movements and changes in the world around him. Then there comes a time when it lies within his grasp to shape the clay of his life into the sort of thing he wishes it to be. Everyone has it within his power to say, "This I am today; that I will be tomorrow.

—Louis L'Amour
The Walking Drum

The population of adults who have survived childhood cancer is growing at a rapid rate. It is estimated that by the year 2000, 1 in every 900 young adults will be a cancer survivor. Thousands of survivors are staying well, growing up, graduating from college, and successfully entering the workforce. Survivors of childhood leukemia are educators, sports figures, radio announcers, doctors, social workers, dancers, lawyers, professionals of all types.

Diane Komp, M.D., in *A Child Shall Lead Them*, writes:

> I lecture about long-term survivors to each new group of medical
> students that comes through pediatrics at Yale. I can see from their faces
> that most of them prefer memorizing the odds that someone will make it

than tasting the sweetness of individual victories. "That's very nice, but how representative is that case?"

Not all of them feel that way, though. I watch their faces and can now pick out from their ranks a special type of young person who is being seen in increasing numbers in medical classrooms. Although their class-mates cannot tell who they are, I can spot a long-term survivor of child-hood cancer five minutes into that lecture.

Despite their numbers, some survivors still face job discrimination due to fears about cancer and its treatment. Under federal law, and many state laws, an employer cannot treat a survivor differently from other employees because of a history of cancer except in certain circumstances involving health, life, and disability insurance. The Americans with Disabilities Act (ADA) prohibits many types of job discrimination by employers, employ-ment agencies, state and local governments, and labor unions. In addition, most states have laws that prohibit discrimination based on disabilities, although what these laws cover varies widely.

The Americans with Disabilities Act of 1990 (ADA) prohibits discrimination based on actual disability, perceived disability, or history of a disability. Any employer with 15 or more workers is covered by the ADA.

The ADA requires that:

- Employer may not make medical inquiries of an applicant, unless:

  1. Applicant has a visible disability, e.g., amputation, or

  2. Applicant has voluntarily disclosed his cancer history.

  Such questions must be limited to asking the applicant to describe or demonstrate how she would perform essential job functions. Medical inquiries are allowed after a job offer has been made, or during a pre-employment medical exam.

- Employer must provide reasonable accommodations unless it causes undue hardship.

- Employer may not discriminate because of family illness.

- Employer is not required to provide health insurance.

The ADA is enforced by the Equal Employment Opportunity Commission (EEOC). Call 1-800-669-4000 for enforcement information. Call 1-800-669-3362 for enforcement publications.

Cancer survivors should not lie about a cancer history during a job interview. However, they should understand the consequences of voluntarily revealing a cancer history prior to receiving a job offer.

If you feel that you have been discriminated against due to your disability or a relative's disability, contact the EEOC promptly. A charge of discrimination generally must be filed within 180 days of the notice of the discriminatory act.

If a survivor of cancer or a member of the family feels that he has been denied a job, fired, forced from a job, denied reasonable accommodation, or discriminated against for promotions or medical leave because of cancer history, contact the Childhood Cancer Ombudsman Program for help at (703) 492-0045. They can provide the following free services:

- Outside review by experts.
- Citations to medical and legal literature.
- Mediation.
- Analysis of employment contracts.
- Instructions in appeal procedures.
- Assistance with filing complaints.
- Explanations of how to respond to questions on job applications and at interviews.

The military

Some survivors of childhood cancer wish to enlist in the military, or qualify for ROTC, the reserves, or the service academies. Currently, regulations allow only for military service by ALL survivors who have no history of recurrence. Others may consider applying for a waiver. The Childhood Cancer Ombudsman Program at (703) 492-0045 can research federal regulations and research previous cases to aid the applicant to the military.

Insurance

Job discrimination can spell economic catastrophe for cancer survivors because most health insurance is obtained from employment. As survivors mature, seek employment, and move away from home, many encounter barriers to obtaining health insurance, such as rejection of application based on cancer history, policy reductions, policy cancellation, preexisting condition exclusions, increased premiums, or extended waiting periods. As current discussions about national health care reform are extremely contentious, it seems unlikely that major reforms of the American health insurance system will occur in the near future.

However, 25 states do offer high-risk individuals, like survivors, access to comprehensive health insurance plans (CHIPS). CHIPS, also called "high-risk pools," are a means for individuals to obtain insurance regardless of their physical condition or medical history. For more information on CHIPS, call your state Office of the Insurance Commissioner. The NCI publication *Facing Forward* (listed in the "Resources" section at end of the chapter) lists contacts by state for insurance coverage for the hard to insure (pages 24-26).

Although neither the states nor the federal government mandate a legal right to insurance, there are some legal remedies to insurance discrimination:

- **COBRA.** The Comprehensive Omnibus Budget Reconciliation Act (COBRA) is a federal law which requires public and private companies employing more than 20 workers to provide continuation of group coverage to employees if they quit, are fired, or work reduced hours. Coverage must extend to surviving, divorced, or separated spouses, and to dependent children. You must pay for your continued coverage, but it must not exceed by more than 2 percent the rate set for your former co-workers. By allowing you to purchase continued coverage, you have time to seek other long-term coverage.

- **ERISA.** The Employee Retirement and Income Security Act (ERISA) is a federal law which protects workers from being fired because of the cancer history of the employee or beneficiaries (spouse and children). ERISA also prohibits employers from encouraging a person with a cancer history to retire as a "disabled" employee. ERISA does not apply to job discrimination (denial of new job due to cancer history), discrimination which does not affect benefits, and employees whose compensation does not include benefits.

Both ERISA and COBRA are enforced by:

Pension and Welfare Benefits Administration
U.S. Department Of Labor—Room N-5658
200 Constitution Avenue, N.W.
Washington, DC 20210
(202) 523-8521

At the end of the chapter is an extensive list of resource organizations which can help if you or your child faces job discrimination or problems with insurance due to treatment for cancer.

Lisa N. Ellis, a survivor of ALL, included the following essay in her application to law schools. Lisa, who will begin law school in 1997, gives much of the credit for her success to her eductional consultant, Joanne Holt.

> *Frustrated by my earlier performance on the LSAT, I began a search this year to uncover possible meaning in the gap between my actual test scores and my capabilities. My search led me to a rather unpredictable place: the sixth floor of Children's Hospital in Seattle, the same wing where I had received treatment for leukemia twenty-three years ago. Prompted by information received from a family friend who was also a former cancer patient, I started to explore the connection between my cancer treatment and my learning.*
>
> *From the colorful murals on the walls to the confusing floor plan of the building, much about the hospital looked the same to me. However, this time I was twenty-three years older and so was my oncologist. I approached her for information to help me further my career just as she was phasing out of hers. The information I hoped to receive would resolve some of the misgivings about my abilities on standardized tests and open new doors for me to retake the LSAT with enhanced opportunities.*
>
> *The cancer-related information that wasn't revealed to me during my years of treatment was laid out on the table for me now. I was told that I was diagnosed at the same time the medical profession was starting to experience some significant breakthroughs in the treatment of childhood cancer. Stringent protocols involving chemotherapy, high doses of cranial and body radiation and painful procedures like spinal taps and bone marrow aspirations were beginning to produce positive results: more children were surviving what was previously viewed as a terminal disease. Caught in this watershed of medical breakthroughs, my cancer quickly responded and went into remission. Yet, I was informed that the same treatments that saved my life may also have affected my learning.*

The statistics spelled out various side effects the treatment could have on former patients. Cited studies showed that some patients had difficulties with academic subjects like math, writing and reading. Other research pointed to differences in processing speeds; including the inability to process information at a rapid pace or difficulty maintaining concentration for extended periods. Because I was only three years old when I was diagnosed, it was impossible to determine my cognitive makeup before treatment. Now, later in life, I had the opportunity to pinpoint the relevance these statistics had upon me.

I elected to go through an evaluation process which disclosed my educational strengths and weaknesses. Overall, the results indicated that I have strong intellectual ability. In particular, I demonstrated strong aptitude in vocabulary, comprehension and verbal reasoning sections. Despite these encouraging results, scores for short-term sequential memory and processing speed sections were discrepant from my overall assessment. Yet, for me, the most significant impact these lower scores have posed is a greater challenge with timed standardized tests. At the advice of an educational consultant, I unofficially took the LSAT under untimed conditions. The substantial improvements in my scores (169 instead of 150) confirmed my ability to deduce logical answers to test questions given adequate time.

The results of this recent evaluation process validated my earlier conceptions about my academic profile. Sophomore year in college, I developed an understanding that I had to study harder than some of my classmates to learn the material and achieve good grades. Yet, instead of feeling defeated, I rose to the challenge. I look back on my college experience and believe that I benefited immensely from my extra efforts. I utilized the knowledge and guidance of my professors to discuss issues and write effectively. I also became highly organized, allowing me the ability to participate in sports, attain school leadership positions and maintain a solid grade point average. At Whitman College, I completed rigorous courses, consistently achieved a competitive grade point average, and received academic distinction with a minimum of accommodations.

Combined with my successful college performance is relevant and challenging work experience. I've held positions at several public law organizations which have utilized my abilities to communicate *articulately, analyze complex issues, and develop rapport with diverse populations in multiple settings. Recently, I have been a Legal Extern for low-income persons at the Legal Action Center. I have direct experience analyzing evidence, interviewing clients, investigating case backgrounds, researching laws, and advocating for clients both orally and in writing.*

With a history of academic and professional accomplishment, I have promising potential as a law student. In the past, I have adapted my learning style to overcome academic or work-related challenges. Now, I have gained insight and knowledge of my learning skills which will carry me with confidence through the demanding field of law.

Resources

Organizations

Candlelighters Childhood Cancer Foundation
7910 Woodmont Ave., Suite 460
Bethesda, MD 20814
1-800-366-2223
Fax: (301) 718-2686

Operates a hotline which provides information and services to survivors, families, and medical professionals on all pediatric cancer-related topics. Candlelighters offers many publications (most free), including: *Introduction to the Americans with Disabilities Act: A Guide for Families of Children with Cancer and Survivors of Childhood Cancer; Insurance—Your Options and Your Child's;* and *Tips on Health Insurance for Long Term Survivors.*

Childhood Cancer Ombudsman Program
(703) 492-0045

Provides services for cancer survivors and their families on employment discrimination and service in the military.

National Information Center for Children and Youth with Disabilities (NICHY)
P.O. Box 1492
Washington, DC 20013
1-800-695-0285
(202) 884-8200

A clearinghouse that provides free pamphlets and information on disabilities and the rights of disabled children and their parents.

The Disability Rights Education and Defense Fund
2212 Sixth Street
Berkeley, CA 94710
1-800-466-4232

Answers questions about the Americans with Disabilities Act, explains how to file an complaint, and provides dispute resolution.

National Coalition for Cancer Survivorship
1010 Wayne Road, Fifth Floor
Silver Spring, MD 20910
(301) 650-8868

Furnishes information about legal rights and advocacy services for cancer survivors of all ages. Publications include: *Health Insurance and Cancer: What You Need to Know*; *Working It Out: Your Employment Rights As a Cancer Survivor*; and *Charting the Journey: An Almanac of Practical Resources for Cancer Survivors*.

Job Accommodation Network
West Virginia University
918 Chestnut Ridge Road, Suite # 1
P.O. Box 6080
Morgantown, WV 26516
1-800-526-7234 or 1-800-ADA-WORK

Provides information about accommodations on the jobs for persons with disabilities.

Reading for adults

Berger, Larry, and Dahlia Lithwick. *I Will Sing Life—Voices from the Hole in the Wall Gang Camp*. Boston: Little Brown, 1992. Stories and pictures of children with cancer.

Leukemia Society of America. *Coping with Survival*. To obtain free copy, call 1-800-955-4LSA. 32-page booklet includes information on diagnosis, communicating with physicians, treatment, life after treatment, and services and support.

Mullan, Fitzhugh, M.D., and Barbara Hoffman, J.D., eds. *Charting the Journey: An Almanac of Practical Resources for Cancer Survivors*. Mt. Vernon, NY: Consumers Union, 1990. Comprehensive guide to the issues of cancer survivorship. Includes sections on dealing with doctors and hospitals; the mind/body relationship; support services; peer support; employment, insurance, and money matters; dealing with the family; appendix on survivor resources.

National Cancer Institute. *Facing Forward: A Guide for Cancer Survivors.* To obtain a free copy, call 1-800-4-CANCER and ask for Publication No. 90-2424. A 43-page booklet written for adult survivors that contains valuable information on caring for your health, feelings, insurance, earning a living, and how to move ahead.

Technical reading: books

Green, Daniel, M.D., and Giulio D'Angio, M.D., eds. *Late Effects of Treatment for Childhood Cancer.* New York: Wiley-Liss, 1992. Technical text covering such issues as neuropsychological function following treatment for leukemia, growth hormone deficiency, precocious and premature puberty, reproductive function after bone marrow transplant, insurance issues, and job discrimination.

Schwartz, Cindy, M.D., Wendy Hobbie, R.N., et al. *Survivors of Childhood Cancer: Assessment and Management.* St. Louis: Mosby-Year Book, Inc., 1994. Excellent, up-to-date technical volume covering all aspects of possible late effects from treatment for childhood cancer. Includes chapters on each body system: central nervous system, neuroendocrine, head and neck, thyroid, cardiovascular, pulmonary, liver, ovary, testes, genitourinary, muscular, and skeletal systems. Also discusses a broad spectrum of survivor psychosocial issues and the need for long-term follow-up.

Pediatric Dentistry Reference Manual. Ask your child's dentist to refer to the current year's manual to help formulate a dental plan for the child. Lists dental complications of chemotherapy, radiation and bone marrow transplantation, management guidelines on care of the teeth, and dental emergencies.

Technical reading: articles

Berkowitz, Robert, D.D.S, et al. "Dental Management of Children with Cancer." *Pediatric Annals* 17:11 (November 1988): 715-25. Discusses the short-term and long-term side effects of chemotherapy, radiation, and bone marrow transplant.

DeLaat, C., and B. Lampkin. "Long-Term Survivors of Childhood Cancer: Evaluation and Identification of Sequelae of Treatment." *CA: A Cancer Journal for Clinicians* 42:5 (Sept/Oct 1992): 263-82. Excellent review article. This article summarizes all known late effects from treatment for childhood cancer and outlines current recommendations for screening.

Fochtman, D. "Follow-up Care for Survivors of Childhood Cancer." *Nurse Practioner Forum* 6:4 (Dec 1995): 194-200. As the large number of survivors of childhood cancer reach adulthood, the need for follow-up for late effects from their cancer therapy is necessary. Discusses the need to educate both survivors and their health care providers.

Hamre, M.R., L.L. Robison, et al. "Effects of Radiation on Ovarian Function in Long-term Survivors of Childhood Acute Lymphoblastic Leukaemia: A Report from the Children's Cancer Study Group." *Journal of Clinical Oncology* 5 (1987): 1759-65. Found craniospinal and/or abdominal radiation to be the primary cause of ovarian dysfunction or failure.

Hays, Daniel M, John Landsverk, et al. "Educational, Occupational, and Insurance Status of Childhood Cancer Survivors in Their Fourth and Fifth Decades of Life." *Journal of Clinical Oncology* 10 (1992): 1397-1406. Study including 219 survivors with individually matched controls found few long-term problems with education, employment, and insurance, with the exception of patients treated for central nervous system tumors.

Hovi, Liisa, M.D., Era Pertti, Ph.D., et al. "Impaired Muscle Strength in Female Adolescents and Young Adults Surviving Leukemia in Childhood." *Cancer* 72(1) (1993): 276-81. Small study evaluated and compared muscle strength of forty-three survivors with that of sixty-nine healthy, age-matched women. Results showed shorter heights and significantly poorer strength in the survivors. Of the various treatment modalities, cranial radiation and L-asparaginase were independently associated with the lower muscle strength values.

Kenney, L. B., and H. S. Nicholson. "Birth Defects in Offspring of Adult Survivors of Childhood Acute Lymphoblastic Leukemia: A Children's Cancer Group/NIH Report." *Cancer* 78:1 (July 1996): 169-76. This is the largest retrospective study to date on birth defects in offspring of ALL survivors. Study analyzed 593 survivors and 409 siblings. Found no difference in the rate of birth defects (3.6% vs. 3.5%) between groups. Concluded that adult survivors of childhood ALL are not at greater risk of birth defects in offspring compared with sibling controls.

Lipshultz, Steven, Steven Colan, et al. "Late Effects of Doxirubicin Therapy for Acute Lymphoblastic Leukemia in Childhood." *The New England Journal of Medicine* 324(12) (1991): 808-15. Assessed the cardiac status of 115 survivors of ALL who had received between 45-550 mg./m^2. They found 57 percent had abnormalities in the thickness of the left ventricular wall of the heart or ability of the heart to contract. Late effects correlated with increased total dose.

Neglia, Joseph P., M.D., Anna T. Meadows, et al. "Second Neoplasms after Acute Lymphoblastic Leukemia in Childhood." *New England Journal of Medicine* 325(19) (1991): 1330-36. Children's Cancer Study Group studied 9,720 survivors of ALL, and found that 2.53 percent develop second cancers within 15 years of diagnosis. Those at highest risk of second cancers, particularly brain tumors, were children at the age of five or less at the time of diagnosis who had undergone cranial irradiation.

Pajari, V. and M. Lanning. "Developmental Defects of Teeth in Survivors of Childhood ALL Are Related to the Therapy and Age at Diagnosis." *Medical and Pediatric Oncology* 24:5 (May 1995): 310-14. Developmental defects of dental enamel and roots were analyzed and compared to age- and sex-matched healthy controls. Study found that chemotherapy alone increased the number of enamel defects, but did not affect the roots. Scattered irradiation from CNS radiation caused developmental defects in both enamel and roots. Younger age was the most important factor in developing tooth defects.

Sklar, Charles, Leslie Robison, et al. "Effect of Radiation on Testicular Function in Long-Term Survivors of Childhood Acute Lymphoblastic Leukemia: A Report from the Children's Cancer Study Group." *Journal of Clinical Oncology* 8(12) (1990): 1981-87. Study of sixty long-term survivors of ALL found high levels of follicle-stimulating hormone (FSH) and/or reduced testicular volume in 55 percent of the group receiving craniospinal and gonadal radiation, 17 percent of those receiving craniospinal radiation, and 0 percent of boys receiving only cranial radiation. Leydig cell function was found to be resistant to direct radiation with doses as high as 12 Gy.

Sonis, Andrew L., D.M.D., Nancy Tarbell, M.D., et al. "Dentofacial Development in Long-term Survivors of Acute Lymphoblastic Leukemia." *Cancer* 66(12) (1990): 2645-52. Compared the dentofacial development of six groups of children and found that 94 percent of all patients and 100 percent of patients treated when less than 5 years old were affected. Abnormalities were greatest in children less than 5 years old who received cranial radiation as well as chemotherapy.

Steinherz, Laurel, M.D., Peter Steinherz, M.D., et al. "Cardiac Toxicity 4 to 20 Years After Completing Anthracycline Therapy." *Journal of the American Medical Association* 266 (1991): 1672-77. Studied 201 patients who had received between 200 to 1275 mg/m2 of anthracyclines (doxirubicin and daunomycin) by using echocardiograms from 4 to 20 years after end of treatment. Twenty-three percent of those studied had abnormal cardiac function.

Steinherz, Laurel, M.D., and Thomas Graham, M.D. "Guidelines for Cardiac Monitoring of Children During and After Anthracycline Therapy: Report of the Cardiology Committee of the Children's Cancer Study Group." *Pediatrics* 89(5) (May, 1992). The anthracyclines are important drugs for treating malignancies, but their use is limited by their cardiotoxicity. In this article, the Children's Cancer Study Group has formulated recommendations for monitoring children before, during, and after chemotherapy to allow for dose modification if cardiac damage is evident.

Van Eys, Jan. "The Truly Cured Child." *Pediatrician* 18 (1991): 90-95. The concept of the truly cured child describes a child on par with her peers in development, maturation, achievement, and aspirations. The term cure has three components: biological cure, psychological cure, and social cure. Includes a description of a true psychosocial cure and methods to achieve it.

Wallace, W. H., S. M. Shalet, et al. "Ovarian Function Following the Treatment of Childhood Acute Lymphoblastic Leukaemia." *Medical and Pediatric Oncology* 21(5) (1993): 333-9. Studied forty survivors of childhood ALL and found the outlook for normal ovarian function to be good. The spinal component of craniospinal radiation, with cyclophosphamide potentially a contributory factor, was shown to be a major risk factor for ovarian damage.

Wallace, W.H., S.M. Shalet, et al. "Male Fertility in Long-term Survivors of Childhood Acute Lymphoblastic Leukaemia." *International Journal of Andrology* 14 (1991): 312-19. Studied long term testicular function in thirty-seven young adult male survivors of ALL. All thirty-seven men had normal puberty and testosterone levels. Six men were sterile (no sperm produced), and all six had been treated with cytoxan or cytoxan and ARA-C (cytosine arabinoside). Concludes that long-term outlook for male fertility improves with time in those with evidence of germ cell damage, but remains poor for at least ten years for those most severely affected.

Relapse

Hold fast to dreams
For if dreams die
Life is a broken winged bird
That cannot fly.

—Langston Hughes

PARENTS FREQUENTLY DESCRIBE the return of their child's leukemia as more devastating than the original diagnosis. Parents feel betrayed. They think that they put their child through a hell for nothing. They are scared, for they know that any recurrence is serious. The anger is back—since they did everything the doctors said, why did the cancer return? They are afraid that if the first battery of treatments didn't work, what will? And the unspoken but most crushing feeling of all: If my child dies, how will I survive?

If your child has relapsed, one point that is well worth remembering: You are not the same person that you were at diagnosis. You've been through this before so you know how to get medical and emotional support. You have a relationship with the medical team, and you can speak the language now. You have developed friendships with other families of children with cancer. You know that something that seems insurmountable can be overcome, one day at a time.

This chapter will explain how doctors determine if a relapse has occurred, emotional responses of the parents, and how to decide on a treatment plan.

Signs and symptoms

Although relapse can happen years after treatment ends, it most commonly occurs during treatment or in the first year off treatment. In fact, most treatment centers do not consider children to be long-term survivors of leukemia until they have been off treatment for at least two years.

The signs and symptoms of leukemia relapse include all of the same telltale warnings that occurred prior to diagnosis. These are:

- Fatigue.
- Fevers.
- Night sweats.
- Bruises.
- Pale skin.
- Back, leg, or joint pain.
- Loss of appetite.
- Enlarged lymph nodes in the neck or groin.
- Enlarged abdomen caused by a large spleen or liver.
- Changes in behavior, such as excessive irritability.
- Dizziness.
- Headaches.

In some cases, parents have no warning. After they bring their child in for a routine bone marrow aspiration or spinal tap, they receive a totally unexpected telephone call from the doctor with the news.

> *I am a long-term survivor (30 years old), who first was diagnosed with ALL at age 8 and subsequently relapsed three times, at ages 13, 15, and 16. The first relapse was by far the worst to deal with emotionally. It had been five years since my diagnosis, so I went in for my last spinal tap and bone marrow. I had been off treatment with good counts for two years. My mother and I didn't even wait for the test results; we went out to lunch and went shopping. Later that day, I called the clinic, and my doctor told me the bone marrow was fine, but she needed to talk to my mother. I heard my mother say, "No, no, oh no," and she started to cry. I just stood there feeling numb, knowing the news was bad. The cancer had returned to my central nervous system. We held each other and cried.*

The three most common sites for relapse are the bone marrow, the central nervous system, and the testes. Bone marrow relapse is the most common form of recurrence of leukemia. Achieving a prolonged second remission or cure after a bone marrow relapse is becoming more commonplace since the use of bone marrow transplantation has increased. Allogenic transplants from an HLA-identical sibling (see Chapter 20, *Bone Marrow Transplantation*) that is performed early in a second remission has resulted in longer leukemia-free survival when compared with chemotherapy. The value of autologous and matched unrelated bone marrow transplantation for relapsed ALL is uncertain.

Since the use of central nervous system prophylaxis was initiated, the likelihood of CNS relapse has dramatically decreased. Currently, CNS relapse is seen in less than 10 percent of young patients. There are various of ways of treating CNS relapse, depending on the amount of prior radiation and intrathecal medication given. Usually, treatment plans include aggressive systemic and intrathecal therapy combined with craniospinal radiation.

Only one percent of boys with leukemia suffer a testicular relapse. Treatment for this type of relapse includes radiation to the testes (2400 cGy to both testes) and chemotherapy. Radiation to the testes at these doses usually causes sterility, and may cause hormonal abnormalities as well. Once a remission is achieved, some oncologists recommend a bone marrow transplant.

Occasionally leukemia reoccurs at other sites, such as the ovary or eye. These cases are usually treated with local radiation to the relapse site, and intensification of chemotherapy.

> Right before Stephan went to camp, he went in for his maintenance spinal tap. I got a bill from a different specialist, and when I asked the oncologist about it, he said that Stephan had a few white cells in his fluid that he wanted to get another opinion on. He assured me that everything was okay, but I just had that feeling that something was about to go wrong. At his next spinal, his count was 88 in the cerebrospinal fluid. A central nervous system relapse.

· · · · ·

> Jody was complaining about pain and a feeling of pressure in his leg bones. I kept bringing him back to the oncologist, saying that something was wrong, that he was in great pain, but the doctor kept insisting that it was just growing pains. He didn't even examine his legs for a month. When he did, he could feel parts of the bone radiating heat. The bone scan showed the cancer in the exact spots that Jody had pointed out.

· · · · ·

Greg was in school, on maintenance, looking great. The night before a routine doctor's appointment, he started crying in the bathroom. But only half his face was crying. It was obvious that something was wrong. The next morning I was watching the doctor as he walked into the room, and when I saw his face I knew that we were in big, big trouble. Greg had Bell's palsy: the lumbar puncture showed that he had relapsed in his central nervous system.

• • • • •

JaNette was diagnosed with AML with the Philadelphia chromosome. Four months into treatment, after a routine bone marrow aspiration, I got a phone call from the doctor saying that she had relapsed. I remember going to the hospital where they did another bone marrow. At exactly four o'clock in the afternoon, they gave me a relapse protocol to read. I was sitting on the floor in the hallway reading it, and it was so horrible because I knew what it meant! I understood what we were in for, and I started to bawl and couldn't stop. After that it was just a blur.

Emotional responses

Parents who have children with leukemia in remission think or speak of relapse with an almost palpable dread. Just the thought can cause the emotions which surged in them at diagnosis to erupt. The depth of the emotions generated by relapse is very hard for parents and survivors to relive and describe. As one survivor said in a shaky voice when being interviewed, "It's been eleven years since I finished treatment, but talking about it shows that you scratch the surface and those overwhelming feelings are still right there."

Parents feel a wide array of emotions at relapse: numbness, guilt, dread, anger, fear, confusion, denial, and grief. Physical symptoms such as dizziness, nausea, fainting, and shortness of breath are common. Parents wonder how they can ask their child to endure it again. They wonder how they will survive it themselves. They oscillate between optimism and panic.

I found that relapse was far worse than the original diagnosis. At diagnosis, after a certain period of adjustment, you think that treatment has a beginning, a middle, and an end. But relapse creates a bigger burden to accept. You begin to feel that maybe the disease is more powerful than the medicine. I found that for awhile I just stopped functioning and thinking rationally. I felt that all the hell of treatment had been just a waste of time. I felt guilt and a tremendous sense of loss of control. I felt like I was on a runaway freight train, hurtling towards an end that didn't look so good anymore. This is the point at which people are willing to use any type of unconventional therapies because they are desperate. I know one mom in our support group who was even willing to try coffee enemas. She looks back on it now and says, "I just went crazy."

• • • • •

My first relapse was the worst emotionally. Neither my parents or me ever thought that after five years it would be back. I also had been so young when I was first treated that I didn't really think of leukemia as cancer and didn't understand that I could die from it. But at 13, I remembered clearly what I had been through and all I could think was that it hadn't worked. I told my parents that I wouldn't do it again. My father sat me down and gave me a reality check. He explained that I would die if I didn't get treatment. He said, "If you don't do it for your-self, please do it for me and your mom." The next morning I went into the clinic and started all over again.

• • • • •

Jesse relapsed four times, and in some ways it got harder and in other ways it got easier. We knew each time that her chances for survival were fading, and that was hard. But, each time we grieved and worked through the feelings, and our skills at handling relapse improved. I turned to God for comfort, and I think that helped me feel that I was standing on a rock out in the ocean, rather than thrashing around in the water. My faith gave me solace. Jesse handled the relapses better than anyone else in the family. She would calmly listen to the doctors' explanations, then she would say, "Okay, what do we have to do?" She was never angry. She was sometimes sad, but mostly accepting.

Deciding on a treatment plan

A rapid response is necessary when faced with a recurrence of childhood leukemia. Treatment plans for a first relapse may be specified in your child's protocol, or your physician may suggest a different approach. Suggestions for treatment may include radiation to the head and spine, radiation to the testes, more intensive chemotherapy, or bone marrow transplantation.

Physicians make recommendations based on knowledge, experience, and consultations with other experts in the field. Do not hesitate to ask your physician why she has suggested a certain approach to your child's relapse. Ask your doctor about treatment goals, methods, and possible side effects. Ask your doctor if she has consulted with others in the decision-making process, and if so, whom. If your child is old enough, include her in the discussion if she wishes to participate.

Just like at diagnosis, time is a pressing concern. Parents know that treatment should begin as soon as possible. But, beware rushing into a new treatment plan if you feel uncomfortable. Your child needs to know that you are 100 percent in favor of proceeding, and children have radar for parents' feelings. There is always time for answers to all of your questions and time to get a second opinion.

Refer to Chapter 6, *Forming a Partnership with the Medical Team,* for ways to obtain a second opinion. One excellent resource is the Childhood Cancer Ombudsman Program. Panels of volunteer pediatric oncologists volunteer to give second medical opinions or medical record reviews at the request of families or the treating oncologist. The program is particularly valuable in helping families make well-informed treatment choices, as well as becoming comfortable with the therapeutic approach chosen. To use this free service, call (703) 492-0045.

Candlelighters (1-800-366-CCCF) can utilize their computer system to give you a PDQ (Physician's Data Query) listing of all the relapse protocols currently being used as well as ongoing clinical trials. They will use information that you provide on the type of leukemia, treatments already given, and your child's condition and will provide a tailor-made list of institutions doing research on that type of relapse. It may well reinforce what your doctor recommended, or it might provide you with some additional treatment options. Either way, it will increase your comfort level during the treatment planning process.

The following are questions that you might want to ask your doctor when discussing the treatment plan:

- What is the goal of this treatment? Is it likely to cure my child, or is it just for comfort?

- Why do you think that this treatment is the best option? What are the other choices, and why did you choose this one?

- Have you consulted with other physicians? If so, whom? Did you all agree on this treatment, or was there a range of choices suggested?

- Is there a standard treatment for this type of relapse? What is it?

- What clinical trials are ongoing for this type of relapse?

- Explain the potential benefits and possible side effects of the suggested treatment.

- What are the known or potential risks of the treatment?

- How often will my child need to be hospitalized?

- How long will my child need this treatment?

- If the treatment is investigational, is there scientific evidence that it works for leukemia?

- Will my child benefit, or is the study to advance medical knowledge?

- Does insurance cover this type of investigational treatment?

> After his CNS relapse while on maintenance, Stephan (8 years old) received cranial and spinal radiation, went through another induction, and they started to give him spinals with ARA-C, methotrexate, and hydrocortisone. Even with ondansetron it's bad. He's very sick to his stomach, and just feels queasy all of the time. After the reinduction, he went back on his maintenance schedule, and will finish at the expected time. But it's much harder for him now. His ankle bones ache, he's limping, and he can't run. Six days after vincristine, he gets severe back pain, like someone is pounding on his back hard. If he is bumped or jarred, he cries out in pain. He creeps along looking like an old man.

. . . . .

> When Greg relapsed, they threw his protocol in the trash can, and our oncologist started making phone calls to other doctors in the Children's Cancer Group network to decide on a plan. Greg was put successively on three different relapse protocols in an attempt to keep him in remission. When his counts went down, the blasts would temporarily disappear, but when his counts rose, the blasts would creep back. His CNS relapse was followed by a bone marrow relapse, and the only option left was a bone marrow transplant, but we didn't know if he would be strong enough to survive it.

. . . . .

Cristie was standard-risk ALL, so when she relapsed six months into treatment, they put her on a high-risk protocol, then when she relapsed again, she was put on even higher doses of chemotherapy. We finally went to them and said, "What are our options here?" They decided to give higher doses to try to get her in remission for a BMT, but by then she had serious heart damage from the ARA-C and was no longer an acceptable risk at most transplant centers. She ended up going to a center 3,000 miles from home which took high-risk cases.

• • • • •

After another relapse, they wanted to try a chemotherapy with limited possible results, and we really didn't want our 11-year-old Caitlin to go through any more. But she talked it over with the doctor and concluded, "Of course I have to do it, I'm a fighting Irish."

In the Spring 1995 issue of the Candlelighters newsletter, Arthur Ablin, M.D. (Director Emeritus of Pediatric Clinical Oncology at the University of California, San Francisco) writes of the importance of goal setting in the decision-making process after relapse:

Before determining which treatment is to be chosen, a decision must be made to determine the goal of treatment—in other words, what is it that we are trying to achieve. This crucial first step is the basis upon which any decision concerning treatment must be made. But it is too often omitted from consideration and/or discussion, even by the most experienced. The frustrations accompanying the previous failure of treatment, the fear of the loss of the hope for cure, the pressure of urgency to find solutions, the new awareness of the possibility or probability of death, lead us all to want to consider treatments first rather than these more difficult considerations involved in establishing goals. These also force us to deal with reality earlier, which could mean the almost intolerable confrontation with the death of a very-much-loved child, a tragedy to be avoided at all cost.

After you have set goals, received answers to all of your questions, obtained a second opinion if desired, and decided on a treatment plan, it is time to proceed. Your knowledge and experience may prove to be a double-edged sword. You have no illusions about the difficulties ahead because you've done it before, but you also will be strengthened by your ties with the cancer community, your comfort with your physicians and hospital routines, and your ability to "work the system" to get what your child needs. Many parents shared how their child took the lead about relapse treatment. While the parents agonized, their child said simply, "Let's just do it." And they did.

I encourage people to try to keep things in perspective. Attitude is 90 percent of survival. As difficult as it is, try to maintain a good attitude and keep focused on the future. I always thought, "I have cancer, this is a bad thing, but I am going to beat it." My analogy was a boxing match. When I relapsed, I was knocked down. But I always got up and kept fighting.

I had a total of three relapses, two of which were on treatment. Every time we relapse, statistics say our chances of survival are less likely. But I survived those three relapses, and now I live a life as normal as if cancer never touched it. After cancer, I finished high school and went to college. I gave birth to a beautiful, healthy baby girl. My daughter (still beautiful) is now seven years old, and with her I'll have a chance to relive some of the childhood I missed. For me, life does go on after cancer.

Resources

Reading for adults

Adams, David, and Eleanor Deveau. *Coping With Childhood Cancer: Where Do We Go From Here?* rev. ed. Toronto: Kinbridge Publications, 1993. Contains an excellent chapter on relapse, which covers such topics as the impact of relapse, how relapse strikes, feelings, pain, siblings, adjustment to living, the adolescent patient, and some thoughts for single parents.

National Cancer Institute. *When Cancer Recurs: Meeting the Challenge Again.* To obtain a free copy, call 1-800-4-CANCER and ask for publication No. 93-2709. Booklet describes different types of recurrence, types of treatment, and coping with the return of the cancer.

National Cancer Institute. *Advanced Cancer: Living Each Day.* To obtain a free copy, call 1-800-4-CANCER, ask for Pub. No. 85-856. 30 pages. Booklet provides practical information to make living with advanced cancer easier.

Technical reading

Hinds, P. S., L. K. Birenbaum, et al. "Coming to Terms: Parents' Response to a First Cancer Recurrence in Their Child." *Nursing Research* 45:3 (May-June 1996): 148-53. Study collected data through interviews, observations, and medical record reviews on thirty-three guardians of children with recurrent cancer. Parents tried to regulate shock, monitor their situation, and evaluate care-limiting decisions in order to help their child have the optimal chance for cure while preparing for the child's possible death.

Kantarjian, H. M., M. Talpaz, et al. "Treatment of Chronic Myelogenous Leukemia in Accelerated and Blastic Phases with Daunorubicin, High-dose Cytarabine, and Granulocyte-macrophage Colony-stimulating Factor." *Journal of Clinical Oncology* 10:3 (1992): 398-405. Study attempted to improve the results of intensive chemotherapy in CML in the accelerated and blastic phases. This treatment did not significantly improve remission rates, mortality, complications, or overall survival.

Ribeiro, R. C., G. K. Rivera, et al. "An Intensive Re-treatment Protocol for Children with an Isolated CNS Relapse of Acute Lymphoblastic Leukemia." *Journal of Clinical Oncology* 13:2 (Feb 1995): 333-8. Study assessed the salvage rate and long-term complications among children treated with an intensive regimen for isolated CNS relapse during first remission of ALL. In this protocol, cranial irradiation was delayed until after an intensive course of systemic chemotherapy was completed. Results were that the therapy was effective (especially for children with no prior cranial radiation) and well tolerated by children. Most patients suffered no significant neuropsychologic impairment.

Sadowitz, P. D., S. D. Smith, et al. "Treatment of Late Bone Marrow Relapse in Children with Acute Lymphoblastic Leukemia: A Pediatric Oncology Group Study." *Blood* 81:3 (Feb 1, 1993): 602-9. Study compared the efficacy of doxorubicin/prednisone and cytarabine/teniposide in treating children with a late bone marrow relapse. On this regimen, 97% achieved a complete remission, with neither treatment proving to be significantly superior. Factors found to be independently associated with a favorable outcome were: age less than ten years at initial diagnosis, white blood cell count less than 5000/microL at relapse, and duration of first remission greater than 54 months.

Well, R. J., S. H. Gold, et al. "Cytosine Arabinoside and Mitoxantrone Induction Chemotherapy Followed by Bone Marrow Transplantation or Chemotherapy for Relapsed or Refractory Pediatric Acute Myeloid Leukemia." *Leukemia* 8:10 (Oct 1994): 1626-30. The purpose of the study was to determine the induction rate, duration of response, and toxicity of cytosine arabinoside and mitoxantrone in pediatric patients with AML. Patients who achieved a complete remission either had a bone marrow transplant or further chemotherapy. Twenty-seven of thirty-seven patients achieved a complete remission. Of the remaining children, 41% remained disease free at two years. Some patients treated achieved prolonged survival.

Wofford, Marcia, Stephen Smith, et al. "Treatment of Occult Late Testicular Relapse in Children with Acute Lymphoblastic Leukemia: A Pediatric Oncology Group Study." *Journal of Clinical Oncology* 10:4 (April 1992): 624-30. Study compared the efficacy and toxicity of two drug treatments: VM-26/ARA-C and doxorubicin/prednisone. The results showed no significant difference between the two treatments. Both were quite effective; only four of eighty patients had a local recurrence.

CHAPTER 20

Bone Marrow Transplantation

The courage of life is often a less dramatic spectacle than the courage of the final moment; but it is no less a magnificent mixture of triumph and tragedy.

—John Fitzgerald Kennedy
Profiles in Courage

BONE MARROW TRANSPLANTATION (BMT) is a complicated procedure used to treat leukemia, other cancers, and some blood diseases that were once considered incurable. In a bone marrow transplant, the patient's bone marrow is totally destroyed by high-dose chemotherapy, with or without radiation. New, disease-free marrow is then infused into the patient's veins. The marrow migrates to the cavities inside the bones where it begins to produce new, healthy blood cells.

A BMT, although frequently life-saving, is an expensive, technically complex, and potentially life-threatening procedure. Understanding the procedure and its ramifications at a time of crisis is tremendously difficult. This chapter will present the basics of bone marrow transplantation in simple terms, as well as share the experiences of several families.

If a bone marrow transplant has been recommended for your child, the "Resources" section at the end of the chapter references several easy-to-read publications, as well as many technical articles which will provide more in-depth coverage of the subject.

When are transplants necessary?

At present, some types of leukemia cannot be cured with chemotherapy and/or radiation. BMT is usually recommended for children with CML in the chronic phase or AML in first or second remission. In other cases, such as relapsed ALL, a bone marrow transplant will be one of several options which will be discussed with the family.

If a BMT has been recommended for your child or teenager, you may want to get a second opinion before proceeding. Chapter 19, *Relapse*, and Chapter 6, *Forming a Partnership with the Medical Team*, give several methods for obtaining an educated second opinion. In addition, to fully understand the issue, you may want to ask the oncologist some or all of the following questions:

- What are all the treatment options?
- For my child's type of cancer, history, and physical condition, what chance for survival does he have with a transplant? With other treatment?
- What are the risks from the transplant? Explain the statistical chance of each risk.
- What are the benefits of this type of transplant?
- What will be my child's short-term and long-term quality of life after the transplant?
- How long will she have to take medicines after the transplant?
- What are the side effects of these medicines?
- Is this transplant considered to be experimental, or is it accepted clinical practice?

> *My daughter was 6 years old when she was diagnosed with AML. When she relapsed four months into treatment, an allogenic bone marrow transplant was her only hope.*

· · · · ·

> *After my son's second relapse from ALL, the doctors told us that a BMT was his last option for a cure.*

· · · · ·

> *The day my daughter was diagnosed with CML, they told us her only chance for a cure was a BMT.*

Types of transplants

Under certain circumstances, BMT is the treatment most likely to provide a cure for some children with leukemia. However, there are several different types of transplants available, each with strengths and weaknesses. It is important to understand the types of transplant to better enable you to evaluate what has been proposed for your child.

What are HLA antigens?

Every individual has proteins, called human leukocyte-associated (HLA) antigens, on the surface of their cells. These protein markers allow the person's immune system to distinguish the body's own cells from those of another person. Scientists look at six different HLA antigens to determine a person's HLA type. Two people are considered to be a match if all six antigen sites are identical. If five or less sites match, it is called a mismatch or partial match.

HLA genes are inherited, so close relatives, especially siblings, are the most likely candidates for a six antigen match. The odds of obtaining an unrelated (from a person not in the immediate family) matched bone marrow were once slim, but are now increasing due to the rapid expansion of persons typed and listed on various national and international marrow registries.

Allogenic

Allogenic BMTs are those in which donor bone marrow is transplanted into the patient. The marrow usually comes from a brother or sister with a matching marrow type or from a parent or sibling whose marrow type nearly matches the patient (a mismatched donor). Sometimes an matched unrelated donor (called MUD) can be located through the U.S. National Marrow Donor Program or similar donor registries in the U.S. or other countries. The risk of complications increases if the donor is mismatched or unrelated.

In an allogenic BMT, the patient's bone marrow is destroyed through a combination of total body radiation and chemotherapy, or high-dose combination chemotherapy alone. The donor's marrow is dripped into the patient's vein in a manner similar to a blood transfusion. The donor marrow enters the cavities in the patient's bones, and if it engrafts properly, begins to produce new and healthy blood cells.

The primary life-threatening complications of an allogenic bone marrow transplant are graft-versus-host disease (GVHD) and infection. GVHD affects approximately 30 to 50 percent of patients who have undergone an allogenic transplant, with a higher percentage of cases occurring after a transplant using mismatched marrow or marrow from an unrelated donor. While GVHD is a serious complication, it may decrease the likelihood that the child will relapse. This not-well-understood phenomenon is called the graft-versus-leukemia effect. GVHD is discussed in detail later in this chapter.

Transplant centers use different and various methods to reduce the risk of infection. The most effective methods are single room isolation, thorough hand washing, and screened and irradiated blood products. Other infection control methods—air filters, requirements to cap and gown before visiting the patient, prohibiting live plants, fruits, and vegetables in the patient's room—remain unproven.

Allogenic transplants are usually recommended only after relapse for most ALL patients, but the proper time to attempt a transplant for AML patients is still controversial. Most physicians recommend transplants for their pediatric AML patients in first remission, but others support transplants only if the youngster with AML relapses. The type of AML and the timing of the relapse also affect the physician's recommendation for BMT. For children or teens with CML, bone marrow transplant is the only hope for cure, and is usually recommended in the chronic phase of the disease.

> Leslee (12-1/2 years old) was diagnosed with AML the day after Thanksgiving, 1991. They tried four different chemotherapy protocols, but she never went into remission. They told us to just take her home to die. We asked Fred Hutchison Cancer Research Center to make an exception to their rules and try a transplant, even though she was not in remission, but they said no. Leslee told her doctor, "Experiment on me. Please. I want to live." He wrote the transplant center, and they agreed to do a three-antigen mismatch (from my husband) transplant, but they cautioned us that she had less than a 5 percent chance of survival. Her dad and I were behind her, but she did it herself. I couldn't believe how much she wanted to live. They did the transplant in July, 1992. It's the end of 1995 now, and she's doing great. But the best friend she made there, who had a very favorable prognosis, died.

Autologous

During an autologous bone marrow transplant, the patient's own marrow is extracted and cryopreserved (a type of freezing). Some transplant centers use various methods to purge the marrow prior to freezing in order to kill any remaining leukemic cells. The patient then undergoes radiation and chemotherapy or high-dose chemotherapy alone to kill all of his existing marrow. The frozen marrow is then thawed, and reinfused into the child or teen intravenously.

Currently, there are ongoing studies to evaluate the risks and benefits of purged versus unpurged autologous transplants. It is clear from gene marker studies that most relapses following autologous marrow transplantation involve leukemic cells infused with the marrow.

Children undergoing autologous transplants do not develop graft-versus-host disease and are therefore less susceptible to infection. This is because the GVHD suppresses the immune system, decreasing resistance to infection. But patients who undergo autologous transplants have higher relapse rates because of residual leukemic cells in the marrow or, perhaps, because there is no graft-versus-leukemia effect from GVHD. Patients who develop GVHD after an allogenic transplant have lower relapse rates than do those children who have an autologous or syngeneic transplant.

Syngeneic

Syngeneic bone marrow transplants are those in which the donor is the patient's identical twin. Because the marrow exactly matches the patient's, the major life-threatening complication of graft-versus-host disease (GVHD) is prevented. As with autologous transplants, any possible graft-versus-leukemia (GVL) benefit is absent in syngeneic transplants.

Peripheral blood stem cell transplant (PBSCT)

When doctors aspirate liquid bone marrow from the cavities in bones, it is full of stem cells—cells from which all other cell types evolve. Stem cells can also be found in the circulating (also called peripheral) blood, although in a much less concentrated form.

In a peripheral blood stem cell transplant (PBSCT), the leukemia patient's own stem cells are harvested in a procedure called apheresis or leukapheresis. Blood is removed through a catheter or vein in the arm and circulated through a machine which extracts the stem cells. The blood is then returned to the patient. Each pheresis session lasts two to four hours, and generally from four to six sessions are required to harvest enough stem cells for a PBSCT. The stem cells are frozen until the transplant is performed.

Placental blood stem cell transplant

Umbilical cord blood is a rich source of stem cells, the ancestral cells from which all other cell types evolve. Some institutions are conducting transplants using the umbilical cord blood obtained during the birth of a sibling or from preserved unrelated donor cord blood. Preliminary results suggest that graft-versus-host disease occurs less frequently in fully matched sibling placenta transplants although GVHD is still a major problem in mismatched placental blood transplants. In addition, cord blood is rarely contaminated by viruses such as cytomegalovirus (CMV) or Epstein Barr virus (EBV) that can cause life-threatening complications after a BMT. Placental blood stem cell transplantation is one of many promising new directions in the research efforts of scientists studying ways to improve bone marrow transplantation.

As with different chemotherapy protocols, bone marrow transplant protocols vary among institutions, and are constantly evolving. Many aspects of bone marrow transplantation, for example, the graft-versus-leukemia effect, are not well understood but are under intense scientific scrutiny. Research is also underway to identify those children most likely to benefit from a BMT, the best time to transplant, which new drugs best reduce the likelihood of infection, and the best methods to reduce post-transplant relapse.

For more information on types of transplants, write or phone the *Blood and Marrow Transplant Newsletter*, 1985 Spruce Avenue, Highland Park, IL 60035, (847) 831-1913, and ask for one of the following:

- "BMTs for AML," September 1994 issue.
- "BMTs for ALL," November 1994 issue.
- "BMTs for CML," March 1995 issue.
- "Cord Blood Transplants," January 1996 issue.

The *BMT Newsletter* is also electronically published on the Internet. You can find it on the World Wide Web at Oncolink (*http://cancer.med.upenn.edu/*) or Gopher (*cancer.med.upenn.edu*).

Finding a donor

Finding a bone marrow donor can be a stressful and time-consuming task. The search begins soon after relapse for children with ALL, in first remission for children with AML or some types of high risk ALL, and during the chronic phase for children with CML. In some lucky families, tests show that a sibling or parent is a partial or identical match. Other patients, especially those from minority groups not well-represented in the donor files, can spend months or years searching for a match.

My advice to parents just beginning the process is do not rely on anyone else to make all the arrangements for a donor search and financial arrangements with the transplant center. We were focused on my son's relapse treatment and thought a donor search was ongoing. We then found out that over two precious months had been lost in a delay for financial approval. I foolishly relied on my doctor and his staff to make arrangements and follow through, and it just slipped through the cracks. I should have been on the phone several times a week making sure that the search had begun and that the transplant center was happy with the financial arrangements. It just never occurred to me that a public, research hospital would have a money-first, treatment-second policy. I have a lot of guilt over whether those months made a difference in my son's outcome. I'll never know.

The first step in determining if a person is an HLA match is obtaining a sample of blood from a vein in the arm and sending it to a laboratory for analysis. Each member of the family is HLA typed, and if a match is not found, then the search widens to the donor marrow registries or placental blood banks. The "Resources" section of this chapter lists registries, foundations, and programs that can assist you in finding a donor.

Many people think, erroneously, that to be entered on a registry a sample of bone marrow is necessary. To determine a person's HLA type, only a tube of blood from the arm needs to be obtained. Educating the public needs to be an important component of a public donor drive.

Christie had a rare Mediterranean trait, and we could not find a match in all the registries worldwide. We decided that we had to do it on our own and began a donor drive in our town, which is predominantly Italian. The Red Cross discouraged us, saying that we probably wouldn't get a good response, that they could not process the blood without the money ($45 per person) in hand, and it would be better to spend quality time with Christie. But when the community of Rochester found out, it just snowballed. Dave and I went on TV and advocated for Christie stressing the importance of Christie's bone marrow drive, and told people that this might help their own child one day. The first day of the drive, people lined up outside and stood for hours in the freezing rain and cold. The response was so overwhelming that late in the day they ran out of supplies. Large corporations became involved; GRC did a telethon that raised over $50,000. We typed over 4,000 people from Rochester and *received letters from all over the country. It was just a beautiful thing. Christie was such a powerful little person, and she came to represent so much to our community.*

• • • • •

We felt that it was an omen that Jody's older sister and younger brother were perfect matches. They chose Marieke because she was older, but after all of the workup and tests, they discovered that she was CMV (cytomegalovirus) positive so they used two-year-old Christoph's marrow. Marieke was very disappointed.

• • • • •

While they were trying to find a match for JaNette, the church started a fund raiser and donor sign-up drive. They signed up over 600 people in two days, and United Blood Service had matching funds available to offset some of the costs. Meanwhile, we found an unrelated donor who lived in Milwaukee. She donated the marrow there, and a nurse from UCLA flew out to pick it up.

• • • • •

In hindsight, I would have insisted that they begin the donor search at first relapse. It's a very complicated and time-consuming procedure, and we just kept losing time and having more relapses. Personally, I think that every child with leukemia should be typed at diagnosis.

If a child needs a marrow transplant from an unrelated donor, the national and international registries are notified to conduct a computerized search of their databases. This will identify any donors with the same HLA type as the child. The registry contacts the potential donor to ask if he will donate more blood samples to determine if complete compatibility exists between donor and child.

If the testing shows compatibility, the donor is given an extensive explanation of the entire donation procedure and a complete medical exam. The donor must then make a final commitment to provide marrow for the child in need.

Choosing a transplant center

Choosing a transplant center is a very important decision. Institutions may just be starting a BMT program, or they may have vast experience. Some may be excellent for adults, but have limited pediatric experience. Some may allow you to room in with your child while others may isolate the patient for weeks. Protocols vary among institutions, as well. The center closest to your home may not provide the best medical care available for your child, or allow the necessary quality of life (rooming in, social workers, etc.) that you need.

To obtain a list of transplant centers, call for the current "Transplant Center Access Directory" from The National Marrow Donor Program (NMDP) Office of Patient Advocacy. The directory lists all BMT Centers affiliated with the NMDP that perform unrelated BMTs. The directory includes the location of the center, diseases treated, and costs. To obtain a free copy, call 1-800-526-7809.

To help you learn about the policies of different transplant centers, here are some questions that you might ask:

- How many pediatric transplants did the institution do last year? How many of the type recommended for my child?

- How successful is your program? What are the one-, two-, and five-year survival rates? (Remember that some institutions accept very high-risk patients, and these statistics would not compare to a place that only transplants healthy children in remission.)

- What are the antigen match requirements? (Some institutions require a six-antigen match, others require five out of six, others permit a minor mismatch at the A or B antigen site, but not at other antigen sites).

- What is the nurse-to-patient ratio? Do all the staff members have pediatric training and experience?

- What are the institution's rules on parents staying in the child's hospital room?

- What are the institution's anti-infection requirements? Isolation? Gown and gloves? Washing hands?

- Describe the BMT procedure in detail. Is radiation part of the pretransplant treatment?

- Explain the risks and benefits of this procedure.

- Assuming all goes well, how soon could my child leave the hospital? Leave the area to go home?

- What will his life be like assuming all goes perfectly? If there are problems?

- What are the long-term side effects of this type of transplant?

- What long-term follow-up is available?

- Explain the waiting list requirements.

- What support staff is available (educator, social worker, play therapist, chaplain, etc.)?

- How much will this procedure cost? What is the down payment necessary to secure a spot on the waiting list? How much will my insurance cover?

Many transplant centers have videos and booklets for patients and their families to explain services and describe what to expect before, during, and after transplant. Call any transplant center that you are considering, and ask them to send you all available materials.

To explore more fully what questions to ask various transplant centers, obtain the *Candlelighters Guide to Bone Marrow Transplants in Children* (listed in the "Resources" section at the end of the chapter). This excellent book has an entire chapter devoted to questions to ask to find the best transplant center for your child.

To obtain additional information on how to choose the appropriate transplant center, write or phone the *BMT Newsletter* to obtain the January 1994 issue "Choosing a BMT Center."

> The head of oncology at UCLA comes to our city every two months to follow-up on the kids who have been treated there. It was a big draw to us to have post-transplant follow-up at home, rather than having to travel a great distance to get back to the center. The other thing was that children are not put in laminar air flow, and families weren't required to cap and gown, only scrub their hands. Since I'm allergic to those hospital gloves, this allowed me to stay with my daughter throughout. We did, however, call around to several centers to compare facilities, costs, and insurance coverage.

· · · · ·

> *We didn't have a choice: Fred Hutchinson in Seattle was the only center that would agree to do a mismatch marrow transplant on a very high-risk relapsed child. We applied to every center on the east coast, and were not accepted.*

Making an informed consent is serious for a life-threatening procedure such as a bone marrow transplant. Do not hesitate to keep asking questions until you fully understand what is being proposed. Ask the doctor to use plain English if she has lapsed into medical jargon. Bring a tape recorder or friend to help remember the information. And include your child or teen in the discussion and decision-making process if she wishes. Do not sign the consent form until you feel comfortable that you understand the procedure and have had every single question answered.

Paying for the transplant

Bone marrow transplants are expensive, averaging from $200,000 to $300,000 for the transplant, hospitalization, and follow-up care. Fees for the donor search, donor blood tests, donor physical exam, and bone marrow harvest can total more than $30,000. Most bone marrow transplants for leukemia are no longer considered experimental, so many insurers cover the procedure without complaint. However, not all insurers cover the donor-related costs. Most insurance plans have a lifetime cap, and many only pay 80 percent of the costs of the transplant up to the cap. Often, transplant centers will not perform the procedure without all of the money guaranteed. With time of the essence, this can cause great anguish for families who struggle to raise funds or mortgage all of their belongings to pay.

> *Our first quote from the transplant center was $350,000, but we were able to negotiate for a lower price.*

· · · · ·

> *My son died soon after the transplant. I hate to talk about the money, because I don't want people to think I begrudge spending it. I know that I would feel differently if the transplant had been successful, but I honestly think that we were misled about the real chance of success for his type of disease. We spent the equity on our house, plus took out a second mortgage. We will be paying it off the rest of our lives.*

If you are having difficulty getting your insurance company to pay for the transplant, call the Childhood Cancer Ombudsman Program for help at (703) 492-0045. If you are not insured (or are underinsured) and must raise all or part of the necessary funds, contact the "Organizations for financial assistance" listed at the end of the chapter. They may be able to offer some financial help, and can supply advice on how to quickly and effectively raise funds. Before working with any of these organizations, ask for all printed information available, and ask questions about any fees or costs associated with their services. Make sure that when the treatment is completed or the child dies, any remaining funds may be applied to outstanding medical debts.

You might also call the *BMT Newsletter* and ask for the November 1993 issue, "Successful Fundraising."

> *Our HMO refused to pay for our daughter's bone marrow transplant because it required an unrelated donor, which they considered to be "experimental." Her oncologist and several doctors from the transplant center gathered data and presented it to the insurance board. The HMO reversed its position and paid for the transplant, but not for the donor search, donor fees, donor harvest, or having the marrow transported from London. It cost us approximately $25,000.*

Donating the marrow

Marrow is withdrawn (harvested) from the large bones of the hips. While the donor is under general anesthesia, the doctor inserts a large needle into the bones of the hips and withdraws bone marrow. This procedure is done up to thirty times to draw out a total of one to two pints. The entire process takes less than one hour. After marrow donation, most hospitals keep the donor overnight.

Because the amount of marrow that is removed contains less than five percent of the donor's developing blood cells, it only takes a few days for the donor's body to replace the marrow. The donor is usually sore for a day or two, and may feel a bit tired for up to two weeks. The recovery time varies from donor to donor.

> *After no match was found for Christie in the 4,000 donors that we signed up and typed, I became her donor. We were just a partial match. Being her donor was just wonderful. It was Mother's Day weekend, and I was just full of faith and love. I thought this is it, God has given me a*

second chance to give life to this child. I had a very powerful feeling that it was so special that I could do this for my daughter. I really felt that this was it, it was going to work.

It was uncomfortable for a couple of days, and I was a little bruised. But the people there were wonderful, and they really followed me closely. I'm still on the registry; if someone called me tomorrow, I'd be on a plane. It's a very rewarding feeling, a gift from God.

• • • • •

Jody's two-year-old brother Christoph was a perfect match. I stayed with him when he donated marrow, and my husband stayed with Jody. Christoph seemed to handle the marrow donation easily. Although he had some nausea in the recovery room, he was up and running around late that afternoon saying, "I the donor." He felt very proud. I knew he was somewhat sore because he said, "My diaper hurts."

The transplant

Prior to the actual transplant, the patient's bone marrow is destroyed using high-dose chemotherapy with or without radiation. This portion of treatment is called conditioning. The purpose of the high-doses of chemotherapy and radiation is to kill all remaining cancer cells in the body, make room in the bones for the new bone marrow, and suppress the patient's immune system so that it will accept the donor's marrow.

Conditioning regimens vary according to institution and protocol, and also depend on the medical condition and history of the patient. Typically, the chemotherapy is given for two to six days, and radiation (if part of conditioning) is given in multiple small doses over several days. The chemotherapy drugs most commonly used are cyclophosphamide, VP-16, or Ara-C. Most institutions give chemotherapy first, then radiation, although there are ongoing clinical trials evaluating the effectiveness of radiation prior to chemo.

They got JaNette into her second remission in December, then gave her maintenance drugs to keep her there until they were ready to start transplant conditioning in April. So, unlike some of the other kids, she went to transplant healthy and strong. JaNette had 1,200 rads of total

*body radiation in five increments—two the first day, two the second day,
and one the third day. Then she had two days of incredibly strong chemotherapy, one day of rest, then the transplant.*

The transplant itself consists of simply infusing the donor marrow through a
catheter or IV into the patient, just like a blood transfusion. The marrow
cells travel through the blood vessels, eventually filling the empty spaces in
the long bones. Engraftment is when the new marrow begins to produce
healthy white cells, red cells, and platelets. This typically occurs from two to
six weeks after transplantation. Complete recovery of all components of
immune function can take from one to two years.

*I couldn't believe how beautiful the bone marrow was—a bag of
shimmering red liquid. It just glistened. It meant life.*

• • • • •

*My dad donated marrow for my transplant. He said he was sore and
doing the "bone marrow hop," but he made it to my room that day to see
his marrow transfused into me. I really felt different as I was getting the
bone marrow, like I was getting so much more energy.*

• • • • •

*I cannot say enough good things about the transplant center. They
were very family-oriented, allowed us in the room 24 hours a day. I was
allowed to sleep in bed with her (I just told the nurses to make sure to
poke her and not me). The nurses were wonderful, and I still think of
them as family. We didn't get very close to the other families; we tended
to stay in our own child's room. One day a family would be there, then
the next day they would be gone. I got to the point where I just didn't
want to know.*

• • • • •

*The transplant was very hard for my daughter, as was the environ-
ment that we all had to live in. I can't even describe the devastating
stories of the families we met, hearing a child dying in the room next
door. It was not a happy place, and my daughter became depressed. She
was a very bright, funny, spunky kid, but yet she became quiet and withdrawn. I knew in my heart that she was beginning to give up. They diagnosed her with ICU psychosis, and recommended just sending her home,
feeling that being home would be better for her emotionally.*

• • • • •

The transplant went well except that it was fifty days in the laminar flow room so that we couldn't touch him. Five years old and we couldn't touch him. We had these gloves that we could use to reach in. But Jody was such an accepting kid, he adjusted. We played a lot of cards and at night we'd turn off the lights, and he'd imagine soaring out the tenth floor window. He'd just fly out of that room. He was on hyperal (IV nutrition) and lots of prednisone and other drugs, and he had a few tantrums. Once he pulled out all of his needles and threw them against the wall. I thought that it was a pretty healthy response, but the social worker showed up immediately.

· · · · ·

We were prepared to stay five months in or near the transplant center, but we went home after only two and a half. She had the normal nausea, so she was on TPN (total parenteral nutrition) from transplant May 5 until the end of June. Until she could take her medications by mouth, I did some IVs at home. She had her last platelet transfusion in July. It took until the following June for her counts to normalize, and for her to start producing T-cells. We feel lucky that things went so well.

Donor and patient confidentiality are closely guarded. The NMDT allows letter exchanges or meetings if both donor and recipient express a strong desire to do so, but only after a year has passed since the transplant.

Emotional responses

Bone marrow transplant takes a heavy emotional toll on the child, the parents, and the siblings. It can be a physically and mentally grueling procedure, with the possibility of months or years of after-effects. Most transplant team members are extensively trained to meet the needs of the patient and family during the transplant and long convalescence. The team is usually comprised of physicians and nurses, as well as psychiatrists, social workers, educators, nutritionists, and play therapists.

Christie had many painful complications after the transplant. I remember lying next to her and saying, "Christie, if Mommy could take this away from you I would." She looked at me and said, "Mommy, I love you so much, I would never want you to go through this." But then she went on to say, "It's not so bad, I met a lot of people, we got to travel,

Daddy didn't have to work, Danielle and Nicole got to spend time with Daddy." She just saw something positive in everything, even this terrible disease.

Christie was also very, very funny. She loved having me be the donor, and she started calling me her "blood sister." She kept saying, "Ma, when am I going to start being funny like you?" and I'd tell her that she was way beyond me. Her humor was contagious.

* * * * *

Leah was feeling good and was very healthy when she went into the laminar air flow room. We lived near the transplant center, and she had at least 20 visitors a day. I think the visits and the nonstop telephone conversations really kept her spirits up.

* * * * *

My daughter is a very tough kid, a fighter. But after making it home from the transplant, then having to go back in for six weeks due to a life-threatening herpes infection, she got very down. She was on massive doses of steroids, and just didn't want to see friends or talk to anyone. Later in her hospitalization, she met another teenager with leukemia, and the light just came back on for her. She became herself again, and began to get better.

* * * * *

I think the hardest part of the transplant was being in the laminar air flow room (LAF). They gave me a sterilization wash, put me in some boots, and told me I couldn't touch anything. I felt like a space person. Then I went into the room for two months. I really missed touching people. I cried when I got out and hugged my mom.

* * * * *

What helped me the most was the decorations and having a positive attitude. My mom decorated the area outside the LAF room with balloons, cards, and posters. It was hard to take the medicine, so my mom made a huge poster to mark off how well I did. Every time I took my medicine, I got a sticker. When I got one hundred stickers, I got some roller blades.

* * * * *

I felt great during the transplant and at the center, but when we came home it was very, very difficult. We had just moved before my daughter was transplanted, so we didn't have a good support system in place. She had been in the hospital, then transplant center for almost a year, and then we had to stay at home for another year. For a few months she would spike a fever every time someone who was not in the family came in the house. So my young son could never go to friends to play or have friends over. We just stayed home. It was very hard, and we all felt very isolated.

Often so much time and energy is focused on the child who needs the transplant that the needs of the sibling donor are overlooked. Siblings need careful preparation for what is about to occur, and all questions need to be answered and concerns addressed. Parents need to be careful that the sibling donor realizes that the results of the BMT are out of everyone's control; that the sibling is not responsible for either her brother's life or death.

Organizations that can offer emotional support to families during the transplant experience are listed in the "Resources" section at the end of this chapter.

Complications

Some children have a smooth journey through the transplant process (especially children in remission with a fully matched sibling donor), while others bounce from one life-threatening complication to another. Some children live, and some children die. There is no way to predict which children will develop problems, nor is there any way to anticipate whether the new development will be merely an inconvenience or a catastrophe. This section will present some of the major complications that can develop post-transplant, and the experiences of several families in facing these problems.

Failure to engraft

Engraftment is when the donated marrow takes up residence in the patient's bones and begins to produce healthy blood cells. In cases where a child has received HLA-matched marrow from a sibling, engraftment failure is less than one percent. In contrast, children receiving marrow from partially HLA matched family members or unrelated donors, graft rejection occurs in five to twenty-five percent of patients.

Infections

Most infections following transplant come from organisms within the body (e.g., CMV, gut bacteria). Staph infections from not washing hands and then touching the patient or, occasionally, exposure to airborne fungi are practically the only preventable forms of infection.

The immune system of healthy children quickly destroys any foreign invaders; not so with children who have undergone a bone marrow transplant. The diseased immune system of these children has been destroyed by chemotherapy and radiation to allow the healthy donated marrow to grow. Until the new marrow engrafts and begins to produce large numbers of white cells (two to six weeks), children post-transplant are in danger of developing serious infections. In the absence of GVHD, the immune recovery by three months is sufficient for the child to safely attend school.

> Since my daughter's temperature starts rising whenever anyone not family enters the home, we've had to take some extraordinary measures. We change clothes before we come in the house, and spray with Lysol. Shoes are left out of doors.

To prevent and combat bacterial infections, children receive large doses of several kinds of antibiotics if their temperature goes above $101°$ F. any time in the first weeks after transplant. Fungal infections can occur, but are rare in children who received a matched BMT. Ironically, the antibiotics used to treat bacteria allow fungi to flourish.

After the first month post-transplant, children are also susceptible to serious viral infections, most commonly, herpes simplex virus, cytomegalovirus, and varicella zoster virus, particularly if they have GVHD. These can occur up to two years after the transplant. Viral infections are notoriously hard to treat, although a few are sensitive to the antiviral agents acyclovir and ganciclovir.

CMV is completely preventable if the patient and donor are both CMV negative and all transfused blood products are CMV negative.

Interstitial pneumonitis, a sometimes fatal form of pneumonia, is most common the second or third month post-transplant. It is a type of pneumonia which can result from an infection or from the conditioning regimen itself.

Preventing infections is the best policy for those children who have had a bone marrow transplant. The following are suggestions to minimize exposure to bacteria, viruses, and fungi:

- Have medical staff and all family members wash their hands before touching the child.

- Keep your child away from crowds and people with infections.

- Do not let your child receive live virus inoculations until the immune system has fully recovered.

- Keep your child away from anyone who has recently been inoculated with a live virus (chicken pox, polio).

- Keep your child away from barnyard animals and all types of animal feces.

- Avoid home remodeling while your child is recovering.

- Call the doctor at the first sign of a fever or infection.

> *Leah had so many problems with infections and getting her counts back up that she spent two years on steroids, cyclosporin, and monthly gammaglobulin.*

For more information on infections, obtain the September 1993 *BMT Newsletter*, "Infections," or read Chapter 8 of *Bone Marrow Transplants: A Book of Basics for Patients*, by Susan Stewart (see the "Resources" section of this chapter).

Graft-versus-host disease (GVHD)

Graft-versus-host disease is a frequent complication of allogenic bone marrow transplants. It does not occur with autologous or syngeneic transplants. In GVHD, the bone marrow provided by the donor (graft) attacks the tissues and organs of the BMT child (host). Approximately 30 to 50 percent of persons who have a related HLA-matched transplant develop some degree of GVHD. The incidence and severity of GVHD is increased for those children who receive unrelated or mismatched marrow. The majority of GVHD cases are mild, although some can be life-threatening.

There are two types of GVHD: acute GVHD and chronic GVHD. Patients can develop one type, both types, or neither one. Acute GVHD usually occurs at the time of engraftment or shortly thereafter. Donor cells identify the patient's cells as invaders, and attack the patient's skin, liver, stomach, or intestines. Allogenic BMT patients are given drugs before and after transplant in an attempt to prevent GVHD. Symptoms of acute GVHD can range from mild skin rash to severe, sometimes fatal infections or liver, stomach, and intestinal problems. Acute GVHD is treated with cyclosporin, steroids (prednisone, dexamethasone), and methotrexate.

> *JaNette's transplant was on May 5 and her ANC was up to 1000 on May 30. That's when her graft-versus-host started. It doesn't look like a regular rash, more like pinpoint red dots under the skin. It's very itchy, and then it starts to peel. She looked like she had leprosy! She had very little internal graft-versus-host disease. She's a year and a half post-transplant, and she still broke out in a rash the last time they tried to taper her off the cyclosporin.*

· · · · ·

> *Ryan died from acute graft-versus-host disease. It destroyed his liver. It was a hard death, and we felt that it robbed us of whatever time he would have had left if he didn't have the BMT.*

Chronic GVHD usually develops after the third month post-transplant. It primarily affects the skin (itchy rash, discoloration of the skin, tightening of the skin, hair loss), eyes (dry, light-sensitive), mouth and esophagus (dry, tooth decay, difficulty swallowing), intestines (diarrhea, cramping, weight loss), liver (jaundice), lungs (shortness of breath, wheezing, coughing), and joints (decreased mobility). This list may seem overwhelming, but remember that only some patients develop chronic GVHD, and those who do may experience all, a few, or only one of these symptoms.

> *A year and a half after the transplant, they tried to taper my daughter off the cyclosporin. Her liver function counts went way up, and she broke out in a rash all over her body. The bottoms of her feet were so blistered that she couldn't walk. She has permanent dark splotches all over her torso, but the ones on her face and neck gradually faded away.*

· · · · ·

> *I wasn't supposed to go out in the sun after my transplant, but I did anyway. The sun aggravated the mild GVHD that I had and I turned blotchy. I had itchy light and dark patches on my stomach and face. I had to go back on steroids.*

Long-term side effects

Increasing numbers of children are being cured of their disease and surviving years after a bone marrow transplant. The intensity of the treatment prior to, during, and after transplant can cause major effects not apparent for months or years. This section will describe a few of the major long-term side effects that sometimes develop after a bone marrow transplant.

Relapse

Despite the intensive chemotherapy and radiation given prior to the bone marrow transplant, some children suffer a recurrence of the original disease. Relapse is most likely to occur in the first two years post-transplant.

> *Jody had his transplant in October, and we thought he was doing wonderfully. In June he just started getting tired and slowing down. We brought him in and found out that he had relapsed. They said there was no hope for a cure, but they thought that they could get him into remission again. He lived for another 15 months.*

Problems with the eyes

Many children treated with total body radiation develop cataracts. How the radiation is administered affects the child's chance of developing this complication. If the total body radiation (TBI) is given in one dose, approximately 80 percent of children develop cataracts. If the TBI is given in smaller doses over several days (fractionated), the chances of developing cataracts is less than 25 percent. Almost all protocols now use fractionated TBI.

> *Lea has developed cataracts in both eyes which will require laser surgery to correct.*

Decreased tear production is common in those children with chronic GVHD, but is also seen in patients with no GVHD.

Growth and dental development

Irradiation can affect growth. If your child had prior cranial radiation, or total body radiation (TBI) as part of preparation for the BMT, she should be closely monitored for learning disabilities, dental problems (facial bone and jaw growth, delayed development of permanent teeth, incomplete root development), and growth hormone deficiency resulting in delayed or decreased growth.

Aseptic necrosis

Long-term use of high-dose steroids can cause, in some people, a problem called aseptic necrosis. This condition is caused by the death of the small blood vessels that nourish the bones. Pain and loss of mobility result.

> Leslee was an athlete who played three sports prior to her AML diagnosis and bone marrow transplant. The steroids saved her life but destroyed her bones. She has had surgery on her shoulders, hips, and knee joints. Her shoulders and hips are much better, but her knees are still painful, and she has trouble getting around. The surgeon is hoping that soon he will be able to use live bone in experimental surgery to help her.

• • • • •

> Leah has problems with her knees, wrists, and ankles. For a while after the transplant, she played basketball with a face mask on. But the doctor finally told her she had to stop playing sports. It was very hard for her to give up gymnastics, soccer, and basketball. But she continued to swim on the high school team, despite having problems getting out of the pool. She's very tough and determined.

Thyroid function

Children who receive cyclophosphamide (CY) only, or CY plus busulphan (BU), do not develop thyroid deficiency as a result of treatment. Those children who receive TBI do, however, have a 25 to 50 percent chance of having low thyroid function due to a decreased production of thyroid hormone. Tablets containing thyroid hormone usually are effective in treating the problem.

Puberty and sterility

For the most part, children who had only cyclophosphamide during the preparative regimen have normal sexual development. Those who had total body irradiation, however, are likely to experience delayed puberty (the incidence is lower if the radiation was given in several smaller doses). All children who received TBI should be followed closely by a pediatric endocrinologist, who can prescribe hormones (testosterone for boys, estrogen and progesterone for girls) to assist in normal pubertal development. Girls are more likely to need hormonal replacement; boys usually produce testosterone but not sperm.

Children who receive total body radiation usually become sterile, that is, after growing up, girls will not be able to become pregnant, nor will boys be able to father children. Ability to have a normal sex life is not affected. Some children treated only with cyclophosphamide have remained fertile, and to date all offspring have been normal.

Secondary malignancy

Children who receive a BMT are at increased risk of developing a second malignancy (cancer), particularly if total body irradiation is used in the preparative regimen. The types of cancer most commonly seen post-transplant are leukemia, lymphoma, carcinoma, and bone and soft tissue sarcomas. To put it all in perspective, however, the overall risk appears to be much less than five percent for any particular child.

The transplant center was very clear about all of the potential problems. That was good, for it prepared me. My attitude is watch for them, hope they don't happen, if they do, then live with them. JaNette has lost about 50 percent of her lung capacity, probably from the radiation. She has to do daily treatments to keep her lungs from tightening up. She still is on cyclosporin one-and-a-half years later and flares up with the GVHD rash periodically. She can no longer tolerate gamma globulin, so her counts go down sometimes and she gets pneumonia. I know that she may get cataracts, develop heart problems, and many other things. But, she had an easy time with the transplant, she's a happy third grader, she's alive, and we feel so, so very lucky.

• • • • •

It's been three years since I had the transplant that they said had less than a five percent chance of working. During the transplant, I developed no mouth sores, no infections, no GVHD. Just a headache the whole time. I do miss being an athlete, I do miss the friends that I lost, and I do miss my blond hair (it came back in brown, so I tried to dye it blond and it turned bright, fluorescent red). But I can deal with those things. To survive I think you need luck, a positive attitude, and a decorated room to help you stay cheery.

Resources

Organizations for donor location

National Marrow Donor Program (NMDP)
3433 Broadway St., NE Suite 500
Minneapolis, MN 55413
Donor Information: 1-800-MARROW-2
Patient Search Information: 1-800-526-7809
Corporate Recruitment Programs: 1-800-526-7809
FAX: (612) 627-5899
World Wide Web: *http://www.marrow.org*

This center was established by Congress to improve the efficiency and effectiveness of the donor search process so that a larger number of unrelated BMTs could be performed. The NMDP has developed the world's largest computerized listing (2,600,000 persons listed in 1997) of potential marrow donors. NMDP has cooperative search arrangements with registries in Canada, France, Australia, England, Austria, Spain, Singapore, and Switzerland.

American Red Cross
430 17th Street, NW
Washington, D.C. 20006
(202) 737-8300

The American Red Cross provides numerous services, including the coordination of bone marrow testing and donation in association with the National Marrow Donor Program. Local chapters are listed in the white pages of the telephone book.

American Bone Marrow Donor Registry, Search Coordination Center
Caitlin Raymond International Registry of Bone Marrow Donor Banks
University of Massachusetts Medical Center
55 Lake Avenue North
Worcester, MA 01655
Donor Information: 1-800-736-6283
Patient Search Information: 1-800-726-2824
FAX: (508) 752-1496

The American Bone Marrow Registry is a nonprofit organization that coordinates donor searches among participating centers in the United States and throughout the world. Approximately 50,000 donors are registered with the

ABMDR, and they have access to more than a million donors worldwide. Currently, the ABMDR is the only organization with an active registry of cord blood donors.

International Bone Marrow Transplant Registry
Medical College of Wisconsin
P.O. Box 26509
8701 Watertown Plank Road
Milwaukee, WI 53226
(414) 456-8325

This research organization collects and analyzes data on transplants from over 250 institutions in 30 countries. It studies factors that affect the success of transplants, but does not make donor matches. It publishes a newsletter, and will supply a publication list upon request.

The HLA Registry Foundation
70 Grand Ave.
River Edge, NJ 07661
1-800-336-3363

Registry of approximately 125,000 bone marrow donors, serving the U.S. east of the Mississippi. It provides coordinators who travel to the site of the donor drive to help individuals or groups with donor recruitment.

Organizations for financial assistance

In addition to those below, there are many state and regional organizations which provide emotional and financial assistance to families of a child undergoing a bone marrow transplant. Appendix B of the *Candlelighters Guide to Bone Marrow Transplants in Children* (see "Reading for adults") lists many such organizations. You could also call Candlelighters at 1-800-366-CCCF to obtain an up-to-date listing.

Children's Organ Transplant Association
2501 Cota Drive
Bloomington, IN 47403
1-800-366-2682

Offers guidance and assistance in all aspects of fund-raising for those who need to raise money for transplants. A COTA staff member will travel to the site of the campaign, help the campaign obtain 501(c)(3) status, provide a toll-free telephone number, and advise on all aspects of fund-raising. Emergency funds available.

National Children's Cancer Society
1015 Locust St. Suite 1040
St. Louis, MO 63101
(314) 241-1600 or 1-800-5-FAMILY
FAX: (314) 241-6949

NCCS offers a multifaceted outreach program, which includes financial assistance, education, information, and emotional support. They provide financial assistance for bone marrow transplantation, donor harvest, donor search, donor recruitment, and family emergency expenses (such as travel, hotel, food). They also have an active advocacy program to help families with insurance companies, hospitals, Medicaid, the National Marrow Donor Program, and the American Registry.

Organ Transplant Fund
1027 South Yates Rd.
Memphis, TN 38119
1-800-489-3863 or (901) 684-1697

Gives financial assistance for transplants as well as helps patients who need a bone marrow transplant organize fund-raisers. It maintains accounts to which tax-deductible contributions can be made and has a support program that provides practical help with arrangements and advocacy.

The Barbara DeBoer Foundation
2069 S. Busse Road
Mount Prospect, IL 60056
1-800-895-8478

Helps to identify and utilize resources in your community to raise necessary funds for transplants.

The Sparrow Foundation
1155 N. 130th, Suite 310
Seattle WA 98104
(206) 745-5403

Nonprofit, charitable organization, which helps families raise funds for any necessary medical procedure. The organization was started by the family of a young boy whose successful BMT was paid for entirely by community donations.

Organizations for emotional support

BMT Family Support Network
P.O. Box 845
Avon, CT 06001
1-800-826-9376

Links families involved in bone marrow transplants for telephone assistance. Also provides information and resources. Serves grieving families.

National Bone Marrow Transplant Link
29209 Northwestern Highway #624
Southfield, MI 48034
1-800-LINK-BMT or (810) 932-8483

Human service agency that encourages contact by families and health professionals. It operates a hot line, and provides peer support, a library, clearinghouse, and suggestions for financial assistance.

Reading for adults

Association of Pediatric Oncology Nurses. *The APON Patient/Family Education Catalog*. Includes description of the BMT process, BMT phases (checklists, education protocols), BMT patient education cards, bone marrow transplant journal. Catalog $2 members, $5 others. APON, 11512 Allecingie Parkway, Richmond, VA 23235.

Johnson, F. Leonard, M.D., and 31 others. *The Candlelighters Guide to Bone Marrow Transplants in Children*. Bethesda, MD: Candlelighters, 1994. 1-800-366-CCCF. Straightforward, informative guide designed to educate parents about what a BMT is, types of BMTs, long-term medical effects, financial issues, psychosocial effects, impact on schooling and family life, what happens if the transplant fails, and seven family stories on their experiences.

Komp, Diane. *A Child Shall Lead Them: Lessons About Hope from Children with Cancer*. Grand Rapids, MI: Zondervan Publishing, 1993. Komp, a pediatric oncologist at Yale, shares stories from her medical practice and describes her related Christian spiritual journey. Includes letters to a patient undergoing a BMT.

National Cancer Institute. *Bone Marrow Transplantation and Peripheral Blood Stem Cell Transplantation*. 1994. To obtain free copy, call 1-800-4-CANCER and ask for NIH Pub. No. 95-1178. Excellent 50-page booklet covers the purpose of BMTs, the types of BMTs, complications, long-term effects, financial considerations, psychosocial considerations, the future of BMTs, clinical trials and PDQ, and resources.

Riley, Shawn. *Borrowed Blood: Victory Over Leukemia.* Rochester, NY: Lion Press, 1992. $12.95 payable to Lion Press, P.O. Box 92541, Rochester, NY 14692. Riley was diagnosed at age 22 with CML, then at age 31 with ALL. This story describes his experiences, focusing on his BMT.

Stewart, Susan. *Bone Marrow Transplants: A Book of Basics for Patients.* Published by *BMT Newsletter*, 1985 Spruce Avenue, Highland Park, IL 60035. Phone: (708) 831-1913. FAX: (708) 831-1943. 170 page book clearly explains all medical aspects of bone marrow transplantation, the different types of transplants, emotional and psychological considerations, pediatric transplants, complications, and insurance issues. Technically accurate, yet easy to read.

"Surviving the Transplant Experience—the Caregiver's Perspective." *BMT Newsletter* Vol 7 No 5 (Nov 1996). Contains numerous families' experiences on how they managed caregiving, travel, and emotions throughout the transplant experience.

Leeland, Jeff. *One Small Sparrow: The Remarkable Real-life Drama of One Community's Compassionate Response to a Little Boy's Life.* Sisters, Oregon: Multnomah Books, 1995. Written by the father of a baby with leukemia, this heartwarming true story describes how a community raised the entire cost of a successful bone marrow transplant. Contains numerous ideas for methods to raise funds. Christian perspective.

Newsletter

BMT Newsletter. 1985 Spruce Avenue, Highland Park, IL 60035. (847) 831-1913. FAX: (847) 831-1943. This extremely informative and up-to-date newsletter is written and published by a former BMT patient. It is published six times a year, and is available by writing or calling the above numbers. It is also electronically published on the Internet (see appendix D). It is free, but donations are accepted (and appreciated). Includes articles on medical aspects of BMTs, personal stories, and reviews of books and videos on the topic.

Reading for children

Amadeo, Diana. *There's a Little Bit of Me in Jamey.* Niles, IL: Albert Whitman & Co., 1989. Wonderfully sensitive book written for young children who will be bone marrow donors for a sibling. Describes feelings and fears about leukemia and bone marrow transplants. Beautifully illustrated and very reassuring for young children.

Leukemia Society of America. *I'm Having a Bone Marrow Transplant.* To obtain free copy, call 1-800-955-4LSA. Coloring book for young children helps to explain what to expect during the BMT.

Technical reading

Barrett A. J., M. M. Horowitz, et al. "Bone Marrow Transplants from HLA-identical Siblings as Compared with Chemotherapy for Children with Acute Lymphoblastic Leukemia in a Second Remission." *New England Journal of Medicine 331* (1994): 1253-58. Study determined that for children with ALL in second remission, bone marrow transplants from HLA-identical siblings result in fewer relapses and longer leukemia-free survival than does chemotherapy.

Billett, A. L., E. Kornmehl, et al. "Autologous Bone Marrow Transplantation After a Long First Remission for Children with Recurrent Acute Lymphoblastic Leukemia." *Blood 81:6* (March 15, 1993): 1651-57. This study reports the outcome of autologous BMT for fifty-one children with ALL whose first remission lasted over 24 months. Three year event-free survival was 53%. Longer remission and the amount of cells reinfused were prognostic factors for survival.

Borgmann A., H. Schmid, et al. "Autologous Bone Marrow Transplants Compared with Chemotherapy for Children with Acute Lymphoblastic Leukaemia in Second Remission: A Matched Pair Analysis." *Lancet 346* (1995): 873-76. Children with ALL in second remission are best treated by allogenic BMT from an HLA matched donor. Only 25% of children have such a donor. This study evaluated chemotherapy versus autologous bone marrow transplant for those children with no matched donor. The study results showed no advantage of autologous transplant over chemotherapy for children with ALL in a second remission.

Bortin, M. M., et al. "Changing Trends in Allogenic Bone Marrow Transplantation for Leukemia in the 1980s." *Journal of the American Medical Association 268(5)* (1992):): 607-12. Compared side effects, treatment-related mortality, and rate of relapse of 7,788 BMT patients with leukemia. Concluded that over the decade there were modest improvements in treatment-related mortality but no change in relapse risk.

Chou, R. H., and G. B. Wong. "Toxicities of Total-body Irradiation for Pediatric Bone Marrow Transplantation." *International Journal of Radiation Oncology/Biology/Physics* 34 (1996): 843-51. Studied fifteen children with immunodeficiency disorders and fifty-eitht children with leukemia to determine the acute and late effects, including cognitive function, of total body irradiation and chemotherapy for BMT. There were extensive acute and chronic problems, including: liver dysfunction, veno-occlusive disease, decreased growth, delayed puberty, cataracts, interstitial lung disease, graft-vs-host disease, IQ reduction, and two secondary malignancies.

Clift, R. A., C. D. Buckner, et al. "Marrow Transplantation for Patients in Accelerated Phase of Chronic Myeloid Leukemia." *Blood* 84:12 (Dec 15, 1994): 4368-73. Reviewed the records of fifty-eight patients treated at Fred Hutchison Cancer Research Center. Study found a low probability of relapse in younger patients transplanted within one year of diagnosis and catagorized as in accelerated phase based on chromosomal abnormalities.

Ferrara, J. L. M., and H. J. Deeg. "Mechanisms of Disease: Graft-versus-host Disease." *The New England Journal of Medicine* 324 (10) (1991): 667-74. Review article covers the causes of GVHD, defines and describes acute and chronic GVHD, and explains current prophylactic and therapeutic interventions.

Johnson, F. Leonard, M.D., and Carl Pochedly, eds. *Bone Marrow Transplantation in Children*. New York: Raven Press, 1990. A technical review of pediatric bone marrow transplantation for a variety of diseases and conditions.

Kernan, N. A., et al. "Analysis of 462 Transplantations from Unrelated Donors Facilitated by the National Marrow Donor Program." *The New England Journal of Medicine* 328(9) (1993): 593-602. This article analyzes the survival rate and percentages of serious side effects from the 462 patients transplanted from unrelated donors in the first four years (1986-1990) of the National Marrow Donor Program.

Kurtzberg, Joanne, Mary Laughlin, et al. "Placental Blood as a Source of Hematopoietic Stem Cells for Transplantation in Unrelated Donors." *New England Journal of Medicine* 335(3) (1996): 157-166. Reports preliminary results of transplantation using partially HLA mismatched placental blood from unrelated donors. The overall 100 day survival rate was 64 percent and the overall event free survival rate was 48 percent.

Ochs, L., X. O. Shu, et al. "Late Infections After Allogenic Bone Marrow Transplantations: Comparison of Incidence in Related and Unrelated Donor Transplant Recipients." *Blood* 86:10 (Nov 15, 1995): 3979-86. Infectious complications are a major source of morbidity and mortality after BMT. This study compared incidence of late infections in recipients of bone marrow from related and unrelated donors. Incidence of infection was higher in unrelated BMT's (84.7%) than related BMT's (68.2%), causing higher death rates in those patients who received marrow from an unrelated donor.

Pizzo, P., and Poplack, David, eds. *Principles and Practice of Pediatric Oncology.* Philadelphia: Lippencott-Raven, 1996. Chapter 14, "Bone Marrow Transplantation" discusses in great detail all aspects of bone marrow transplantation for pediatric patients. Extremely technical.

Audio/video

Christiansen, Otteau. *A Critical Decision.* 20 minutes, VHS. To obtain free copy, call the Leukemia Society of America at 1-800-955-4572. Excellent introduction to the various types of bone marrow transplants, procedures, and short-term side effects. The story follows five patients with leukemia (one preschooler, one teenager, and three adults) through the entire BMT process.

Syrjala, Karen, et al. *Coping Skills for Bone Marrow Transplantation.* Audio tape and handbook teaches imagery and relaxation to help BMT patients control physical discomfort and stress. Appropriate for mature teens and adults. $10 to Fred Hutchison Cancer Center: Karen Syrjala, Ph.D. FHCRC, 1124 Columbia Street, Seattle, WA 98104.

Death and Bereavement

The loss of my son has illuminated for me the true definition of love: the giving
of oneself, body and spirit, to another. His death, like that of any child, is a story
of withered hopes and unfulfilled dreams. In this book I have tried to capture
a few remembered strains of the brief, glad music of his life. These are all I
have of him now, and they comfort me even as they break my heart.

—Gordon Livingstone, M.D.
Only Spring

THE DEATH OF A CHILD causes almost unendurable pain and anguish for loved
ones left behind. Death from cancer comes after months or years of debilitating treatment, emotional swings, and financial crises. The family begins
the years of grief already exhausted from the years of fighting cancer. It is
truly every parent's worst nightmare.

In this chapter many parents share their innermost thoughts and feelings
about deciding to end treatment, dying at home or in the hospital, and grief.
It didn't matter whether the parents had recently lost their child, or it had
happened decades ago, tears flowed when talking about it. Because family
members and friends can be strong sources of support, or casualties of the
grieving process, parents describe things that really helped them, and they
make suggestions on what to avoid. Grief has as many facets as there are
grieving parents, so what follows are the experiences of a few.

Making the decision to end treatment

Whatever necessity lays upon thee, endure; whatever she
commands, do.

—Goethe

For children who have had a series of relapses, medical caregivers and
parents need to decide when to end active treatment and begin to work
toward making the child comfortable for his remaining days. This is an

intensely personal decision. Some families want to try every available treatment and exhaust all possible remedies. Others reach a point where they feel they have done all they can and they simply do not want their child to suffer any more. They hope for time to share memories, express love, and prepare for death.

> *After Christie came home from the transplant center, she started to perk up and feel a bit better. But she had pretty massive problems with graft-versus-host disease, infections, fragile bones, and a very weak heart. She had a stomach abscess that they thought was causing her vomiting and eating problems, so they decided to biopsy it. They came out and said they found a cluster of tumors on her ovary, which turned out to be malignant leukemic cells. In my rational mind, I knew it was time to stop. I could imagine stopping the treatment, but I just couldn't picture life without her.*

Dr. Arthur Ablin, Director Emeritus of Pediatric Clinical Oncology at the University of California, San Francisco, wrote in the Spring 1995 Candlelighters newsletter about the difficulties of deciding to end active treatment:

> *All too often, the decision to abandon the goal for cure and, reluctantly, accept the reality of inevitable death of a child is too painful and, therefore, never made. This paralyzing pain occurs with equal frequency, perhaps, for the family and the doctor. We of the medical profession have no equal in our ability to prolong dying. We have a powerful array of mechanical, electronic, pharmaceutical, and biotechnical interventions at our command. We can keep people dying for months and even years. Applying or withholding this armamentarium is an awesome responsibility and it requires infinite wisdom to know how to manage wisely and correctly. We can do great good by applying these tools correctly but can also do incalculable harm through over-utilization. Physicians and families alike must work together to avoid the possible pitfalls....When cure is beyond all of us, then the challenge is to make the rest of life as worthwhile and rich as possible. There is much to do for the terminally and critically ill child and his or her family. They have that right, we have the privilege, to be of service.*

Many children know when it is time to stop. In the Spring 1995 issue of the Candlelighters newsletter, Grace Monaco describes how her four-year-old daughter told her, "I don't think I can come home, Mommy! All my machinery is worn out, and I don't think they have any more parts."

When my six-year-old son Greg was in the hospital in intensive relapse treatment, he would repeat over and over again, "I want to go home." When he was finally well enough to come home for awhile, he kept saying, "I want to go home." In frustration, I said, "Greg, you are home, why do you keep saying that?" He looked up and quietly said, "I want to go to my heavenly home. I want to go to God." I said, "Honey, please don't say that," and, knowing how much we loved him, he replied, "Okay, Mom, I'll fight, I won't go." And he did fight hard for several more months. But he was way ahead of us in acceptance, he was at peace, and he knew it was time to let go.

• • • • •

The history of Jody's battle with leukemia is long, and to me, marked with his resilience, strength, and incredibly strong spirit. He was diagnosed with ALL shortly after his second birthday. He relapsed just before he turned three, then not again until he was five and a half, seven months after he went off chemotherapy treatment. He underwent a bone marrow transplant approached with the good omen of having a perfect match with both his older sister and younger brother, and thrived until another relapse at age six and one half. Realistic hope for Jody's long-term survival was dashed at that time. Jody achieved another remission which lasted for several months, then experienced a bone marrow relapse. We realized that the disease was systemic, and all conventional means of treating the leukemia was, finally, hopeless.

While the doctor was ready to present us with medical options that Thursday afternoon, we already knew our decision. It was rational: Jody should go off all chemotherapy treatment. Jody's leukemia was clearly very resistant to chemotherapy drugs. It was ethical: With no chance of further good health and high-quality living, allowing death to come naturally was surely the best choice. It was humane: Jody would be treated for pain, and we would bring him home to die in familiar surroundings with his family. And it was sad: Jody's laughter wasn't to be heard again, he wasn't to feel good again, he was to become sicker and sicker and die. The unfathomable reality of life without Jody's presence was marching to meet us without reprieve.

When it is clear that death is inevitable, parents struggle with the thought of how to "tell" the ill child and siblings. All too often in our culture, children are perceived as having to be protected from death, as if this somehow makes their last days better. On the contrary, any pediatric nurse or social worker can tell you that children, often as young as four, know that they are dying. If the parents are trying to spare the child, an unhealthy situation develops. The child pretends everything is okay to please the parents, and the parents try to mask their deep grief with a false smile. Everyone loses.

This scenario is replayed on a daily basis at hospitals all over the country: scared, lonely children dying without being able to tell the people they love the most how they are feeling. This type of denial keeps children and parents alike from finishing up business—distributing belongings, telling each other how much they love one another, saying good-bye. It also strips parents of their ability to prepare their child for the journey from life to death. Children need to know what to expect. They need to know that they will be surrounded by those they love, that their parents will be holding them, and they need to know what the family's beliefs are about what happens after death.

> *Jennifer contracted a respiratory fungal infection that resulted in her being hospitalized on a ventilator. She was given lots of morphine so that she wouldn't feel air hungry. She was alert off and on for a few days. We read to her and played tapes. After one week on the respirator she took a turn for the worse. She didn't respond to me after that. Her kidneys were ceasing to function, and she started to get puffy. Her liver was deteriorating, and her painful pancreatitis had come back. After ten days on the respirator, I couldn't bear it any longer. I lay down in her bed, took her in my arms, and kissed her at least 200 times. I talked to her for a long time, and told her that we would take care of her cats, and that I was sorry that she had to suffer so much, and how beautiful Heaven is. I told her to go be with Jesus, her Grandpa, and her dog. I also told her how much we all loved her and how proud we were of her. I got off the bed to change positions, and the nurse rushed in. Her heart had suddenly stopped the second I got up. I believe she heard me and just needed to know it was okay to go. She didn't want to leave until she knew her Mommy was ready.*

> *Because of her Christian upbringing, Jennifer knew all about Heaven. She had told me that she wasn't afraid to die, and this has been a great source of comfort to us. I believe that she was preparing for her death, even as we hoped for her remission. Before she went to the hospital, she spent all her money, gave away some of her possessions to her sisters, and said a final good-bye to her home, cats, teachers, and friends.*

· · · · ·

After Caitlin decided she wanted no more treatments, we brought her home. She asked me to give her clothes to the poor, and her special things to her brothers. She gave them the last of her money, saying she no longer had any use for it. She had already bought them Christmas presents for the coming Christmas and given them ahead of time. Her affairs were oh so in order. She asked my friend to make me laugh after she died. She told me that it wasn't dying she minded, because her friend who had already died had come in a dream and told her that heaven was a good place, but she did not want to leave her father and me. They were agonizing conversations yet, I am so glad that we were able to have them.

Supportive care

In the U.S., there is a very active and effective hospice system. Hospices ease the transition from hospital to home and provide support for the entire family. Hospice personnel ensure adequate pain control, allow the patient to control the last days or weeks of his life, and provide active bereavement support after death.

Usually, if the family wishes the child to die at home, a smooth transition occurs from the oncology ward to hospice care. Unfortunately, sometimes pediatric patients are not referred to hospice, and the parents are left to deal with their child's last days at home with no experienced help and no clear idea of what is to come. Before you leave the hospital, it is wise to find out the name of a contact person at the agency that will be taking over the home care of your child.

When Jody came home, he was assigned both a pediatric visiting nurse and a hospice nurse. On their first visits, I was handed a great deal of literature to read, including a whole notebook from hospice. I lacked both the desire and energy to read the literature and learn a whole new medical system—let alone two. I just wanted one phone number to call for help, with two or three consistent people to answer.

In actuality, the care we received was wonderful. The primary nurse would call, offer to visit if we wanted it, assess Jody's condition over the phone, handle any questions we had, and would ask if we wanted a call the next day. She would tell us who would be calling if she was not working at the appointed time. Interestingly, the service that I found most beneficial at that time was the nurse running interference for us with the doctor. The pain medications needed to be adjusted and changed at times;

advice was needed about his intake, his mouth sores, and his hand and foot inflammation. As I, along with Jody, became quieter and more removed from outside activities, even the thought of calling the clinic and being made directly aware of the bustle and demands of that world was very unappealing.

If you have questions about hospice or what support is available, you can contact Children's Hospice International at 1-800-2-4-CHILD.

Dying in the hospital

Some children die in the hospital suddenly, while others slowly decline for weeks or months. If your child is slowly dying, you may have choices about where your child will spend her last days. There are no right or wrong choices. Much depends on the number of people available to provide care at home, and how comfortable they are doing so. Many parents ask their child where they prefer to be. Some like to be with the nurses in a hospital environment, while others want to stay at home with brothers, sisters, friends, and pets. Parents, children, and staff need to talk honestly to decide on the appropriate place for the child, and then obtain the support (hospice, private nurses in the hospital, family members) needed to make the choice a comfortable reality. Remain flexible so that as the situation changes, options remain open.

Although we had been advised that it didn't look good for Greg, we were trying one last time to get him to transplant. He was sleeping quietly in his hospital bed. He had been complaining of severe head pain, and was on a low morphine drip. The afternoon nurse woke him to take vitals, and he chatted with her. He told me, "Mom, I'm going to go back to sleep, I love you." Two hours later the night nurse tried to wake him up to give him some medicine, and she couldn't wake him. They called the doctor in from his home, and he ordered a CAT scan. When the film came up to the floor, the doctor took me out in the hall and said, "He's not going to live through the night." He held up the film showing a massive cerebral infarction; Greg was bleeding into the brain. He quietly died less than an hour later. Family and staff were in total shock. Nobody expected it. But, looking back, Greg had decided that he had had enough, he was ready to go. I am grateful that he didn't die on a transplant floor in a strange city. We were able to call in friends and family, and we were

*surrounded and supported by the wonderful nurses whom we knew so
intimately. I couldn't leave him until three nurses promised to stay with
him and escort him to the morgue. They are still dear friends.*

. . . . .

*I felt bad for my daughter, because like any good child, she wanted
permission, even to die. My husband had promised her that he would
never give up. He kept on saying, "Fight. Fight. Don't give up, don't leave
me. We'll do another transplant, we'll try different medicine. It's too early
to give up." I looked at him and said, "She's not going anywhere until you
tell her that it's okay." Then he told her, and she took her last breath. He
still feels guilty to this day because of his promises. He just doesn't understand that it was time; that she needed to know that it was okay with us.*

Parents of children who died in the hospital stressed the importance of clear
communication. Parents need to be strong advocates for adequate pain control, and they need to clearly tell the staff how they would like things to be.
For instance, in most hospitals, patients are routinely resuscitated using CPR
and electric shocks to the heart (this is called a "code"). Parents need to
discuss their wishes with the oncologist and ensure that an order of "NO
CODE" is put in the chart and on the child's door. Parents also should
discuss whether they want nurses or doctors present when their child dies.
Many families feel very close to the hospital staff and feel supported by their
presence, while others prefer to have only family and close friends at the
bedside. Advance planning helps to ensure that as death approaches, the
family's wishes are understood and respected.

Dying at home

A child's death at home can be a peaceful or a frightening experience,
depending on the preparation and support provided to the family.

*It was scary to be taking Caitlin home to die, but she was so happy
to be there. Her brother was fourteen years old, six foot three, and he
carried her everywhere she wanted to go. We let her be in charge,
whoever she wanted to see would be allowed in. My parents bought her a
television and a VCR, each with remotes. She'd sit in bed with a remote
in each hand, glad not to have to compete with her brothers, and say, "I
got the power."*

The night of her death her vomiting was too bad for us to stay at home. We brought her to the hospital in our car; we fixed a bed for her in the back with me and her aunt on the floor and her dad driving. She was taken directly to the pediatric floor, where they started an IV and gave her something to stop the vomiting. My husband and I were in such denial that we had packed enough for at least a two-week stay. No one on the staff had told us that her death was very near.

Ten days after her death we had to return to the peds floor with our son, and one of the doctors asked me if I had known Caitlin was dying when we came in with her. I said, "No, did you?" He replied, "Yes, because her breathing had changed." This new information hurt me deeply. It would have been good to have been told that her death was near and been given some choices about how we would like to handle it. I truly believe this could have been done quickly and as gently as all of her care had been given. I would like to have had the chance to hold Caitlin in my arms as she left our world, cradling her as closely as possible for the last time. Instead, I was hanging over the railing, holding her hand.

· · · · ·

We decided to bring Jody home to die for several reasons. First of all, the medical profession was offering no more realistic hope. Secondly, Jody was young enough and small enough to be easily held, carried, cared for by us. Thirdly, nothing violent or terrifying happened which made us seriously debate whether to go back in the hospital with him.

I saw many life values in a new way from the experience of Jody dying at home. What comes to my mind is a sunny, breezy afternoon, September 13. Only Jody and I were home. I held him outside under the plum tree for perhaps an hour and a half or longer. I couldn't support him well and read to him at the same time, so we didn't do anything. I spoke to him some, but mostly just held him quietly. I was aware as I looked up into the sky that my normal reaction on such a day would be to want to be hiking, biking, "doing" something. A surprise recognition burst and spread gently through my consciousness: I was exactly where I wanted to be and no doing of anything could mean as much as being there with Jody.

Jody's last day, September 16, was peaceful. A spiritual healer, whom Jody had known for two years, came and spent time with him. A massage therapist/healer/friend, who had visited him several times during the five

*weeks he was home, gave him a long, gentle massage. My husband Tom
stayed home from teaching that day (by chance?). Jody lay in his arms or
on my lap most of the day. The visiting home nurse came by briefly,
offered to stay, but we preferred to be alone. I was holding Jody; Tom was
next to me holding his feet. His breathing became labored and irregular.
His eyes were unblinking long before he took his last breath, then a heartbeat, then another, then silence.*

Siblings

Whether your child is dying at home or in the hospital, if there are siblings
they should be included in the family response. Being part of things, having
jobs to do, helps brothers and sisters remain involved, contributing
members of the family. Young children can answer the doorbell, go on
errands, or make tapes to play for the sibling. Older children can help with
meals, stay with the ill child to give parents a break, answer the phones, or
help make funeral arrangements. These jobs should not be "make-work"—
children should truly be helping. This allows them not only to clarify their
role in the family, but helps them to prepare for the death as well as have an
opportunity to say good-bye. These jobs help siblings feel themselves to be a
useful part of the family rather than a forgotten and perhaps less loved
brother or sister.

The Compassionate Friends, an organization for both parents and siblings,
is listed in the "Resources" section at the end of this chapter.

The funeral

Funerals and related rituals (memorial services, wakes, burial, shiva) are
important not only as a time to say good-bye and to begin to accept the
reality of death, but they also provide an opportunity to recognize the relationships and impact that the child or teen has had on others. Funerals
allow a gathering together to share memories and to show support for the
remaining family members. A funeral is a tangible demonstration of love.

*We had Greg's minister, godparents, and kindergarten teacher come
to our house to help plan the service. We did not want it to be scary,
because we wanted all of his young friends to come. They needed to say
good-bye, too, and above all, we wanted them to be comfortable. During
the service several songs were sung, and the minister didn't stand up at a
pulpit. He stood on our level with his hand on Greg's casket, and talked*

about Greg's life. It was simple and good. On the way to the cemetery it rained lightly, and the sky was filled with three rainbows. Sadness and hope.

Children of all ages should be allowed to attend the funeral if they wish, but only after they have been prepared first about what to expect. They need an explanation of where they will be going (funeral, shiva, wake, memorial service, burial) and what these words mean. They need to know what type of room they are going to, if the casket will be there, if it will be open, if there will be flowers, who will be there, how the mourners will be acting, who will stay with the them, what they will be expected to say, and how long they will be there. All questions should be answered honestly and children's feelings respected.

Many siblings also benefit from giving one last gift to the departed, such as writing a private note and dropping it in the casket, or bringing some of their sister's favorite flowers to put in her hands. If you have any questions or concerns about what to tell the remaining children or whether they should attend the services or burial, read *How Do We Tell the Children? A Parent's Guide to Helping Children Understand and Cope when Someone Dies* by Dan Schaefer and Christine Lyons (listed in the "Resources" section of this chapter, under Helping the Siblings).

> *One of our pastors was a very close personal friend who stayed with us for the last three days in the hospital at Jesse's bedside. When she died, we were physically and emotionally weary; we just couldn't think. He and the other pastors planned the whole service and walked us through it.*
>
> *There were hundreds of people there—Jesse had touched so many lives. The pastors had known Jesse her whole life and they loved her, truly loved her. They told personal stories; reminisced about the last hugs they had shared with her. They told the story of her faith and of her death, which comforted many of those who attended. Each family member walked up during the service and brought some of her favorite flowers.*
>
> *We had given our children free rein to pick out the clothes that Jesse would be buried in. They made very thoughtful choices: her favorite, very comfortable pajamas with little tea cups on them, and her teddy bear. The service was very special; a celebration, a testament to her faith and ours.*

Ministers, priests, and rabbis have a unique opportunity to provide support, love, and comfort to the grieving family and friends. They usually know the family well, and can evoke poignant memories of the deceased child or teen during the service. Members of the clergy often have excellent counseling skills, and can visit the family after the funeral to provide ongoing help during mourning.

The role of family and friends

Family members and friends can be a wellspring of deep comfort and solace during grieving. Some people seem to know just when a hug is necessary or when silence is most welcome. Unfortunately, in our society there are few guidelines for handling the social aspects of grief. Many well-meaning persons voice opinions concerning the time it is taking to "get over it" or question the parents' decision to not give away their child's clothing. Others do not know what to say, so they are silent, pretending that life's greatest catastrophe has not occurred. Many friends never again mention the deceased child's name, not knowing that this silence, as if the cherished child never existed, only adds to parents' pain. Holidays can become uncomfortable, as they bring sadness as well as joy.

In an attempt to alleviate these difficulties, bereaved parents helped compile the following lists of what helps, and what does not, in the hope that it may guide those family members and friends who deeply care, but just don't know how to help. These suggestions are offered with the understanding that what works for one person may not work for another. Try to use your knowledge of the bereaved family to choose options that you think will make them comfortable. If in doubt, ask them.

Things that help

Kind words can be short and easy to say, but their echoes are truly endless.

—Mother Theresa

The long lists of things that help from Chapter 5, *Family and Friends*, (e.g., keeping the household running, feeding the family, and helping with bills) are still appropriate here. The following lists are specific suggestions for grief.

Helpful things to say:

- I am so sorry.

- I cannot even imagine the pain that you are feeling, but I am thinking about you.

- I really care about you.

- You and your family are in my thoughts and prayers.

- We would like to hold a memorial service at the school for your son if you think that it would be appropriate.

- I will never forget John's sunny smile.

- I will never forget Jane's gentle way with children and animals.

Parents also offer a list of helpful things to do:

- Go to the funeral or memorial service.

    We were overwhelmed and touched by all of the people who came to the funeral. Even people that I had not seen in years—like some of my college professors—attended. Her oncologist and nurse drove 100 miles to be there.

- Show genuine concern and caring by listening.

    What has helped me the most is for people to just listen. Finding time to remember and reminisce is sometimes very difficult and painful, yet other times I feel much pride and happiness. Friends whose children also have cancer have been the greatest help to me during my daughter's illness and after her death.

- Help the siblings.

    When Jody was dying, his two well siblings, ages nine and four, presented concerns. I witnessed extremely tender moments, also flares of anger and hurt feelings. I assumed they felt neglected as I spent more and more time with Jody, just being his companion and caretaker. Christoph, four, wanted to be near, to talk, to play. His energetic pace and my feelings of guilt became nearly intolerable to me the last ten days or so. I decided to get the help of close friends and relatives to play with and lovingly attend to Christoph as many hours as possible when Tom was not home. Often they were in the same room with Jody and me.

• • • • •

We had friends just call and say, "We will pick up Nick on Saturday and take him to Water World, then to our house for dinner. We were hoping he could spend the night. Will that be all right?" They did this many times, and it not only was fun for him, but gave us a chance to be alone with each other and our grief.

· · · · ·

The day my daughter died, a close friend—herself a bereaved parent—did something wonderful. She took over my three kids, and prepared them for the funeral. She sat down with them and they read a book entitled, "Today My Sister Died," and talked about it. She described in great detail what would happen at the funeral, and more importantly, she prepared them for some of the not-so-helpful comments that they would hear. So, when the first person said, "You're the big sister now," they had a response. She listened to them and prepared them and it truly helped them cope.

- Write the parents a note instead of sending just a preprinted sympathy card with your signature. Include special things you remember about their child or your feelings about their child. Letters, poems, or drawings from classmates and friends allow children to share their feelings with the family of the deceased, as well as provide poignant testimonials that the family will cherish.

- Talk about the child who has died. Parents forever carry in their heart cherished memories of their child and enjoy hearing others' favorite recollections.

Months after the funeral, we gathered family members and some close friends to share memories on tape. We did a lot of laughing as well as shed a few tears. But I will always cherish those tapes.

· · · · ·

I think most of all parents want their child to be remembered. It really comforts me to go to Greg's grave and find flowers, notes, or toys left by others.

- When parents express guilt over what they did or did not do, reassure them that they did everything they could. Remind them that they provided their child with the best medicine had to offer.

- Remember anniversaries. Call or send a card or flowers on the anniversary of the child's death.

- Respect the family's method of grieving.

- Give donations in the child's name to a favorite charity of the child or parents, for instance, the child's school library, Candlelighters, the local children's camp, The Leukemia Society, American Cancer Society, or Hospice.

> *Every year we still get a card saying that Caitlin's occupational therapist donated money to Camp Goodtimes. It makes me feel good that she is remembered so fondly and that the money will help other kids with cancer and their brothers and sisters.*

- Commemorate the child's life in some tangible way. Examples are planting trees, shrubs, or flowers, erecting a memorial or plaque, displaying a picture of the child.

> *One of our Candlelighters fathers was on the city council. He encouraged the city to dedicate a new park to the children who had never grown up. They agreed, and named it "Children's Memorial Park." A local nursery offered to sell trees at a special discount for families or groups to buy and dedicate to a deceased child. A kiosk was built at the front of the park with the location of each tree and the name of the child to whom it is dedicated. Our Candlelighters board bought a grove of trees and a plaque with the names of the more than seventy children from our organization who have died since 1978 when we were founded. Last summer, we reserved the park for a "memorial picnic" and remembered and celebrated our departed children.*

- Be patient. Acute grief from the loss of a child lasts a long, long time. Expectations of a rapid recovery are unrealistic and hurtful to parents.

- Encourage follow-up from medical personnel.

> *Caitlin had a very kind, very gentle radiation oncologist. I went back to see her after Caitlin died; she said, "We were so happy when we saw the progress that Caitlin made, from a stretcher to sitting to talking and walking again; and then our hearts broke when she relapsed. I wept." It was so human and so wonderful for her to let me know that she cared.*

· · · · ·

> *We have had several phone calls from Jesse's oncologist, surgeon, and primary nurse. They were so wonderful to our entire family for years, and we miss them. We also had one call from the grief counselor at Children's, but we never heard from her again. We named our cat after one of*

the doctors, and it had been a running joke at the hospital. He wrote my children a funny letter about that. But, after the death of my child, I realized that they were busy and we really didn't have a relationship left. It is hard, after such intimacy. But my job now is grieving, and their job is trying to save other kids.

Things that do not help

He who sees a need and waits to be asked for help is as unkind as if he had refused it.

—Dante

Please do not say to the parents:

- I know exactly how you feel.
- It's a blessing her suffering has ended.
- Thank goodness you are young enough to have another child.
- At least you have your other children.
- Be brave.
- Time will heal.
- God doesn't give anyone more than they can bear.
- It was God's will.
- He's in a better place now.
- God must have needed another angel.
- It's lucky this happened to someone as strong as you.
- Don't worry, in time you'll get over it.
- Why did you decide to cremate him?
- How is your marriage holding up?
- You need to be strong for your other children.

Please do not say to the siblings:

- You need to be strong for your mom and dad.
- Don't cry, it upsets your parents.
- You're the man of the house now.
- How does it feel to be the big sister?

Even if a bereaved parent has deep religious faith, it is often tested by their child's death. Parents are not comforted by well-meaning friends who assume faith is making the grief bearable; indeed, many parents find it to be infuriating. Better to just say "I'm sorry."

In the months and years following the child's death, any of the following might not be appreciated:

- Don't you think it's time to get over it?

- It's been six months; it's time to put the past behind you.

- Life goes on.

- You need to get on with your life.

- You shouldn't be feeling that way.

- Don't you think you should give away all of his clothes?

- Don't cry.

- Don't be sad.

- Don't worry.

- Doesn't it bother you to have her pictures around?

- Please don't talk about Johnnie, it just stirs up all those memories.

- It's not good to just sit around, you need to get out and have some fun.

Don't let your own sense of helplessness keep you from reaching out. Pretending that nothing is wrong or being afraid to talk about the child who has died hurts grieving parents.

The following are suggestions from parents on what not to do:

- Don't remove anything which belonged to the child who died, unless specifically asked to by the parents.

> One family member took my son's toothbrush out of the bathroom and threw it away. I missed it immediately. She probably felt that she was doing me a favor, but it made me so angry. I needed to keep things. I have his hair from the second time it fell out, because he wanted to save it, and I've kept his teeth which had to be pulled during treatment. I just need to have those things, and I resent people who insist you must clear out a child's things. Parents should be able to keep things or get rid of them— whichever is comfortable—regardless of others' opinions.

- Don't offer advice.

*Christie's room is still her room. We still refer to it as Christie's room.
People just don't have the right to say you shouldn't leave that room
empty: it's not empty, it's full of her life. I know that they are not trying to
hurt us. It just bothers them to see that room. Sometimes it is just a
reminder of death; yet, there are times when being in there and surrounded by all her things brings us closer to her and her time with us.*

- Don't say anything which in any way suggests that the child's medical
care was inadequate. Parents already feel intense guilt over what should
have been or could have been.

*I can't tell you how many people said things like "If only you had
gone to a different treatment facility" or "if only you had used this or that
treatment." What people need most is support for what they are doing or
did do.*

- Don't look on the bright side or find silver linings.

*I became unexpectedly pregnant the month after my daughter died. I
can't tell you how many people said things like "The circle of life is complete" or "God is taking one and giving you another." or "God is replacing
her." She can never be replaced. It was horrible to hear those things, and
I felt it was unfair to both the unborn baby and to my daughter who died.*

- Don't come and pray over the child who is dying unless you have been
asked.

*The mother of one of my son's friends called and asked to pray. I
said okay, but was surprised when she showed up in person with a friend,
and in a very loud voice, began exhorting the devil to leave. My son was
only seven, and very sick, and it was scary for him.*

• • • • •

*The sister of my son's bus driver, whom I had never met, came by the
hospital with a bit of holy cloth to put under my son's pillow. It required
us to say a special prayer over and over again. We declined, but it was
awkward. People need to respect the parents' beliefs, not push their own.*

- Don't drop bereaved parents from the support group. Talk about your
options; grief-stricken parents have enough silence in their lives.

*When my daughter was terminal, in really bad shape, I went to the
support group. We had all bonded and were very close. I felt guilty
because I really wanted to cry and was trying to hold it back because I*

didn't want to upset everybody else. All of the sudden, I felt like I was the alien, like you feel when your child is diagnosed. Here I was in a room full of people I loved, where I had felt safe. Now I was alone again, this time with no hopes of Christie's recovery. It was truly the end. I never felt more scared or alone.

• • • • •

Our support group was run by two social workers from the two local hospitals. The rule was that bereaved parents could come for one visit after the funeral to say good-bye and that was it. They were out. Two parents in our group lost their children, and we had a struggle with the social workers about changing the rules. They were adamant that the two groups of parents should not mingle, that it would be too upsetting for the parents of kids on treatment. My son was on treatment, and I felt strongly that we shouldn't abandon our friends in their time of greatest need and that we would all benefit from sharing their experiences and grief. In the end, we compromised by having the bereaved parent(s) stay in the group for a year, then he or she would become a member of the new bereaved group. Both groups meet at the same time and place, so we socialize together after the meetings.

• • • • •

We don't have a support group or a bereaved group per se, we just have frequent gatherings. So we all see each other almost monthly, and there is no issue of losing your friends if your child dies.

- Don't make comments about the parents' strength.

   People would say things to me like "You're so strong" or "I just couldn't live through what you have." It makes me want to scream. Do they mean I loved my child less than they love theirs because I have physically survived?

- Losing all contact with the medical community.

   My son's doctor came to his funeral and said that he would call me, but he never did. I bumped into him four months later, and he said, "Call me and make an appointment, I want to talk to you." I felt that it was important to talk, so I went, and he wanted to know what had I done with my son's room.

• • • • •

Caitlin's caregivers were all very good to her; she felt such a connection and love for them. After her death, they were so important to us as a link to her, and at times that was either horrible or tender. I wanted Caitlin to still be a part of their thoughts, but at the same time I intellectually knew that there is only so much investment they can make. One growth I have made is to realize that I have as little notion of their pain as they do of mine.

· · · · ·

While the change in medical personnel is inevitable, I feel that periodic calls would be very helpful to the patient and family. It is such a loss, that the sense of continuity with the primary physician, even if intermittent and infrequent, is emotionally reassuring and satisfying. A follow-up conference after the death of the patient is also important to provide closure—perhaps some medical reminiscing, some feedback, good-byes.

Sibling grief

Siblings are sometimes called the "forgotten grievers" because attention is typically focused on the parents. Children and teens hesitate to express their own strong feelings in an attempt to prevent causing their parents additional distress. Indeed, adult family members and friends may advise the brothers and sisters to "be strong" for their parents or to "help your parents by being good." These requests place a terribly unfair burden on children who have already endured months or years of stress and family disruption. Siblings need continual reinforcement that each of them is an irreplaceable member of the family and that the entire family has suffered a loss. They have a right to mourn openly and in their own way.

The family requires such reorganization after a child's death, and there is nowhere to look for an example. Each person in the family constellation has different feelings and different ways of grieving; there is just no way to reconcile all of this when the supposed leaders of the group are totally out of it. Not to mention the fact that both my husband and I wanted more understanding and compassion from each other than we were possibly able to give.

Children express grief in many ways, including physically (changes in eating habits, toileting, sleeping, stomachaches); emotionally (regression to earlier behaviors, risk taking); fears (of the dark, being away from parents); guilt (said "I wish you would die" to sibling and sibling died); and emotional changes (tantrums, crying, sadness, anxiety, withdrawal, depression).

Many families pull apart because it is too painful to share their deep, but different feelings of grief. Some parents worry that if they start talking, they will "break down" in front of the children. But, children who are excluded from the family's mourning may begin to feel alienated from the family. Here are suggestions from families to help pull together while mourning.

• Let the siblings go to the funeral. They have suffered a loss; they need to say good-bye; they need support for their grief just as much as adults.

> *I grew up going to my relatives' funerals. Having those positive experiences really helped me deal with the loss of my son. There is nothing more natural than to take a child to the funeral, where they are part of families loving each other, crying together, and laughing at some of the memories. Too many people try to protect kids from death and it does them a great disservice.*

• Children and teens experience the same feelings as adults. By sharing your own feelings, it can encourage them to identify their own. (For example, "I'm really feeling sad today. How do you feel?")

• Some families establish a regular meeting time to talk about their feelings. Both tears and laughter erupt when family members talk about funny or touching memories of the departed child. One family even had theme nights, such as trying to remember every practical joke he ever pulled, or things that he did that were not so nice (nobody needs to remember a saint).

• Jointly discuss how holidays and anniversaries should be observed. Some families hang a Christmas stocking every year for the departed child, while others merely mention her name during the blessing. Each family devises different ways to handle the child's birthday and anniversary of her death.

• Encourage all family members to join a group such as a Candlelighters bereavement group or Compassionate Friends (see the "Resources" section at the end of the chapter).

Parental grief

Parental grief is particularly intense. It is unusually complicated and has extraordinary up-and-down periods. It appears to be the most long lasting grief of all.

—Therese A. Rando
*Grieving: How to Go On Living
When Someone You Love Dies*

There are as many ways to grieve as there are bereaved parents. There is no timetable, no appropriate progression from one stage to the next, no time when parents should "be over it." Losing a child is one of life's most horrific and painful events.

The death of a child shatters the very order of the universe—children are not supposed to die before their parents. It seems unnatural, incomprehensible. Losing a child entails mourning not only the child herself, but all of our hopes, dreams, wishes, fantasies, and needs relating to her. When you lose a child, you lose part of yourself, part of your future.

This book will not go through the numerous psychological descriptions of the grieving process. There are excellent reference books available, several of which are listed in this chapter's "Resources" section. Here, the parents themselves will tell you about grief.

> *I truly think that it is the worst thing in the entire world. Nothing worse can happen than losing your child. There is no reprieve. None.*

· · · · ·

> *I was having a very hard time grieving when a wonderful therapist that I was seeing said to me, "You are beating yourself up about grieving. Think about it: When you enter marriage, what are you called? A wife. When your spouse dies, what are you called? A widow. When you don't have a home and you are living on the street, what is the name for that? A homeless person. When you lose a child, what's it called, what's the name?" I said, "I don't know." She said, "Exactly. There is not even a word in our vocabulary. That's how terrible it is. It doesn't even have a name."*

· · · · ·

The biggest thing that I had to learn was just to cope with whatever I was feeling on that particular day. When I feel angry, I just need to let myself be angry. If I need to cry all day, I do. I still have plenty of those days. If someone calls me and wants to take me out to lunch to cheer me up, I have learned to say no when I'm not feeling like going out. I know that it hurts other people to see me cry, but I need to do that sometimes. I just miss her so much.

· · · · ·

Every day when I walk out of my house I tell myself to grab the mask. I feel like I walk different than everybody and talk different than everybody and look different than everybody. It's the worst part of bereavement, the isolation caused by people who just don't know how to talk to you, when really all they need to do is listen and remember with you.

· · · · ·

I found myself getting busier and busier, thinking that I could outrun the pain. I realized that I couldn't avoid the hurt; I just had to grit my teeth, cry, and live through it.

· · · · ·

My daughter was our firefly; she lit the whole scene up. When she died, that spirit was gone, and there was just a hole left. We just didn't feel like a family anymore.

· · · · ·

I feel jealous when I hear about people who have lost their fear when their child dies. I became more fearful, of everything. I am a very strong person, but I really picked up a lot of fear, and, four years later, I still have it.

· · · · ·

I felt like our sick daughter was the center of our universe for so long, that now I need to start feeling some responsibility for my other kids whom I've been away from for so long, both physically and emotionally. I told my husband the other night that I didn't even know if I loved the three kids anymore. I cannot feel a thing. Pinch me, I don't feel it. Hug me, I don't feel it. I'm numb.

· · · · ·

It's hard to admit, but there was an element of relief when my daughter died. Not relief for myself, but for her. I was almost glad that she wouldn't face a life full of disabilities. That she wouldn't face the numerous orthopedic surgeries that would have been required to repair the damage from treatment. That she wouldn't face the pain of not having children of her own. I just felt relief that she would no longer feel any pain.

· · · · ·

At first we didn't feel like a family anymore. Now it's better, but it's still not the family that I was used to, that I want. I still feel like the mother of four children, not three. I find it very hard to answer when someone asks me how many children I have. I also can't sign cards like I used to, with all of our names, so now I just write "from the gang." I guess that's not fair to the boys, but I just can't bear to leave her name off.

· · · · ·

I had a visual image of our family of five. When Jody died, it became this physical square thing with only mom, dad, boy, girl, and it bothered me so much.

· · · · ·

I thought this morning of how I used to listen to Jesse breathe. Now I can't hear her breathe or laugh. I can't feel her arms around me. I remember missed kisses and late-night times. I ache. Heaven seems so far away.

· · · · ·

It seems that sometimes she is still so near that during conversations I can hear her comments or answers, and yet I fear the memories might fade and I so cherish the nearness. We each wear articles of her clothes or jewelry every day. One daughter is sleeping on the floor in our room, and the other two are sleeping in her bed.

· · · · ·

The worst times were the first two Christmases. We had to grit our teeth, put our heads down, and just get through it. We had to keep moving, never stop moving. I would have ignored it altogether if I didn't have another child.

· · · · ·

Birthdays are hard for us. Greg's birthday was June 10, and his brother's is June 9. So it's pretty hard to ignore. On Greg's birthday and the anniversary of his death, we blow up balloons, one for every year he would have been alive, write messages on them with markers, and release them at his grave.

. . . . .

It seems like just about every holiday has some difficult memory attached to it now. He was diagnosed on Easter, and then relapsed the next year on Valentine's Day. I hate them both now. Christmas is always hard. And Halloween is tough because he so loved to dress up. I see all those little ones in their costumes and I'm just flooded with pain.

. . . . .

I keep wondering if I should have put a stop to the bone marrow transplant because I had no peace about it. I felt such fear and dread about her platelets and liver. And what I feared happened. I still pray to have peace over making that choice. To have peace over giving a teenager the weight of deciding all that herself. I still feel so guilty and know I'd still be kissing her goodnight if we hadn't gone forward—and how I miss those kisses.

. . . . .

I feel like Job 3: 25-26:

What I feared has come upon me
What I dreaded has happened to me
I have no peace, no quietness;
I have no rest but only turmoil.

. . . . .

This evening my heart was so saddened. I paced up and down in front of the mantel pausing to look at each picture of my daughter. Something that I cannot describe catches in my chest, and I can't breathe right. I look at her face and try to will it to life for a kiss and a touch, for softly spoken endearments at night. How we love all of our children, yet one missing leaves such a stabbing pain.

. . . . .

I worry that missing one child so desperately pervades my very ability to be a good mom to my other three. I so wish to find joy again, to find things in life to smile about. I so wish my children could see me smile again. I pray that God will give me this thing, because it is beyond my finding in this world.

· · · · ·

I had always heard that time heals all things. I was afraid of healing, because I didn't want to feel any farther away than I felt when he died. It's been seven years, and he still feels really close, a presence. But I still ache to touch his body so, that little back and fat tummy.

· · · · ·

It's been two years, and I still feel a lot of rage. I walk down the street and see kids hanging out, smoking, doing drugs, being rude, wasting themselves, and I am filled with rage that my son—such a straight arrow, so decent, so strong—is gone.

· · · · ·

I feel strongly that parents should seek out other parents who have lost children. Nobody else understands as well. Nobody else is as comfortable with it. We have our own sense of humor, and we often laugh hard about things that make other people uncomfortable.

· · · · ·

It's hard when people I have just met ask, "How many children do you have?" In the beginning I always felt that I had to explain that I had two but one died. Now, I just say one. I don't want their sympathy, I don't want their pity, but most of all I just don't want to have to explain. After two years or so, I started to feel uncomfortable giving out my life history and then having to deal with other people's discomfort. So now I just say one, and yet it still feels like I'm betraying him every time I do it.

· · · · ·

That one-year rule, when you are supposed to start feeling better, I've found to be true. Not that any of the pain is lessened, but I realized that I had managed to live through a year of holidays and anniversaries. I knew it was possible to do it a second, then a third time. One year isn't magic, but it does prove to you that you can survive.

· · · · ·

On the anniversary of Ryan's death we all went to the cemetery, and his girlfriend's parents planted a cherry tree at the foot of his grave. That was on a Sunday. I woke up on Monday feeling just as bad as I did the day before. All I could think was, "Oh hell, I have to go through that whole cycle again." The first year did not bring me any peace.

. . . . .

This morning was the four-year anniversary of my daughter's death. While I was at church I wanted to write in the intentions book, "I want my daughter back," but then I didn't because nobody would understand. I guess I'm pretty unreal in my thoughts a lot of the time.

. . . . .

From the minute I turn the calendar over to August, I'm on a knife edge. The twentieth of August just pulses on the calendar. I become depressed, spacey, I'm just in a very bad mood. I get sick a lot those first three weeks of August. But when it's over, I begin to relax and look forward to fall.

. . . . .

At church, we always sit with the same group of close friends who helped us through Jesse's illness and are helping us grieve her death. If they begin to sing a hymn that reminds one of us of Jesse, we all start to cry, and someone produces a box of tissues which gets passed down the aisles. People must wonder at the group that sobs through services. But it has helped me so much to have a community of grievers, it's been a very cleansing thing. It has spread out the tears.

. . . . .

I think parents need to know that it hurts like hell and they will feel crazy. But it is a normal craziness. If they talk to other bereaved parents, they will know that pain, guilt, rage, and craziness are how normal human beings feel when their child dies.

Bereaved parents are frequently reassured that "time will ease the pain." Most find that this is not the case. Time helps them understand the pain; the passage of time reassures them that they can adjust and they will survive. The acute pain becomes more quiescent, but still erupts when parents go to what would have been their child's graduation, hear their child's favorite song, or just go in the grocery store. Grief is a long, difficult journey, with many ups and downs. But, with time, parents report that laughter and joy do return. They acknowledge that life will never be the same, but it can be good again.

Looking back after many years

Certain smells, certain moments when I feel unloved, certain aspects of the Christmas rituals, and hundreds of other ordinary details of life, will reopen the wound. But at least now I can let it bleed for awhile and go on. At least now I can be open, not only to those painful moments, but also to the many joys of my life.

—Judith Barrington
Grief Postponed

Four parents whose children died many years ago share their thoughts on grief and how they changed:

My 15-year-old son was diagnosed with leukemia in 1962, and he lived until February 1963. He was tall, sturdy, wonderful. He inspired us all. Although it was very painful when he died, I truly felt that I had done all that I possibly could. I had four younger children, and I'd parceled myself out as best I could. Jennifer was born in October 1965, and my mother always said David had asked Our Lord to send her "to help me mend my heart."

I felt that I had done my best for David, he was at peace, and I also needed peace. Our deep faith greatly helped. David was strong enough to tell me, "I don't want you to worry, Mom, God knows what he is doing." I also had a flock of kids who were hurting and needed me. So I threw myself back into life and carried on.

There are many imponderables that I think of. What would David be like if he had survived? Would the lives of his brothers and sisters have been different if they had not lived through his illness and death? How would my marriage have been different? What would I be like if he was still alive? These thoughts serve no purpose; you just have to give yourself credit for doing your best and leave it at that. But, at times when I feel desperate, I simply look up at the night sky, and I know that one of those stars is mine.

· · · · ·

My daughter died in March 1971. That feeling that I had a hole in my solar plexus and was walking around with a heart literally broken in two lasted for over a year. I didn't go to a movie for four years, and it was very difficult for me to find pleasure in anything. But I have healed and am again a fully functional person. I have fun, tell jokes, play guitar, make speeches, and love my children.

There are many things that I did to heal. I linked up with another bereaved parent. Our relationship worked wonderfully; we clung to each other and we helped each other survive the holidays. During my daughter's illness and a catastrophic diagnosis of mental illness in my other daughter, I began to take too many tranquilizers. So I entered a 12-step program, and think that it literally saved my life. I gave up pills, quit smoking, rediscovered faith, and learned a new way to live.

At that time I also became very involved in a church, which was perhaps the most comforting, healing thing of all. I decided never to visit my daughter's grave. I know it comforts some people, but not me. I never thought for a second that she was there, just her bones. She, I will meet again. And finally, I had more children. I caution newly bereaved parents to think long and hard about the timing of the next child. But I look at my children, and I thank God for them.

Grieving was such hard work. For years her birthday was a black time for me, but that has faded away with the years. For a long time I felt like I was only going through the motions of life. But I just decided to act cheerful, force myself to go out, count my blessings, and reach out to people who were less fortunate than me. It worked.

· · · · ·

Life does go on after the death of someone you love...even if it's your child. It isn't always easy or fun or purposeful, but it's like anything else...life is what YOU make of it.

My son Cory died on Mother's Day 1985 after five and a half years of battling leukemia. When he left this existence a big part of my heart died with him. At first, the sky wasn't as blue as it once was...the mountains weren't as majestic...the ocean wasn't as magnificent, and yeah, it was hard to get out of bed and put one foot in front of the other. But, I had to do it. I had to go on, not only for my daughter, but for myself, too.

One day the fog lifted, and I knew in what remained of my heart, that my little boy wanted me to continue on loving life and all it has to offer. Before he died, Cory told me, "Don't weep for me, Mama. Just remember me and all the love I brought with me. I chose this life to be with you, but I was never meant to grow up."

I wrote a poem based on the things he said to bolster my courage and to help me cope with his leaving. I hope anyone who reads it can derive some comfort from it as well.

The Freedom of Flight

Don't weep for me when I have gone away...
Death is not like the end of the play.
It's like the freedom of the butterfly's first flight.
I won't really be gone—only from sight.
All the love that I brought with me from birth,
Will always be with you, while you are on earth.
I will be back in God's loving embrace...
So please wipe those tears of sadness off of your face.

Be happy I'm free from pain and despair,
Free like the birds that soar through the air.
I will always be with you, in everything you see...
Wherever you look it will remind you of me...
A flower in bloom, a new bud on a tree...
Or even a dandelion growing in the lawn,
But please don't think of me as gone.
A kid's game of soccer, a familiar song you will hear...
Comic books, cartoons, and "Danger," my favorite bear.
Don't think of death as the end of me.
It's just the beginning of my flight to be free.
Don't mourn my passing, because I will be
As one with God, all knowingness and light.
I will dance on the stars that shine in the night,
Or glide like a leaf caught in a gentle breeze...
Or soar on the wind with a bird's grace and ease...
Maybe hitch a ride on the tail of a kite,
All with the magic and freedom of a butterfly's first flight.

I will never stop missing him. Thankfully he gave me the strength to move forward. Cory loved life so much and fought so courageously during the short time he was here, it would be an insult to his memory if I didn't cling to and enjoy life as tenaciously as he taught me to. The memories of the fun we had, the love we shared, and the vision of him dancing on the stars sustain me.

• • • • •

The old adage that "time heals" is a myth. You need to choose to heal and then find out how to help yourself. As I look back on our journey, our first instinct was to huddle as a family; to bask in what was left. We were hurting together; we loved him; we missed him; we needed to celebrate who he was. We intuitively knew that we were going to make it, we just didn't know how.

When Donnie died 13 years ago, we didn't know much about grief. There wasn't as much written about it then as there is now. But we were committed to healing individually and as a family. One of the important things that we did for one another was to give each other lots of space. My husband and I knew the distancing was necessary but temporary. We were on a teeter-totter. We each had a different schedule, a different way of handling pain. He allowed me my "craziness," and I respected his silence. I found that it helped me to wallow in it, to feel it all, to cry. I've grieved clean.

If you have children, learn about how kids grieve. They revisit their grief at each developmental stage. Keep the door open so that they can talk about it.

After Donny's death, I found that I just had to be with kids. I volunteered at the school, and followed all of his friends until they graduated from high school. A friend carried his cap and gown, and they made a speech about how a very important person was missing from the ceremony. I cried, but it was good.

I think it is very important for people to choose to feel. If you attend a grief support group or Compassionate Friends, or read about the grief process, you will quickly realize that your feelings are normal and that each person goes through grief differently. Another good reason to go to a group is that other people can give voice to your feelings when you just don't have any words. In the beginning you are just a ball of pain. You learn that every person feels that way; that it is normal, human. Many people come to group and never speak, but they are comforted. I found it *was far better for me to be in the same room with real people who had walked down the same road, rather than just to read about it in books. Feel the pain and you will heal.*

I just wish that I had armfuls of time.
—Four-year-old with cancer
Armfuls of Time

Resources

Organizations

Children's Hospice International
2202 Mt. Vernon Ave. Suite 3C
Alexandria, VA 22301
(703) 684-0330
1-800-2-4-CHILD

This organization serves as an information clearinghouse, promotes hospice support through pediatric care facilities, sponsors seminars for professionals, and distributes publications, a newsletter, and audio cassettes. CHI will refer families to the nearest hospice program.

The Compassionate Friends
National Office
P.O. Box 3696
Oak Brook, IL 60522-3696
(630) 990-0010
FAX: (630) 990-0246
email: tcf_national@prodigy.com
World Wide Web: *http://www.jjt.com/~tcf_national/index.html*

A self-help organization that offers understanding and friendship to bereaved parents and siblings. Its primary purpose is to assist them in the positive resolution of their grief and to support their efforts to achieve physical and emotional health. It sponsors local chapters, which hold support meetings as well as provides telephone numbers of members who can be contacted for telephone support (they match persons with similar losses). It publishes a newsletter for parents and one for siblings, and offers a Resource Catalog with a comprehensive list of books, audio, and video materials on adult and sibling grief.

Grief Recovery Institute
8306 Wilshire Blvd. #21A
Beverly Hills, CA 90211
(213) 650-1234 or 1-800-334-7606

Organization that sponsors workshops, supports people who are grieving, and provides publications on recovery.

The Grief Recovery Helpline
1-800-445-4808

Free service staffed by trained personnel to help anyone who is grieving.

Candlelighters Childhood Cancer Foundation
7910 Woodmont Ave. Suite 460
Bethesda, MD 20814
1-800-366-CCCF
FAX: (301) 718-2686
World Wide Web: *http://www.candlelighters.org*
email: *info@candlelighters.org*

The *Candlelighters Bibliography and Resource Guide* contains a comprehensive listing of books and journal articles on grieving the child who dies from cancer. Call and ask them to send you the newest edition of the *Bibliography and Resource Guide.*

Candlelighters Childhood Cancer Foundation Canada
National Office
Suite 401, 55 Eglinton Avenue East
Toronto, ON Canada M4P 1G8
1-800-363-1062 (Canada only)
(416) 489-6440
FAX: (416) 489-9812
World Wide Web: *http://www.candlelighters.ca*
email: *staff@candlelighters.ca*

The Canadian Candlelighters Resource Catalogue contains an extensive listing of resources for bereaved children, parents of bereaved children, bereaved parents, and bereaved grandparents. Call for the most current catalogue.

The Centering Corporation
1531 N Saddle Creek Road
Omaha, NE 68104
(402) 553-1200

Call to ask for their free catalog which contains an extensive listing of books, cards, audio and videotapes on death and grieving.

Reading for adults: terminal illness

Adams, David, and Eleanor Deveau. *Coping With Childhood Cancer: Where Do We Go from Here?* rev. ed. Toronto: Kinbridge Publications, 1993. Chapters 6, 7, and 8 of this excellent parent's guide deal with children's knowledge of death, if your child is dying, and after death: how families survive through grief and mourning.

American Cancer Society. *Caring for the Patient with Cancer at Home: A Guide for Patients and Families.* 1-800-ACS-2345. Publication Number 4656-PS. 40 pages. Provides information to make caring for patients at home easier.

Callanan, Maggie, and Patricia Kelley. *Final Gifts: Understanding the Special Awareness, Needs, and Communications of the Dying.* New York: Poseidon Press, 1992. Written by two hospice nurses with decades of experience, this book helps families understand and communicate with terminally ill patients. Compassionate, comforting, and insightful, *Final Gifts* movingly teaches us how to listen to and comfort the dying. Highly recommended.

Deits, Bob. *Life After Loss: A Personal Guide Dealing with Death, Divorce, Job Change, and Relocation.* Tucson, AZ: Fisher Books, 1992. One parent was given this book soon after her son became ill, long before he died. She found it very comforting because "we all begin to grieve from the moment of diagnosis—we grieve the loss of our child's health, the loss of our dreams, our innocence."

Modlow, D. Gay, and Ida M. Martinson. *Home Care for the Seriously Ill Child: A Manual for Parents.* 1991. $9.95 from Children's Hospice International (703) 684-0330. Helps parents explore the possibility of home care for the dying child. It contains practical information on what to expect, methods for pain relief, and control of medical problems. There are appendices on medications, bibliographies, and do's and don'ts for helping bereaved parents.

Grief

Compassionate Friends. *We Need Not Walk Alone: After the Death of a Child.* Bereaved parents and siblings write about their grief in prose and poetry. 235 pages. $14.95 + $3.50 shipping. P.O. Box 3696, Oak Brook, IL 60522. (708) 990-0010

Conley, B. *Handling the Holidays.* 1986. C.O.P.E. booklet available from Human Services Press, P.O. Box 2423, Springfield, IL. 62705. (217) 528-1756.

Donnelly, Katherine Fair. *Recovering from the Loss of a Child*. New York: Macmillan, 1982. Part 1 of this moving book contains firsthand accounts of how husbands, wives, siblings, and friends have survived the pain caused by a child's death. Part 2 contains extensive listings of support organizations.

James, John, and Frank Cherry. *The Grief Recovery Handbook: A Step by Step Program for Moving Beyond Loss*. New York: Harper Collins, 1988. Exposes cultural myths about grieving ("time heals all wounds") and gives grievers choices to help them actively work through their grief.

Kubler-Ross, Elisabeth, M.D. *On Children and Death*. New York: Macmillan, 1983. In this comforting book, Dr. Kubler-Ross offers practical help in living through the terminal period of a child's life with love and understanding. She discusses children's knowledge about death, visualization, letting go, funerals, help from friends, and spirituality.

Kubler-Ross, Elisabeth, M.D. *On Death and Dying*. New York: Macmillan, 1969. Discusses attitudes toward death, emotional stages of dying (anger, bargaining, depression, acceptance, hope), interviews with the terminally ill, family reactions, and therapy.

Lauren, Phoebe, J.D. *How to Live When Your Child Dies*. Sausalito, CA: Center For Attitudinal Healing, 1995. Book written by a mother whose only child died. This is a personal book full of practical guidelines and approaches to working through grief. Debunks many myths about grief and provides great comfort to parents struggling through grief in a society that is neither understanding nor supportive.

Morse, Melvin, M.D. *Closer to the Light: Learning from Near Death Experiences of Children*. New York: Villard Books, 1990. Dr. Morse, a pediatrician and researcher into children's near-death experiences, writes about the startlingly similar spiritual experiences of children who almost die. Dozens of children' moving stories will comfort bereaved parents who believe, or are trying to believe, that their child is in a better place, where all will meet again.

Rando, Therese, Ph.D. *Grieving: How to Go On Living When Someone You Love Dies*. Lexington, MA.: Lexington Books, 1988. Written by a nationally known grief counselor, this comprehensive and compassionate book explains the phases of grief, dispels unrealistic expectations, and guides the reader through the hard work of grief into healing. Helpful chapters on loss of a child, family reorganization, resources, and solving practical problems.

Rando, Therese, Ph.D, ed. *Parental Loss of a Child*. Champaign, IL: Research Press, 1986. Thirty-seven articles, including death from serious illness; guilt; grief of fathers, mothers, siblings, single parents; professional help; advice to physicians, clergy, funeral directors; support organizations.

Rosof, Barbara. *The Worst Loss: How Families Heal from the Death of a Child*. New York: Henry Holt & Co., 1994. Describes the work of grieving, how children grieve, barriers to grieving and their resolution, and the rest of your life.

Sander, Seryl. *Times of Challenge*. New York: Mesorah Publications, 1988. 1-800-MESORAH or (721) 921-9000. Collection of true stories describing joy, strength, and triumph under the most unlikely of circumstances. Written by people who were challenged by and conquered adversities such as cancer, paralysis, retardation, and others. Includes a chapter on death and dying according to Jewish philosophy.

Staudacher, Carol. *Men and Grief: A Guide for Men Surviving the Death of a Loved One*. Oakland, CA: New Harbinger Publications, 1991. $11.95 + $2 shipping to New Harbinger Publications, 5674 Shattuck Avenue, Oakland, CA 94609. (510) 652-0215. Written by a health care professional, this book uses case studies to explore how men cope with grief, and provides insight and coping strategies for healing.

Wheeler, Sara, and Margaret Pike. *Goodbye My Child*. Omaha, NE: The Centering Corporation, 1992. (402) 553-1200. Helps with funeral planning, answers practical questions, discusses the death of children of all ages, differences in men's and women's grief, healing, phases of mourning, caring for ourselves, red flags of grief, and unfinished business. Uses examples from the experiences of bereaved parents.

Wild, Laynee. *I Remember You: A Grief Journal*. San Francisco: HarperCollins, 1994. A journal for written and photographic memories during the first year of mourning. Beautiful book filled with quotes and comfort.

Helping the siblings

Doka, Kenneth, ed. *Children Mourning, Mourning Children*. Hemisphere Publications, 1995. A collection of chapters (first presented at The Hospice Foundation of America conference) written by many health care professionals who work with grieving children. Topics include children's understanding of death, answering grieving children's questions, the role of the schools and many others. To obtain, write: Taylor and Francis, 1900 Frost Road, Suite 101, Bristol, PA, 19007. $14.95 plus $2.50 for shipping and handling.

Fox, S. *Books and Films on Death and Dying for Children and Adolescents: An Annotated Bibliography and First Supplement.* Boston: The Good Grief Program, 1985 and 1988.

Grollman, Earl. *Talking About Death: A Dialogue Between Parent and Child.* Boston, MA: Beacon Press, 1990. One of the best books for helping children cope with grief. It contains a children's read-along section to explain and explore children's feelings. In very comforting language, this book teaches parents how to explain death, understand children's emotions, understand how children react to specific types of death, when to seek professional help; it also contains a resource section.

Jarratt, Claudia Jewett. *Helping Children Cope with Separation and Loss.* rev. ed. Cambridge, MA: Harvard Common Press, 1994. Written by a child and family therapist, this book covers many types of loss: hospitalizations, divorce, death. Describes simple, yet effective, techniques that adults can use to help children through grief.

Rosen, Helen, Ph.D. *Unspoken Grief: Coping with Childhood Sibling Loss.* Lexington, KY: Lexington Books, 1986.

Rudman, Masha Kabakow, Kathleen Dunne Gagne, and Joanne E. Bernstein, eds. *Books to Help Children Cope With Separation and Loss : An Annotated Bibliography,* 4th ed. Serving Special Needs Series. New York: R.R. Bowker Company, 1993. Reviews more than 600 books that deal with helping children cope.

Schaefer, Dan, and Christine Lyons. *How Do We Tell the Children?: A Step-by-Step Guide for Helping Children Two to Teen Cope When Someone Dies.* updated ed. New York: Newmarket Press, 1993. If your terminally ill child has siblings, read this book. In straightforward, uncomplicated language, the authors describe how to explain the facts of death to children and teens and show how to include the children in the family support network, laying the foundation for the healing process to begin. Also includes a crisis section, for quick reference on what to do in a variety of situations.

Biographies

Additional biographies are listed in the "Resources" section of Chapter 6, *Forming a Partnership with the Medical Team.*

Kruckeberg, Carol. *What Was Good About Today.* Seattle: Madrona, 1984. A mother writes of her daughter's battle with AML, their interactions with doctors and nurses, the support and love of an entire town, and grieving

Sara's death. A heartwarming story of family bonds, and the search to find something good about each day.

Livingstone, Gordon, M.D. *Only Spring: On Mourning the Death of My Son*. San Francisco: Harper, 1995. This book, written in stunning language by a physician whose six-year-old son died from complications of a bone marrow transplant, chronicles the months of Lucas' struggle to live and the subsequent years of his parents' heartbroken grief. A deeply moving, haunting yet hopeful book about loss, grief, and love.

Mann, Bruce W. *Leukemia: A Family's Challenge*. Traverse City, MI: Prism, 1987. 121 S. Union Street, Traverse City, MI 49684. Written by the father of 14-year-old Michele, this book describes Michele's life with, and death from acute granulocytic leukemia. Covers topics faced by all cancer families: diagnosis, second opinions, assertiveness with the medical team, feelings ranging from hope to terror, siblings, friends, and many others. Includes a step-by-step description of a bone marrow transplant.

Magazine

Bereavement: A Magazine of Hope and Healing. Magazine was founded in 1987 by a bereaved mother to provide support for those grieving, allow direct feedback from the bereaved to helping professionals, and help the non-bereaved learn what helps and what hurts. Also publishes booklets on numerous grief-related topics. For a free copy or to subscribe, write or call: Bereavement Publishing, Inc., 8133 Telegraph Drive, Colorado Springs, CO 80920. (719) 282-1948.

Reading for young siblings

Buscaglia, Leo. *The Fall of Freddy the Leaf: A Story of Life for All Ages*. New York: Holt, Rinehart and Winston, 1982. This wise yet simple story about a leaf named Freddy explains death as a necessary part of the cycle of life.

Dodge, Nancy C. *Thumpy's Story: A Story of Love and Grief Shared*. Springfield, IL: Prairie Lark Press, 1984. This compassionate, yet practical tale is helpful in explaining to children normal reactions to the loss of a loved one.

Hickman, Martha. *Last Week My Brother Anthony Died*. Abingdon, TN: 1984. Touching story of a preschooler's feelings when her infant brother dies. The family's minister (a bereaved parent himself) comforts her by comparing feelings to clouds—always there but ever changing.

Mellonie, Bryan, and Robert Ingpen. *Lifetimes: The Beautiful Way to Explain Death to Children.* New York: Bantam Books, 1983. Beautiful paintings and simple text explain that dying is as much a part of life as being born.

Reading for school-aged siblings

Coburn, J. *Annie and the Sand Dobbies.* New York: Seabury, 1980. Narrated by an eleven-year-old boy whose young sister and beloved dog both die. In simple yet profound words, his parents explain their Christian beliefs about death and the afterlife.

Houston, Gloria. *My Brother Joey Died.* New York: J. Messner, 1982. Simple, caring book describes one child's journey through grief after the death of her sibling. Describes the sister's feelings about the funeral, the changed family, her parents' grief, her grandparents' role, and the comfort of a support group.

Temes, Roberta, Ph.D. *The Empty Place: A Child's Guide Through Grief.* Far Hills, NJ: New Horizon Press, 1992. To order, call (402) 553-1200. Explains and describes feelings after the death of a sibling, such as the empty place in the house, at the table, in a brother's heart.

White, E.B. *Charlotte's Web.* New York: Harper, 1952. Classic tale of friendship and death as a part of life. (The videotape is widely available to rent.)

Reading for teenage siblings

Gravelle, Karen, and Charles Haskins. *Teenagers Face to Face with Bereavement.* Englewood Cliffs, NJ: J. Messner, 1989. The perspectives and experiences of seventeen teenagers comprise the heart of this book, which focuses on teens coping with grief.

Grollman, Earl. *Straight Talk About Death for Teenagers: How to Cope with Losing Someone You Love.* Boston, MA: Beacon Press, 1993. Wonderful book that talks to teens, not at them. Discusses denial, pain, anger, sadness, physical symptoms, and depression, as well as charts methods to help teens actively work through their feelings at their own pace.

Richter, Elisabeth. *Losing Someone You Love: When a Brother or Sister Dies.* New York: G.P. Putnam, 1986. Fifteen young people describe the sorrow, fear, loneliness, anger, and desire to protect their parents after their sibling dies. Valuable book for both teens and parents to read.

Rofes, Eric. *The Kid's Book About Death and Dying.* Boston, MA: Little, Brown, and Co., 1985. Fourteen young people between the ages of 11 and 14 share their thoughts and perceptions on death and dying.

Raiment, Janis. *Children Facing Grief: Letters from Bereaved Brothers and Sisters*. Saint Meinard, IN: Abbey Press, 1989.

Rosen, Helen. *Unspoken Grief: Coping with Childhood Sibling Loss*. Lexington, MA: Lexington Books, 1986. Provides an overview of children's comprehension of death, childhood bereavement, methods to explore the child's emotions, and ways to acknowledge the significance of the child's loss. Includes numerous surveys and case histories.

Audio/video

Drying Their Tears. Produced by CARTI, Communication Division, Markham University, P.O. Box 55050, Little Rock, AR 72215. For information call 1-800-482-8561 or (501) 660-7614. Ask for Mary Machen. Video and manual to help counselors, teachers, and other professionals help children deal with the grief, fear, confusion, and anger that occur after the death of a loved one. There are three segments: training facilitators, section for children aged five to eight, and one for ages nine to teens. Each includes interviews with children and video from children's workshops.

The Healing Path. The Compassionate Friends sibling video addresses concerns of surviving siblings, such as sadness, pain, anger, and fear. The video explores eight topics: facing the reality of death, who will listen, changed family life, special days, visiting the cemetery, parental overprotection, feelings and expectations, and looking to the future. For information call (630) 990-0010 or FAX (630) 990-0246.

Mr. Rogers Talks with Parents About Childhood Cancer. Videotapes (2) guidebook, pamphlet. 47 mins. VHS. Available from the American Cancer Society. 1-800-ACS-2345. The first tape consists of interviews with parents about ways to deal with emotions during diagnosis and treatment. The second tape includes sensitive interviews with three bereaved parents.

The Compassionate Friends has dozens of audiotapes available on all aspects of grief, including such topics as the holidays, marriage, fathers, siblings, anger, guilt, the grief process, writing and grief, emotional healing, recovery, religion and grief, music and healing, and moving from anger to positive growth. To explore all of the available titles, contact the Compassionate Friends and ask for their Resource Catalog. (See "Organizations" at the beginning the "Resources" section.)

Photographs of Our Children

Children during and after treatment

YOUR CHILD WILL PROBABLY be changed in appearance or attitude by the drugs that he takes for treatment. However, when treatment ends, your child's appearance, energy, and personality will recover. It's hard to tell yourself "this too will pass" when you are looking at a child who has lost his hair, is swollen from prednisone, and has frequent rages. The parents of the children below make these photos public so that you can more fully believe that you will "get your child back" after chemotherapy is over.

JEREMY

471

KIM

 JUDD

KRISTIN

BRENT

JUSTIN

KATY

JOHN

LESLEE

MEAGAN

CARRIE BETH

GINA

❦
In Memoriam

Despite major advances in treatment, some children still die from childhood leukemia. Some of the grieving parents who helped create this book wished to share a photograph of their beloved child. In loving memory, we dedicate this page to them—departed but not forgotten.

GREGORY SMITH

RYAN REDDELL

CHRISTIE SIMONETTI

CAITLIN
McCARTHY-KING

JENNIFER
HAWKINSON

Blood Counts and What They Mean

KEEPING TRACK OF THEIR CHILD'S BLOOD COUNTS becomes a way of life for parents of children with leukemia. Unfortunately, misunderstandings about the implications of certain changes in blood values can cause unnecessary worry and fear. To help prevent these concerns, and to better enable parents to help spot trends in the blood values of their child, this appendix explains the blood counts of healthy children, the blood counts of children being treated for leukemia, and what each blood value means.

Values for healthy children

Each laboratory and lab handbook has slightly different reference values for each blood cell, so your lab sheets may differ slightly from the charts below. There is also variation in values for children of different ages. For instance, in children from newborn to four years old, granulocytes are lower and lymphocytes higher than the numbers listed below. Geographic location affects reference ranges as well.

Values for Healthy Children

Hemoglobin (Hgb.)	11.5–13.5 g/100ml.
Hematocrit	34–40%
Red Blood Count	3.9–5.3 m/cm or 3.9-5.3 x 10^2/L
Platelets	160,000–500,000 mm³
White Blood Count	5,000–10,000 mm³ or 5–10 K/ul
WBC Differential:	
Segmented neutrophils	50–70%
Band neutrophils	1–3%
Basophils	0.5–1%
Eosinophils	1–4%
Lymphocytes	12–46%
Monocytes	2–10%
Bilirubin (total)	0.3–1.3 mg./dl
Direct (conjugated)	0.1–0.4 mg./dl

Indirect (unconjugated)	0.2–0.18 mg./dl
AST (SGOT)	0–36 IU./l.
ALT (SGPT)	0–48 IU./l.

Values for children on chemotherapy

Blood counts of children being treated for leukemia fluctuate wildly. White blood cell counts can go down to zero, or be above normal. Red cell counts go down periodically during treatment, necessitating transfusions of packed red cells. Platelet levels also decrease, requiring platelet transfusions. Absolute neutrophil counts (ANC) are closely watched as they give the physician an idea of the child's ability to fight infection. ANCs vary from zero to in the thousands.

Oncologists consider all of the blood values to get the total picture of the child's reaction to illness, chemotherapy, radiation, or infection. Trends are more important than any single value. For instance, if the values were 5.0, 4.7, 4.9, then the second result was insignificant. If, on the other hand, the values were 5.0, 4.7, 4.6, then there is a decrease in the cell line.

The explanations below will describe each blood value. If you have any questions about your child's blood counts, ask your child's doctor for a clear explanation. Especially in the beginning, many parents agonize over whether the rapid changes in blood counts (often requiring transfusions, changes in chemo dosages, or whether the child can have visitors) are normal or expected. The only way to address your worries, and prevent them from escalating, is to ask what the changes mean.

What do these blood values mean?

The following sections explain each line of the above list of blood values. See Figure 7, Sample lab data sheets, to get an idea of the different ways these values might be displayed on the actual lab reports prepared for your child.

Hemoglobin (Hgb)

Red cells contain hemoglobin, the molecules that carry oxygen and carbon dioxide in the blood. Measuring hemoglobin gives an exact picture of the ability of the blood to carry oxygen. Children will have low hemoglobin

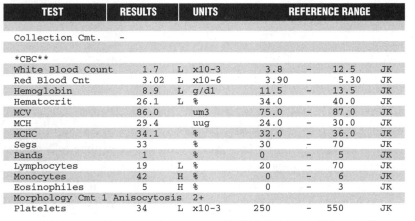

```
NAME:                                    LOCATION: 6000
DOB:                      SEX: F         REQUEST#: 342491
COLLECTED: 08/25/1992    08:34           ACCOUNT#:
REPORTED: 08/25/1992 @ 11:02             DR:
PATIENT PHONE#:                          COPY TO:
TESTS: **CBC**
ORDERED:
```

TEST	RESULTS		UNITS	REFERENCE RANGE			
Collection Cmt.	-						
*CBC**							
White Blood Count	1.7	L	x10-3	3.8	–	12.5	JK
Red Blood Cnt	3.02	L	x10-6	3.90	–	5.30	JK
Hemoglobin	8.9	L	g/dl	11.5	–	13.5	JK
Hematocrit	26.1	L	%	34.0	–	40.0	JK
MCV	86.0		um3	75.0	–	87.0	JK
MCH	29.4		uug	24.0	–	30.0	JK
MCHC	34.1		%	32.0	–	36.0	JK
Segs	33		%	30	–	70	JK
Bands	1		%	0	–	5	JK
Lymphocytes	19	L	%	20	–	70	JK
Monocytes	42	H	%	0	–	6	JK
Eosinophiles	5	H	%	0	–	3	JK
Morphology Cmt 1 Anisocytosis	2+						
Platelets	34	L	x10-3	250	–	550	JK

```
Speciman ID:                        August 20 1992 11:36
Patient:                            Operator ID     SVT
Sex:            DOB:                 Sequence #      7358
DR:                                 Open Sampler
Param Set 1    Limit Set 4

WBC:   0.7 K/uL
NEU:   0.4   68.6 %N                S                    D
LYM:   0.1   17.8 %L                I                    E
MONO:  0.1   10.9 %M                Z                    P
EDS:   0.0    2.2 %E                E                    O
BASO:  0.0    0.5 %B                                     L

                                    COMPLEXITY        ORTHOGONAL
RBC: 3.03 M/uL
HGB:  9.2 g/dL
HCT: 26.9 %
MCV: 88.7 fL
MCH: 30.4 pg
MCHC: 34.2 g/dL
RDW: 13.6 %

                                        RBC               PLT
PLT: 147. K/UL
```

```
              INTERPRETATION              MANUAL DIFFERENTIAL    RBC MORPHOLOGY
-------WBC--------RBC--------PLT-------
```

NEU	META	NORMAL	MICRO
BAND	MYELD	PLYCHROM	MACRO
LYMPH	PRO	HYPCHROM	ANISO
MONO	BLAST	POIK	BASOSTIP
EOSIN	VAR LYM	TARGET	
BASO	TOXGRAN	SPHERO	NRBC

```
SUSPECTED ABNORMAL POPULATIONS:
   Variant Lymphocytes

USER-DEFINED ABNORMALITIES:
   Leukopenia           Anemia
   Neutropenia          Macrocytic RBC
   Lymphopenia

              PATIENT LIMITS SET 4

WBC:  5.0-13.0                  RBC:  4.20-5.20   PLT: 142.-424.
NEU:  1.0-6.6  35.0-75.0 %N     HGB:  12.5-15.0   MPV: 0.0-99.9
LYM:  2.5-9.0  16.0-56.0 %L     HCT:  33.0-45.0
MONO: 0.0-1.2   0.0- 8.0 %M     MCV:  76.0-87.0
EDS:  0.0-0.8   0.0- 5.0 %E     MCH:  24.0-33.0
BASO: 0.0-0.4   0.0- 3.0 %B     MCHC: 31.4-35.8
                                RDW:   8.0-14.0
```

COMMENT: _____

DIFF BY _____

Figure 7. Sample lab data sheets

levels at diagnosis and during the intensive parts of treatment. This is because both cancer and chemotherapy decrease the bone marrow's ability to produce new red cells. During maintenance, your child's hemoglobin level will be higher than during induction and consolidation, but still lower than that of a healthy child. Usually, signs and symptoms of anemia—pallor, shortness of breath, fatigue—will start to show when the hemoglobin gets to or below 10g/dl.

Hematocrit (HCT)
also called packed cell volume (PCV)

The purpose of this test is to determine the ratio of plasma (clear liquid part of blood) to red cells in the blood. Blood is drawn from a vein, finger prick, or from a Hickman or Port-a-cath and is spun in a centrifuge to separate the red cells from the plasma. The hematocrit is the percentage of cells in the blood; for instance, if the child has a hematocrit of 30 percent, it means that 30 percent of the amount of blood drawn was cells and the rest was plasma. When the child is on chemotherapy, the bone marrow does not make many red cells, and the hematocrit will go down. Usually the child will be given a transfusion of packed red cells when the hematocrit goes below 18 to 19 percent. Even during maintenance the bone marrow is partially suppressed, so the hematocrit is often in the low to mid-thirties. This results in less oxygen being carried in the blood, and your child may have less energy.

Red blood cell count (RBC)

Red blood cells are produced by the bone marrow continuously in healthy children and adults. These cells contain hemoglobin which carries oxygen and carbon dioxide throughout the body. To determine the RBC, an automated electronic device is used to count the number of red cells in a liter of blood.

Red cell indices (MCV, MCH, MCHC) are mathematical relationships of hematocrit to red cell count, hemoglobin to red cell count, and hemoglobin to hematocrit. This gives a mathematical expression of the degree of change in shape found in red cells. The higher the number (low teens are fine) the more distorted the red cell population is.

White blood cell count (WBC)

The total white blood cell count determines the body's ability to fight infection. Treatment for cancer kills healthy white cells as well as diseased ones. Parents need to expect prolonged periods of low white counts during treatment. To determine the WBC, an automated electronic device counts the number of white cells in a liter of blood. If your lab sheet uses K/ul instead of mm³, multiply by 1000 to get the value in mm³. For example, on the lab sheet at the end of this appendix, the total WBC is 0.7 K/ul. Therefore, 0.7 x 1000 = 700 mm³.

White blood cell differential

When a child has blood drawn for a complete blood count (CBC) one section of the lab report will state the total white blood cell count and a "differential." This means that each type of white cell will be listed as a percentage of the total, as in the chart below.

White Blood Cells (WBC) - 1,500 mm³

Segmented neutrophils	49% (also called polys or segs)
Band neutrophils	1% (also called bands)
Basophils	1% (also called basos)
Eosinophils	1% (also called eos)
Lymphocytes	38% (also called lymphs)
Monocytes	10% (also called monos)

You might also see cells called metamyelocytes, myelocytes, promyelocytes, and myeloblasts listed. These cells are nonfunctional and are seen in a variety of serious illnesses. The appearance or disappearance of these immature cells are early signals of change.

The differential is obtained by microscopic analysis of a blood sample on a slide.

Absolute neutrophil count (ANC)

The absolute neutrophil count (also called the absolute granulocyte count or AGC) is a measure of the body's ability to withstand infection. Generally, an ANC above 1,000 means that the child can go to school and participate in normal activities.

To calculate the ANC, add the percentages of neutrophils (both segmented and band) and multiply by the total WBC. Using the example above, the ANC is 49% + 1% = 50%. 50% of 1,500 (.50 X 1,500) = 750. The ANC is 750.

Platelet count

Platelets are necessary to repair the body and to stop bleeding through the formation of clots. Because platelets are produced by the bone marrow, platelet counts decrease when a child is on chemotherapy. Signs of lowering platelet counts are small vessel bleeding such as bruises, gum bleeding, or nosebleeding. Platelet transfusions are usually given when the count is between 10,000-20,000 mm^3. Platelets are counted by passing a blood sample through an electronic device.

Approximately one third of all platelets spend a great deal of time in the spleen. Any splenic dysfunction such as enlargement may cause the counts to drop precipitously. If the spleen is removed, platelet counts may sky-rocket. This transient thrombocytosis (elevated platelet count) will abate within a month.

ALT (alanine aminotransferase)
also called SGPT (serum glutamic pyruvic transaminase)

When doctors talk about "liver functions," they are usually referring to tests on blood samples that measure liver damage. If the chemotherapy is proving to be toxic to your child's liver, the damaged liver cells release an enzyme called ALT into the blood serum. ALT levels can go up in the hundreds or even thousands in some children on chemotherapy. Each institution and protocol has different points at which they decrease dosages or stop chemo-therapy to allow the child's liver to recover. If you notice a change in your child's ALT, ask for an explanation and plan of action (for example, "John's ALT is now 450, what is your plan to reduce or stop the chemotherapy to allow his liver to recover?")

> *I was very interested in my daughter's blood counts throughout her treatment. I also tried to get information without making people mad. If I asked a question and received an unsatisfactory answer, I would reply in a nice way, "I am worrying about this and would really appreciate a few minutes of your time to explain it to me." I found the attendings and*

clinic director to be the most willing to provide explanations. If you get a ridiculous reply (once a fellow patted me on the head and said, "It's our job to think about these things, not yours") go find someone else to ask.

AST (aspartate aminotransferase)
also called SGOT (serum glutamic oxaloacetic transaminase)

SGOT is an enzyme present in high concentrations in tissues with high metabolic activity, including the liver. Severely damaged or killed cells release SGOT into the blood. The amount of SGOT in the blood is directly related to the amount of tissue damage. Therefore, if your child's liver is being damaged by the chemotherapy, the SGOT can rise into the thousands. In addition, there are other causes for an elevated SGOT, such as viral infections, reaction to an anesthetic, and many others. If your child's level jumps unexpectedly, ask the physician for an explanation and a plan of action.

Bilirubin

The body converts hemoglobin released from damaged red cells into bilirubin. The liver removes the bilirubin from the blood, and excretes it into the bile, which is released into the small intestine to aid digestion.

Normally there is only a small amount of bilirubin in the bloodstream. Bilirubin rises if there is excessive red blood cell destruction or if the liver is unable to excrete the normal amount of bilirubin produced.

There are two types of bilirubin: indirect (also called unconjugated), and direct (also called conjugated) bilirubin. An increase in indirect (unconjugated) is seen when destruction of red cells has occurred, while an increase of direct (conjugated) is seen when there is a dysfunction or blockage of the liver.

If excessive amounts of bilirubin are present in the body, the bilirubin seeps into the tissues producing a yellow color called jaundice.

If your child's total bilirubin rises above normal levels, ask the physician for an explanation and plan of action.

Your child's pattern

Each child develops a unique pattern of blood counts during treatment, and observant parents can help track these changes. This appendix contains a record-keeping sheet that you can use to record your child's blood values (see Figure 8). If there is a change in the pattern, show it to your child's doctor and ask for an explanation. Doctors consider all of the laboratory results to decide how to proceed, but they should be willing to explain their plan of action to you so that you better understand what is happening and worry less.

If your child is participating in a clinical trial and you have obtained the entire clinical trial protocol (discussed in Chapter 4, *What Is a Clinical Trial*), it will contain a section that clearly outlines the actions that should be taken by the oncologist if certain changes in blood counts occur. For example, my daughter's protocol has an extensive section which lists each drug and when the dosage should be modified. For vincristine it states:

Vincristine

1.5 mg/m^2 (2 mg maximum) IV push weekly $\times$ 4 doses days 0,7,14,21.

Seizures:

Hold one dose, then reinstitute.

Severe foot drop, paresis, or ilius:

Hold dose(s): when symptoms abate, resume at 1.0 mg/m2; escalate to full dose as tolerated.

Jaw pain:

Treat with analgesics; do not modify vincristine dose.

Withhold if total bilirubin >1.9 mg/dl. Administer 1/2 dose if total bilirubin 1.5-1.9 mg/dl.

Resources

If you would like more information on laboratory diagnostic tests, two good books that can often be found in the reference section of your local library are:

Sobel, David, M.D., and Tom Ferguson, M.D. *The People's Book of Medical Tests* New York: Summit Books, 1985,

Everything You Need To Know About Medical Tests, written by 70 doctors and medical experts. Springhouse, PA: Springhouse Corporation, 1996.

Blood Counts									
Date:									
WBC *ref. range* _____									
Neutrophils *(polys or segs)*									
Neutrophils *(bands)*									
ANC *(polys + bands,* *multiplied by WBC)*									
Hematocrit *ref. range* _____									
Platelets *ref. range* _____									
Chemistries									
Chemotherapy									
Side Effects									

Figure 8. Example of a record-keeping sheet

APPENDIX C

Resource Organizations

Service organizations

The services provided by the five organizations listed in this section are described in detail in the "Resources" section of Chapter 1, *Diagnosis.*

Candlelighters Childhood Cancer Foundation
7910 Woodmont Avenue, Suite 460
Bethesda, MD 20814
1-800-366-CCCF
FAX: (301) 718-2686
World Wide Web: *http://www.candlelighters.org*
email: *info@candlelighters.org*

Candlelighters Childhood Cancer Foundation Canada
National Office
Suite 401, 55 Eglinton Avenue East
Toronto, ON Canada M4P 1G8
1-800-363-1062 (Canada only)
(416) 489-6440
FAX: (416) 489-9812
World Wide Web: *http://www.candlelighters.ca*
email: *staff@candlelighters.ca*

The Leukemia Society of America
600 Third Avenue, 4th Floor
New York, NY 10016
(212) 573-8484 or 1-800-955-4LSA
FAX: (212) 856-9686
World Wide Web: *http://www.leukemia.org*

American Cancer Society
1599 Clifton Road NE
Atlanta GA 30329-4251
1-800-ACS-2345
World Wide Web: *http://www.cancer.org/*

Canadian Cancer Society
565 W 10th Avenue
Vancouver, BC Canada V5Z 4J4
(604) 872-4400
World Wide Web: *http://www.bc.cancer.ca/ccs/*

Organizations that provide information

National Cancer Institute (NCI)
Cancer Information Service
Building 31, Room 10A16
9000 Rockville Pike
Bethesda, MD 20892
1-800-4-CANCER
FAX: (301) 231-6941
CANCERFAX: (301) 402-5874

Provides a nationwide telephone service for people with cancer, their families, friends, and the professionals who treat them. They answer questions and send out informational booklets on a huge variety of cancer-related topics.

CANCERFAX provides treatment guidelines, with current data on prognosis, staging, and histologic classifications. To use CANCERFAX you need a fax machine with a telephone set to touch tone dialing. You do not need to send anything. Pick up the receiver and enter the CANCERFAX number. A recording will come on to guide you.

National Coalition for Cancer Survivorship
1010 Wayne Avenue
Silver Spring, MD 20910
(301) 650-8868
FAX: (301) 565-9670

Organization that strives to identify and address the needs of long term cancer survivors, advocate for change in health care delivery and policy to maximize survivor's access to optimal treatment and support. Write or call for a list of available publications.

PDQ (Physician Data Query)
1-800-4-CANCER

PDQ is the National Cancer Institute's computerized listing of accurate and up-to-date information for patients and health professionals. PDQ provides information on the latest cancer treatments, research studies, clinical trials, and organizations and doctors involved in caring for people with cancer.

Childhood Cancer Ombudsman Program
12141 Pineneedle Court
Woodbridge, VA 22192
(703) 492-0045

This is a free service provided by the Childhood Brain Tumor Foundation of Virginia to support children with cancer and their families who are experiencing difficulties in gaining access to an appropriate education, medical care, coverage of the costs of health care, and meaningful employment. Services include medical library searches, a second opinion program, and help resolving problems with insurance or discrimination.

Organizations that provide emotional support

Center For Attitudinal Healing
33 Buchanan Dr.
Sausalito, CA 94965
(415) 331-6161

The Center for Attitudinal Healing in Sausalito, California, is a nonprofit, nonsectarian group, founded by a child psychiatrist, which sponsors a program for children with catastrophic or life-threatening diseases and their siblings. They use music and art in a loving, supportive program to help children ages 6 to 16 share their feelings about their situation. They sponsor local and national workshops and publish several excellent books.

Cancer Cured Kids
PO Box 189
Old Westbury, NY 11568
1-800-CCK-7525
(516) 484-8160
FAX: (516) 484-8160 (call first)

Organization dedicated to the quality of life of kids who have survived cancer. Cancer Cured Kids supplies information about the educational and psychosocial needs of survivors.

Chai Lifeline/Camp Simcha
National Office
48 West 25 Street, 6th Floor
New York, NY 10010
(212) 255-1160 or 1-800-343-2527
FAX: (212) 255-1495

National nonprofit Jewish organization dedicated to providing support service programs to children and their families in crisis. They are discreet, confidential, and provide all services free of charge. Some of the many services provided are visits to hospital and homebound children, medical referrals, support groups, Grant-a-Wish, respite program, negotiating insurance claims, financial aid, transportation, home tutoring for Judaic studies and many others. This organization sponsors the only kosher camp in North America for children with cancer.

Child Life Council
11820 Parklawn Dr. Suite 202
Rockville, MD 20852
(301) 881-7090
FAX: (301) 881-7092

The Child Life Council seeks to promote the well-being of children and families in health care settings by supporting the development and practice of the child life profession and providing training conferences, publications, and information to the membership and the general public about the child life profession.

Parents Caring and Sharing
c/o Chumie Bodek
109 Rutledge Street
Brooklyn, NY 11211
(718) 596-1542 or 596-9002 (call business hours, Eastern time)

Provides outreach and support network and writes a newsletter for Jewish Orthodox families with children with cancer. Holds monthly meetings and links families of children with similar diseases.

Association of the Care of Children's Health (ACCH)
7910 Woodmont Avenue, Suite 300
Bethesda, MD 20814
(301) 654-6549
FAX: (301) 986-4553

A nonprofit, multidisciplinary organization of health professionals and parents that promotes psychosocial health of children and their parents in health care settings. It sponsors conferences, provides advocacy resources, and publishes journals, newsletters, and booklets.

ChemoCare
231 North Avenue West
Westfield, NJ 07090
1-800-55-CHEMO (outside New Jersey)
(908) 233-1103 (within New Jersey)
FAX: (908) 233-0228

Provides one-to-one emotional support to cancer patients (children or adults) and their families undergoing chemotherapy, radiation, and/or surgery, from trained and certified volunteers who have undergone the treatments themselves.

Coping Magazine
PO Box 682268
Franklin, TN 37068
(615) 790-2400
FAX: (615) 794-0179

A bi-monthly publication devoted to people whose lives have been touched by cancer.

Friends Network
PO Box 4545
Santa Barbara, CA 93140
Attention: Kenon Neal

A national nonprofit organization which distributes an activities newsletter printed in color, called *The Funletter,* to children with cancer.

Famous Phone Friends
9109 Sawyer Street
Los Angeles, CA 90035
(310) 204-5683

Links children who are confined to the hospital or home due to injury or illness by telephone with entertainers and athletes. Specific requests are honored, if possible. Referral by physician, nurse, hospital volunteer, or treatment center social worker.

Free air services

Air Care Alliance
1-800-296-1217
World Wide Web: *http://www.angelflightfla.org/aircareall.org/acahome.html*

ACA is a nationwide association of humanitarian flying organizations. Founded in 1990, ACA members have safely flown 24,000 patients to and from medical treatments.

Corporate Angel Network, Inc. (CAN)
Westchester County Airport, Building 1
White Plains, NY 10604
(914) 328-1313
FAX: 1-800-328-4226

A nationwide nonprofit program designed to give patients with cancer the use of available seats on corporate aircraft to get to and from recognized cancer treatment centers. Patients must be able to walk and travel without life-support systems or medical attention. A child may be accompanied by up to two adults. This service will also fly donors. There is no cost or financial need requirements.

Mission Air Transportation Network
Proctor & Gamble Building
4711 Young Street
North York, ON Canada M2N 6K8
(416) 222-6335
FAX: (416) 222-6930

A Canadian charitable organization that provides free air transport to Canadians in financial need who must travel from their own communities to recognized facilities for medical care. Mission Air arranges flights for children with cancer, using donated seats on corporate, commercial, or government aircraft.

A child and parent using Mission Air must:

• Be Canadian residents.

• Be financially unable to buy airline ticket.

• Have medical clearance to fly and not require medical treatment on board the aircraft.

- Be able to sit in a regular aircraft (no stretchers).

- Have an appointment with a pediatric oncology treatment center.

National Patient Air Transport Hotline
24-hour hotline: 1-800-296-1217

Refers callers to the most appropriate, cost effective charitable or commercial service. Specialists who staff the hotline are familiar with more than three dozen volunteer pilot organizations and special airline transport programs.

How to Get Information From Your Library or Computer

Libraries and bookstores

Almost every book and article listed in the "Resources" sections of this book was obtained through the public library in a very small town. I was able to obtain materials by utilizing the capabilities of the local library and the medical library in our local hospital. There is a wealth of information available.

How to find a book in a public library

Your library will either have a card catalog or computers, which list all of the materials available. If you do not know how to use the computer or catalog, ask a librarian to help you.

A computer system will tell you if the book is available in your library or any of the other branch libraries in the system. If it is in the library, go get it from the shelf. If it is in at another branch, drive there to pick it up or ask the librarian how to put in a "request" to have it sent to your local library. Library systems usually have a van, which shuttles between all of the branches several times a week, so it often only takes a few days to arrive.

If the book has been checked out by someone else, ask the reference librarian to put a "hold" on it for you. When the book is returned, you will be notified to come pick it up. Libraries usually only hold books for a week, so it needs to be picked up promptly, or if there are special circumstances, you should call to ask if they can extend the hold.

If the book is not in the collections of any library in the system ask the reference librarian to arrange for an "inter-library loan." This means that the librarian will do a quick computer search to see where the book is available, then borrow it from another library system for you. This is a very common practice. You can even obtain medical texts from university or medical school libraries. Your local librarian will receive the book in the mail, and will call you or send you a postcard to tell you of its arrival.

If the book is not available for interlibrary loan, you can ask the library to purchase it for their collection. They will usually do this only if it has been published fairly recently.

How to find a magazine article in a public library

If you are looking for a magazine article, go to the area where the library displays magazines. Often, the previous year's monthly issues are stacked below the display area. For an older issue of a popular lay magazine, ask the reference librarian for its location. Public libraries sometimes stock well known medical journals such as the Journal of the American Medical Association and the New England Journal of Medicine. You will probably have to visit a specialized library to find all other medical journals.

To find a medical journal at a university, medical school, or hospital library, check first in the computer to see whether the library carries that journal. Then go to the area of the library that contains the journals, and look through them alphabetically to find the area you need. Medical journals are usually boxed by year with the binding out, so that you can quickly scan the issues to find the one you want. If you get lost on any of the above steps, ask for help from the reference librarian.

If you cannot locate a journal article that you want to read, call your city or county central library headquarters and ask to speak to the person who arranges "interlibrary loans." Ask this person to check whether the journal is available from any of their sources. Some hospital libraries will also use a similar system to get a copy of an article from a journal they do not stock. Usually the library that has the journal will make a copy and send it to you by mail. This may be a free or a fee service.

Using a medical library

To find the nearest medical library open to the public, call the National Network of Libraries of Medicine at 1-800-338-7657.

Hospitals have libraries of various sizes which may have the information you need. Large pediatric hospitals have both resource rooms, which contain non-technical information, and hospital libraries, which contain medical texts and journals. Medical school libraries usually have the largest and most comprehensive collections.

Most medical libraries subscribe to computer services such as Medline, PDQ (Physician's Data Query), or Grateful Med, which provide summaries (called abstracts) of medical articles. Know the topics that you want to research, and ask the librarian to help you use the computer service. The machine will print out a list of abstracts (a paragraph summarizing the information contained in the article) dealing with the requested topic. After reviewing the list, choose the articles that you would like to read, and ask the librarian to help you locate the correct issue of each journal. Rather than feeding dimes into their copying machine, ask if they have a card that can be purchased at a discount for quantity copying. If you are going to advocate for a different treatment or changes in your child's protocol, bring the appropriate articles with you to the next appointment with the doctor.

If the library does not have Medline or a similar computer database, ask the librarian to show you how to use the Index Medicus.

To find copies of technical books to borrow, see if the computerized system has understandable directions to help you to locate the book. If not, ask the librarian for help. Do not be shy; librarians love to help people find what they need. Many times when I was doing research, I appeared at the librarian's desk obviously exhausted and said, "I have a seriously ill child, and I need some information...." Every librarian I ever met literally flew into action.

Using a university library

If you live closer to a university library than a medical library, call the librarian to ask if they subscribe to Medline or other medical databases. Ask if the public is allowed to use it, and if so, whether an appointment is required.

If you have a computer with a modem, you may be able to research their collection without leaving your home. Ask the librarian if this is possible, and, if so, get a copy of the preprinted directions on how to access the collection by modem.

Bookstores

If you prefer to buy books rather than borrow them from the library, you can do so at your local bookstore, or through an online or mail order bookstore, depending on what is most convenient for you. To save time, call ahead to ask if they have the book in stock. If they don't, ask them if they can order it. They will check via computer, and will tell you if it is available, the cost, and the estimated time of arrival. If you plan to pick it up at your local bookstore, ask them to call you when it arrives.

Computer sources of information and assistance

There is an astonishing amount of information available through the Internet. What used to take hours or days of research is now available at your fingertips in the comfort of your own home. Libraries from all over the world can be accessed, and you can download information in minutes from huge databases like Medline or Cancerlit. Obtaining information from large medical databases, established journals, or large libraries is exceedingly helpful for parents at home with sick children. However, the huge numbers of people using the Internet has spawned chat rooms, bulletin boards, and thousands of FAQ's (frequently asked questions), which may or may not contain accurate information. You may want to adopt the motto "Let the buyer beware."

Information flow through the Internet is an ever-changing and fluid phenomenon. The information listed below was current when this book went to press. Of course, our listing of computer sources of information does not constitute an endorsement of any information available from these sources.

Methods to find out what is available

CANSearch
World Wide Web: *http://www.access.digex.net/~mkragen/cansearch.html*

A guide to cancer resources on the Internet produced by the National Coalition for Cancer Survivorship.

CancerGuide
World Wide Web:
http://asa.ugl.lib.umich.edu/chdocs/cancer/CANCERGUIDE.HTML

An index of cancer information for patients and their families.

GrannyBarb and Art's Leukemia Links
World Wide Web:
http://www.acor.org/diseases/hematology/Leukemia/leukemia.html

Where to get leukemia information on the Internet. Covers topics such as what is leukemia, CancerNet, PDQ, abstracts, cancer lit, internet support groups, leukemia-specific sites, bone marrow transplant sites, cord blood transplant sites, leukemia organizations.

Yahoo
World Wide Web:
http://www.yahoo.com/Health/Diseases_and_Conditions/cancer/Leukemia

Cancer Help
World Wide Web: *http://members.aol.com/abiaca/cancer.htm*

Links include cancer sites, clinical trials, databases, mailing lists, and support groups.

CANCERFAQ
World Wide Web: *http://otpt.ups.edu/Conditions/CancerFAQ.html*

A comprehensive listing of sources of cancer information available by computer. It is maintained by E. Loren Buhle, Jr., Ph.D. (Last updated in 1995.)

Steve Dunn's CancerGuide
World Wide Web: *http://www.cancerguide.org*

A great place to start when looking for information. Steve Dunn, a cancer patient, clearly explains the pros and cons of researching your own cancer, understands cancer types and staging, recommends books, and includes patient stories. He has links to many of the best cancer sites on the web.

Medical information

CancerNet
1-800-4-CANCER
World Wide Web: *http://pdqsearch@icicc.nci.nih.gov/*
email: *CancerNet@icicc.nci.nih.gov* Subject: none or use a dash if required. Message: help (if you use a signature, delete it). You will receive a list of available publications and instructions on how to get the information you want.

By far the most comprehensive and up-to-date source of information about cancer. It is maintained by the U.S. National Cancer Institute. Many of the resources listed in this book are available from the database.

If you would like to be notified by email when CancerNet is updated each month, send email with the word subscribe or subs as the body of the message. CancerNet will then send you a message each month telling you what has been updated. To cancel this service, send email with the word unsubscribe or unsubs as the body of the message.

TeleSCAN-Telmatics Services in Cancer
World Wide Web: *http://telescan.nki.nl/*

The first European Internet service for cancer research, treatment, and education, providing a hypermedia interface to primarily European information resources and services related to cancer.

Oncolink tm
World Wide Web: *http://cancer.med.upenn.edu/*

A text and multimedia service available through the Internet. This service was started by E. Loren Buhle, Jr., Ph.D., the parent of a child with ALL. Oncolink offers a wide variety of cancer-related information, including articles, handbooks, case studies, writings by patients and their families, and visual images, including "Children's Art Gallery."

Oncolink tm, Pediatric Leukemia Page
World Wide Web: *http://cancer.med.upenn.edu/disease/leukemia*

Contains a large amount of information on childhood leukemia, including bone marrow transplantation.

Medicine Online
World Wide Web: *http://www.meds.com/*

Provides patients and professionals with in-depth educational information on specific diseases. Also includes information on reimbursement and a treatment guide.

Med help International
World Wide Web: *http://medhlp.netusa.net/*
telnet: *medhlp.netusa.net*
ftp: *medhlp.netusa.net*
or dialup modem to 516-423-0472 (N81-ANSI)

A nonprofit organization which provides medical information written in nontechnical language in order to support patients and their families. The all-volunteer staff is comprised of physicians and other health care professionals who are electronically connected.

List of medical resources

MedWeb: Oncology
World Wide Web: *http://www.gen.emory.edu/medweb/medweb.oncology.html*

Hypermedia Clinical Practice Guidelines for Cancer Pain
World Wide Web: *http://www.stat.washington.edu/TALARIA/TALARIA.html*

The Multimedia Medical Reference Library
World Wide Web: *http://www.med-library.com/*

PharmInfoNet tm
World Wide Web: *http://pharminfo.com/*

Devoted to delivering useful, up-to-date, and accurate pharmaceutical information to health care providers, pharmacists, and patients.

Rx List—The Internet Drug Index
World Wide Web: *http://www.rxlist.com/*

Alternative Medicine Homepage
World Wide Web: *http://www.pitt.edu/~cbw/altm.html*

The Anthony Nolen Bone Marrow Trust
World Wide Web: *http://wombat.doc.ic.ac.uk/bone-marrow/index.html*

A leading research center and the United Kingdom register for potential donors. This site references other international BMT sites.

The BMT Newsletter
World Wide Web: *http://oncolink.upenn.edu/speciality/chemo/bmt/newsletter*

All issues of the BMT newsletters are on line, as well as the book *Bone Marrow Transplants: A Book of Basics for Patients.*

Bone Marrow Donors Worldwide
World Wide Web: *http://BMDW.LeidenUniv.NL*

The National Marrow Donor Program
World Wide Web: *http://www.marrow.org/*

Medical journals

Numerous medical journals are on the World Wide Web. If you do not have access to a medical library, the Web may be your best bet for finding abstracts from technical journals.

American Medical Association Home Page
World Wide Web: *http://www.ama-assn.org*

Allows access to current and past issues of the Journal of the American Medical Association (JAMA), as well as other journals published by the AMA.

British Medical Journal
World Wide Web: *http://www.bmj.com/*

Links to sites of medical interest

The Multimedia Medical Reference Library
World Wide Web: *http://www.med-linrary.com/*

Provides links to many medical journals.

The New England Journal Online
World Wide Web: *http://www.nejm.org*

Contains full text of editorials, opinion pieces, and letters, but has only abstracts of most other articles.

Medical institutions

HospitalWeb
World Wide Web: *http:/neuro-www.mgh.harvard.edu/hospitalweb.nclk*

A list of hospital sites on the Internet.

Fred Hutchison Cancer Research Center
World Wide Web: *http://www.fhcrc.org/*

Fox Chase Cancer Center
World Wide Web: *http://www.fccc.edu*

Stanford Medical Center
World Wide Web: *http://www.med.Stanford.edu/*

University of Texas M.D. Anderson Cancer Center
World Wide Web: *http://utmdacc.mda.uth.tmc.edu*
gopher: *utmdacc.mda.uth.tmc.edu*

H. Leo Moffitt Cancer Center Home Page
World Wide Web: *http://daisy.moffitt.usf.edu/*

University of Michigan Comprehensive Cancer Center
World Wide Web: *http://www.cancer.med.umich.edu/*

Pediatric Bone Marrow Transplant Program at University Of Nebraska
World Wide Web: *http://www.unmc.edu/Pediatrics/BMT/mainmenu.html*

Psychosocial support

Ped-Onc Mailing List
email: *listserv@medinfo.org*

Email support group for parents of children with cancer. To subscribe, leave
the subject line blank and in the body of the message type: subscribe PED-
ONC [your] first name last name (if you have a signature, delete it).

BMT-Talk Mailing List
World Wide Web:
http://www.ai.mit.edu/people/laurel/Bmt-talk/bmt-talk.html
email: *bmt-talk-request@ai.mit.edu*

A monitored email discussion group. To subscribe, leave the subject line
blank and in the body of the message type: subscribe. For digest form, send
email to: *bmt-talk-digest-request@ai.mit.edu* with the same message.

Hem-Onc Mailing List
email: *listserv@maelstrom.stjohns.edu*

Email support group for leukemia, lymphoma, and multiple myeloma. To
subscribe, leave subject blank (or add dash if required) Message: subscribe
hem-onc your first and last name (if you have a signature, delete it.)

CML-Talk Mailing List
email: *listserv@listserv.aol.com*

Email support group for chronic mylogenous leukemia. To subscribe, leave
subject blank. Message: subscribe CML-Talk your first and last name (if you
have a signature, delete it).

Cancer-L Mailing List
email: *listserv@wvnvm.wvnet.edu*

Email support group for all cancers. To subscribe, leave subject blank. Message: Subscribe Cancer-L your first and last names (if you have a signature, delete it).

Sickkids Mailing List
email: *listserv@maelstrom.stjohns.edu*

Moderated (with adult supervision) email support group for children under 18 who have serious illnesses. The children exchange information, establish friendships, ask questions, and exchange humor. There is a team of children who serve as discussion managers. To subscribe, leave subject blank. Message: subscribe SICKKIDS your first and last name (if you have a signature, delete it). Although adults may not participate in the group, they can email questions or concerns to an adult advisor at: *Sickkids-request@maelstrom.stjohns.edu.*

Touchstone Support Network
World Wide Web: *http://www-med.stanford.edu/touchstone/*

A nonprofit, nonsectarian, completely volunteer organization that provides emotional and practical support services for children with chronic and life-threatening illnesses. They help seriously ill children and their families cope with the day-to-day stresses of their overwhelming situations to help them maintain as much stability as possible at home, school, work, and in the community.

SpeciaLove
World Wide Web: *http://minuteman.com/specialove/*

A resource devoted to parents and children with cancer to facilitate networking. This resource is oriented to the family aspects of childhood cancer. SpeciaLove, Inc. was started in 1983 by Tom and Sheila Baker, who lost their thirteen-year-old daughter to leukemia.

Emotional Support Resources
World Wide Web: *http://asa.ugl.lib.umich.edu/chdocs/support/emotion.html*

Patient Advocacy Numbers
World Wide Web: *http://infonet.welch.jhu.edu/advocacy.html*

Cancer Discussion List Archives
World Wide Web: *http://medinfo.org*

Other resources for cancer patients

National Community of Charitable Aviators
World Wide Web: *http://www.angelflightfla.org/aircareall.org/acahome.html*

A nationwide association of humanitarian pilots who help needy patients travel to facilities for necessary treatment.

EMF-Link
World Wide Web: *http://infoventures.microserve.com/*

Information on biological and health effects of electric and magnetic fields (EMF).

EMF and Leukemia Fact Report from the National Cancer Institute
World Wide Web: *http://www.feb.se/NCI_ChildhoodLeukemia*

Federal agencies

Food and Drug Administration
World Wide Web: *http://www.fda.gov/*

For information on specific drugs, telnet to *fdabbs.fda.gov* and login as "bbs".

National Institutes of Environmental Health Sciences
World Wide Web: *http://www.niehs.nih.gov/*

Americans with Disabilities Act information available on electronic bulletin boards

The following are telephone numbers of electronic bulletin boards from which ADA documents can be downloaded if you have a computer with a modem.

U.S. Department Of Justice 202-514-6193
Disability Law Foundation 205-854-9074
205-854-2308
205-854-0698

Compuserve Disability Forum   call 1-800-635-6225 for your local access number

GEnie Disability Round Table   call 1-800-638-9636 (GEnie subscribers only) for your local access number

Project Enable	304-755-7842
Washington State access to self-help	206-767-7681

Commercial online services

America Online

Go to Clubs and Interest, then click on The Health Channel. From there you can access community forums on blood and lymph disorders. You can access MEDLINE under health resources. Speakers and Support Groups can be found under Health News. As of May 1997, the following support groups were active:

Sunday, 7 PM Eastern time	Living With CancerSelf Help Group
Monday, 9 PM EST	Compassionate Friends
Monday, 10 PM EST	Cancer Survivors Mutual Support
Tuesday, 7 PM EST	Loved Ones of Cancer Survivors

Compuserve

Compuserve's forum (GO CANCER) opened in 1988, and is comprised of cancer patients, friends, relatives, and medical professionals. The forum is divided into three areas: the message base, the libraries, and the conference areas. The message base is where people share information. The libraries are updated on a daily basis, and contain the latest PDQ (lay and medical) information on many cancers. In the conference area large numbers of people participate in real-time conferences, sometimes with expert guests.

Prodigy

There are medical bulletin boards, with several topics listed under cancer. Select Special Interest Groups and scroll to Health & Fitness. You can get to a Health chat room by selecting Highlights and scrolling to Home & Family.

Wish Fulfillment Organizations

FOR MANY CHILDREN WITH CANCER, having a dream fulfilled by a wish organization creates a special, joyous memory. Dreams range from trips, to taking friends out for high tea, to getting a computer. Often parents think that wishes are available only for children in the last stages of their life, but this is not the case. Many organizations grant wishes to children in remission from cancer and other diseases or chronic conditions. Some questions you might ask when determining which organization to apply to are:

- Who is eligible for a wish fulfillment?
- Are there any geographic or other restrictions?
- Who makes the arrangements for the wish?
- What costs are covered by the wish organization?
- Who can accompany the child?
- Are there appropriate medical facilities where the wish will take place?
- How do we apply?
- When do we hear if the wish will be granted?

Listing these organizations does not constitute endorsement. The best way to choose is through careful questioning of the organization and through recommendations from other families who have experience with the organization.

B.A.S.E. Camp Children's Cancer Foundation
c/o Terri Jones
4651 North Pine Hills Road
Orlando, FL 32808
(407) 297-9648 (call for information and request form well in advance of arrival date)
Fax: (407) 298-3928

Does not grant wishes, but does help obtain free or reduced price tickets to Walt Disney World, Universal Studios, and other central Florida attractions, for children with a hematology/oncology disease and their immediate family.

The child with cancer must be on treatment when tickets are used. B.A.S.E. needs to receive a written request and doctor's statement (containing child's name, disease, and whether he/she is medically able to visit any central Florida attraction) between two and three weeks prior to your arrival date in Florida.

The Children's Dream Factory of Maine
Doris Simard or Skip Welch
400 U.S. Rte. 1
Falmouth, ME 04105
(207) 781-3406 or 1-800-639-1492

Grants wishes for chronically or seriously ill children from Maine.

Children's Happiness Foundation
PO Box 266
Marshfield, MA 02050
(617) 837-9609 or 1-800-424-3543
FAX: (617) 837-5229

Serves New England children ages 3 to 18 with life-threatening or chronic degenerative diseases.

Children's Wish Foundation International
7840 Roswell Road, Suite 301
Atlanta, GA 30350
(770) 393-WISH
1-800-323-WISH
FAX: (404) 393-0683

U.S. or Europe. Fulfills wishes of terminally ill children.

The Children's Wish Foundation
Joel Jones, Director
c/o New Hope Center
100 E. Sybelia Suite 300
Maitland, FL 32751
(407) 629-8920
FAX: (407) 629-7206

Orlando-based organization that grants wishes for children with life-threatening illnesses who have not yet reached their 18th birthday. Focuses primarily on children who reside in Florida, but has also granted wishes to children from other parts of the U.S., Canada, England, and Russia.

Dreams Come True, Inc.
Emory Clinic-Peds. Heme/Onc
1365 Clifton Road NE
Atlanta, GA 30322
(778) 248-3496

Serves any child with cancer or chronic blood disease treated at Emory University Heme/Onc Clinic. Dreams submitted by children.

The Dream Factory, Inc.
PO Box 3942
Louisville, KY 40202
1-800-456-7556
FAX: (502) 584-0023

Chapters in 30 states. Grants wishes of children ages 3 to 13 who are seriously or chronically ill.

Fulfill A Dream
PO Box 3989
Fort Smith, AR 72913
(501) 785-4130

Serves eastern Oklahoma and western Arkansas. Fulfills dreams of children 17 or younger with life-threatening illness.

Grant A Wish Foundation
c/o Brian Morrison, Executive Director
PO Box 21211
Baltimore, MD 21228
(410) 242-1549 or 1-800-933-5470
FAX: (410) 242-8818

Provides a variety of special services and programs (such as beach and mountain retreats, attending Orioles games) to any child up to 18 years of age who is being treated for cancer. Services are provided free of charge and are available on an ongoing basis throughout treatment.

High Hopes Foundation of New Hampshire, Inc.
Box 172
North Salem, NH 03073
(603) 898-5333 or 1-800-639-6804

Grants wishes of chronically ill children and children with life-threatening diseases in New Hampshire.

Kids, Inc.
9300-D Old Keene Mill Road
Burke, VA 22015
(703) 455-KIDS

Grants unfulfilled wishes to gravely ill children 16 and younger anywhere in the U.S.

The Lisa Madonia Memorial Fund
409 Veloit
Forest Park, IL 60130
(708) 366-2057
FAX: (708) 366-2065

Charitable organization dedicated to granting wishes and providing support to 18 to 25 year olds with cancer. No geographic boundaries.

Magic Moments
c/o Children's Hospital of Alabama
1600 7th Avenue South
Birmingham, AL 35233
(205) 939-9372
FAX: (205) 939-9189

Grants wishes to children 4 to 19 living or being treated in Alabama, who have chronic, life-threatening diseases, or who have severe trauma (burns, spinal cord, head trauma).

Make A Wish Foundation of America
100 W. Clarendon, Suite 2200
Phoenix, AZ 85013
(602) 279-WISH or 1-800-722-WISH
FAX: (602) 279-0855

U.S. and international chapters and affiliates. Grants wishes to children under the age of 18 with life-threatening illnesses.

Marty Lyons Foundation
333 Earle Ovington Blvd. Suite 600
PO Box 9323
Mitchell Field, NY 11553
(516) 745-8966 or 1-800-232-7887

Chapters in New Jersey, New York, and Florida provide a special wish to children ages 3 to 17 who are terminally ill or have a chronic life-threatening disease.

Operation Liftoff of Ohio
PO Box 1094
Gallipolis, OH 45631

Fulfills a dream for children in Ohio and surrounding states who have a life-threatening illness.

Rotary Wishing Well, Inc.
Jim Hogue
10900 NE 8th Street #900
Bellevue, WA 98004
(206) 462-4606
FAX: (206) 454-4383

Serves Washington, Oregon, Idaho, Montana, and Arkansas. Provides significant life experiences for children 4 to 19 with life-threatening or chronic diseases.

Sunshine Foundation
PO Box 255
5400 County Road 547 N
Loughman, FL 33858
(813) 424-4188 or 1-800-457-1976

No geographic boundaries. Grants wishes to chronically or terminally ill children, ages 3 to 21.

Teddi Project
c/o Camp Good Days and Special Times
1332 Pittsford-Mendon Road
Mendon, NY 14506
(716) 624-5555 or 1-800-785-2135
FAX: (716) 624-5799

Priority given to children from Central Florida and the upstate New York area, especially Buffalo, Rochester, Syracuse, Albany, and Binghamton. Serves chronically or terminally ill children ages 7 to 17.

Thursday's Child
PO Box 259279
Madison, WI 53725
(608) 988-4234 or (608) 278-4234

Grants wishes to seriously ill children who live in or are being treated in southwest and south central Wisconsin.

Wish Upon a Star
California Law Enforcement
Maureen Logan, Director
PO Box 4000
Visalia, CA 93278
(209) 733-7753

Serves children in the state of California. Nonprofit, law enforcement effort designed to grant wishes of children afflicted with high-risk and terminal illnesses.

Wish With Wings, Inc.
Pat Skaggs or Kim Clark
PO Box 3479
Arlington, TX 76007
(817) 469-9474
FAX: (817) 275-6005

Serves children living in or being treated in Texas. Grants wishes for children 3 to 16 with life-threatening diseases.

The Wishing Star Foundation
Doug Raper, Director; Sharon Johnson, Wish Coordinator
539 W. Sharp
Spokane, WA 99201
(509) 325-9803 or 1-800-685-6956
FAX: (509) 325-1778

Serves Idaho, eastern Washington, and some areas of Oregon and Nevada. Grants wishes to children 3 to 19 with life-threatening diseases.

Wishing Well Foundation
Jim Reid
PO Box 717
St. Louis, MO 63188
(314) 272-6190

Grants wishes to children in the St. Louis area only who are chronically or terminally ill.

Glossary

Absolute Neutrophil Count (ANC)
Also known as absolute granulocyte or AGC:

> Total count of the neutrophils in the blood, which provides an indication of a person's ability to fight infection. To calculate the ANC, add the percentages of seg neutrophils and band neutrophils, divide by 100, and multiply by the total white blood count.

ALL (Acute Lymphoblastic Leukemia)

> An acute form of leukemia occurring predominantly in children, characterized by the unrestrained production of immature lymphoblasts (a type of white cell) in the blood forming tissues, particularly the bone marrow, spleen, and lymph nodes.

AML (Acute Myeloid Leukemia)

> An acute form of leukemia characterized by a massive proliferation of mature and immature abnormal granulocytes (a type of white cell).

Allogenic Transplant

> Type of bone marrow transplant in which the marrow is donated by another person.

Alopecia

> Hair loss; a common side effect of chemotherapy.

Anemia

> Condition in which there is a reduction in the number of circulating red blood cells.

Anesthesia

> Partial or total loss of sensation, with or without loss of consciousness, induced by the administration of a drug.

Anorexia

> Loss of appetite.

Anesthesiologist

A doctor who specializes in the study and administration of anesthesia.

Attending Physician

Doctor on the staff of a hospital who has completed medical school, residency, and fellowship.

Acute Lymphoblastic Leukemia (ALL)

An acute form of leukemia occurring predominantly in children, characterized by the unrestrained production of immature lymphoblasts (a type of white cell) in the blood forming tissues, particularly the bone marrow, spleen, and lymph nodes.

Asymptomatic

Without symptoms.

Autologous

From the same person. An autologous bone marrow transplant is a procedure in which bone marrow that has been removed from a patient is given back to that patient.

B-cells

Type of lymphocyte (white cell) that helps produce antibodies that destroy foreign substances.

Basophil

Type of granulocyte (white cell) which plays a special role in allergic reactions and helps in the healing of inflammations.

Blast Cell

An undifferentiated normal cell in an early stage of development; also means a leukemic cell of indeterminable type.

Blood-Brain Barrier

A network of blood vessels located around the central nervous system with very closely spaced cells that make it difficult for potentially toxic substances—including anticancer drugs—to enter the brain and spinal cord.

Blood Type

Identification of the proteins in a person's blood cells so that transfusions can be given with compatible blood products. Examples of blood types are A+, A-, B+, B-, AB+, AB-, O+, O-.

Bone Marrow

Soft, inner part of large bones that makes blood cells.

Bone Marrow Aspiration

Process in which a sample of fluid and cells is withdrawn from the bone marrow using a hollow needle.

Bone Marrow Biopsy

The removal of a sample of solid tissue from the bone marrow.

Bone Marrow Transplant

A procedure in which doctors replace bone marrow that has been destroyed by high doses of chemotherapy and/or radiation.

CBC (Complete Blood Count)

Measurement of the numbers of white cells, red cells, and platelets in a cubic millimeter of blood.

CML (Chronic Myelogenous Leukemia)

A disease which progresses slowly and is characterized by increased production of granulocytes in the bone marrow. It is usually associated with a specific chromosomal abnormality called the Philadelphia chromosome.

CNS (Central Nervous System)

The brain, spinal cord, and nerves.

Cancer

A term for diseases in which abnormal cells divide without control.

Carcinogen

A substance or agent that produces cancer.

Centigray

Measurement of radiation-absorbed dose; same as a rad.

Central Nervous System

Brain, spinal cord, and nerves.

Cerebrospinal Fluid (CSF)

Fluid which surrounds and bathes the brain and spinal cord and provides a cushion from shocks.

Children's Cancer Group (CCG)

An organization which designs and monitors pediatric clinical trials.

Chemotherapy

Treatment of disease with drugs. The term usually refers to cytotoxic drugs given to treat cancer.

Chromosome

A structure in the nucleus of a cell that contains genetic material. Normally, 46 chromosomes are inside each human cell.

Chronic Myelogenous Leukemia (CML)

A disease which progresses slowly and is characterized by increased production of granulocytes in the bone marrow. It is usually associated with a specific chromosomal abnormality called the Philadelphia Chromosome.

Clinical Trial

A carefully designed and executed investigation of a drug, drug dosage, combination of drugs, or other method of treating disease. Each trial is designed to answer one or more scientific questions and to find better ways to prevent or treat disease.

Consolidation

Portion of the protocol which consists of new combinations of drugs to destroy any cancer cells that survived induction.

Cytomegalovirus (CMV)

One of a group of herpes viruses that can cause fatal infections in immuno-suppressed patients.

Cytotoxic

Causing the death of cells.

Delayed Intensification

Portion of treatment which comes after the initial induction, consolidation, and interim maintenance. The purpose of this phase is to destroy any remaining cancer cells.

Differentiation

The process by which cells mature and become specialized.

Echocardiogram

A diagnostic test that uses ultrasound to visualize the interior of the heart and determine how effectively it is functioning.

Electrocardiogram (ECG, EKG)

A graphic record of the electric current produced by the contraction of the heart.

Electromagnetic Fields

Magnetism produced by electrical fields.

Eosinophil

A type of white cell which responds to allergic reactions as well as foreign bacteria.

Erythrocytes

Red blood cells.

External Catheter

Indwelling catheter in which one end of the tubing is in the heart and the other end of the tubing sticks out through the skin, for example, a Hickman catheter.

Fellow

A physician who has completed four years of medical school, several years of residency, and is pursuing additional training in a specialized field.

Finger Poke

When a laboratory technician pricks the finger tip to obtain a small sample of blood.

Graft

Tissue taken from one person (donor) and transferred to another person (recipient or host).

Graft-Versus-Host Disease

A condition that may develop after allogenic bone marrow transplantation in which the transplanted marrow (graft) attacks the patient's (host's) organs.

Granulocytes

A type of white cell which destroys foreign substances in the body such as viruses, bacteria, and fungi.

Hepatitis

Inflammation of the liver by virus or toxic origin. Fever and jaundice are usually present, and sometimes the liver is enlarged.

Hematocrit

The measurement of the proportion of cells to plasma in a sample of blood. Sometimes called packed cell volume (PCV).

Hematologist

Physician who specializes in the diagnosis and treatment of disorders of blood and blood forming tissues.

Hemoglobin

The protein found in red blood cells that carries oxygen.

Hemorrhagic Cystitis

Bleeding from the bladder, which can be a side effect of the drug cytoxan.

Heparin Solution

An anticoagulant injected into indwelling catheters between uses to prevent clots.

Hickman Catheter

An indwelling catheter that has one end of the tubing in the heart and the other end outside the body.

HIV (Human Immunodeficiency Virus)

The virus which causes AIDS.

Host

In bone marrow transplantation, the person who receives the marrow.

Human Leukocyte Antigens (HLA's)

Proteins on the surface of cells that are important in transplantation and transfusion. For BMT's, the HLA's on white cells of the patient and potential donor are compared. A perfect HLA match occurs only between identical twins.

Infusion Pump

A small, computerized device which allows drugs to be given at home through an IV or indwelling catheter.

Immune System

Complex system by which the body is able to protect itself from foreign invaders.

Immunosuppression

When the immune system is suppressed, leaving the body susceptible to infection.

Induction

The first part of the chemotherapy protocol for treating some types of leukemia in which several powerful chemotherapy drugs are given to kill as many cancer cells as possible.

Institutional Review Board (IRB)

Group made up of scientists, clergy, doctors, and citizens from the community which approves and reviews all research taking place at an institution.

Intern

Recent medical school graduate who is receiving his/her first year of supervised practical training in medical and surgical care of patients in hospitals.

Intrathecal

Injecting drugs into the cerebrospinal fluid during a spinal tap.

Intravenous-access Line (IV)

A hollow metal or plastic tube which is inserted into a vein and attached to tubing, allowing various solutions or medicines to be directly infused into the blood.

Leukemia

Disease characterized by the unrestrained growth of abnormal white cells in the bone marrow, and often in the spleen and liver; these cancerous cells usually appear in the peripheral blood and may also invade other organs.

Leukocytes

White blood cells.

Leukopenia

A below normal number of white cells.

Lidocaine

Drug most commonly used for local anesthesia.

Lumbar Puncture (Spinal Tap)

Procedure in which a needle is inserted between the vertebrae of the back to obtain a sample of cerebrospinal fluid and/or inject medication.

Lymph

A clear, colorless fluid found in lymph vessels throughout the body, that carries cells to fight infection.

Lymph Nodes

Rounded bodies of lymphatic tissues found in lymph vessels.

Lymph System

A system of vessels and nodes throughout the body which helps filter out bacteria as well as performs numerous other functions.

Lymphocytes

Type of white cell, formed in the lymphoid tissues, that prevents infection and helps provide immunity to disease.

Maintenance

Part of a leukemia protocol for treating ALL. It follows the intensive induction and consolidation phases and helps to destroy any remaining cancer cells.

Medical Student

Student who has completed four years of college and is enrolled in medical school.

Monocytes

Type of white blood cell.

Neurotoxic

Substance which is poisonous to the brain, spinal cord, and/or nerve cells.

Neutropenia

Condition when the body does not have enough neutrophils (a type of infection fighting white cell).

Neutrophils

The most numerous of the granulocytic white cells, they migrate through the bloodstream to the site of infection, where they ingest and destroy bacteria.

Nutritionist

A professional who analyzes nutritional requirements and gives advice on how to eat an appropriate diet for any condition.

Oncologist

Doctor who specializes in the treatment of cancer.

Oncology

Study of cancer.

Pancreas

A gland situated behind the stomach which has two vital functions: It secretes enzymes into the intestines which aid in the digestion of food and it produces and secretes insulin, a hormone essential for regulating carbohydrate metabolism by controlling blood sugar levels.

Pancreatitis

Inflammation of the pancreas which can cause extreme pain, vomiting, hiccoughing, constipation, and collapse.

Pathologist

Doctor who specializes in examining tissue and diagnosing disease.

Pediatrician

Doctor who specializes in the care and development of children and the treatment of their diseases.

Pediatric Oncology Group (POG)

An organization which designs and monitors pediatric clinical trials.

Petechiae

Small, reddish spots under the skin caused by hemorrhage.

Plasma

The liquid part of the lymph and the blood.

Platelet

Disc-shaped blood cell which aids in blood clotting.

Port-a-cath

Indwelling catheter which has a small portal under the skin of the chest attached to tubing which goes into the heart.

Prognosis

Expected or probable outcome.

Prophylaxis

An attempt to prevent disease.

Protocol

The "recipe" for a child's cancer treatment. Outlines the drugs that will be taken, when they will be taken, and in what dosages. Also includes the dates for procedures (e.g., bone marrow aspiration schedule).

Rad

Radiation absorbed dose. A unit of measurement of the absorbed dose of radiation.

Radiation

High-energy rays which are used to kill or damage cancer cells.

Radiologist

Doctor who specializes in using radiation and radioactive isotopes to diagnose and treat disease.

Randomized

Chosen at random. In a randomized research project, a computer chooses which patients receive the experimental treatment(s), and which patients receive the standard treatment.

Relapse

A return of the cancer after its apparently complete disappearance.

Remission

Disappearance of detectable disease.

Resident

Physician who has completed four years of medical school and one year of internship, and who is continuing his or her clinical training.

Right Atrial Catheter

Indwelling catheter with tubing that extends into the heart which provides access for drawing blood and injecting medication.

Side Effect

Unintentional or undesirable secondary effect of treatment.

Somnolence Syndrome

Syndrome which can occur from three to twelve weeks after cranial radiation. It is characterized by drowsiness, prolonged periods of sleep (up to twenty hours a day), low-grade fever, headaches, nausea, vomiting, irritability, difficulty swallowing, and difficulty speaking.

Spinal Tap

Procedure in which a needle is inserted between the vertebrae of the back to obtain a sample of cerebrospinal fluid and/or inject medication. Also called a lumbar puncture (LP).

Staphylococcus Epidermidis

Bacteria normally present on the skin which can infect the blood through an indwelling catheter.

Stem Cells

Cells from which all blood cells develop.

Streptokinase

Enzyme sometimes used to dissolve blood clots in catheter tubing.

Stroke

Loss of consciousness and paralysis caused by bleeding into the brain or clotting that blocks blood flow to a portion of the brain causing injury or death to brain tissue.

Subcutaneous Port

Type of indwelling catheter comprised of a portal under the skin of the chest attached to tubing leading into the heart.

Systemic

Affecting the body as a whole.

T-Cell

Type of lymphocyte (white cell), derived from the thymus, that attacks infected cells, foreign tissue, and cancer cells.

Thrombocytes

Another name for platelets.

Thymus

Small gland located behind the breast bone and between the lungs that plays a major role in the immune system.

Tumor Board

A meeting held at hospitals, attended by oncologists, pathologists, radiologists, fellows, and residents, where complicated cases are discussed to develop a treatment plan.

Urokinase

Enzyme sometimes used to dissolve clots in catheter tubing.

Vancomycin

Antibiotic commonly used to treat infections in indwelling catheters.

Vital Signs

Term which describes a patient's pulse, rate of breathing, and blood pressure.

White Blood Cells

Cells that help the body fight infection and disease.

X-ray

High-energy electromagnetic radiation used in low doses to diagnose disease or injury and in high doses to treat cancer.

X-ray Technician

Certified technician who positions patients for x-rays, monitors equipment, and takes X-rays of the body.

Index

6-MP (Mercaptopurine), 185–186
6-TG (6-Thioguanine), 191

A

absolute neutrophil counts (ANCs)/
absolute granulocyte
counts (AGCs),
209–212, 481–482
acupuncture, 47
acute lymphoblastic leukemia. *See*
ALL
acute myeloid leukemia. *See* AML
adjunctive treatments
with chemotherapy, 197
for pain relief, 47–48
for stressed children, 350
See also emotional support
Adriamycin, 183–184
air travel, assistance with, 87,
491–492
ALL (acute lymphoblastic leukemia)
bone marrow transplants, 400,
403
diagnosis, 25
possible late effects (chart), 376
risk levels and prognosis, 25–26
treatment, 26–29, 73. *See also*
clinical trials
allergic reactions. *See* immune system
reactions
allogenic transplants, 31, 402–403.
See also bone marrow
transplants
alopecia (hair loss), 204–207,
238–239

ALT (alanine aminotransferase),
482–483
alternative treatments, 198–200
Americans with Disabilities Act
(ADA), 378–379
AML (acute myeloid leukemia)
bone marrow transplants for, 400,
403
diagnosis and occurrence, 29
possible late effects (chart), 377
prognosis, 30
treatment, 30–32. *See also* clinical
trials
ANC, AGC, 209–212, 481–482
anemia, 20, 480
anesthesia/sedation
during procedures, 48–50
during radiation treatments, 234,
238
for catheter implantation, 138,
142
for catheter removal, 358, 359
local/topical, 49, 52, 54, 56, 58,
196–197
psychologic method, 47–48
tolerance to, 50, 234
See also medications
anesthesiologists, 49–50
anger
in children, 335–337
following diagnosis, 9–10
at doctors, 113, 118–119,
122–126
in parents, 341-342
in siblings, 311

523

anorexia (appetite loss), 262–263. *See also* food and meals; nutrition
antibiotics
    as chemotherapy, 174
    following bone marrow transplants, 417
    for catheter infections, 140
    lactose intolerance from, 264
    prior to dental visits, 223
    See also infections
antinausea drugs, 194–196. *See also* nausea and vomiting
appetite loss (anorexia), 238–239, 262–263. *See also* food and meals; nutrition
ARA-C, 181–182
art therapy, 157, 346–347. *See also* play and play therapy
aseptic necrosis, 421
Asp (L-asparaginase), 178–179
aspirin, avoiding, 212
assistance. *See* emotional support; financial assistance; "Resources" at the end of chapters and Appendices C and D
AST (aspartate aminotransferase), 483
Ativan, 195
autologous transplants, 32, 403–404. *See also* bone marrow transplants

B

baldness (alopecia), 204–207, 238–239
basophils, (basos), 21, 209. *See also* white blood cells
bed-wetting, 221–222
behavioral changes. *See* emotional and behavioral responses
bilirubin, 483
billing errors, 251–254. *See also* financial records
biofeedback, 47

blast cells, 21, 24, 52. *See also* white blood cells
blood
    counts, 477–485. *See also* blood counts
    donating, 94
    general information about, 20, 21–22, 24
    tests
        for bone marrow donors, 406
        culturing, 139
        at diagnosis, 2, 24
        drawing samples for, 57–58
        peak and trough levels, 140
    transfusions, 58–60
    transplants, 404–405
blood counts
    ALT or SGPT, 482–483
    ANCs/AGCs, 209–212, 481–482
    AST or SGOT, 483
    bilirubin, 483
    CBCs (complete blood counts), 2, 57, 373
    charts for tracking, 248, 485
    hematocrit, 58–59, 480
    hemoglobin (Hgb), 20, 478–479
    individual patterns, 483–484
    interpreting, 478–83
    normal values, 58, 59, 477–478
    platelet counts, 60, 482
        transfusions with low, 60
    RBC (red blood counts), 58, 480
        transfusions with low, 58–59
    SGOT, 483
    SGPT, 482–483
    values during chemotherapy, 478
    WBCs (white blood counts), 3, 481
        dental care with low, 223
        differentials, 209, 481
        doctors visits during low, 211
        exercise with low, 135
        infection risks with low, 139, 210–216
        following radiation, 239

bone marrow
    analysis, 24, 29, 52
    aspiration, 51–53
    donors, finding, 402, 405–407,
        423–424
    functions, 1, 20
    relapse in, 390–391
    registries, 402, 423–424
    See also bone marrow transplants
bone marrow transplants (BMTs)
    allogenic, 31, 402–403
    autologous, 32, 403–404
    conditioning, 412
    confidentiality of donors, 414
    donors, locating, 402, 405–407,
        423-424
    emotional responses to, 414–15
    emotional support during, 426
    graft rejection, 416–417
    graft-versus-host disease
        (GVHD), 402, 404, 405,
        418–419
    infections following, 403,
        417–418
    paying for, 410–411, 424–425
    procedures, 411–413
    questions to ask about, 401
    second opinions, 401
    side effects, long-term, 420–422
    syngenic, 404
    transplant centers, 408–410
    when needed, 29, 31–32, 34,
        400–401
Broviac's catheter. *See* catheters

C

calendars, for record-keeping,
        247–248
calories in diet, increasing, 271–272.
        See also food and meals;
        nutrition
camps, summer, 166–168, 328
cardiovascular disorders, 65–66, 237,
        368–369

catheters
    advantages, 137
    choosing, 147–148
    comparison chart, 147
    external
        care requirements, 138,
            140–141
        description of, 137–138, 139
        implantation procedures,
            138
        pros and cons, 141
        removal, 358
        risks from, 138–141
    not using, 146–147
    removal, 359
    subcutaneous ports
        care requirements, 145
        description, 142, 143–144
        implantation procedures,
            142–143
        risks from, 145–146
CBCs (complete blood counts), 2, 57,
        373. *See also* blood
        counts
celebrations, end-of-treatment,
        359–361
centigrays, 229. *See also* radiation
        treatment
central lines. *See* catheters
cerebrospinal fluid (CSF), 54
Cerubidine, 182
charts, for blood counts, 248, 485. *See
        also* blood counts
chemotherapy
    administration, 53–54, 174–175
    for ALL, 27–28
    for AML, 30–31
    antinausea drugs during,
        194–196
    for CML, 32, 33–34
    drugs, 176–193
    dosages, calculating, 174–175
    general information, 173–177
    long-term side effects, possible,
        65–66, 226, 367–374

chemotherapy (*cont'd*)
    prior to bone marrow transplants, 412
    questions to ask about, 175–176
    short-term side effects, possible, 204–226, 262–265
    types of, 173–174
    when to call doctor during, 176
    See also side effects/complications and individual chemotherapy drugs
chicken pox, 214–215, 289–290, 291. *See also* infections
child life specialists, 43–45, 150–152
chronic leukemia. *See* CML
clinical trials
    design and supervision, 73–76
    enrollment, 72, 77–78
    informed consent, 76–77
    pros and cons, 72–73, 75, 81–82
    questions to ask about, 75–76
    randomization, 74
    relapse protocols, 394
    right to refuse to participate, 80–81
    right to withdraw 81
    standard and experimental treatments, 73, 79
    study document, 79–80
    treatment protocols, 77–79
CML (chronic myelogenous leukemia)
    adult CML, 33
    bone marrow transplants, 400, 403
    juvenile CML, 32
CNS prophylaxis, 27–28, 53, 73. *See also* ALL
COBRA health insurance, 380
cognitive problems/late effects. *See* learning difficulties
communicable disease risks
    chicken pox, 214–215, 289–290
    infections, preventing, 417–418
    from pets, 215–216
    pneumonia, 212–213
    at school, 286–287, 289–291
    from transfusions, 59, 60
    See also infections
communications
    about alternative treatments, 200
    between child and medical team, 45, 115, 120, 444
    conflict-resolution, 90, 104–105, 122–126, 256, 298
    about death and dying, 291–292, 338, 432–435, 436, 442–449
    within the family, 34–38, 40, 44–45, 308, 311–312, 323–328, 331–34, 345–350
    with friends, 90–91, 99–100
    with health insurance agencies, 255–257
    honesty, importance of, 34–39, 123, 126, 200, 332–334, 340, 433–435
    with hospital billing departments, 251–254
    during hospitalizations, 87, 88, 133
    with medical team, 44, 75–77, 108, 112–121, 122–125, 200, 234
    about over-the-counter medications, 216, 218
    post-treatment, 365, 374–377
    with relatives, 84–86
    with school administration and teachers, 283–290, 291–292, 298–299
    with schoolmates, 96, 284, 292
    See also counseling; grief and bereavement
Compazine, 195–96
complementary treatments. *See* adjunctive treatments.
complete blood counts. *See* CBCs

comprehensive health insurance plans
(CHIPS), 380
computers
for learning difficulties, 299
on-line information and support,
157, 496–504
conflict-resolution. *See* communications
consolidation, 28
constipation, 218–219
counseling, individual and family
for children, 161–169, 336, 337,
338–350
for parents, 161–165
interviewing, 163–164
preparing children for, 165–166
referral sources, 163
for school-related problems, 289
support groups, 153–160
types of, 161–163
See also emotional support; mental health services
cranial radiation, 235–237
CSF (cerebrospinal fluid), 54
cyclophosphamide, 179–181
Cytarabine, 181–182
cytomegalovirus (CMV), 59, 60, 417
Cytosar, 181–182
cytosine arabinoside, 181–182
Cytoxan, 179–81

D

daunomycin, 182, 368–369
daunorubicin, 182
death and dying, 431–469
ending treatment, 431–432
family and friends, 441–449
funerals and memorial services,
292, 439
at home, 437–439
hospice care, 435–436
in the hospital, 436–437
parental grief, 451–461
school-related responses,
291–292

siblings, 439, 449–450
sources of support during,
461–462
talking about, 338, 432–435
See also communications; grief
and bereavement
Decadron, 187–91, 194
deductible medical expenses, 250
delayed intensification, 28
Demerol, 197
dental needs, 223, 370. *See also* developmental delays
depression
in children, 337
in parents, 340
in siblings, 310–11
See also counseling, individual
and family; mental
health services
developmental delays, 27, 223,
241–243, 372, 420, 421
dexamethasone
for chemotherapy, 187–191
for nausea relief, 194
weight gain with, 263–264
See also emotional and behavioral
responses
diagnosis
children's responses, 34–38, 331
parent(s) responses, 4–13
process of, 1–4, 23–24, 51–58
siblings' responses, 307–338
telling others about, 85–86,
90–91, 283
diarrhea, 216–217
diet. *See* food and meals; nutrition
disabilities
accepting, 301–302
employment issues, 377–379
learning disabilities, 226,
240–241, 381–383
military service, 379
resources, 383–388
special education programs,
295–299

discipline, maintaining, 334, 336, 342–343, 345–346

DMR, DNR, 182

doctors

anger towards, 9, 113, 119

changing during treatment, 112, 125–126

changing post-treatment, 375–377

communicating with, 112–21, 122–125, 200

desirable qualities in, 111–112, 121–122

educating about possible late effects, 374–377

as helpers with decision-making, 76–77, 78, 82, 147–48

qualifications, board-certified, 109

relationship styles, 112–114

resolving conflicts with, 122–126

role during diagnosis, 2, 5, 108

when to call

during blood transfusions, 58

during chemotherapy, 176

for dehydration, 208, 217

for fever, 64

for fluid retention, 264

for infection, 214

post-treatment, 367

for skin problems, 226

Doxorubicin, 183–184

drug interactions, avoiding, 199–200, 212, 216

drugs. *See* medications and individual drugs

E

eating problems. *See* food and meals; nutrition

echocardiograms, 65, 369

educational problems. *See* school

electrocardiograms (ECG, EKG), 369

electromagnetic fields (EMFs), 7, 23

Elspar, 178–79

EMLA cream (topical anesthetic), 49, 54, 56, 58, 196

emotional and behavioral responses

to bone marrow transplants, 414–416

in children, 331, 334–339

anger, 335

comfort objects, 337

common behavioral changes, 334-339

coping skills, 339

at diagnosis, 34–38

talking about death, 338

tantrums, 336–337

trusting your child, 338

coping with, 345–351

counseling for, 336, 337

to dying and death, 431–469. *See also* grief and bereavement

at diagnosis, 4–13

during treatment, 332–344

to end of treatment, 355-362

from friends, 90–91, 99–100

in grandparents, 88–90

from medications, 188–191, 346

in parents, 4–13, 339–344

anger, 9–10

coping skills, 344

depression, 340

at diagnosis, 4-13

dishonesty, 340

fear, helplessness, 8–9

guilt, 7–8

inconsistency, 342

overindulgence, 343

overprotection, 343

sadness, grief at diagnosis, 10-11

showing too much/little emotion, 340–341

siblings, not spending time with, 344

substance abuse, 344

temper, losing, 341–342

post-treatment, 362–367
at relapse, 389, 392–393
from relatives, 84–86
in siblings, 40, 307–24
See also communications; emotional support; grief and bereavement; siblings; school
emotional support, sources of
bereavement groups, 447, 450, 461–462
for bone marrow transplants, 426
counselors, individual and family, 161–166
friends and community, 11, 90–100
groups for children, 156–158
groups for parents, 153–156, 447
groups for siblings, 158–159, 328, 439
hospice care, 435–36
in-hospital, 43–45, 150–161
on-line, 157, 496–504
organizations, 488–490
parent-to-parent programs, 159–160
relatives, 11, 84–90
religious community, 97, 160–161
from schoolmates, 96–97
employment issues
for children post-treatment, 377–379
Family and Medical Leave Act, 101–102
for parents, 95, 101–105
Endoxan, 179–181
enteral nutrition (tube feeding), 279
environmental risk factors, 7–8, 23
eosinophils (eos), 21, 209. *See also* white blood cells
erythrocytes. *See* red blood cells
etoposide, 184
exercise, 134–35, 347, 369
eye problems, possible late effect, 420

F

Family and Medical Leave Act, 101–102
family and relatives
emotional responses to diagnosis, 84–86
handling anger towards, 9–10
notifying about diagnosis, 85–86
ways to be helpful, 86–88, 441–449
See also grandparents; siblings
family life
disruption and restructuring, 8, 10, 100–105, 310, 449–450
maintaining discipline and communications, 334, 336, 342, 345–351
marital stress, ways to handle, 102–105, 161–65
returning to normalcy, 346–348, 356, 362–365
See also emotional support
fatigue and weakness, 219–221, 238–239, 370–372
fear and anxiety, 8–9, 43–47, 124, 389. *See also* emotional and behavioral responses
fentanyl, 49
fertility, 367–368
fever. *See* infections; temperature-taking
filing systems, for record-keeping, 249–250
financial assistance, sources of
for bone marrow transplants, 410–411, 424–425
for computer purchases, 299
Family and Medical Leave Act, 101–102
free air transportation, 491–492
free medicine programs, 258
friends and community, 95–96, 256, 259, 410–411
government programs, 258

financial assistance, sources of (*cont'd*)
  in-hospital, 257
  service organizations, 15–16,
      259–260
financial records, keeping track of, 96,
      249–254, 256–257
finger pokes, 58
fluid retention, 263–264
folic acid supplements, avoiding, 186
follow-up care, post-treatment,
      372–377
food and meals
  boosting calories and protein,
      270–272
  for constipation, 218–219
  coping with, 274–277
  for diarrhea, 217
  food aversions, 225
  improving appeal, 268–270
  menu suggestions, 265–267
  for mouth sores, 224
  for nausea and vomiting, 208
  snack suggestions, 272–273
  See also nutrition; supplemental
      feeding
food supplements, commercial,
      277–278
friends and community
  emotional responses, 90–91,
      99–100
  fund-raising activities, 259,
      410–411
  helpful/unhelpful acts or com-
      ments, 91–99, 441–449
  losing, 99–100
  notifying about diagnosis, 90–91
funerals/memorial services, 292, 439

G
genetic risk factors, 22–23, 33
government services
  employment protection,
      101–102, 372
  financial assistance, 258
  insurance protection, 380

graft rejection, 416. *See also* bone mar-
      row transplants
graft-versus-host disease (GVHD),
      402, 404, 418–419
graft-versus-leukemia (GVL) effect,
      402, 404
grandparents, 88–90. *See also* family
      and relatives
granulocytes, 21, 29. *See also* white
      blood cells
grief and bereavement
  in friends and family, 88,
      441–449
  in parents, 10–11, 451–461
  school's participation in, 292
  in siblings, 449–450
  support services, 461–462
  See also emotional support
guilt feelings, 7–8, 244, 309, 344, 443
GVHD. *See* graft-versus-host disease
GVL effect. *See* graft-versus-leukemia
      effect

H
hair loss, 204–207, 238–239
HCT, 58, 480
health insurance
  for bone marrow transplants,
      410–411
  claim denials, appealing,
      256–257
  contact person, establishing, 255
  for dental treatments, 370
  EOBs (explanations of benefits),
      253
  financial assistance, 257–260,
      and Appendices C and D
  HMOs, 110, 111
  negotiating with, 256
  payment and billing problems,
      251–254
  policies, types of, 255
  post-treatment, 379–381
  for wigs, headwear, 205
health records. *See* medical history

heart damage, monitoring for, 65–66, 369
help, accepting, 97
hematocrit (HCT), 58, 480. *See also* red blood cells
hemoglobin (Hgb), 20, 478–479. *See also* red blood cells
heparin solutions, 138, 144
hepatitis, 59, 60, 374
Hexadrol, 194
Hickman's catheter. *See* catheters
HLA (human leukocyte-associated) antigens, 402, 406, 416
hospice care, 435–436
hospitalizations
  for antibiotic therapy, 140
  continuity of care during, 109, 115
  coping with, 129–135
  during treatment, 26, 30–31
  for feeding, 278–279
  initial, 3–4
  schooling during, 283–285
  siblings fears about, 311–312
  staying entertained during, 132, 134–135
  for treatment of chicken pox, 214
  visiting and calling during, 86, 292
  ways to help during, 86–88
hospitals
  billing
    financial assistance, 257–260, Appendices C and D
    insurance, 254–257
    procedures and problems, 251–254
  child life programs, 43–45
  mental health services, 150–161
  parents living in, 130–131
  parking arrangements, 131
  play areas, 134–135
  for radiation treatment, 231
  referrals to, 112

rooms, brightening, 87, 129–131
sleeping in, 129, 133
staff
  anesthesiologists, 49–50
  billing supervisors, 252–253
  chaplains, 160–161
  child life specialists, 43–45, 150–152
  doctors and nurses, 108–111
  endocrinologists, 242, 421
  financial counselors, 252
  mental health professionals, 283
  nutritionists, 273–274
  radiation specialists, 231–232
support groups
  for children, 156–158
  for parents, 153–156
  for siblings, 158–159, 439
waiting in, 132
See also medical centers; medical teams
Hydrea, 184–185
hydroxyurea, 184–185
hypnosis. *See* adjunctive treatments

I

idarubicin, 368–369
IDEA (Individuals with Disabilities Education Act), 295–296
IEPs (Individual Education Plans), 297–299
IFSPs (Individualized Family Service Plans), 300
imagery. *See* adjunctive treatments
immobilization devices, 232–234. *See also* radiation treatments
immune system reactions, 21
  to bone marrow transplants, 402, 404, 416, 418–419
  to L-asparaginase treatment, 179
  to platelet transfusions, 60

immune system reactions (*cont'd*)
    to red cell transfusions, 58
    See also blood counts; infections;
        side effects/complica-
        tions
immunizations
    against chicken pox, 215
    post-treatment, 373
    for siblings, 211–212
Individual Education Plans (IEPs),
        297–299
Individualized Family Service Plans
        (IFSPs), 300
Individuals with Disabilities Educa-
        tion Act, 295–296
induction, 26–27, 30–31. *See also*
        treatments
infections
    following blood transfusions, 59,
        60
    following blood transplants, 405
    following bone marrow trans-
        plants, 403, 417–418
    with catheters, 139–140, 146
    chicken pox, 214–215, 289–90
    detecting and diagnosing, 57, 63,
        64, 211–212
    from pets, 215–216
    pneumonia, 212–213
    preventing, 210–212, 223, 286,
        289–290, 417–418
    shingles (herpes zoster), 215
    signs and symptoms of, 64
    when to call doctor, 212
    See also blood counts
information, keeping track of
    financial records
        deductible expenses, 250
        general, 96, 249
        hospital billing, 251-254
        insurance 254–257
    medical records
        blood counts, 248, 485
        chemotherapy dosages, 175
        general, 245–249, 374–377

informed consent, 76–77, 410
insurance. *See* health insurance
IVs (intravenous lines), 55–57, 174,
        263. *See also* catheters

J, K
ketamine, 50

L
laboratory tests, interpreting,
        478–483. *See also* blood,
        tests
L-asparaginase, 178–179
late effects, possible, monitoring for,
        374–377
learning difficulties
    accepting, 301–302
    identifying and evaluating,
        293–296
    overcoming, 381–383
    services for children with,
        295–299
    services for infants and preschool-
        ers with, 299–300
    treatment-related, 226, 240–241,
        372
    See also late-effects; special educa-
        tion programs
legal rights
    during clinical trials and treat-
        ment, 80–81, 116, 117
    employment-related, 377–378
    health insurance issues, 257, 380
    military service issues, 379
    special education services,
        295–300
    See also post-treatment; special
        education programs
leukemia
    causes, possible, 22–23,
    definition, 1, 20
    diagnosis, 1–4, 23–24, 33
    prognosis and survival rates, 11,
        24, 25–26, 30, 32, 34

signs and symptoms, 1–3, 20–21,
    22, 23–24, 29, 32, 33
treatment, obtaining optimal, 24
types of, 22, 24–34
See also ALL; AML; CML; clinical
    trials; treatments
leukocytes. *See* white blood cells
libraries, using, 493–495
lorazepam, 195
low blood counts. *See* blood counts
lumbar punctures (spinal taps), 53–55
lymphocytes (lymphs), 21, 209. *See*
    also white blood cells

M

maintenance, 28–29, 346
marriage, strains and coping,
    102–105, 161–165
masks, immobilization, 232
medical centers
    for bone marrow transplants, 408
    for radiation treatments, 231
    as research sites, 72
    as teaching hospitals, 109
    as treatment sites, 3, 24, 26, 30,
        231
    See also clinical trials; hospitals
medical expenses
    deductible, 250
    keeping track of, 96, 249–254
    See also financial records
medical history, keeping track of,
    245–49, 375–376
medical libraries, using, 494–495
medical teams, 3
    bone marrow transplants, 414
    communicating with, 44, 108,
        112–121, 122–125,
        132, 448–449
    follow-up care, 372–373
    information providers, 35–36
    members of
        anesthesiologists, 49–50
        doctors/oncologists,
            108–110

endocrinologists, pediatric,
    242, 421
mental health professionals,
    43–45, 150–152
nurses, 110
nutritionists, 273–274
pediatricians, 115–116
radiation therapists, 231–32
specialists, 116
See also communications; doctors
medications
    avoiding negative interactions,
        199–200, 212–216
    behavioral changes from,
        188–191, 346
    importance of taking during
        maintenance, 61–63
    for mouth sores, 224
    for nausea, 194–196
    oral, 60–63, 174
    over-the-counter, 216, 218
    for pain, 48–50, 52, 54–56, 58,
        196–197
    for stress, 349
    taking at school, 286
    See also chemotherapy
meditation. *See* adjunctive treatments
mental health services
    behavior modification programs,
        336
    counselors, individual and family,
        161–166
    in-hospital, 143–145, 150–161
    See also emotional support
meperidine, 197
mercaptopurine, 185–186
"meters squared" (m2), 174–175
methotrexate, 186–187. *See also* CNS
    prophylaxis
Mexate, 186–187
military service, 379
monocytes (monos), 21, 209. *See also*
    white blood cells
morphine, 49, 196–197
mouth sores, 224
MTX (methotrexate), 186–187

MUGA scans, 67–68
music therapy, 157

N

nausea and vomiting, 207-208,
        238–239
neutropenia (low white counts), 135
neutrophils, 21, 209. *See also* white
        blood cells
nursing staff, 110
nutrition
    commercial supplements,
        277–278
    food sources, 265–266, 270–273
    importance of, 262, 265
    problems
        from chemotherapy treat-
            ment, 226, 262–265
        from diarrhea, 216–217
        malnutrition, 265
        from nausea and vomiting,
            207–208, 219
    by tube or IV, 263, 278–279
    vitamin supplements, 267–268
    See also food and meals
nutritionists, 273–274

O

oncologists
    finding and choosing, 111–112
    pediatric, 24, 26, 109
    radiation, 231
    relationship with home pediatri-
        cian, 115–116
    See also doctors
Oncovin, 191–193
ondansetron, 195
organizations, Appendix C, also "Re-
        sources" at the end of
        each chapter
outpatient treatment, 26, 109, 115

P

pain relief
    medications, 48–50
        EMLA cream, 49, 54, 56, 58,
            196
        fentanyl, 49
        ketamine, 50
        lidocaine, Xylocaine, 50, 52
        meperidine (Demerol), 197
        morphine, 49, 196–197
        propofol, 49–50
        valium/versed, 49
        tolerance to, 50, 234
    psychological methods, 46–48,
        197–198
    See also anesthesia/sedation; med-
        ications
PDQ (Physician Data Query), 29, 32,
        374, 487–488
pediatricians, 115–116. *See also* doc-
        tors
peripheral blood stem cell transplants
        (PBSCT), 404
pets, risks from, 215–216
Physician Data Query (PDQ), 29, 32,
        374, 487–488
physicians. *See* doctors
pill-taking techniques, 60–63
placental blood stem transplants,
        404–405
plasma, 20. *See also* blood
platelets (thrombocytes), 21
    platelet counts, 482
    transfusion with low, 60
play and play therapy, 43, 44,
        129–134, 346–348
pneumonia, 212–213
ports. *See* catheters
post-treatment
    changing doctors, 374–377
    emotions during, 362–367
    employment issues, 377–379
    follow-up care, 372–377
    health histories, maintaining, 375
    health insurance issues, 379–381

long-term effects, possible,
367–372
military service, 379
safe sex, 374
smoking risks, 373–374
prednisone, 187–191, 263–264. *See
also* emotional and be-
havioral responses
pregnancy, monitoring during,
367–368
procedures
assisted feeding, 278–279
blood draws (non-catheter), 57
blood transfusions, 58–59
bone biopsies, 53
bone marrow aspiration, 51–53
bone marrow donation, 411–412
catheter implantation, 57
external, 138
subcutaneous, 142–143
catheter removal, 358–359
diagnostic, 2–4, 23–24
echocardiograms, 65
end of treatment, 357–358
finger pokes, 58
HLA-matching for bone marrow
transplants, 406
intravenous (IV) lines, starting,
55–57
last day of treatment, 357–358
MUGA scans, 65–66
neurophysiological testing,
296–297
pain relief methods
pharmacological, 48–50
psychological, 46–48
pill-taking, 60–63
preparing for, 43–45, 46
questions to ask before, 51
for radiation treatments, 232–235
scheduling, 44
spinal taps (lumbar punctures,
LPs), 53–55
temperature taking, 63–64
urine samples, 64
prochlorperazine, 195–196

prognosis, 11
ALL, 25–26
AML, 30
adult CML, 34
juvenile CML, 32
propofol, 49–50
protein in diet, increasing, 270–271
protocols for treatment, 77–80. *See
also* clinical trials
psychological counseling
in hospital, 143–145, 150–161
individual and family, 161–166
puberty, alterations in, 242, 368
Purinethol, 185–186

Q, R

radiation oncologists, 231
radiation therapists, 231–232
radiation treatments
for ALL, 26, 28
for AML, 31
for bone marrow transplants, 412
craniospinal, 235–337, 391
general information, 229–230
immobilization during, 232–234
long-term effects, possible,
240–242, 369, 370
preparation for, 232–235
questions to ask about, 230–231
short-term side effects, 238–240
simulations, 235
testicular, 237, 391
total body (TBI), 237–238
RBCs (red blood counts), 480
record-keeping
financial, 249–254, 256–57
importance of, 245
medical, 245–249, 375–377
for special education services,
300–301
red blood cells, 20, 58, 58–59
red blood counts (RBC), 480
relapse
with bone marrow transplants,
404, 420

relapse (*cont'd*)
    emotional responses, 389, 392–393
    fears of, 356
    setting treatment goals, 396–397
    signs and symptoms, 389–392
    treatments, 391, 393–397
relaxation techniques. *See* adjunctive treatments
religious support. *See* spiritual support
reproductive system effects, 237, 242, 367–368, 421–422
research
    libraries, using, 493–496
    computer resources, 496–504
resources. *See* emotional support; financial assistance; "Resources" at end of each chapter and Appendices C and D.
Rubidomycin, 182

S

sadness. *See* emotional and behavioral responses; grief and bereavement
school
    administration
        communicating and dealing with, 283–290
        educating about leukemia, 284
        parental notification procedures, 287, 289–290
    alternative learning activities, 284
    during hospitalizations, 283–285
    learning disabilities, treatment-related, 226, 240–241
    for preschoolers, 290–291
    preventing infection at, 286, 289–290
    returning to, 286–289
    siblings' needs at, 285–286

    special education programs, 295–299
    and terminal illness, 291–292
schoolmates and teachers
    educating about leukemia, 284, 288, 291–292
    emotional responses to illness, 289
    ways of being helpful, 96–97, 284, 292
second opinions, 6, 77, 121–122, 394, 401
self-help groups. *See* support groups and services
sexual activity, post-treatment, 374
SGOT (serum glutamic oxaloacetic transaminase), 483
SGPT (serum glutamic pyruvic transaminase), 482–483
siblings, 307-330
    attention needs, 310, 312, 344
    behavioral problems, 40, 327
    as bone marrow donors, 402, 405, 416
    emotional responses, 308–311
    communicating with, 332, 333–334
    educating about leukemia, 311–312, 324–325
    grief and bereavement, 439, 449–450
    helpfulness of, 328
    informing about diagnosis, 38–39
    poems and stories by, 312–324
    school-related problems, 285–286, 327
    summer camps, 166–168
    support groups, 158–159, 439
    unequal treatment of, 342–343
    ways to help with, 92–93, 324–328, 442–443
side effects/complications, possible, 520
    from anesthesia/sedation, 50, 234)

from antinausea drugs, 194–196
behavioral and emotional chang-
    es, 188–191, 346
from blood transfusions, 59–60
from bone marrow transplants,
    402, 416–419, 420–422
from chemotherapy
    bed-wetting, 221–222
    constipation, 218–219
    dental problems, 223
    diarrhea, 216–218
    eating problems, 226,
        262–281
    fatigue, weakness, 219–221
    hair loss, 204–207
    late effects, possible,
        293–295, 367–372
    learning disabilities, 226,
        293–300
    low blood counts, 209–216
    mouth and throat sores,
        224–225
    nausea and vomiting,
        207–208, 238–239
    skin and nail problems,
        225–226
    taste and smell changes, 225
with external catheters, 138–141
late effects, 367–377
learning difficulties, 293–302
from pain medications, 196–197
from radiation treatments, 27,
    237–240
following spinal taps, 55
with subcutaneous ports,
    145–146
See also individual medications
    and treatments
signs and symptoms
    chronic GVHD, 419
    dehydration, 208, 217
    infection, 64, 139, 212
    learning difficulties, 293–295
    leukemia, 1–3, 20–21, 29, 32, 33
    malnutrition, 265

pneumonia, 213
relapse, 389–392
treatment-related problems, 176
6-MP, 185–86
6-Thioguanine (6-TG), 191
skin problems, 225–226, 238–239
sleep changes, cranial radiation, 239
smell changes, 225, 238–239,
    264–265
smoking risks, 373–374
somnolence syndrome, 239–240, 520
special education programs, 295–301
sperm banking, 368
spinal taps (lumbar punctures, LPs),
    53–55
spiritual support, 97, 160–161,
    439–441
SSI (Supplemental Security Income),
    258
sterility, possible, 368, 421
subcutaneous ports. See catheters
substance abuse, 4, 340, 344
sun, avoiding, 225
supplemental feeding
    commercial liquids, 277–278
    enteral nutrition (tube feeding),
        263, 279
    TPN (total parenteral nutrition)
        (IV-feeding), 263,
        278–279
    vitamins, 267–268
    See also food and meals
Supplemental Security Income (SSI),
    258
support groups and services
    camps, 166–167
    for children with cancer,
        156–158
    for parents, 153–155, 159–160
    for siblings, 158–159
    See also Appendices C and D
swollen glands, 238–239

T

tantrums, 336–337
taste changes, 225, 238–239, 264–265
tax deductions, medical, 250
TBI (total body radiation), 237–238. *See also* radiation treatments
team approach
    to follow-up care, 372–373
    to medical care, 3
    to special education, 296
    See also medical teams
temper problems
    in children, 335–337
    in parents, 341–342
temperature-taking, 63, 211
testicular radiation, 237
tests. *See* procedures
therapy, psychological. *See* counseling, individual and family
thermometers, types of, 63
throat sores, 224
thyroid damage, possible, 237, 421
total body radiation (TBI), 237–238
total parenteral nutrition (TPN) (IV-feeding), 263, 278–279
transfusions, blood, 58–60
treatment centers. *See* medical centers
treatments
    adjunctive, 197–198
    for ALL, 26–29
    alternative, 198–200
    for AML, 30–32
    bone marrow transplants, 400–422
    chemotherapy, multiagent, 173–177
    choosing a hospital, 3
    for CML, 32, 33–34
    deciding about, 24
    discontinuing, 431–435
    information about, 29, 32
    last day of, 355–61

    protocols, 77–79
    radiation, 229–238
    relapse, 393–397
    See also clinical trials
tube feeding, 263, 279

U, V

vaccinations
    against chicken pox, 215
    for siblings, 211–212
    post-treatment, 373
valium, 49
Valsalva maneuvers, 141
vancomycin, for infections, 140
VCR (vincristine), 191–193
VePesid, 184
versed, 49
vincristine, 191–193
visitors for child
    during periods of low ANGs, 220
    during hospitalizations, 86
    by schoolmates, 96, 292
visualization. *See* adjunctive treatments
vitamin supplements, 267–268. *See also* supplemental feeding
vomiting and nausea, 207–208, 238–239
VP–16, 184

W

WBCs (white blood counts), 481
weakness and fatigue, 219–221, 238–239, 370–372
weight gain
    promoting, 271–272
    from steroid treatments, 263–264
white blood cells (leukocytes), 21–22, 24, 29. *See also* blood counts
    white blood cell count (WBC), 481

white blood cell differential, 209, 481
wigs, headwear, 205
wish fulfillment organizations, 505–510
worry and fear. *See* emotional and be-havioral responses

X

x-rays. *See* radiation treatments.

Z

Zofran, 195

About the Author

Nancy Keene is one of the original developers of the O'Reilly Patient-Centered Guides health series. Before coming to work for O'Reilly, Nancy spent years advocating for and supporting her young daughter through intensive treatment for acute leukemia. She had already devoted much time to developing a personal philosophy of patient empowerment through knowledge and attitude because of her own hospitalizations for various medical problems.

Prior to parenthood, Nancy worked as an air traffic controller at two major airports on the east coast. While obtaining a degree at the University of Virginia, she worked as a paramedic at a busy rescue squad and taught adults basic and advanced emergency life support skills.

Nancy lives in Washington state and is busy writing and raising her two daughters. She spends her limited free time volunteering at school, talking with parents of children newly diagnosed with cancer, reading an eclectic mix of books, and dreaming of travel.

Colophon

Patient-Centered Guides are about the experience of illness. They contain personal stories as well as a mixture of practical and medical information.

The faces on the covers of our Guides reflect the hard-won experiences contained within and the human side of the information we offer. Where possible the photos used for our covers are people who have shared the experience we are writing about and who have contributed their stories to the book. For books about children, we prefer to use stock photos.

The cover of Childhood Leukemia was designed by Edie Freedman using Photoshop 4.0 and QuarkXpress 3.32. The fonts on the cover are Onyx and Berkeley. Photograph © Rubberball Productions.

The interior design of this book is by Nancy Priest and Edie Freedman using Berkeley and Franklin Gothic fonts. Text was prepared with QuarkXpress and FrameMaker. Illustrations are by Christopher Reilley, created with Photoshop 4.0 and Freehand 7.